Politics
in Zambia

# Perspectives on Southern Africa

# Politics
# in Zambia

by William Tordoff *editor*
Robert Molteno, Anirudha Gupta
Thomas Rasmussen, Ian Scott
and Richard L. Sklar

University of California Press
Berkeley and Los Angeles, California

University of California Press
Berkeley and Los Angeles, California

ISBN: 0 520 02593 8
Library of Congress catalog card No. 73 86660

Printed in Great Britain

# Contents

# List of maps

# Preface

This book is a study of politics in Zambia in the post-independence period (1964–72) and can therefore be regarded as a sequel to David C. Mulford's *Zambia: the Politics of Independence, 1957–64* (London, 1967). It concentrates on domestic politics, though the chapter on Zambia's response to the Rhodesian unilateral declaration of independence shows the interaction between internal and external events.

The book traces the growth of sectionalism in Zambia and identifies sectional groups as essentially interest groups competing for scarce economic resources. It analyses the effect of sectionalism on the United National Independence Party, Zambia's ruling party. It examines the nature of the political competition between UNIP and the various opposition parties which existed until December 1972 through a study of the 1968 general election, the 1971 by-elections, and the working of the National Assembly. The book outlines the relationship between the UNIP government and the trade union movement, and assesses the effectiveness of the machinery of government for implementing the former's goals; these goals are based on the philosophy of Humanism. It points out that Humanism entails a profound change in the values of Zambian society and examines the difficulties involved in its further institutionalisation. The book concludes with a review of the achievements of the UNIP government since independence and assesses future prospects now that a one-party State has been formally established.

All the contributors (see p. x) have been closely associated with the University of Zambia, which generously made research and other facilities available. We are heavily indebted to the many persons who have willingly given us the benefit of their knowledge and opinions, though we remain, of course, solely responsible for the use which we have made of both. As editor and co-author, I wish to thank particularly Robert Molteno, of the University of Zambia, for assisting me to keep abreast of Zambian politics, as well as for the warm hospitality which he and his wife, Marion, have provided during my return visits to Lusaka. I am grateful, too, to Colin Leys, of the University of Sheffield, for his perceptive and most helpful comments on the typescript. My thanks are also due to Douglas Anglin, first Vice-chancellor of the University of Zambia and now Professor of Political Science at Carleton University, to Dennis Austin and Ralph Young of the University of Manchester, Charles Elliott of the University of East Anglia, Cherry Gertzel and Morris Szeftel of the University of Zambia, and Denis Benn of the University of Guyana, for their advice and encouragement. I extend my regrets, as well as thanks, to those who prepared chapters for what, initially, was to have been a more comprehensive volume: John Omer-Cooper, Charles Elliott, Morris Szeftel, James Scarritt, Robert Bates, Dennis Dresang, Sheridan Johns, Alan Greenwood, Robin Fielder and Ruud Kapteyn. It is hoped to incorporate many of these chapters into a second volume, focusing on administration in Zambia.

The authors and the editor also owe thanks to several secretaries for the typing, in particular to Mrs Joyce Ingham and Miss Marilyn Dunn of the Department of Government at Manchester, Mrs Clare Walker of the Department of Political Science, University of California (Los Angeles), and Mr Joseph Chipote of the University of Zambia. Finally, we are grateful to Mrs Angela Young for preparing the index.

William Tordoff
*University of Manchester, 1974*

# Notes on contributors

William Tordoff, Professor of Government at Manchester University, was seconded to the University of Zambia as Professor of Political Science, 1966–68. He is the author of *Ashanti under the Prempehs, 1888–1935* (London, 1965) and *Government and Politics in Tanzania* (Nairobi, 1967).

Robert Molteno was Research Fellow in Political Science and is now Lecturer in Public Administration at the University of Zambia. He is author of *The Zambian Community and its Government* (Lusaka, 1973). His other publications include 'South Africa's forward policy in Africa', *The Round Table*, No. 243 (July 1971).

Anirudha Gupta, Associate Professor of African Studies, Jawaharlal Nehru University, New Delhi, was Research Associate at the Institute of Social Research, University of Zambia, in 1965 and subsequently. He is author of *Politics in Nepal* (Bombay, 1964) and *Reporting Africa* (New Delhi, 1969), and editor of *Indians Abroad— Asia and Africa* (New Delhi, 1971). He is now completing a study of Zambian politics.

Thomas Rasmussen, Assistant Professor of Political Science, Alfred College, New York, was Lecturer in Political Science, University of Zambia, 1967–70. His contributions to scholarly journals include 'Political competition and one-party dominance in Zambia', *Journal of Modern African Studies*, vol. 7, No. 3 (October 1969).

Ian Scott, Assistant Professor, Department of Economics and Political Science, University of Saskatchewan, was Lecturer in Political Science, University of Zambia, 1967–70. He is completing a University of Toronto doctoral thesis on party organisation in Zambia.

Richard L. Sklar, Professor of Political Science at the University of California, Los Angeles, was Senior Lecturer in Political Science at the University of Zambia, 1966–68. His publications include *Nigerian Political Parties: Power in an Emergent African Nation* (Princeton, 1963) and *Corporate Power in an African State: the Political Impact of Multinational Mining Companies in Zambia* (California, in press).

# A note on currency

The kwacha replaced the Zambian pound in January 1968; two kwacha were worth one old pound, which was at par with sterling before the British devaluation. One kwacha then equalled 58p, but its sterling value fell to 54p when the kwacha was pegged to the United States dollar in December 1971. Since the floating of the British pound the sterling value of the kwacha has varied widely; for example, it stood at 70p in May 1972 and at 53p in February 1974.

# A note on copper prices

Between 1939 and 1953 the price of Zambian (then Rhodesian) copper was controlled by the British government. Thereafter, apart from interludes between 1955–57 and 1964–66, Zambian copper has been sold at prices determined daily on the London Metal Exchange (LME). The average daily price per ton in March 1970, just three months after the Zambian government had acquired a 51 per cent ownership interest in the copper mines, was K1,241 (£730). This was substantially higher than the estimated minimum price (K750, £437) required for Zambia to make compensation payments entirely out of her copper dividend earnings. However, by the end of 1970 the average price for the month of December had declined to K740. The average price for 1971 and 1972 was K750 and K796 per ton respectively. In 1973 political threats to the Zambian transport system, among other causes, resulted in a sharp rise of the price level to a record peak of more than K1,500 (over £1,000) in November.

Zambia adopted the metric system under the Metric System Act of 1970. There are 2,205 lb in one metric ton, compared with 2,240 lb in one long ton, and 2,000 lb in one short ton.

# I

# Introduction

## William Tordoff and Robert Molteno

This book is a study of the politics of the First Zambian Republic, which began when Northern Rhodesia, a British protectorate in Central Africa, became the independent republic of Zambia on 24 October 1964 and ended in December 1972. The independence constitution, which had allowed multi-party competition, was then amended to provide for a 'one-party participatory democracy'. The Second Republic was inaugurated and its governmental institutions elaborated during 1973.

This introduction will provide a historical perspective—both before and after independence—in which to place the more analytic chapters which follow. It is trite, but true, that every nation is a product of its past. Zambia is no exception. Indeed, the problems, policies and patterns of the First Republic cannot be understood without a knowledge of the country's history. A significant number of works have been devoted to both Zambia's pre-colonial[1] and colonial[2] past, and the first part of the present chapter therefore

1. See, *inter alia*, H. W. Langworthy, 'A history of Undi's kingdom to 1890' (Ph.D. thesis, University of Boston, 1969); M. M. Bull, 'A history of the Lozi people to 1900' (Ph.D. thesis, University of London, 1968); A. D. Roberts, 'A political history of the Bemba: North-eastern Zambia to 1900' (Ph.D. thesis, University of Wisconsin, 1966). More general works include B. Fagan (ed.), *A Short History of Zambia from the Earliest Times to A.D. 1900* (Nairobi, 1966); H. W. Langworthy, *Zambia before 1890: Aspects of Pre-colonial History* (London, 1972); *About Zambia*, No. 6: *History* (Lusaka, 1973) [author, Q. N. Parsons]; A. D. Roberts, 'The nineteenth century in Zambia' in T. O. Ranger (ed.), *Aspects of Central African History* (London, 1968); and A. J. Wills, *An Introduction to the History of Central Africa* (Oxford, 1967).

2. For example, L. H. Gann, *The Birth of a Plural Society: Northern Rhodesia, 1894–1914* (Manchester, 1958) and *A History of Northern Rhodesia: Early Days to 1953* (London, 1964); and A. D. Roberts, 'The political history of twentieth-century Zambia' in Ranger (ed.), *Aspects of Central African History, op. cit.*

makes no claim at comprehensiveness. Our modest aim in this introduction is to highlight and relate to current events the salient
features of Zambia's history before 1964, and then to provide a
synoptic account of events since independence.

## The imposition of colonial rule

European rule was imposed on Zambia only at the extreme end of
the nineteenth century. While the causes were those underlying the
general 'scramble for Africa', the immediate occasion was the
large gold discoveries of 1886 in South Africa. Unfortunately from
the British point of view, the new mines were located in the Boer-
controlled Republic of the Transvaal. Cecil Rhodes, businessman and
imperialist (he already dominated the diamond fields of Kimberley
and was Prime Minister of the Cape Colony), decided to bypass and
contain the two Boer republics by establishing British colonies to
their north; he hoped to find new minerals there. To this end he
founded his British South Africa Company (BSA) which established
itself in what is today Rhodesia and at once sent agents north of the
Zambezi to sign treaties with the various chiefs. The most important
treaty was that signed with Lewanika, the king (Litunga) of Barotseland, in 1890, for it became the basis of the company's subsequent claim to mineral rights over country far beyond Lozi
control.

The characteristics of the colonial absorption of Northern
Rhodesia are of continuing importance. First, the new colony embraced not one traditional State but a large number of often rival
polities of varying sizes and with different State systems, languages
and cultures. The period of colonial rule was too short for the members of these pre-colonial polities to be fully integrated into a single
national community. Secondly, the fact that the imposition of
European rule did not involve the prolonged and destructive wars
which characterised the spread of colonial rule in other parts of
southern Africa also helped the traditional authority systems to
survive, albeit in an increasingly modified and weakened way. To
this day, to take only the most important example, the Litunga of
Barotseland is a major focus for sub-national group loyalty which has
repeatedly threatened national integration in the new State. Thirdly
and finally, the BSA Company, although chartered in London, was
really initially a South African enterprise. Colonial rule came to
Northern Rhodesia from the already white minority-ruled and
racialist south so that the country was, and continued to be, the
major northernmost outpost of southern African European settler

rule. As we shall see, this has had enduring consequences which continue to hamper the Zambian government's freedom of action.

*Colonial rule—its consequences*

The BSA Company ruled Zambia from the 1890s until 1924, when, for mainly economic reasons, it handed over its administrative role to the British Colonial Office. Britain, although allowing local European settlers a progressively larger say in the government, retained ultimate control of the territory until independence. However, in 1953 she did permit the creation of the Central African Federation, which united Southern and Northern Rhodesia with Nyasaland under the control of predominantly Southern Rhodesian whites.

Economically both the company and later the Colonial Office alienated considerable quantities of the best land to European settlers. Then, in the 1930s, copper from one of the world's richest deposits began to be exploited on a large scale. On the one hand this led to a rapid and large increase in the number of Europeans (their numbers rose to some 75,000 by 1960), and on the other to the formation of the powerful African Mineworkers' Union in 1949.

Even before this, African protest against colonial rule had begun. The vehicle initially was religious sects, in particular the African Watch Tower movement. This soon, however, stressed not opposition to, and replacement of, foreign rule, but its imminent supersession by divine intervention. Watch Tower and related religious movements rejected all governmental authority and, since they retained large numbers of followers even into the post-independence period, they came into sometimes violent conflict with the United National Independence Party (UNIP) government after 1963. More overt political resistance began with the voluntary welfare societies organised by the tiny minority of Africans with a Western primary school education. These societies became widespread with the urbanisation of the 1930s and amalgamated into the Federation of African Societies in 1946; within two years the Federation had transformed itself into the Northern Rhodesia African National Congress (NRANC). The African National Congress (ANC)—as NRANC soon became—led the unsuccessful anti-Federation struggle of the early 1950s. But a more militant offshoot, the Zambia African National Congress (succeeded by UNIP after it was banned in 1959), spearheaded the final stages of the independence struggle which was victorious in 1964.

The Northern Rhodesian colonial system, as it developed in the first half of the twentieth century, not only shaped the nationalist

Miles 10 0 10 20 30 40 50 60 70 80 90 100 Miles

| | |
|---|---|
| Provincial Boundaries | |
| Provincial Headquarters | ● |
| Towns | • |
| Roads | |
| Railways | |
| Aerodromes | ✈ |

ZAIRE

ANGOLA

Mwinilunga

Solwezi

Chingol

West Lunga

Kabompo

West Lunga Nat. Park No. 14

N O R T H    W E S T E R N    C O P P E

Zambezi

Kabompo

Kasempa

Liuwa Plain Nat. Park No. 15

Zambezi

Kaoma

Mumbwa

Kalabo

E

Mongu

Kafue National Park No. 11

C

Kafue

Lochinvar Nat. Park No. 13

Mazabu

2

W E S T E R N

Monze

Sananga

S O U T H E R N

Gwen

Choma

KA

ANGOLA

Sioma Ngwezi Nat. Park No. 16

Sesheke

Kalomo

Livingstone

Zambezi

NAMIBIA

BOTSWANA

Mosi-Oa-Tunya N.P. No. 17

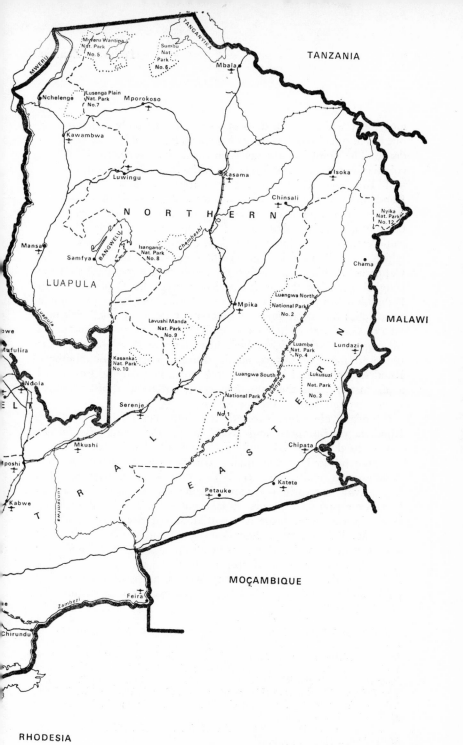

Fig. 1.1. The Republic of Zambia (*by courtesy of the Ministry of Development Planning and National Guidance, Lusaka*)

movement which emerged to oppose and eventually overthrow it, but has also had continuing consequences for Zambia since independence. The point has already been made that Northern Rhodesian colonialism was an extension of the white south. It was South Africa and Rhodesia which were the sources of most of Northern Rhodesia's white immigrants; it was through Rhodesia that Northern Rhodesia's first and major railway outlet to the sea ran; it was from the south, therefore, that most of its imports came; and with trade came companies, including the giant Anglo-American Corporation, which, with Roan Selection Trust, monopolised the mines of the Copperbelt. This orientation to the south continued throughout the colonial period and was intensified during the Central African Federation (1953–63).[3] It has created vast problems for Zambia since 1964: the severe fuel and other shortages after Rhodesia's unilateral declaration of independence (UDI) in 1965, which hampered the implementation of Zambia's first National Development Plan; the even more serious economic disruption caused by Southern Rhodesia's closure of its railway to Zambia in 1966 and threatened again in 1973; and the immensely costly construction of alternative routes through Tanzania to the sea after 1965.

Colonial rule also involved the introduction into Northern Rhodesia of European and Asian minorities.[4] While the former monopolised managerial, professional and skilled artisan occupations, the latter (although much smaller) controlled much of the country's middle-range retail commerce. Both groups were deeply committed to a private enterprise economy, although at the same time few of them were prepared in 1964 to take out Zambian citizenship or to invest in long-term projects essential to the development of the economy. Paradoxically, their dominant position in the economic structure forced on UNIP a non-racialist policy at a time when many of its African supporters deeply resented the wealth, exploitation, social exclusiveness and arrogance of these minorities. Citizenship policy and fears of 'paper Zambians' were recurrent issues throughout the First Republic.

3. On the federal period, see E. Clegg, *Race and Politics: Partnership in the Federation of Rhodesia and Nyasaland* (London, 1960); T. M. Franck, *Race and Nationalism: the Struggle for Power in Rhodesia–Nyasaland* (New York, 1960); R. Gray, *The Two Nations: Aspects of the Development of Race Relations in the Rhodesias and Nyasaland* (London, 1960); P. Keatley, *The Politics of Partnership* (Harmondsworth, 1963); C. Leys and R. C. Pratt (eds), *A New Deal for Central Africa* (London, 1960); and P. Mason, *Year of Decision* (London, 1960).

4. F. and L. O. Dotson, *The Indian Minority of Zambia, Rhodesia and Malawi* (New Haven, 1968).

The European minority also successfully institutionalised racialist practices against the African majority—wage discrimination, exclusion from many occupations and social facilities, segregated public services, and the establishment of a virtual political monopoly for Europeans until 1959.[5] While racialism created a convenient target for the nationalist movement (for example, the boycott of butchers' shops in the 1950s), it also created a series of post-independence problems. Many Europeans left precipitately after 1963, before citizens had been trained to replace them. There have been periodic racialist incidents, especially in social clubs and in work places. Several acts of sabotage followed Rhodesia's UDI in 1965. And perhaps most important of all, the continuing economic cleavage between Africans and other racial groups has diverted popular attention from the evolving intra-African class formation which has taken place as independence paved the way to African entry into the private sector and domination of the public bureaucracy.[6]

Colonialism also moulded the developing Zambian economy in distinctive ways.[7] Though most of the country continued to be occupied by African peasant farmers, land was also alienated to settlers. Alienation led both to agricultural production for the market being dominated by often racialist European farmers along the line of rail, and to serious land shortages among the Ngoni of Eastern Province and in parts of the Tonga-dominated Southern Province. It was no accident that these rural areas were among the first to be politicised by the ANC. The exploitation of copper from the 1930s also had certain unintended consequences which were in fact beneficial in the long run. As already noted, a powerful trade union movement arose in the towns, while the migrant labour system, which compelled a circulation of workers between country areas and town, played a major role in mobilising certain of the rural provinces

5. J. W. Davidson, *The Northern Rhodesian Legislative Council* (London, 1948) and D. C. Mulford, *Zambia: the Politics of Independence, 1957–64* (London, 1967).

6. See chapter 3.

7. R. E. Baldwin, *Economic Development and Export Growth: a Study of Northern Rhodesia, 1920–60* (Berkeley, 1966); J. A. Bancroft, *Mining in Northern Rhodesia* (London, 1961); W. J. Barber, *The Economy of British Central Africa* (Stanford, 1961); M. Bostock and C. Harvey (eds), *Economic Independence and Zambian Copper* (New York, 1972); C. Elliott (ed.), *Constraints on the Economic Development of Zambia* (Nairobi, 1971); M. L. O. Faber and J. G. Potter, *Towards Economic Independence: Papers on the Nationalisation of the Copper Industry in Zambia* (London, 1972); J. A. Hellen, *Rural Economic Development in Zambia, 1890–1964* (London, 1972); and A. Martin, *Minding their own Business: Zambia's Struggle against Western Control* (London, 1972).

against colonial rule. On the other hand, most of the typical features of a colonial economy emerged in acute degree: an export-oriented mono-economy based on copper, which was mined by vast foreign multi-national corporations; underdeveloped manufacturing and agricultural sectors; and an infrastructure almost solely geared to the needs of the mining industry. The rural sector off the line of rail was badly neglected, and there was a wide income gap between rural and urban dwellers. Despite measures since independence to restructure the economy, these characteristics continued in modified form throughout the First Republic.

Another consequence of colonial rule, and one which proved to be of increasing importance towards the end of the First Republic, was that the colonial system was an authoritarian one. The colonial government of Northern Rhodesia had wide-ranging and arbitrary powers which contravened all the important civil liberties. The Zambian government inherited these powers from the Governor of Northern Rhodesia, and has not found it necessary to enlarge upon them in any important respect. It can be argued, of course, that certain objective circumstances faced both the colonial and Zambian governments and made such powers inevitable. But it remains indisputable that the colonial era did little to develop a political culture in Zambia which placed a high valuation on limited government and respect for individual rights.

The last major consequence of the colonial era has already been discussed briefly—namely, its impact on national integration. Of course, in one sense the Zambian nation would not have existed in its present form without colonial rule. Moreover colonialism, and especially the imposition of federation upon a reluctant people in 1953, evoked a nationalist response and was therefore itself functionally integrative. But the colonial authorities also took certain measures whose effect was to retard the growth of national consciousness. Indirect rule was introduced after 1929 and prolonged some degree of loyalty to the pre-colonial governmental authorities.[8] Thus in many areas UNIP ran into opposition from chiefs as it tried to mobilise the rural people against foreign rule. Moreover the deliberate withholding of secondary education until the 1940s, and of locally based higher education throughout the colonial period,[9] both retarded the emergence of a nationalist leadership and meant that Zambia entered independence with a relatively smaller pool of educated manpower than any other former British dependency.

8. W. M. Hailey, *An African Survey* (London, 1957), *passim*.
9. J. M. Mwanakatwe, *The Growth of Education in Zambia since Independence* (Lusaka, 1968).

## *The nationalist struggle*[10]

The nature of the nationalist struggle has also had important effects
on the political culture, structure of political conflict, and party and
State institutions of the independent republic. First of all, though the
struggle was more bitter than in several other British-ruled African
territories such as the Gold Coast, Nigeria and Tanganyika, it was
not prolonged. ANC was formed only after the second world war in
1948. The failure to stop federation had a demoralising effect and
the organisation was almost quiescent in the middle and late 1950s.
A new phase of nationalist–colonialist conflict began in 1958, when
certain ANC leaders, led by Kenneth Kaunda, broke away to form
their own party in order to wage a more miltant struggle and to
break the Central African Federation. The struggle had been won
by early 1962 (a bare three years later), by which date the near
chaos in three rural provinces caused by the 'Cha Cha Cha' campaign had forced the British government to revise the new constitution so as to clear the way for majority rule. UNIP and ANC together did in fact win a majority of Legislative Council seats against
the settler United Federal Party (UFP) in the election held at the
end of 1962. And in December they participated in the government
of Northern Rhodesia in an uneasy coalition. A year later, and only
nine months before independence, an all-UNIP government was
formed following the first general election held under universal
franchise, in which UNIP won fifty-five of the sixty-five main roll
seats, and 69·6 per cent of the votes cast. Almost immediately
negotiations took place with the British government over the timing
of independence and the constitution of the new State.

Secondly, the nationalist movement's impact was uneven. Its
roots go back furthest in the urban areas, in the Southern and
Eastern Provinces, which were affected by land alienation, and in
Northern and Luapula Provinces, which developed close ties with the
Copperbelt through returning migrant workers. At the other extreme, parts of Western and North-western Provinces only heard
the nationalist message to any significant extent at the very end

10. A. L. Epstein, *Politics in an Urban African Community* (Manchester,
1958); K. D. Kaunda, *Zambia shall be Free: an Autobiography* (London,
1962); R. Hall, *Zambia* (London, 1965); W. Kirkman, *Unscrambling an
Empire: a Critique of British Colonial History* (London, 1966); H. Meebelo,
*Reaction to Colonialism* (Manchester, 1971); D. C. Mulford, *The Northern
Rhodesia General Election, 1962* (Nairobi, 1964) and *Zambia: the Politics of
Independence, op. cit.*; and R. I. Rotberg, *The Rise of Nationalism in
Central Africa: the Making of Malawi and Zambia, 1873–1964* (Cambridge,
Mass., 1967).

of the 1950s. Again, a small number of Africans remained faithful to the colonialists throughout, while religious groups such as Watch Tower and Alice Lenshina's Lumpa Church in Northern and parts of Eastern Provinces never responded to the nationalist call. The unevenness of the nationalist impact, as well as the short duration of the anti-colonial struggle within a culturally and linguistically fragmented society, meant that the unity which UNIP established was fragile. The Zambian government, as in most new States, was formed out of the party (UNIP) which had led the movement for independence. As President Kaunda has admitted, his party was mainly designed for agitational purposes, with colonialism seen as the 'Common Enemy in opposition to which a people, traditionally divided along tribal, linguistic and regional lines, achieves unity'.[11] It was to be expected, therefore, that such unity was to be severely strained after independence as different parts of the country competed with each other for a share in the limited economic resources available for distribution.

Other features of the nationalist struggle demand attention. The movement was subject to repeated splits even before independence. In October 1958 ANC spawned ZANC. When this was banned, two successor parties were formed early in 1959—the African National Independence Party and the United National Freedom Party—which fused in August 1959 to form UNIP. Three months later ANC split again, and the breakaway group under Mainza Chona merged with UNIP. In 1962, under UFP sponsorship, a sectionally based and short-lived Barotseland National Party was formed, while the following year an ANC official, Job Michello, broke away temporarily and established his own People's Democratic Party. The party splits, therefore, which both UNIP and ANC have experienced since independence clearly have precedents in the earlier phase of the nationalist struggle.

Another feature of the pre-independence rivalry between the African political parties was widespread and vicious violence. The early 1960s saw large numbers of clashes between UNIP and ANC activists with bloody and sometimes fatal consequences. There is therefore a clear continuity between the pre- and post-independence eras in the use of violence by parties as a political tactic.

Finally and most fundamentally, the leadership of the nationalist movement at regional and national levels remained firmly in the hands of members of the African elite and what has been called the

11. *A Humanist in Africa: Letters to Colin Morris from Kenneth Kaunda, President of Zambia* (London, 1966), p. 53.

'lumpen-elite' (i.e. semi-educated townsmen).[12] This was facilitated by the fact that the methods of the nationalist struggle did not involve a popular armed revolt and there was no ideological commitment to reject the colonial system in all its aspects. The result was a fairly peaceful and evolutionary, albeit hasty, transition to political independence in which Britain eventually co-operated with the nationalist movement. Even the symbols of this transition were familiar: a cordial pre-independence constitutional conference in London; the graceful presence of a member of the royal family at the independence celebrations; and the constitutional entrenchment of British-style parliamentary institutions and a civil service still for the time being in the hands of British officials. The conservatism of government policy in certain respects since 1964 and the growing involvement of the political leadership in the private sector can probably be best explained in the light of the preceding process of an evolutionary transition to independence.

## Independence[13]

1964, the year of independence, was a hectic year in every way. Following its handsome electoral victory in the January general election,[14] UNIP formed its first Cabinet under Kaunda as Prime Minister, although the process was marred by considerable tension within the party over the composition of the Cabinet.[15] Nevertheless, preparations began at once for the transition to independence of a country less than 0.5 per cent of whose 3½ million population had even full primary education. The first urgent steps were taken to prepare Zambians for senior posts in the civil service. At the end of the year, two months after independence, the first three permanent secretary posts were Africanised, along with twenty-seven other senior civil service positions.[16] A planning unit was set up for

12. J. R. Scarritt, 'Adoption of political styles by African politicians in the Rhodesias', *Midwest Journal of Political Science*, vol. x, No. 1 (February 1966).

13. Useful general works, not already mentioned, on Zambia include W. V. Brelsford, *The Tribes of Zambia* (Lusaka, 1965); E. Colson and M. Gluckman (eds), *Seven Tribes of British Central Africa* (London, 1951); D. H. Davies (ed.), *Zambia in Maps* (London, 1971); and G. Kay, *A Social Geography of Zambia* (London, 1967).

14. D. C. Mulford, 'Northern Rhodesia—some observations on the 1964 election', *Africa Report*, vol. 9, No. 2 (February 1964).

15. Mulford, *Zambia: the Politics of Independence, op. cit.*, pp. 329–30.

16. D. L. Dresang, 'The Zambia civil service: a study in development administration' (Ph.D. thesis, University of California, Los Angeles, 1971).

the first time to give coherence to the new government's economic goals and the nucleus of a Zambian officer corps for the Defence Force was created. In addition, the dissolution of the Central African Federation at the end of 1963 and the approach of independence itself required an exceptionally large volume of legislation. Thus several new parastatal bodies, such as the Zambia Youth Service and the Agricultural Rural Marketing Board, were established. In this way the party took early steps to fulfil the promises which it had made to its young unemployed urban supporters and its even more deprived village followers.

While responsible government enabled UNIP to begin implementing its substantive policies in the social and economic fields (including the decision to tackle the skilled manpower shortage on a localised basis by building the University of Zambia), difficult political issues also had to be dealt with. In April 1964 Kaunda held talks with the Litunga of Barotseland, who consented reluctantly to his province remaining part of the forthcoming independent State, but with a somewhat special status enshrined in the Barotseland agreement. Immediately following this, in May, leaders of UNIP and the two opposition parties, ANC and the National Progress Party (formerly the settler UFP), flew to London to agree on the details of the independence constitution. The result was the acceptance of UNIP's demands for republican status, a unitary State and an executive presidency, modified, however, by elements of the British parliamentary system and certain concessions with regard to British property, citizenship and the political position of local Europeans.[17]

The euphoria as independence day approached mounted, but it was to suffer two serious setbacks. In July large-scale violence broke out between the Lumpa Church followers of Alice Lenshina in Northern Province and the surrounding pro-UNIP village population; the army had to be brought in to deal with a deteriorating situation. The fighting went on sporadically for several months and some 700 lives were lost.[18] The government declared a state of public emergency: this gave the executive increased powers and was in fact continued throughout the First Republic. Then, in August, the ANC finally rebuffed UNIP's discreet approaches for a national front

17. S. V. S. Mubako, 'The Presidential system in the Zambian constitution' (M.Phil. thesis, University of London, 1970).

18. J. W. Fernandez, 'The Lumpa uprising: why?', *Africa Report*, vol. 9, No. 10 (November 1964), and A. D. Roberts, 'The Lumpa Church of Alice Lenshina', in R. I. Rotberg and A. A. Mazrui (eds), *Protest and Power in Black Africa* (New York, 1970).

government based on a merger of the two parties. Nevertheless, the independence celebrations went off with great enthusiasm and ceremony all over the country.[19] On 24 October Zambia became a new member of the United Nations, the Commonwealth and the Organisation of African Unity.

Economic prospects for the new State were auspicious. The copper price was rising, and at the very beginning of 1964 the two copper-mining giants, Anglo-American Corporation and Roan Selection Trust, had decided to lift their self-imposed restrictions on output. Equally important, the UNIP government fought successfully to abolish the dubious treaty rights (still scheduled to run for twenty-two years) under which the BSA Company milked the economy annually of many millions of pounds in mineral royalty payments. On the very eve of independence, in a dramatic encounter between Arthur Wina, Minister of Finance, and Emrys Evans of the BSA Company the latter surrendered its claims to the Zambian government.[20]

In contrast, Zambia's geopolitical environment looked much less promising. Freedom fighters began their war against the Portuguese in Moçambique in the very year of Zambia's independence; this raised the spectre of future Portuguese pressures on the young republic.[21] In addition, most of the Southern African liberation movements already had representatives in Lusaka and looked forward to Zambian independence as creating more favourable circumstances for their own struggles. Moreover, South Africa rudely rebuffed Zambia's offer to exchange ambassadors, and the white Rhodesians were considering a UDI increasingly seriously.[22] Zambia's own actions, though taken for sound political and economic reasons, did not defuse the situation. In June she ended Rhodesia's preferential tariff in the Zambian market and in December gave notice of cancellation of her trade agreements with South Africa and Portugal. At the same time the government announced its intention to build a railway linking Zambia with Tanzania (the Tanzam railway) and initiated friendly relations with China. While the latter move indicated Zambia's determination to adopt a foreign policy of 'positive nonalignment', it caused growing fears in the

19. For a description of the independence celebrations see R. V. Molteno, *The Zambian Community and its Government* (Lusaka, 1974), chapter 4.

20. R. Hall, *The High Price of Principles—Kaunda and the White South* (London, 1969), chapter 5.

21. The London *Times* news team, *The Black Man in Search of Power* (London, 1969).

22. R. Brown, 'Zambia and Rhodesia: a study in contrast', *Current History*, vol. 48 (April 1965).

reactionary white minority regimes of southern Africa and also alarmed many conservative-minded Zambians.

In retrospect, it is clear that all the main issues which dominated the Zambian scene during the First Republic (1964–72) already existed in embryo in 1964: national integration, the form of governmental institutions, the manpower shortage, policy towards the mining industry and private sector generally, and relations with the white south.[23] The years which followed saw a maturation of these problems, and a series of attempts to solve them.

The new State certainly set out with several advantages. Its executive president, Dr Kenneth Kaunda, was a remarkable person—sensitive, humane, hard-working, committed to change, and politically skilful. The country's constitution, within which he had to act, largely conformed to the wishes of the ruling party and in any case was flexible for the most part. The President himself was supported by a Cabinet which combined both highly educated and able Ministers as well as Ministers who commanded the confidence of the party. And the Cabinet in turn could rely on an administrative machine whose revenue, because of soaring copper prices, was already rising and continued to rise considerably for the next six years.[24] Finally, the government not only had overwhelming popular support at the end of a victorious freedom struggle but was also based on a party which had a clear set of broad goals. These included the abolition of what racial discrimination and segregation remained, the maintenance of individual liberties, and the achievement of 'African democratic socialism'. The latter was spelled out to embrace raising the standard of living, achieving a more equitable distribution of wealth, humanising conditions of labour, and maximising social security (in particular, free health services and expanded educational facilities), and generally promoting 'trade, industry, and agriculture in the interests of the people'.[25]

At the same time, the UNIP government laboured under serious disadvantages. At independence, President Kaunda and his Cabinet colleagues had been in office for less than two years and had next to no experience of operating a political system on a national scale. Initially they had to rely heavily on their largely expatriate senior

23. D. G. Anglin, 'Confrontation in southern Africa: Zambia and Portugal', *International Journal*, vol. xxv, No. 3 (summer 1970).

24. Government revenue, which was K63·7 million in 1963–64, rose to a peak of K432.4 million in 1970. The value of mineral production rose from K299 million in 1964 to a peak of K759 million in 1969. *Monthly Digest of Statistics* (Lusaka, 1971), vol. vii, No. 3, tables 15 and 29.

25. K. D. Kaunda, *Humanism in Zambia and a Guide to its Implementation* (Lusaka, 1967), pp. 9–10.

civil service advisers, but in the racially charged atmosphere of Central Africa in 1964 they were not certain of the loyalty of many of them. The problem arising from lack of experience was compounded by the ill-feeling which, though rarely allowed to surface before 1967, existed between certain Ministers. In making appointments to his Cabinet Kaunda tried to balance the various factions within UNIP—the old guard of freedom fighters, of whom a majority were Bemba-speakers from the Northern, Luapula and Copperbelt[26] Provinces, and the new, university-educated men who had been brought into government as Parliamentary Secretaries in January 1963; the militants and the moderates; and the main linguistic and tribal groups. Such balancing was a necessary political tactic in order to maintain the immediate unity of the party. Nevertheless, it did not avoid the alienation of those sections in the party which successively felt themselves disadvantaged.

Another of UNIP's difficulties was that the party's central machinery was never strong enough to control fully its up-country organisation. Local-level supporters of the major African nationalist parties in Northern Rhodesia, as in Tanganyika[27] and several other African dependencies, seem to have played a vital role in crystallising anti-colonial sentiment in the villages and transmitting felt grievances—for example, over unpopular taxes and agricultural regulations—into anti-colonial action.[28] Kaunda and his Ministers were aware that the strength of the rural protest (culminating in the 'Cha Cha Cha' campaign of 1961) had contributed a great deal to the ultimate success of the independence movement and that the local political leaders and their supporters, who had made that protest, expected their reward now that independence was achieved. The government's dilemma was that it was committed to developing the rural areas but could only do so by keeping in force at least some of those very agricultural regulations and practices against which the rural villagers had protested in the colonial era. In the event, some regulations had to be allowed to lapse because local UNIP officials were unwilling to enforce them. Another dimension to this problem was that, while the government required an efficient administrative machine in order to implement its policies, considerable numbers of often ill-educated party activists demanded government employment. Again, a compromise was reached with the principle of merit appointments to the public service being modified

26. Known as the Western Province until 1969.
27. See, for example, R. Young and H. A. Fosbrooke, *Smoke in the Hills: Political Tension in the Morogoro District of Tanganyika* (Evanston, 1960).
28. See chapter 2.

on occasion by a number of political appointments and a steadily growing establishment of ambiguously defined posts filled by politicians who spent most of their time controlling (some civil servants would say 'interfering with') public officers.

The government also had to face the rising expectations of urban dwellers. Newcomers to town wanted jobs and houses, and schools for their children. Although employment rose rapidly in the early years after 1964, many were often disappointed and had to eke out a precarious existence in the overcrowded and insanitary slums which ringed Lusaka, the capital, and to a lesser extent Kitwe and the other Copperbelt towns. Urban residents who were employed wanted better wages and working conditions. They belonged to trade unions which retained much of their pre-independence autonomy and were prepared to take strike action to press their demands, with inflationary consequences for the economy as a whole. The problem was most acute on the Copperbelt, where African miners considered themselves 'poverty-stricken' as compared with their white co-workers. Throughout the First Republic Dr Kaunda's government sought to win voluntary support for its development labour policy (which included wage restraint) by making use of the two major national structures (the Mineworkers' Union and UNIP) which penetrate the local level of the African labour force on the Copperbelt.[29]

A more purely economic problem was the over-dependence of the country on copper. This was part of Zambia's economic legacy from the Central African Federation. During the ten-year period that the Federation lasted, the African agricultural sector was neglected and Southern, rather than Northern, Rhodesia was purposely developed as the manufacturing base of the Federation. By 1964 Zambia had become dependent on Southern Rhodesia for a very large proportion of her manufactured imports, while essential foodstuffs were already being imported in large quantities.

Guided by the Seers report,[30] the government in 1964 laid down the policies which it would follow to overcome this dismal economic legacy; these policies were subsequently embodied in the first (four-year) National Development Plan.[31] First, top priority was to be given to massive investment in infrastructural development, particularly education and transport; secondly, employment was to be

29. See R. H. Bates, *Unions, Parties and Political Development—a Study of Mineworkers in Zambia* (New Haven and London, 1971).

30. *Economic Survey Mission on the Economic Development of Zambia: Report of the UN/ECA/FAO Mission* (Ndola, 1964).

31. *First National Development Plan, 1966–70* (Lusaka, 1966).

increased as rapidly as possible; and thirdly, the economy was to be diversified away from copper by developing a productive African agricultural sector and by establishing a manufacturing sector, founded in the first instance on import substitution.[32] While no one could seriously challenge the attempt to promote African agriculture in a country where over 70 per cent of the people lived off the land, the other objectives have been called into question by at least one economist.[33] Thus it is argued that it was rash, as part of the infra-structural programme, to expand education (and especially primary education) at a very rapid rate when there was scant prospect of an equally rapid rise in job opportunities, and that, though diversification of the economy was intrinsically desirable, it was unwise to develop a manufacturing sector without satisfying certain precon-ditions—for example, that it would be possible to produce goods in Zambia at anything like import parity prices. An alternative strategy (the argument continues) would have been to encourage the rapid development of the copper industry through investment in new mines; for this to take place, the regressive tax royalty formula[34] would need to have been adjusted (as happened eventually in 1969). As it was, despite the favourable prospects for copper in 1964, Zambia's production fell in subsequent years,[35] while other copper-producing countries, particularly Chile, Peru and South Africa, in-vested heavily in new mines.

From an economic standpoint such arguments may (or may not) be sound. But it would have been difficult politically for the govern-ment of newly independent Zambia to deny the universal demand for education and not to attempt to create new employment oppor-tunities through the creation of a strong manufacturing sector. More-over, to be seen to be collaborating too closely with white-owned and -managed mining companies would have been politically damaging for the government. Even so, the latter was quickly caught in a dilemma not of its own making. On the one hand, in allocating investment funds the attempt was made to divert resources to the rural areas and away from the line of rail, and to promote the de-velopment of such neglected parts of the country as the Northern, Luapula, Western (then Barotse) and North-western Provinces. On

32. Elliott (ed.), *Constraints on the Economic Development of Zambia, op. cit.*, pp. 10–15.

33. See Elliott, *loc. cit.*

34. The effect of the tax formula was both to increase tax liability pro-portionately when prices were low and to increase the liability of post-tax earnings. See C. R. M. Harvey, 'The fiscal system', in Elliott, *op. cit. supra*, pp. 155–62.

35. Fortunately, however, this was offset by rising prices.

the other hand, it was also recognised that it was vital to 'invest in
growth', and in the event it proved impossible to reconcile fully the
concept of regional balance with that of investment in the growth
areas of the economy. Government capital investment was highest in
the Central Province, followed by the Southern Province (stronghold of the ANC opposition).[36]

Another adverse economic legacy of federation and the European
settler rule which it perpetuated was a weak manpower situation.
Indeed, one of the ironies facing Zambia at independence was that,
though she was much richer than the great majority of tropical
African States to the north, she was worse off than many of them
in terms of the indigenous trained and experienced personnel available to implement her development policies.[37] In 1964 there were
only 109 African graduates in the country and 1,200 Africans with
secondary school certificates. Outside the formal educational sphere
the picture was equally gloomy. Artisan training had been neglected
under the Federation and until 1959 no African in Northern
Rhodesia could be apprenticed.

A further difficulty was

the inadequacy of economic and politico-economic institutions inherited
from the federal era alike in the government, private and parastatal
sectors. Very few civil servants were experienced in the formulation and
implementation of policies for rapid economic development. In the
private sector, local managers had hitherto been entirely dependent upon
policies originating in Rhodesia or South Africa. Almost by definition,
the parastatal organisations were federal in character and management.
Thus upon independence, parastatal institutions from the Agricultural
Rural Marketing Board to the Bank of Zambia had to be created *ex-nihilo*
in a very short space of time.[38]

A final problem, already touched on, confronting the Zambian
government in October 1964 arose from Zambia's geographical
position. She was a land-locked country, ringed by States many of
which were unfriendly or unstable: Angola to the west; Moçambique
and Malawi to the east; Zaïre (formerly Congo Kinshasa) and
Tanzania to the north-west and north-east respectively; and
Rhodesia and the South African-controlled Caprivi Strip across the
Zambezi to the south. The country was perhaps most exposed on its
western and southern flanks, since UNIP's hold over the Lozi-
dominated Western Province (the former Barotseland) was un-

36. *First National Development Plan, op. cit.*, p. 81.
37. *Manpower Report: a Report and Statistical Handbook on Manpower,
Education, Training and Zambianisation, 1965–66* (Lusaka, 1966).
38. C. Elliott, 'The Zambian economy' (Lusaka, 1968, mimeo.).

certain,[39] and ANC controlled the Southern Province. Zambia's only certain escape route, particularly after Rhodesia's UDI at the end of 1965, lay northwards through friendly Tanzania, with which the Zambian government has therefore continuously sought to develop and extend communication, trading and other links.

It is against this background of advantages and disadvantages that the history of the First Zambian Republic must be seen. What follows is a basic chronology of events until the Second Republic was inaugurated in 1973.

## *Events since independence*[40]

*1965*. The looming threat of a Rhodesian UDI, which finally materialised on 11 November 1965, dominated the year. Despite the Zambian government's announcement in January that it was imposing strict controls over the liberation movements, relations with the south deteriorated steadily. In June it was revealed that South Africa was beginning the construction of a large air and military base in the Caprivi Strip of Namibia (South West Africa), just across the border from Zambia's Western Province. In the same month Portugal and South Africa stopped transhipping arms for the Zambia Defence Force and in October Rhodesia went so far as to seize military consignments bound for Zambia. Threats from the south escalated: the Smith government accused UNIP of helping Rhodesian 'saboteurs' and the Portuguese Foreign Minister threatened 'legitimate retaliation' against African States helping guerrillas in Moçambique. Zambia responded to Rhodesia by demanding that Britain introduce majority rule there. She also started to reduce her reliance on Rhodesia Railways by using the Benguela Railway through Angola to Lobito on the Atlantic Ocean in order to bring in a small quantity of imports; at the same time, she continued exploratory moves towards building a Tanzam railway to Dar es Salaam on the east coast and held trade talks with the three principal East African States. Despite these steps, UDI caused immediate problems. Rhodesian sympathisers blew up the Kariba–Copperbelt power line on 26 November, and, on the same day, the

39. See Mulford, *Zambia: the Politics of Independence, op. cit.*, chapter VI, and G. L. Caplan, *The Elites of Barotseland, 1878–1969: a Political History of Zambia's Western Province* (Berkeley and Los Angeles, 1970), *passim*.

40. Sources for the rest of this chapter include the *Times of Zambia*, *Zambia (Daily) Mail*, the *Government Gazette* (Lusaka), the collected *Laws of Zambia*, and Zambia Information Service press releases.

railways were temporarily paralysed by a strike of 300 white Rhodesian railway workers in Livingstone. Racial incidents, which had been initiated by whites after independence the previous year, recurred and threatened both law and order and racial harmony. Zambia was faced with several difficult issues: how to find alternative ways of bringing in vitally needed petrol and other supplies; what to do with the common services (railways, airways and electricity) jointly owned by the two countries at a time when Zambia lacked both local staff and repair facilities; and lastly how far and fast to go along with Britain's sanctions policy against Rhodesia, when her only other link with the Indian Ocean was a mud track to Dar es Salaam.

One small advantage which Zambia had was her soaring public revenues due to still rising copper prices. In January the Transitional Development Plan was inaugurated, with its emphasis on educational expansion, while planning accelerated for the first National Development Plan, due to begin in July 1966. The levels of both public and private sector activity continued to rise dramatically.

Administratively, nothing spectacular happened. Apart from the creation of a Ministry of Mines, no significant restructuring of the government machinery took place. But localisation of senior administrative personnel proceeded at a very fast rate; by the end of the year almost all Ministries and the Zambia Police were headed by Zambians. Government also initiated what proved to be an enduring phenomenon: increasing the scope of the public sector at the expense of the private sector. In July the *Central African Mail* was bought out by government and renamed the *Zambia Mail*; at the end of the year radio also was taken over, and television in early 1966. Finally, at district level, the field staff of a growing number of departments began to proliferate at the same time as the number, quality and powers of provincial and district government staff, who alone could co-ordinate the work of these departments, were reduced.[41]

Politically, the decision was taken to proscribe the Lumpa Church permanently, while offering to welcome back the thousands of Alice Lenshina's followers who had fled to Zaïre. A more constructive event was the passage of the Local Government Act, which established a basically uniform pattern of democratic local authorities throughout Zambia. One consequence was a resurrection of tension between the central government and Barotse traditional leaders, who refused to co-operate with the five rural councils which had been established under the Act in Western Province in place of the

41. W. Tordoff, 'Provincial and district government in Zambia', *Journal of Administration Overseas*, vol. VIII, Nos 3 and 4 (July and October 1968).

Barotse National Council.[42] Moreover, the government made clear its abiding determination to pay no more than lip service to the status of traditional authorities by announcing the imminent removal of chiefs from presiding over the local courts. This dealt a further blow to the declining powers and prestige of traditional authorities. The weakening of the traditional system, however, was in part counteracted by the ruling party's attempt to create alternative structures for rural mobilisation. The party had already spearheaded an impressive wave of self-help projects in many parts of the country. President Kaunda sought to reinforce this move by his Chifubu declaration on co-operatives in April.[43] This ideological initiative extolled the virtues of a co-operative approach to economic development. Only later years were to show the difficulties of institutionalising co-operative organisation and of keeping at a high level enthusiasm for self-help projects.

*1966.* The year 1966 began to see the full impact of Rhodesia's UDI and Britain's policy of trying to regain control of the situation through economic sanctions. The consequences for Zambia were primarily economic:[44] the virtual collapse of her tourist industry; supply shortages (especially oil) and a rise in the cost of imports (both of which resulted in inflation by the end of the year); costly and hasty attempts to diversify copper export routes away from Rhodesia; and an escalating series of problems affecting the common services still owned jointly by Zambia and Rhodesia. Rhodesia Railways quietly accumulated over 70 per cent of the jointly owned rolling stock inside Rhodesia. Then, in May 1966, it reacted to Zambia's attempt to implement financial sanctions against Rhodesia through the railway system by refusing to accept any Zambian traffic through Rhodesia without prior payment.[45] The Zambian government, faced with the total paralysis of the economy, bowed down to this demand in July; but this blackmail hastened its decision to accelerate measures designed to reduce, and ultimately end, dependence on the white south. Thus began a vast diversion of resources to build a new copper-mining and export-oriented infrastructure independent of that of Rhodesia. This policy only got off the ground in late 1966, when a start was made on an oil pipeline from Dar es Salaam to the

42. Caplan, *The Elites of Barotseland, op. cit.,* pp. 212–13.

43. B. de G. Fortman (ed.), *After Mulungushi—the Economics of Zambian Humanism* (Nairobi, 1969), pp. 110–14. See also *A Humanist in Africa, op. cit.*

44. R. Hall, 'Zambia and Rhodesia: links and fetters', *Africa Report,* vol. 11 (January 1966).

45. See chapter 9.

Copperbelt, and on tarring the Great North Road. In subsequent years the policy was extended to include local repair facilities and coal supplies, railway construction (the Tanzam railway), and the Kafue and Kariba North Bank electric power projects—all of which could not be completed before the mid-1970s.

The consequences of Rhodesia's UDI, however, were not only economic. They seriously exacerbated black–white relations in Zambia. These had never been good in the colonial period. They were not improved by the spectacle of continuing white supremacy in the countries to Zambia's south after 1964, and the ill-concealed sympathy for such supremacy among many Europeans in Zambia (10,000 of whom were still white Rhodesians and South Africans). As far back as December 1964 the government had had to introduce legislation to curb racial insults. The following year UNIP was visibly shocked by a Copperbelt by-election for a reserved roll seat when its candidate received only a derisory ninety-six votes. In 1966 the NPP dissolved itself. But this formal abdication by the European community from the pursuit of political power had little effect compared with the accusation in July that a large number of senior expatriate Special Branch officers were passing State secrets to the Rhodesian regime. Further difficulties were caused when freedom fighters in Angola opened up a new front in the eastern part of the country, adjacent to Zambia's Western and North-western Provinces. The results were an influx of several thousand refugees to swell the ranks of those who had already entered Zambia's Eastern Province from Moçambique in 1965. At the same time, the Portuguese began in July what proved to be a series of armed raids into Zambian territory.

Economically and politically the year was far less gloomy. The ambitious first National Development Plan was launched amid high expectations and increasing revenue. True, neither the civil service nor the ruling party had been fundamentally reorganised to assume a developmental role. But it was mainly the shadow of UDI and economic discontent in the towns which held popular attention. A number of serious strikes by mineworkers and others took place and affected in all 152,000 workers, or nearly half the work force, in the first half of the year. The situation was only restored by large, inflationary wage and salary increases in the mining and public sectors following the Brown and Whelan Commissions' awards in October and November.[46]

Politically, UNIP was not seriously troubled by the dismissal for

46. Bates, *Unions, Parties and Political Development, op. cit.*, and R. B. Sutcliffe, 'Crisis on the Copperbelt', *The World Today*, vol. 22, No. 12 (December 1966).

alleged financial impropriety of two Lozi Cabinet Ministers (N. Mundia and M. Nalilungwe) in January. It neglected to consult the House of Chiefs three months later when it introduced the Local Courts Bill, depriving traditional leaders of their judicial role; and the party also ignored the House's subsequent protests. UNIP reacted confidently to the formation of the new United Party (UP) by two Lozi-speaking ANC and UNIP MPs in July by persuading ANC to join it in amending the constitution to provide for the compulsory resignation of any MP who changed his political party allegiance after his election. UNIP was elated at its easy trouncing of most ANC candidates in the country-wide local government elections in September. The year closed with an air of optimism: the worst of the UDI storm had been successfully ridden out; the ruling party was not yet internally divided or externally challenged; implementation of its policies had been taken a long step forward with the opening of the University of Zambia and the setting up of the Zambia National Provident Fund; heavy emphasis on expanding social services and the provision of what were in effect grants to many village farmers helped the government to project a favourable image; and the economy (and employment opportunities) continued to grow at a very fast rate.

*1967.* The next year (1967) was very different, at least on the home front. Despite President Kaunda's Far Eastern tour (including China) and his successful mediation in the Kenya–Somali border dispute, the spotlight of national attention focused on domestic political events. In February by-elections were held in the two constituencies vacated by the UP MPs who had been compelled to surrender their seats under the terms of the constitutional amendment referred to above. UNIP won both, including the Mazabuka constituency in ANC's stronghold of Southern Province. However, only one-third of the electorate cast their ballots amid a clear distortion of the democratic process due to widespread intimidation and violence by UNIP activists. 'Mazabuka tactics' became part of the political folk-lore of both parties. On the one hand, they signified the fragility of UNIP's commitment to multi-party competition and, on the other, they gravely shook ANC's confidence in the legitimacy of the system—so much so that four of the remaining nine ANC MPs anticipated the early demise of their party and crossed the floor to join UNIP.

Meanwhile, the UP was quietly organising in Western Province. It was able to exploit the economic discontent which resulted from the government's decision to stop the Witwatersrand Native Labour

Association (WENELA) recruiting men in the province to work for
very low wages as migrant labourers in the South African mines. The
UP also benefited from UNIP's decision to expel Mr Mundia in
March, and he became the new UP president. The results of UP's
work manifested themselves in renewed secessionist agitation in
Western Province at the end of the year[47] and in the defection of
large numbers of voters there from the ruling party in the 1968
general election.

A different and more important political event took place at the
UNIP national council meeting in April. President Kaunda resumed
and expanded upon his ideological initiative of 1965 by outlining his
philosophy of Humanism.[48] This was not merely a rhetorical attempt
to legitimate UNIP's leadership in the eyes of the masses by moving
away from the more exploitative aspects of capitalism and incor-
porating various traditionalist values. Zambian Humanism, as it was
elaborated by the President in subsequent years, came to provide
certain guidelines—admittedly flexible and sometimes vague—within
which the party could tackle the unfolding problems of Zambian
society.

Perhaps unfortunately, the second step in revealing his philosophy
coincided with the first serious intra-party crisis which UNIP had to
face. In August the triennial general conference of the party was
held. For the first time, contested elections for posts on the central
committee (the top party organ) were allowed. The result was that
Bemba-speaking leaders, whose followers had taken a prominent role
in the independence struggle and who felt relatively under-represented and unrewarded, joined up with the party's weak Tonga-speaking
minority to unseat leading Lozi- and Nyanja-speaking office-holders.
The openly sectional appeals by both sides generated a vast amount
of ill-feeling in the party and lowered its prestige in the country.[49]
The consequences were manifold, damaging and permanent. One
was a major Cabinet reshuffle. Although not the first since independence, it introduced an era of frequent Cabinet reshuffles (sometimes three a year) which proved very disruptive of continuity in the
making and implementation of policy. Another result was the
accession of Mr Simon Kapwepwe to the vice-presidency of both
UNIP and Zambia, thereby increasing the impression that the party

47. G. L. Caplan, 'Barotseland: the secessionist challenge to Zambia',
*Journal of Modern African Studies*, vol. 6, No. 3 (October 1968).
48. K. D. Kaunda, *Humanism in Zambia*, reproduced in Fortman, *After
Mulungushi, op. cit.*
49. R. I. Rotberg, 'Tribalism and politics in Zambia', *Africa Report*,
vol. 12, No. 9 (December 1967), and chapter 4.

was Bemba-dominated. The party's image was further tarnished by the necessity in December of setting up a commission of enquiry into the affairs of the Lusaka city council, and the commission's subsequent revelations that certain UNIP councillors were feathering their own nests.[50]

The August 1967 crisis within UNIP did not, however, stop the government from continuing vigorously to implement its policies. Sanctions against Rhodesia were tightened. The government set up some ten new parastatal bodies during the year. Some (for example, Zambia Railways and Zambia Airways) were the result of the splitting up of the remaining common services with Rhodesia;[51] others (such as the Legal Aid Act) reflected UNIP's continuing commitment to a Welfare State. This goal, however, was becoming somewhat imperilled by the growing inefficiencies of the government machine.[52] The first National Development Plan was behind schedule in some Ministries and the Auditor General reported 'a widespread breakdown of normal controls and checks' in the government's accounting system. Things were not made any easier by the reluctance of the largely foreign-owned private sector either to help citizens break into its monopoly or to invest in essential long-term projects in the agricultural and mining sectors.

The country's foreign situation was also becoming more difficult. Liberation movement activity in Rhodesia, Angola and Moçambique continued to escalate. Rhodesia retaliated in February by putting a temporary embargo on all traffic bound for Zambia, and the following month Portugal suspended Benguela Railway traffic through Angola. The discovery of a Rhodesian spy ring led to the passage of a tough new Official Secrets Act.[53] In May, and again in August, military clashes took place for the first time between Rhodesian forces and freedom fighters. Rhodesia reacted by inviting in South African troops which have remained in Rhodesia ever since. She also countenanced minor acts of sabotage inside Zambia and made threats of military retaliation against Zambia. These threats were repeated in more crude and undisguised language by the South African Prime Minister, Mr Vorster, in October. Clearly, Zambia was facing growing problems with her domestic private sector, the ruling party itself, and the white minority regimes.

50. *Report of the Commission of Enquiry into the Affairs of the Lusaka City Council* [chairman: Chief Justice Blagden] (Lusaka, 1968).
51. Only one was left after 1967—the Central African Power Corporation.
52. *National Convention on the Four-year Development Plan, Kitwe, 11–13 January 1967* (Lusaka, 1967).
53. *Report of the Tribunal on Detainees* (Lusaka, 1967).

*1968*. It was indeed with these three problem areas that most of the important events of 1968 were concerned. In April President Kaunda took the economic bull by the horns by springing his 'Mulungushi economic reforms' on the nation, in terms of which the government bought a 51 per cent (i.e. a controlling) share in twenty-six major companies and used its State power to restrict certain economic, especially retail trading, opportunities to Zambian citizens.[54] While the goals of the reforms were not socialist, they did increase local—both public and private—participation in, and control over, the economy. And they provided the pattern for similar, albeit much more extensive, reforms in ensuing years. The reforms did, however, run into several difficulties: the management contracts which were given to the companies being taken over reduced the reality of State control; the acute shortage of African Zambian entrepreneurs with capital enabled a small number of Asian and European Zambians to benefit disproportionately from the reforms; and the foreign-owned private sector that remained was seriously antagonised at a time when the public sector did not have the appropriate structures, skills, policies or (from 1971 onwards) capital to become the main engine of economic growth. These problems remained throughout the First Republic and they contributed to the failure of the first National Development Plan to attain certain of its goals, especially in the fields of employment, agricultural production and overall physical output.

Sectional tensions within UNIP continued, notably in the Eastern Province, where a 'Unity in the East' movement sprang up in opposition to Bemba elements in the party. In February President Kaunda contained them temporarily by walking out of a national council meeting and resigning for a few hours. Party leaders begged him to return and he did so with the stipulation that Ministers and other UNIP MPs could not leave Lusaka without written permission. This attempt to prevent sectional campaigning in the party was repeated once or twice in later years, but proved ineffective. In 1968, however, various other factors helped keep sectional disputes quiescent. The economy grew fast (averaging a 10 per cent growth rate in real terms during the year). The economic reforms became a major focus of attention, as did further difficulties in Zambia's

54. K. D. Kaunda, *Towards Economic Independence* (Lusaka, 1968), reproduced in Fortman, *After Mulungushi, op. cit.*; F. Soremekun, 'The challenge of nation-building: neo-humanism and politics in Zambia, 1967–1969', *Genève–Afrique*, vol. IX, No. 1 (1970); J. B. Zulu, *Zambian Humanism* (Lusaka, 1970); and P. A. Thomas, 'Zambian economic reforms', *Canadian Journal of African Studies*, vol. 2, No. 1 (spring 1968).

international position. Portuguese bombing of Eastern and Western Provinces became more frequent, and the vital Luangwa river bridge—the gateway to Eastern Province—was blown up. A particularly serious Portuguese incursion resulted in twenty-six Zambian casualties in April and, in the same month, the South African Minister of Defence again threatened retaliation against Zambia because of freedom fighter activities in Rhodesia. President Kaunda tried to reduce this pressure by initiating a secret, desultory and eventually abortive correspondence with Mr Vorster.[55] At the same time, he stated that Zambia must arm herself. He also improved relations with Malawi;[56] opened negotiations to join the East African Community; and stepped up diplomatic attempts to get more effective international (in particular Western) action on southern Africa. Towards the end of the year the new oil pipeline was completed, thereby solving Zambia's fuel problems, and China began a feasibility survey of the Tanzam railway.

However, political events increasingly held attention at home. For 1968 was general election year for both the National Assembly and the presidency.[57] Dr Kaunda initiated elaborate measures to ensure free elections: he set up an independent Electoral Commission and a well staffed and lavishly financed Parliamentary Elections Office, and exhorted all concerned to ensure that the elections were fairly conducted (exhortation was his favourite style of government until 1970). ANC had won the four by-elections held earlier in the year in Southern Province, its area of greatest strength, and UNIP had accepted this defeat. But in August, when inter-party conflict culminated in a UNIP–UP clash on the Copperbelt resulting in six deaths, the government took the opportunity to ban the UP. This move proved ineffective, as the party had already won majority support in Western Province, and its activists continued to campaign, but now under an ANC umbrella.[58] The results of the general election (polling day was 19 December) came, therefore, as a shock

55. *Dear Mr Vorster . . . Details of Exchanges between President Kaunda of Zambia and Prime Minister Vorster of South Africa* (Lusaka, 1971).

56. However, Zambia's relations with several other African States deteriorated because of her recognition of Biafra in May 1968. D. G. Anglin, 'Zambia and the recognition of Biafra', *African Review*, vol. 1, No. 2 (September 1971).

57. See chapter 5, and I. Scott and R. Molteno, 'The Zambian general elections', *Africa Report*, vol. 14, No. 1 (January 1969).

58. The ANC–UP merger was cemented in January 1969, when ANC made Mr Mundia its vice-president. The creation of the Zambia African National Democratic Union (ZANDU) a few months later in May did not alter the position, since the new party never attained any prominence.

to UNIP, although it still won by a large margin. ANC wrested control of Western Province from it and, over the country as a whole, won twenty-three seats (plus one Independent) compared to UNIP's eighty-one. The comparable results in 1964 when the National Assembly was smaller had been UNIP fifty-five and ANC ten, while the settler NPP had won the ten reserved-roll seats which were abolished in 1968.

The 1968 general election was significant in many ways. It led to more extensive Cabinet changes than in the previous and frequent reshuffles of the past two years. The balance of power within UNIP began to swing away from the Northern Province group; this led ultimately to the formation of the United Progressive Party (UPP) two and a half years later. Violence was confirmed as a major feature of Zambian political culture and UNIP activists renewed their demands for a one-party State. There was another event, equally important for the future. During the campaign President Kaunda not only renewed commitment to rural development but also announced his plans to bring this about by decentralising the machinery of government.[59]

*1969.* These decentralisation measures were implemented in 1969.[60] A Cabinet Minister was appointed to head each province and fifty-three District Governors were put in charge of the districts. The initial reforms were more cautious than the President's announcement had indicated, but they pointed a direction in which the government has continued to move. Other important administrative changes were made: a new post of Secretary General to the Government (held by a Cabinet Minister) was created to head the civil service, and a greater politicisation of the service was initiated. The number of central Ministries was almost halved, but the resultant umbrella Ministries failed to improve co-ordination. Later in the year a new National Agricultural Marketing Board was set up and a Finance (Control and Management) Act was passed to discipline civil servants in their handling of public funds. While all these measures were part of the government's plan to develop the rural areas, success was hampered by a continuing lack of professional manpower, failure to find an appropriate strategy for helping farmers, and a growing shortage of capital.

Indeed, as it turned out, it was again the urban economy which

59. K. D. Kaunda, *Zambia's Guidelines for the next Decade* (Lusaka, 1968).

60. W. Tordoff, 'Provincial and local government in Zambia', *Journal of Administration Overseas*, vol. IX, No. 1 (January 1970).

held the limelight in 1969. In January a tough anti-inflation budget brought 30,000 new people into the tax-paying bracket and cut government's capital spending. A partial wage freeze and ban on strikes followed. But the most startling events took place in August, when Dr Kaunda told the UNIP national council that the government would extend the economic reforms not only by further protecting citizen entrepreneurs from foreign competition but also by taking a 51 per cent stake in the country's main industry—copper.[61] The two giant companies accepted State participation, particularly when negotiations made it clear that they would be rewarded with a management contract and the enormous compensation of K209 million payable over eight to twelve years in US dollars, the outstanding debt bearing interest at 6 per cent. The Zambian government's acceptance of capitalist premises became clear when it did not deduct from the compensation (as Chile did) the exploitative profits taken out of the country by the companies over the previous four decades. Nevertheless, the take-over did create the possibility of increased State control over mining policy, opportunities to invite additional companies to prospect, and the hope that the balance of payments would be more favourable once the period of generous compensation was over.

The President's timing of this dramatic move towards restructuring the Zambian economy was probably advanced in a bid to ease the renewed tension inside the ruling party. This tension, however, continued to mount and came to a head when Vice-president Kapwepwe resigned on the alleged grounds that his fellow Bemba were being persecuted.[62] Dr Kaunda persuaded him to withdraw his resignation, but placated party dissatisfaction with Mr Kapwepwe by stripping him of his major portfolios. The President also assumed supreme powers over the party as secretary general and dissolved the controversial central committee elected in 1967. He replaced this committee with a more balanced and representative 'interim executive committee' and, at the same time, appointed the Attorney General, Mr Fitzpatrick Chuula, to head a commission to examine the party's constitution with a view to reducing sectional competition within the party. To show his impartiality between the country's sectional groups, President Kaunda abrogated the 1964 Barotseland agreement in October, and renamed Barotse Province 'Western

61. K. D. Kaunda, *Towards Complete Independence* (Lusaka, 1969), and Bostock and Harvey, *Economic Independence and Zambian Copper*, *op. cit.*

62. W. Tordoff, 'Political crisis in Zambia', *Africa Quarterly*, vol. x, No. 3 (October–December 1970).

Province'. He also tried to strengthen his position by releasing all prisoners who had been convicted of criminal offences arising out of political activities in a general amnesty to celebrate the fifth anniversary of independence. The following month (November) he held talks with ANC leader, Mr Harry Nkumbula, on a possible merger of the two parties.

Other important political events included UNIP's victory in the June 1969 referendum, which made Parliament solely responsible for amending the constitution. The campaign which preceded the referendum also resulted in a flare-up of violence between UNIP and its opponents; ANC was banned in Mumbwa District and new curbs were placed on the activities of the Watch Tower movement. Immediately after the referendum an unexpected conflict arose between the executive and the judiciary over the release of two Portuguese soldiers. This clash led both to the departure of the Chief Justice and two other judges and the beginning of the Africanisation of the Bench.[63] The independence of the judiciary was not, however, seriously affected.

1969 also marked important steps in Zambia's handling of the south. Portuguese land and air violations, in particular, continued; and more refugees from Moçambique arrived. Zambia tightened internal security by passing the State Security Act and arranged with Italy to replace the Royal Air Force in order to accelerate training of the Zambia Air Force. At the same time, Zambia crept a little closer towards economic independence from the south by becoming nearly self-sufficient in coal and beginning construction of the large Kafue hydro-electric scheme. She also continued her negotiations to join the East Africa Community, although she eventually realised that, given the high-cost structure of Zambian industry, her manufactured goods would not be competitive in the East African market without a substantial devaluation. She therefore quietly allowed her application to lapse despite the political attractions of membership. Finally, she persuaded the East and Central Africa Summit Conference to accept the important 'Lusaka manifesto' on southern Africa as a strategy for change in the region.[64] In years to come the white minority regimes may come to regret their refusal to negotiate with black Africa on the basis of this manifesto.

63. A. D. Roberts, 'White judges under attack', *Round Table*, No. 236 (October 1969).
64. Fifth Summit Conference of East and Central African States, *Manifesto on Southern Africa* (Lusaka, 1969); B. V. Mtshali, 'Zambia's foreign policy', *Current History*, vol. 58, No. 343 (March 1970).

*1970* turned out to be a pivotal period in Zambian history. It was the last year of the great copper boom—and the effects of plummeting copper prices in the second half of the year (from a peak of K1,252 a ton in March 1970 to K721 at the end of the year) were tragically intensified by the huge Mufulira mine cave-in disaster in September. This disaster affected a quarter of the country's production and was particularly serious since production in other sectors was also reduced by a rash of strikes. The gross domestic product fell 5.5 per cent in real terms, and the first National Development Plan was so far behind schedule that it had to be extended by eighteen months. Secondly, the year was the first in which the government's strategy for reducing the hold of international capitalism received a major setback when the banks successfully resisted the State's intended take-over, announced by President Kaunda in November.[65] Nevertheless, both the building societies and insurance companies were taken over, and without management contracts. Thirdly, real independence from the south became a certainty when work began on the Kariba North Bank Power Station and China began construction of the Tanzam railway. Rhodesia underlined the need for this new outlet by first of all slapping a surcharge on Zambia's maize imports (as she had done before with coal) and then in November holding up urgently needed fertiliser supplies. Fourthly, the year marked a significant change in the strategy for containing sectional tensions. Previously exhortation, diversionary tactics, generous patronage and delicate sectional balancing acts had been relied on.[66] Henceforth structural change, and, if that failed, coercion, were to be increasingly used. ANC was banned in a second district (Livingstone) and two of its MPs were detained following violent incidents; by the middle of the year, ninety-two Zambians (including six UNIP officials) were in detention. Meanwhile the Chuula Commission held its hearings and reported in September. But its report on a new constitution for UNIP did not succeed in resolving tensions within the ruling party; instead, it triggered off the most serious split in the party's history. A virtual party within the party was formed by mainly Northern Province elements, although they only came out into the open in the middle of the following year. Finally, 1970 was a turning point because the Zambia Defence Force embarked upon a sizeable expansion and the first Zambian was appointed commanding officer of the Zambia army at the very end of the year.

65. K. D. Kaunda, *Take up the Challenge* (Lusaka, 1970).
66. T. Rasmussen, 'Political competition and one-party dominance in Zambia', *Journal of Modern African Studies*, vol. 7, No. 3 (1969).

There were other events which at least captured the headlines. Zambia played host to the prestigious third Non-aligned Summit Conference, attended by representatives of over fifty States. Subsequently President Kaunda, as chairman of the OAU and with a mandate also from the non-aligned nations, set out on an abortive tour of Western countries to persuade them to reduce their support for minority rule in southern Africa.

At home several important policies were put on a new basis. Technical education received a boost with the creation of a new parastatal organisation, the Commission for Technical Education and Vocational Training, which had ambitious plans. This was an important move, since Zambianisation of technical jobs was proceeding very slowly. In agriculture several new steps were taken. A Land Acquisition Act was passed to allow government to take over without compensation large tracts of land abandoned by their foreign owners. Agricultural credit was put on a sounder footing when a new parastatal body replaced the Credit Organisation of Zambia. And an attempt was made to save the co-operative movement by passing very detailed legislation governing the organisation of co-operatives. All these measures were essential in view of the continuing decline of agricultural output in most fields.

The second half of the year saw several political events of note. Local government elections were held in which UNIP won over 85 per cent of the 968 wards. Mr Kapwepwe was replaced as Vice-president by Mainza Chona from Southern Province, and a financial scandal led to the suspension (later lifted) of four Ministers in November. This episode was used by the various sectional factions within UNIP as yet another stick with which to beat one another and reflected the general entrenchment in the private sector of many senior and middle-level party leaders. An equally important event occurred in November, when the President announced a tough leadership code which he wanted the party to adopt in order to reduce the growing materialism of UNIP's leadership.[67] Although the implementation of the code was again postponed at the start of the Second Republic in 1973, it remained a leading issue in national politics.

*1971.* The next year proved to be a difficult one in every respect: the copper price continued at a very low level; unemployment and urban crime increased as the national income contracted further; sectional tensions mounted; and the southern African situation worsened.

67. Kaunda, *Take up the Challenge, op. cit.*

Politically, the year opened with serious allegations by two Northern Province politicians that the government had shown tribal bias in criminal prosecutions. President Kaunda responded by appointing a commission of enquiry, chaired by Chief Justice Doyle, to investigate these and other allegations.[68] While the hearings of the Doyle Commission were bringing to light a good deal of the government's dirty linen, divisive politicking behind the scenes went on over the proposed new UNIP constitution. Unusually vituperative debates in the National Assembly showed the mounting discontent of a Northern Province faction. In April another Minister had to be suspended for sectional activities in Luapula Province, and the President tried to suppress two opposed 'tribal mafias'—the Committee of Twenty-four and the Committee of Fourteen. Nevertheless, in May the party weathered the publication of the Doyle Commission's report, which was severely critical of the financial probity of several Ministers, and the party general conference both adopted the new constitution and unanimously elected a slate of leaders to the central committee. This deceptive peace was soon shattered. President Kaunda dismissed the Ministers criticised in the Doyle report and the Cabinet Minister who had made the original allegation. On 1 August it was reported that a new party, the United Progressive Party (UPP), had been formed on the Copperbelt by UNIP dissidents. Two weeks later the President disciplined four Bemba-speaking MPs for their links with the new party. This at once forced former Vice-president Kapwepwe to admit the existence of the UPP and his own role as its leader.[69] The reaction of UNIP was swift and hysterical. Party-sponsored demonstrations demanded a one-party State; some 100 UPP activists (including all its leaders except Kapwepwe) were detained; large placatory salary increases were handed out throughout the public sector, including the armed forces; and considerable violence and other intimidatory measures were used against suspected UPP supporters. The year ended with twelve by-elections, of which UPP won only one—Kapwepwe's seat at Mufulira West.[70] UNIP had emerged victorious but badly shaken from the most serious crisis in its existence.

68. *Report of the Commission of Enquiry into the Allegations made by Mr Justin Chimba and Mr John Chisata* [chairman, Chief Justice Doyle] (Lusaka, 1971).

69. R. V. Molteno, 'Zambia and the one-party State', *East Africa Journal*, vol. 9, No. 2 (February 1972), pp. 6–8.

70. C. Gertzel, K. Mutukwa, I. Scott, and M. Wallis, 'Zambia's final experience of inter-party elections: the by-elections of December 1971', *Kroniek van Afrika*, vol. 2 (June 1972).

Internationally, events proceeded scarcely any better. In January Britain's new Conservative government reaffirmed its intention of resuming arms sales to South Africa. In the same month the government of President Obote in Uganda was overthrown in a military coup and Zambia lost a valued ally. Pressure from the white south continued. By March 1971 the Portuguese had committed forty acts of aggression, in which fifty Zambians had been killed, over the preceding twenty-one months; Portuguese soldiers also kidnapped five Zambians in March. Nor was this all: Portugal imposed a partial blockade on Zambia-bound cargo at the ports of Beira and Lobito Bay. The following month the South African Prime Minister, Mr Vorster, sought to embarrass President Kaunda by alleging that the latter had had secret contact with his government.[71] Although Kaunda published the correspondence and showed that he had turned down repeated South African invitations to dialogue, student leaders at the University of Zambia criticised the President's conduct and the university was closed for some weeks. Border incidents continued and tension flared up in October when a South African patrol entered Zambian territory from the Caprivi Strip, where Namibian freedom fighters had succeeded in laying land mines. Zambia responded by taking steps to increase her military preparedness. A Home Guard Bill was introduced in the National Assembly in November and this supplemented the Zambia National Service Act which had been passed earlier in the year.

Other potentially important statutes were passed. The Registration and Development of Villages Act laid the legal basis for a long-awaited (and still not achieved) 'rural reconstruction'. The Act formalised the existence of village and ward-level development committees, which the government had been struggling to get going for several years.[72] The Industrial Relations Act, although not brought into operation for over a year, created the legal framework for workers' participation in industry.

*1972.* This was the last year of the First Republic, and several very important changes took place. The most spectacular was the banning of the UPP in February, accompanied by more detentions and the setting up of a Commission, under Vice-president Chona, to recommend what form a 'one-party participatory democracy' in Zambia should take.[73] The Commission was notable alike for the

71. *Dear Mr Vorster . . ., op. cit.,*

72. *Village Productivity and Ward Development Committees: a Pocket Manual* (Lusaka, 1971).

73. *Report of the National Commission on the Establishment of a One-*

broad base of its membership, the painstaking way in which it took evidence in every district of the country, and for the high quality of the report which it produced. This report was an impressive blue-print for the Second Republic. Legislation to establish the one-party State was passed in December. This not only abolished the ANC but also put paid to the two attempts made by UPP supporters during the year to resurrect their party under a new label. It was left to the following year, however, for the new institutions of the Second Republic to be set up. In announcing its intentions the government indicated that it would depart in many respects from the recom-mendations of the Chona Commission.

There were other political events of note during 1972. President Kaunda failed in his persistent attempts to persuade ANC and UPP leaders to merge with the ruling party. And though the Chona Com-mission recommended a rigorous code of leadership embracing all political, administrative, military and judicial leaders, the govern-ment postponed implementation once again. Not content with increased salaries, MPs also voted themselves gratuities for the first time. Finally, Zambianisation of the armed forces was taken a step further with the appointment of the first Zambian commander of the Air Force.

Economically, Zambia felt the pinch as a result of prolonged low copper prices. The government's capital budget for development fell drastically, thus continuing an alarming trend which had begun in 1970. More economic reforms were introduced, and the second National Development Plan was inaugurated.[74] From the outset this plan proved to be an unrealistic document both in its estimates of resources available and in its targets for development. One stark figure which it did reveal was that the country's labour force would grow by 67,000 annually (37,000 in the urban areas), while on the most optimistic projection the plan would create only 20,000 jobs a year.

## The Second Republic

Indeed, the Second Republic was inaugurated in the most in-auspicious circumstances. The economic scene was dominated by low copper prices, though these were soon to be given an artificial boost as a result of the events which followed Rhodesia's closure of her

*party Participatory Democracy in Zambia* [chairman, Vice-president Mainza Chona] (Lusaka, 1972), and *Government Paper No. 1 of 1972: Summary of Recommendations Accepted by Government* (Lusaka, 1972).

74. *Second National Development Plan: 1972–76* (Lusaka, 1971).

border with Zambia. Not only was there almost no development spending on new projects but there were also a disgruntled private sector, rising unemployment, and an urban–rural income gap[75] which was continuing to grow. The Second Republic also started without the active support of the large number of people who had belonged to former opposition parties which had either, like the UPP, been proscribed or, like the ANC, legislated out of existence. UNIP had not oriented itself to the tasks of economic mobilisation and had still not undertaken the intensive political education of its cadres, to which it had pledged itself in 1972. The efficient working of the machinery of government was impeded by continuing shortages of professional manpower, internal weaknesses in the civil service, poor co-ordination between central Ministries and the huge parastatal sector, as well as delays in carrying through further decentralisation. There were almost no institutionalised controls over the Zambia Defence Force and, though the problem was being tackled, the Zambia Police Force still lacked the capacity to handle an increasing load. Again the problem of South Africa[76] remained unsolved, and in January 1973 Rhodesia caused further difficulties by once more closing the border in retaliation for what she claimed to be Zambia's support for the serious and sustained guerrilla activity which broke out inside Rhodesia in December 1972. This pressure was made more worrying when several Zambians were discovered to be collaborating with the white south. A spate of treason and espionage trials had to be held.

It would be rash to deny that as Zambia enters her second decade of majority rule she faces formidable problems. For some of these problems—notably the continuing uneasy relations with the white south and the economic dislocation that will again be caused by fluctuations in the world price of copper—the Zambian government is not to blame. But other problems are a direct legacy of the First Republican period and stem less from the government's inability to formulate sound policies than from its failure to implement many of them—like that relating to the development of rural agriculture. One result is that when, as frequently happens, Zambia is compared to her neighbour, Tanzania, the comparison is usually to

75. D. Rothchild, 'Rural–urban inequities and resource allocation in Zambia', *Journal of Commonwealth Political Studies*, vol. x, No. 3 (1972); and R. H. Bates, 'Input structures, output functions, and systems capacity: a study of the Mineworkers' Union of Zambia', *Journal of Politics*, vol. 32 (November 1970).

76. R. V. Molteno, *Africa and South Africa* (London, 1971) and 'South Africa's forward policy in Africa', *Round Table*, No. 243 (July 1971).

Zambia's detriment. It is not always recognised how different, despite geographical propinquity and ideological similarity, the two countries really are. Despite Zambia's greater wealth, her political leaders have had to operate within even greater constraints than those which have faced President Nyerere and his government. At the end of the introduction to a book which examines critically the political record of post-independence Zambia, we therefore seek to shade a little light into the sombre picture which we have painted immediately above.[77]

Since independence, and especially in the period between 1964 and 1970, economic growth has been rapid, despite UDI and the persistence of acute sectional tensions. These tensions, which are in part to be explained in terms of Zambia's social heterogeneity, have so far been contained with remarkable fairness. The resolution of conflict may prove to be 'an essential mechanism' of national integration;[78] a hopeful sign is that even disgruntled Barotse leaders no longer think of secession as a desirable political end. Moreover, the intense factional fighting among UNIP national leaders has not, over much of the country, had a serious impact at the local level. Though party officials in UNIP-monopolised rural areas such as Luapula Province have had indifferent success in converting UNIP into a mobilising agent for development, they have in other ways maintained the vigour of the party organisation.[79] Like their counterparts in Tanzania, these officials have tended to 'become personally involved in the full range of personal problems',[80] thus weaving the party into the very fabric of local society. While such close involvement has its dangers—it may mean, for example, that the party organisation is able to articulate local grievances but shies away from helping to impose unpopular agricultural regulations—the cumulative effect has probably been to make UNIP a more important agency of national integration than of social fragmentation. Other potential unifying institutions exist, though not all reach down (as UNIP does) to the lowest levels. They too recruit their members

77. For a fuller discussion of Zambia's achievements, see chapter 10.

78. Cf. A. A. Mazrui, 'Pluralism and national integration', in L. Kuper and M. G. Smith, *Pluralism in Africa* (Berkeley and Los Angeles, 1969), p. 335.

79. Zambia affords little evidence to substantiate the thesis of S. P. Huntington: 'Political development and political decay', *World Politics*, vol. xvii, No. 3 (1965). For a convincing refutation of this thesis, see P. R. Brass, 'Political participation, institutionalisation and stability in India', *Government and Opposition*, vol. 4, No. 1 (1969).

80. N. N. Miller, 'The rural African party: political participation in Tanzania', *American Political Science Review*, vol. 64, No. 2 (1970).

from all parts of the country, either ignoring, or maintaining a balance between, the various social divisions based on language, region or tribe. These institutions include (with some qualification) the civil service, the judiciary, the press and other mass media, the Police Force, and the Zambia Defence Force.[81] The latter, which comprises two arms (the Zambia Army and the Zambia Air Force), has not so far been drawn into politics and plays a guardian-type role.[82]

Again, despite the powerful presence of foreign capital and a large domestic capitalist system, the UNIP government has carried through radical measures which have placed the control of the economy in Zambian hands. In this way, President Kaunda has shown that Humanism amounts to something more than a personal creed. It is true that as an ideology Humanism is not fully comprehensive, systematised and coherent, or sufficiently explicit on certain key issues; nor is there any 'ideological primary group' dedicated to spread its values.[83] But what Humanism has lacked in doctrine it has made up for in action-programme since 1968.[84] Examined within its own cultural and political context,[85] Humanism had become a more powerful ideology by the end of the First Republic than had seemed possible when it was first elaborated by Dr Kaunda more than five years earlier.

Finally, despite a colonial legacy of extreme dependence on the south and vulnerability to its pressures, Zambia has been consistently in the forefront of the struggle to liberate southern Africa. Dr Kaunda said when he was being sworn in as President of the new Republic on 24 October 1964:

I am very much aware of the trial and troubles that beset us; but we will face them with courage and determination not only to conquer them, but

81. For example, there is a belief among many civil servants that tribal discrimination exists in making appointments and promotions; this weakens the civil service as an integrative agency. For this and other qualifications see pp. 103–4 and 286.

82. R. Luckham, 'A comparative typology of civil–military relations', *Government and Opposition*, vol. 6, No. 1 (winter 1971).

83. See E. Shils, 'The concept and function of ideology,' reprint from vol. 7 of *International Encyclopedia of the Social Sciences* (New York, 1968), pp. 66–76.

84. The distinction between two basic elements in ideology—doctrine and action–programme—is made by Z. K. Brzezinski in *The Soviet Bloc: Unity and Conflict* (London, rev. edn, 1967). Cf. also F. Schurman, *Ideology and Organisation in Communist China* (Berkeley and Los Angeles, 1966), where the distinction is made between 'pure' and 'practical' ideology.

85. Cf. C. Geertz, 'Ideology as a cultural system', in D. E. Apter (ed.), *Ideology and Discontent* (New York, 1964).

to profit by our experience. For we do not shout from the rooftops that we are great. Rather we realise that now we must work to prove our right to greatness.[86]

He and his government have gone a long way towards fulfilling that declaration.

86. Quoted in Molteno, *The Zambian Community, op. cit.,* p. 30.

## 2

# The popular basis of anti-colonial protest

*Thomas Rasmussen*

The African nationalist struggle against colonial rule has more often been approached from the vantage point of a politically conscious nationalist elite than from the viewpoint of the ordinary rural villager. The latter experienced the full impact of colonial rule, but his interests and concerns were parochial rather than national in scope. National-level leaders indicted the philosophy and practice of colonial rule and put forward demands for independence on the basis of 'one man, one vote'. They conducted the often delicate negotiations which determined the timetable for independence and the conditions under which new States would emerge out of former colonies. They went to the people in the townships and the country-side, spoke to them about the evils of colonial rule, sold membership cards, organised meetings and demonstrations, and promised a better future when Africans governed themselves. Urban-based, nationally oriented leaders spread the gospel of nationalism and mobilised support among the isolated, parochial and largely apathetic rural masses.[1]

The attitudes and activities of the emerging nationalist leadership did provide an attractive and useful starting point for analysing the politics of decolonisation. Furthermore, nationalist leaders were often willing to talk about their grievances, to analyse the impact of European rule on African society, and to articulate their hopes for the future to sympathetic listeners. Thus the leadership became a primary source of information about its own central role in the decolonisation process, and the leaders tended to put the best light on the organisational successes of their parties and the strength of their following among the people in the rural areas.

1. See, for example, I. Wallerstein, *Africa: the Politics of Independence* (New York, 1961), chapter 3; R. S. Morgenthau, *Political Parties in French-speaking West Africa* (Oxford, 1964), pp. 10–21; T. Hodgkin, *African Political Parties* (Harmondsworth, 1961), pp. 27–31.

Records of the colonial administration were another important source of information. These records often exaggerated the role played by a handful of politically conscious leaders and minimised the amount of anti-colonial discontent discernible in the rural village. The vast African majority was represented as simple, law-abiding people who were satisfied with administrative rule, and any expressed discontent was attributed to a handful of malcontents in the locality stirred up by outside agitators from the towns. Prominent nationalist leaders were the main target of the colonial counter-attack: it was believed that if they were silenced the rank and file would not be polluted by anti-colonial ideas.

A number of recent students of African politics, however, have taken a different view and have suggested that national political leaders played a somewhat marginal role in the anti-colonial struggle. They have directed their attention to the political initiative taken by rural villagers.[2] Following their example, we re-examine in this chapter the popular basis of anti-colonial protest in Northern Rhodesia, particularly from the vantage point of local politicians and rural villagers. Our evidence suggests that the bargaining which took place between the colonial administration and nationalist leaders in Northern Rhodesia and the efforts of those leaders to build up a broad base of support for territorial political change is only half the nationalist story. The experience of colonial rule was direct and immediate for the rural villager, too, and it is therefore necessary to find out in what ways and to what extent he participated in anti-colonial protest. We must also consider why support for the nationalist movement developed earlier and grew more rapidly in some districts than in others. Apparently rural villagers in all parts of Zambia did not feel the weight of European domination equally, nor were they equally able to give political expression to their grievances. We also ask what effect political traditions developed during the struggle against colonial rule have had upon patterns of political support for UNIP and ANC since 1964.

The most comprehensive and scholarly account of the nationalist movement is David Mulford, *Zambia: the Politics of Independence, 1957–64*. Mulford's book contains valuable material on local-level politics and protest, especially on the 1961 disturbances and the efforts made by top UNIP leaders to build up effective local party organisations and to establish effective control over them. But Mulford's principal concern was the politics of independence, and he paid particular attention to constitutional developments, election

2. See M. Kilson, *Political Change in a West African State* (Cambridge, Mass., 1966); H. F. Weiss, *Political Protest in the Congo* (Princeton, 1967).

campaigns, and the attitudes and activities of politicians who were prominent in territorial politics during these critical years. In general he views the independence struggle from the vantage point of prominent nationalist political leaders, not from the perspective of the rural villager.

In the four consecutive years between 1958 and 1961, disturbances occurred in Northern Rhodesia serious enough to warrant a full-scale investigation by the colonial administration. In 1958 approximately 29,000 villagers in the Gwembe Valley had to be resettled owing to the spread of the waters of Lake Kariba over the lands which they had occupied. While most of these villagers were resettled in the more thinly populated areas of the valley, 6,000 people had to be moved to Lusitu, 100 miles from their traditional area via a poor road. It was among the latter people that serious resistance to the proposed resettlement took place. The resistance culminated in an armed clash with the police on 10 September 1958 in which eight people were killed and thirty-four injured.[3] In 1959 the colonial administration used the numerous but scattered instances of arson, intimidation and malicious damage which seemed to have a political motivation to justify banning UNIP's predecessor, the Zambia African National Congress (ZANC), and restricting its leaders.[4]

Within a two-week period in March 1960 serious outbreaks of indiscipline took place among students at six schools located in five different provinces. The grievances which sparked off the strikes, demonstrations, boycotts and non-co-operation at the various schools were purely local in nature—most frequently complaints over the food served or grievances against school administrators. The inevitable tensions between students and school officials were aggravated by the fact that most of these officials were European, often young and inexperienced. The commission of enquiry appointed to investigate these occurrences found that the general atmosphere of deepening discontent with the colonial administration undoubtedly contributed to the mood of student unrest. The commission concluded that while UNIP and ANC were not directly involved in provoking the school incidents, the political climate of nationalist opposition to the colonial administration did contribute to the local

3. *Report of the Commission Appointed to Inquire into the Circumstances Leading up to and Surrounding the Recent Deaths and Injuries Caused by Firearms in the Gwembe District and Matters relating thereto* (Lusaka, 1958).

4. *Report of an Inquiry into all the Circumstances which Gave Rise to the Making of the Safeguard of Elections and Public Safety Regulations* (Lusaka, 1959).

students' challenge to duly constituted authority in their own schools. European schoolmasters were seen as the local expression of colonial rule.[5]

The outbreaks of anti-colonial violence in the rural areas which had the greatest significance for the national independence movement occurred in July and August 1961. Hundreds of bridges were destroyed, schools burned and roads blocked in four rural provinces. The disturbances reflected a growing mood of discontent with the efforts of the white settler population to retain a firm grip on the nation's political life and the failure of the Colonial Office to force the pace of constitutional change. The scope of African participation in the disturbances, particularly in the Northern and Luapula Provinces, demonstrated conclusively that anti-colonial sentiment was not the monopoly of a discontented, urban minority but was deeply felt by many rural Africans.[6]

One of the most interesting features of these four disturbances is that in all of them national political leaders played a very marginal role. The protest against some feature of colonial rule was stimulated on all four occasions by local activists who could articulate local grievances and state the anti-colonial case in locally meaningful terms. It does not appear that nationalist leaders came from Lusaka or the Copperbelt to agitate among the local people; quite the contrary: they seemed often to be embarrassed by the excesses of their more exuberant followers. For example, the Gwembe Valley resistance was led by local villagers, most of whom were ANC members, and the participants were drawn from among those most affected by the proposed resettlement scheme. The commission of enquiry found no evidence that they were acting on directions from their ANC superiors, and both Nkumbula and Kaunda denied that ANC had ever encouraged villagers whose traditional lands were to be flooded to resist resettlement in new areas.[7]

The 1959 government enquiry attempted to demonstrate that ZANC leaders were responsible for the scattered acts of arson and malicious damage cited in the report. In fact it seems more plausible that these acts of violence were organised by local political leaders, not by the national party leadership. All ZANC's leaders affirmed their party's commitment to non-violence, although one witness did suggest than an occasional inflammatory statement may have been

5. *Report of the Commission of Inquiry into Disturbances in Certain African Schools* (Lusaka, 1960).

6. *An Account of the Disturbances in Northern Rhodesia, July to October 1961* (Lusaka, 1961).

7. *Report of the Commission . . . Gwembe District, op. cit.*, p. 10.

made in the excited atmosphere of a political meeting.[8] Mulford emphasises that the colonial administration knew that ZANC was not well enough organised to carry out large-scale violence, and concludes that the banning of ZANC in March 1959 was part of a carefully planned attempt to decapitate the major nationalist parties in Central Africa.[9] But restriction of the leaders failed to stem the tide of African nationalism, because the many local politicians, whose roots were in their local communities, were also crucial to the expression of anti-colonial sentiment. Restriction of ZANC leaders simply provided local activists with yet another issue to use against the administration.

The disturbances in the schools in March 1960 demonstrated that anti-colonial, nationalist sentiment was widely distributed and deeply felt among ordinary Zambian students. They showed, too, that the students acted without prompting from national political leaders and in ways that embarrassed the colonial administration and threatened the security of its rule. The issues were expressed in local terms, and the politically conscious opinion leaders, publicists and strike organisers emerged from the ranks of the students themselves.

The commission considered carefully the possibility that UNIP (the successor of ZANC) might have been behind the school disturbances, particularly since the disturbances were well organised and occurred almost simultaneously.[10] Certainly the commission was urged to conclude that the strikes in the schools were organised by a political party, a conclusion which would have justified continued administrative harassment of UNIP and enabled the authorities to blame a handful of malcontents and agitators for stirring up trouble. Such a conclusion would have reinforced the colonial conviction that the great majority of Africans were content to remain under colonial rule. But the commission reported that there was no evidence of any party official at any school before or during the strikes; that no speaker at political meetings advocated strikes in the schools; and that no participating students produced politically oriented statements.[11] Also, the acting president of UNIP claimed no responsibility for the strikes and denied that it had ever been part of UNIP's programme to stir up trouble in the schools.

8. *Report of an Inquiry . . . Elections and Public Safety Regulations*, *op. cit.*, p. 11.

9. Mulford, *Zambia: the Politics of Independence*, *op. cit.*, pp. 102–4.

10. *Report of the Commission of Inquiry Into Disturbances in Certain African Schools*, *op. cit.*, para. 165.

11. *Ibid.*, para. 170.

The launching of UNIP's 'master plan' in 1961 is a particularly important episode in the nationalist struggle in view of its scope, intensity and overtly political character. Because of the great significance of this massive outbreak of violence and the crucial importance of the UNIP conference at Mulungushi which immediately preceded it, it is interesting to consider the relationship between top party leaders and party rank and file at the conference. Did the national party leadership guide and direct the campaign, inspiring their local comrades to begin the disturbances upon their return home? Or were the local UNIP delegates, discontented and frustrated with the lack of progress towards African government, ready to use force to achieve what negotiations had failed to accomplish?

The evidence available seems to support the latter view. Mulford suggests that the behaviour of Kaunda and other top UNIP leaders during late July and early August strongly suggested that UNIP's master plan was launched largely on the strength of local initiative in the Northern Province. At first, Kaunda called unsuccessfully for an end to the violence, but as the disorders spread to other provinces he seized the initiative and sought to turn the situation to UNIP's advantage.[12] The official report of the colonial administration also expressed doubt that the top party leadership could be held responsible for instigating the wave of arson, intimidation and obstruction. The report concluded:

Whatever the instructions of the leaders of the party may have been, it is clear that the call for positive action was interpreted by the lower formations of the party as the signal for the adoption of violent methods... There is no doubt that the root cause of the unrest has been the dissatisfaction over the British government's plans for constitutional change. When negotiations failed to achieve UNIP's objectives, the advocates of violence gained ground and disorders followed. Party officials at the lower level took the initiative and promoted the campaigns of violence, particularly those in the Northern and Luapula provinces.[13]

In short, top party leaders did not need to serve as an inspirational force and did not have to whip up enthusiasm for an intensified campaign against European domination. On the contrary, the delegates assembled at Mulungushi expected to hear that the anti-colonial campaign was to be stepped up and they were pushing the leaders in this direction. In announcing the master plan, national party leaders reflected the sentiments of the aroused party delegates.[14]

12. Mulford, *Zambia: the Politics of Independence, op. cit.*, pp. 201–2.
13. *An Account of the Disturbances in Northern Rhodesia, op. cit.*, p. 73.
14. This interpretation is supported by the reminiscences of two UNIP officials in Serenje District, who were delegates at Mulungushi in 1961.

The evidence presented here suggests that the national political leaders, whose attitudes and activities have often been regarded as the most crucial factor in the success of the independence struggle, played in fact rather marginal roles. First, they were not able to exercise firm control over local party branches and leadership. They were hampered by poor communications, lack of skilled manpower and limited material resources with which to reward loyal followers. Secondly, national political leaders had a vested interest in modera-tion. To some extent, their firm denials of any central direction or involvement in the various disturbances may have been motivated by the knowledge that they would be the target of colonial repression and by desire to stay out of gaol or restriction. More importantly violent and uncontrolled expressions of anti-colonial sentiment both created an opportunity for, and posed a threat to, the nationalist leadership. Acts of resistance to the colonial administration provided an opportunity in so far as they served to discredit the colonial government and to undermine the foundations of its rule; this was an important consideration until 1962, since the outcome of the independence movement was still uncertain. At the same time, how-ever, such acts of resistance proved an embarrassment to national political leaders who were anxious to demonstrate their ability to govern the country responsibly and to build confidence in the future of an African-ruled Zambia.

A corollary of the view that national political leaders played a marginal role in the anti-colonial struggle is therefore the con-tention that the anti-colonial attitudes and activities of many rural villagers and their local spokesmen effectively served to hasten the end of colonial rule. One important source of information on local political activity is the annual reports on African affairs which colonial District Commissioners submitted to their provincial superiors. During the 1950s and early 1960s these reports assessed the amount of political activity in a district and also attempted to define sources of discontent among the village population. These reports are replete with colonial paternalism and interpretations of the primitive African mind, and to some extent they seem to have been written to conform with what the Provincial Commissioners expected to hear. But the reports are an important source of in-formation, particularly for the decade of the 1950s when most DCs tried to minimise the amount of discontent in their districts.[15]

15. Unfortunately, party records and most colonial records on political activity are not available for inspection. This assessment of the importance of local grievances and the role of local activists in exploiting them for political purposes must be regarded as tentative.

In the rural areas of Northern Rhodesia discontent with the existing distribution of power and wealth in society was widespread. In
virtually every province of Zambia expressions of local discontent
with colonial government were of sufficient importance and concern to find their way into official government reports. Nationalism
as a large-scale popular political movement drew much of its
strength by capitalising on essentially local grievances, and national
political issues were essentially defined in local terms.

Local-level supporters of the major African nationalist parties
seemed to play a very important part in crystallising anti-colonial
sentiment in the village and translating felt grievances into anti-
colonial action. Local politicians organised boycotts, led demonstrations, conducted political meetings and encouraged non-compliance
with administrative regulations. These politicians were crucial in
translating the gospel of African nationalism into locally relevant
terms, thereby providing an essential link between national political
leaders and the ordinary rural villager. One DC reported in 1961:

It would still be true to say that the political awareness of the normal
Kalabo villager with regard to territorial affairs is not by any means keen.
A situation is in the process of developing however whereby this 'norm' is
undergoing a transformation. Youths with a certain education who hitherto
left for urban areas to seek employment no longer find this easy, and are
now obliged to become villagers in every sense of the word. Their aspirations politically speaking are not those of old. They find themselves subject to political haranguing not only from individuals but from newspapers
with a wide distribution. They are forced to become aware of territorial
affairs. Some are able to talk quite lucidly on questions once the acknowledged preserve of the local intelligentsia who are becoming less the leaders
of political thought with the passage of time.[16]

For the villager, local issues having to do with agricultural prices,
administrative regulations, traditional family and tribal disputes, and
the growing discontent with poor employment prospects were the
core of anti-colonial sentiment. Political advancement was generally
defined in terms of redressing these local grievances. The politics of
the Eastern Province and of the rural areas of the Southern and
Central Provinces, where most of the African cash crop farming was
concentrated, frequently centred on questions of prices and marketing arrangements for the two most important crops, maize and
tobacco. Dissatisfaction with producer prices was a regular feature
of annual reports on agriculture in the Eastern Province during the
1950s; there were several short-lived boycotts of district markets in

16. Annual report on African affairs: Kalabo District, 1961, Sec./Nat. 66c,
Lusaka archives.

1959 and 1960. While these boycotts were not successful in achieving an increase in producer prices, they did signify the activist mood of villagers when their immediate economic interests were affected.

Tobacco producers often assigned responsibility for annual fluc-tuation in the profitability of tobacco—a much less predictable crop than maize—to the manipulations of Europeans. The DC for Katete pointed out the political implications of fluctuations in tobacco prices:

In addition to the fall in prices, the unpredictable criteria of the buyer in what is unquestionably a buyers market are also a most irritating factor and had a direct bearing on the prices realized. In previous years, for example, top leaves had been rated the most valuable whereas in 1960 they realized the lowest price of any grade. There may be an economic explanation for these fluctuations but they are certainly not understood by the African producer who simply and perhaps not without justification, jumps to the conclusion that he is being cheated by the Europeans. The village politician is always eager to seize and exploit such dissatisfaction.[17]

Several DCs indicated that the various restrictions and administra-tive regulations introduced by the colonial administration and native authorities were a constant source of irritation to the villager. Local politicians were not slow to take advantage of these grievances:

In the villages, political advancement is normally misunderstood to be steps taken in the direction of the removal of all sorts of irksome restric-tions, so that the day of independence is seen by the villager as the day on which he will enjoy complete freedom to hunt, cultivate and collect fire-wood all without the least regard to the regulations which at present govern these activities.[18]

There are in Namwala two things calculated to stir up the Ba-Ila: ques-tions affecting the land and hunting rights. By unfortunate coincidence, new and severe measures for protecting Red Lechwe coincided with the impact of external politics and provides the disaffected with a first class grievance to exploit which was not slow in being taken up.[19]

Local political conflicts between local people over local issues very much affected the course of nationalist politics in the rural areas, a fact which can easily be overlooked when the anti-colonial struggle is viewed from the vantage point of the urban political elite rather than that of the rural villager. The new political parties opened up a new avenue of political competition, just as the extension of

17. Annual report on African affairs: Katete District, 1960, *ibid.*
18. Annual report on African affairs: Fort Jameson District, 1960, *ibid.*
19. Annual report on African affairs: Namwala District, 1957, Sec./Nat. 66F, Lusaka archives.

European influence had done half a century earlier.[20] With the
appearance of the nationalist political parties, a potentially important new influence was added to the local complex of political
forces, and some local competitors were able to turn the new circumstances to their own advantage.

For example, traditional disputes between neighbouring tribes
were occasionally revived by competing political parties. Thus the
DC for Mankoya District reported:

> It cannot be said that [refusal to register political parties] has put an end
> to their political activity, however, and it continues surreptitiously. The
> UNIP's platform was based on territorial issues which have not as yet
> captured the interest of the average villager but the ANC has concentrated
> on the theme of self determination for the Mankoya district, i.e. freedom
> from Lozi domination together with secession from the protectorate, and
> this has attracted both interest and support from certain sections of the
> Mankoya and Bameshasha tribes.[21]

Members of the traditional aristocracy, whose position had been
diminished under colonial rule, sometimes engaged in anti-colonial
activities and openly supported the nationalist parties. The Provincial Commissioner for Barotse Province reported that in Mongu
District 'an extraordinarily complex situation arose when the
nationalists were joined by some traditional leaders who were
out of power at the time and whose motives and aims were different
from those of their new found allies'.[22]

Several years earlier a disinherited traditional leader had stirred up

20. See, for example, Meebelo, *Reaction to Colonialism, op. cit.* Meebelo
points out that African reactions to the white man were largely influenced
by local conditions, and that the reaction of political and social competitors in the Northern Province was based on their estimation of whether
they needed or could win European support. In the period 1895–1939
African reaction to the Europeans was largely determined by the various
cleavages in society between Bemba and non-Bemba, between rivals within
the Bemba ruling class, and between chiefs and commoners.
  For other examples of European impact upon the local balance of power,
see J. A. Barnes, *Politics in a Changing Society* (London, 1954), pp. 60, 125;
and M. Gluckman, 'The Lozi of Barotseland in north-western Rhodesia', in
Colson and Gluckman (eds), *Seven Tribes of British Central Africa, op. cit.*,
  21. Annual report on African affairs: Mankoya District, 1961, Sec./Nat.
66A, Lusaka archives. Molteno states that in 1969, following UNIP's
defeat at the polls in Western Province, local UNIP politicians from
Mankoya District attempted to stem the anti-UNIP tide by appealing to the
same anti-Lozi sentiments. See p. 90. Local politicians can readily change
the basis of their political appeal when their political interests so require.
  22. Annual report on African affairs: Barotse Province, 1961, Sec./Nat.
66A, Lusaka archives.

an anti-administration protest in North-western Province. Approximately 250 people took part in the Vakakaye riots in the Luvale portion of Balovale District. According to the DC, the riots were instigated by Nyampenji, a chieftainess from whom the colonial administration had withdrawn recognition ten years previously. Among the contributing factors to the Vakakaye riots were Nyampenji's long-standing resentment of the Luvale Native Authority, over whose decisions and patronage she had no control, the low economic prospects of the area, and an increase in Native Authority levies. The DC concluded: 'The tightening of controls which replaced the old order . . . coupled too with increased taxes, were sufficient cause for those involved to support Nyampenji in her hatred for the Native Authority.'[23]

So far we have seen that the growth of nationalism in Northern Rhodesia was deeply rooted in the anti-colonial grievances of villagers and that the strength of rural protest contributed much to the ultimate success of the independence movement. National political leaders did not have to mobilise an apathetic and isolated peasantry; their biggest concern was to establish some measure of control over the expression of rural discontent so that it could be utilised to hasten an orderly transition to full independence. But not all Africans perceived that their interests were neglected under colonial rule, and not all Africans were equally prepared to organise in defence of their interests. In the rural areas, anti-colonial sentiments were voiced particularly by cash crop farmers and returned labour migrants who had worked for a period of years on the Copperbelt.

African cash crop farming in Northern Rhodesia tended to be concentrated along the line of rail and in the areas adjacent to settler farms in the Southern Province. The rapid growth of copper production in the 1920s created a growing demand for maize and cattle, since employers made substantial payments in kind to their workmen. The price of maize was set at a high level in the hope of attracting European farmers from the south, a policy which also encouraged African farmers to offer maize for sale. Africans in the Southern Province responded readily to the new opportunities for cash crop farming. European farmers along the line of rail undoubtedly had a positive demonstration effect, and the colonial administration quickly came to concentrate its scarce agricultural expertise in the Southern Province, where soil conditions were favourable. More basically, it is possible that the Ila–Tonga peoples

23. Annual report on African affairs: Balovale District, 1956, Sec./Nat. 66E, Lusaka archives.

were receptive to change because they had no cultural bias against farming. Had they been people of migratory and raiding tradition who considered agricultural labour to be a low-status occupation, as did the Bemba in the Northern Province, they might not have responded so readily to the opportunities offered by cash crop farming. Miracle suggests that the destructive effect of European colonisation on traditional African trading patterns may account for the receptivity of the Ila–Tonga peoples to agricultural change. The influx of cheaper and better manufactures from 1890 to 1930 drove African traders out of business, and Europeans and Asians took over the field of commercial trade. Miracle's view is that the adoption of modern techniques of production in agriculture was spear-headed by this growing body of unemployed traders who were receptive to change because, using traditional farming techniques, they could not maintain the same level of income. They preferred to adopt new methods than to accept a decline in their real standard of living.[24]

The farmers of the Southern Province had a number of deeply felt grievances which were to find political expression at a relatively early date. First was the problem of land hunger. Many Europeans had settled on the most fertile land along the line of rail, and the British South Africa Company pursued a policy of encouraging European settlement. Considerable quantities of the best land were alienated in this way, and the local Tonga were denied the right to use large acreages of their traditional lands. Moreover, the establishment of the Native Reserves in 1928 further reduced the areas Africans were permitted to cultivate, a policy intended to hold down African production of maize in order to keep high the price received per bag by the predominantly European producer. The policy of the colonial government therefore meant that, in order to protect the position of the European farmer, the interests of the African farmer were neglected.[25]

Land hunger became an acute problem in the Southern Province,

24. M. P. Miracle, 'Plateau Tonga entrepreneurs in historical inter-regional trade', *Rhodes-Livingstone Journal*, No. 26 (December 1959), p. 49. N. Long, *Social Change and the Individual: a study of the Social and Religious Responses to Innovation in a Zambian Rural Community* (Manchester, 1968), seems to support Miracle's hypothesis. Long found that in Serenje District many farmers who adopted improved techniques were older, returned labour migrants. Presumably, they were accustomed to a higher standard of living which they could not maintain by using traditional agricultural techniques and consuming their savings.

25. See Baldwin, *Economic Development and Export Growth, op. cit.*, pp. 149–52.

and subsequent overgrazing and overploughing led to soil erosion and declining yields.[26] Furthermore, following the establishment of the Maize Control Board in 1936, the problem of land hunger was aggravated by the fact that expanding maize production became more attractive for the African farmer. From 1932 to 1935 African producers sold an average of 58,000 bags of maize each year. In the next four-year period African maize sales nearly tripled, to 156,000 bags per annum, due largely to the establishment of improved marketing facilities and attractive, guaranteed producer prices. The annual report of the Department of Agriculture for 1936 stated:

One of the most obvious conclusions from the first years working is that hitherto only a small fraction of the native crop has been sold in years of plenty. In providing a cash market for all surplus maize, control has been of the utmost value to native growers, but there have been a number of repercussions. Ploughing has increased considerably (this can hardly be regarded as a healthy development at the present time) and there is a tendency to crowd in towards the railway line ... The new wealth may make farm labour scarce and more expensive.[27]

The cash crop farmers of the Southern Province felt the full weight of colonial regulations, discriminatory treatment and the vagaries of the market, and they became more politically conscious at an earlier date than did subsistence farmers.[28] The latter were little affected by production and marketing restrictions, and as a result political consciousness based on agricultural issues developed more slowly among them.

In the early 1930s three of the most vocal African welfare associations were located in the Southern Province—at Livingstone, Mazabuka and Choma.[29] One of the first attempts at territory-wide organisation occurred in 1937, when a group of successful farmers in the Mazabuka area formed the Northern Rhodesia African Congress. Although it was short-lived, the organisation represented a new high point in the development of African political consciousness.[30]

26. Gann, *A History of Northern Rhodesia, op. cit.*, pp. 306–7.
27. *Annual Report of the Department of Agriculture* (Lusaka, 1936).
28. Evidence to support the hypothesis that cash crop farmers are more politically conscious than subsistence farmers has been found in several countries. See S. M. Lipset, *Political Man* (New York, 1960), p. 244. Discriminatory practices against African farmers on behalf of white farmers and the pressure of the African population on the land due to land alienation and land reservation policies have been major sources of African discontent over much of the continent.
29. Rotberg, *The Rise of Nationalism in Central Africa, op. cit.*, pp. 124–134.
30. Gann, *A History of Northern Rhodesia, op. cit.*, p. 306.

Southern Province Africans also played a leading role in the ANC, which was formed in 1948–49; under the leadership of Harry Nkumbula (from August 1951), it expressed widespread African opposition to the proposed Central African Federation. While little is known about the organisation of the ANC and the strength of its following during the height of the campaign against federation, the Southern and Northern Provinces provided much of its support.[31]

The considerable regulation and discriminatory treatment which Africans experienced in their daily lives were an important source of anti-colonial sentiment in the Southern Province. Discontent over low wages and poor conditions of service on European farms was frequently expressed during the 1950s. The availability of alternative sources of employment within the province reduced the dependence of the African on the European farmer so that the African was not afraid to express his grievances. Thus the African farm labourer was in a strong bargaining position, and labour difficulties were frequently reported.[32]

The administration's cattle inoculation campaign, intended to prevent the spread of trypanosomiasis from African to European-owned cattle, was viewed with deep suspicion by the African cattle owner. In Choma, Monze and Mazabuka Districts local ANC supporters warned people against the dangers of having their cattle inoculated. A serious incident occurred at Choma in 1958 when the men refused to permit their cattle to be inoculated and the women obstructed the police who came to arrest their menfolk.[33]

The Department of Agriculture was always concerned that over-cultivation would permanently damage the land through soil exhaustion and erosion. It introduced numerous regulations to prevent African farmers from overworking the land. The African cultivator regarded 'conservation measures' as unwarranted interference with the use of his own land, extra work for no return and a restriction on the amount of money he could earn each year. Thus regulations on land use were a major grievance among Southern Province farmers. The land issue only failed to become explosive because a badly understaffed colonial administration could not enforce unpopular restrictions, and evasion was commonplace.

The observation that cash crop farmers are more politically conscious than subsistence farmers helps to explain the early development of African political consciousness in the Southern Province.

31. Rotberg, *The Rise of Nationalism*, *op. cit.*, p. 264.
32. Annual report on African affairs, Mazabuka District, 1956, Sec./Nat. 66F, Lusaka archives.
33. Annual report on African affairs, Choma District, 1958, *ibid.*

But it does not explain why the other centre of African nationalism was the Northern Province, and to account for this we must consider the contribution of the Copperbelt to stimulating African political consciousness.

The city has frequently been called the birthplace of nationalism over most of the African continent. In the towns and cities men discovered their identity of interest as African workers, a discovery which led to trade unionism and/or nationalist political activity. The first important signs of awakening political consciousness among Africans on the Copperbelt appeared in the strike actions of 1935 and 1940.[34] During the strikes African miners expressed several grievances. First, the basic wage rates were thought to be too low, housing and food rations inferior, and fringe benefits and working conditions inadequate. These judgements were reached in large part by comparing the wages and working conditions of the African miners with those of European miners. Secondly, Africans knew that most jobs in the mines were reserved for Europeans. The colour bar prohibited African advancement, a factor of growing importance as Africans extended the length of time they spent working on the mines and became a more highly skilled labour force.[35] Experienced miners became aware that they could do a reserved job at least as well as their privileged white counterparts. Thirdly, the African miner came to resent the insulting and frequently brutal behaviour of Europeans underground and in the location.

The labour disturbances in May 1935 were immediately preceded by an increase in the tax rate. In protest, miners refused to report for work, shouted abuse at mine authorities, voiced numerous grievances, and threw rocks at security forces and unsympathetic Africans. This first expression of African political consciousness on the Copperbelt achieved little. The strike was short-lived, African demands were very limited, and the mine management refused to recognise that any real grievances existed.

The strike action in 1940 followed a five-year period of prosperity for the copper companies, a prosperity in which only white workers shared. In March 1940 European miners struck for higher pay, and won some of their demands. African miners also resorted to strike action to force a pay increase. Clearly, African miners were comparing their conditions with those of the white workers, and they were much more militant in 1940 than they had been five years earlier. The strike was effective at several mines for over a week, and ended only

34. For a description of the 1935 and 1940 strikes, see Rotberg, *The Rise of Nationalism, op. cit.*, pp. 161–78.

35. Baldwin, *Economic Development, op. cit.*, chapter 4.

after seventeen strikers were killed and sixty-five injured by police during a workers' attack on a mine compound office.[36]

During the 1950s ANC activity on the Copperbelt was sporadic and not particularly energetic or effective. In part, ANC's limited effectiveness was due to the fact that many politically conscious Africans worked through the African Mineworkers' Union (AMWU) and the urban advisory committees rather than ANC.[37] They articulated their demands and expressed their grievances through organisations recognised by the dominant Europeans. Also, European control on the heavily populated Copperbelt was far more secure than it was in the outlying rural areas. Not only had Europeans the power to hire and fire Africans but security forces were concentrated in the towns to protect European interests. Thus the official account of the 1961 disturbances stated:

> In the Copperbelt Province, the swift and resolute action taken by the police on the outbreak of violence upset the plans for sustained disorder and secured the arrest of most of those responsible for the disturbances. Extensive patrolling and the tightening up of security measures stabilised the security situation. The same is true of the other areas along the line of rail.[38]

Paradoxically, the city in Northern Rhodesia provided the skills and experiences so important in developing African political consciousness, but the result of this increased consciousness came to fruition in the rural areas. From 1959, when most of the ANC Copperbelt organisation went over to UNIP, the latter articulated the anti-colonial grievances and expressed the nationalist sentiments of Copperbelt Africans. Many UNIP supporters in Zambia received their political education on the Copperbelt, and there was considerable social interaction between the Copperbelt and those provinces (Northern and Luapula) which supplied the bulk of its manpower.[39] Workers on the Copperbelt were socialised into UNIP politics, and they spread the UNIP message to their kinsmen when they returned home. In the Luapula and Northern Provinces, where urban associations like the AMWU were not relevant and where the range of social contact and activity was severely curtailed,

36. Rotberg, *The Rise of Nationalism, op. cit.*, pp. 168–86.
37. Epstein, *Politics in an Urban African Community, op. cit.*, chapter v.
38. *An Account of the Disturbances in Northern Rhodesia, op. cit.*, p. 73.
39. Data compiled by George Kay suggest that the percentage of males in a given area who are employed on the Copperbelt and the strength of UNIP in that area may be directly related. In Northern and Luapula Provinces approximately 60 per cent of employed males were at work on the Copperbelt. See Kay, *A Social Geography of Zambia, op. cit.*, p. 76.

ex-Copperbelt workers were drawn into political party activity. UNIP's earliest and strongest areas of support were therefore the Northern and Luapula Provinces rather than the Copperbelt itself. In 1959 UNIP registered sixty-three branches in the Luapula Province, seventeen in the Northern Province, and only four in the Copperbelt Province.[40] The strength of UNIP in the two provinces which constituted the most important labour reserves for the mines was crucial for the eventual success of the independence movement.

The political significance of labour migration patterns may also be approached from the vantage point of local employment opportunities. It appears that there is a relationship between the rate of labour migration for a given area and the availability of opportunities for earning a cash income within that area. The greater the local opportunities for wage employment, the lower will be the rate of labour migration to the towns. In the Southern Province, where cash crop farming is highly developed, the percentage of men employed outside the province is very low.[41] In Serenje District (Central Province) in 1957 approximately 70 per cent of all ablebodied men were away from the district in search of work. The DC remarked, 'The proportion in the north of the district falls to 58 per cent and it is significant that this is in the midst of a fishing industry along the Lulimala and Luapula rivers.'[42]

Many of the administrative regulations and personal obligations which weighed most heavily upon the rural villager and were most keenly resented by him in the colonial era have been continued after independence. If the anti-colonial sentiments and activities of the people living in the rural areas were an important factor in the success of the independence movement, what happens to rural protest after independence? Does it fade away in the glow of African self-government or do local interests flare up in protest again? To what extent do local politicians agitate among the people against the government as they did against the colonial administration? Certainly Weiss found a revival of rural radicalism directed against

40. *Report of an Inquiry . . . Elections and Public Safety Regulations, op. cit.*, p. 17.

41. In Southern Province approximately 60 per cent of tax-paying males are employed within the province. See Kay, *A Social Geography, op. cit.*, p. 76. Present government policy for rural development certainly assumes a positive relationship between rate of migration and local employment opportunities. Government's way of slowing the alarming rate of population drift to the cities is to increase the profitability of cash crop farming and to develop small-scale, labour-intensive rural industries.

42. Annual report on African affairs, Serenje District, 1957, Sec./Nat. 66D, Lusaka archives.

the government in the Congo, most clearly in the Kwilu rebellion of 1963. This second chapter of rural radicalism was launched in the face of a decline in the local standard of living and the lack of influence of local leaders in national politics.[43]

In Zambia since independence local disaffection with the policies of the UNIP government has largely been expressed at the polls, most notably in the general election of December 1968 in the Western (formerly Barotse) Province. But incidents of rural violence with political implications have occurred. Incidents directed against the government seem to have been concentrated in areas of ANC strength, while rural violence in strong UNIP areas seems to have as its target anti-government minorities, usually Jehovah's Witnesses or suspected ANC supporters. The events in Mumbwa District on 17 June 1969 are perhaps the most important example of violent anti-government disturbances in the rural areas since independence. Local ANC organisers not only campaigned actively against the referendum but also prevented voters from casting their ballot on election day. President Kaunda, in banning ANC in Mumbwa District and restricting its local organisers, stated that Mumbwa had been the scene of violent incidents in the past. He presented a list of fourteen separate incidents of personal assault, property damage, intimidation and crop destruction occurring between March and June in which the victims were UNIP supporters and the motivation for the attacks seemed political.[44]

Prior to independence, local political leaders were quick to encourage local discontent with colonial policies and to suggest that conditions would be much better after independence. While villagers did appreciate the dramatic expansion in social services after 1964, in some respects these achievements fell considerably short of popular expectations. According to the Provincial and Local Government Report for 1965, 'The "Crisis of Expectation" amongst the African community continued throughout the year and there was some criticism of Government amongst the uninformed with its alleged lack of progress in implementing the election promises made by U.N.I.P.'[45]

Local people sometimes invoked past political promises to resist paying taxes, as the following example illustrates:

43. Weiss, *Political Protest in the Congo, op. cit.*, pp. 252–4, 297–9.
44. *Text of President Kaunda's Address in which he declared ANC in Mumbwa District an Unlawful Organisation, 19 June 1969*, ZIS press release No. 198/69.
45. *Annual Report of the Provincial and District Government, 1965* (Lusaka, 1966), p. 4.

It is not true to say people who stop others from paying taxes come from other areas. People at Chitanda used to pay but since the Chipepo fish traders refused to pay, they have also followed suit. This is a political issue. Chitanda is ANC and Chipepo (Waya) is UNIP. The former used to be co-operative but not the latter. Revenue collectors can prove that the Chitanda people pay more than the Waya fish traders. Chipepo–Waya people flatly refuse to pay fish levy and say that during the struggle for independence they were promised to pay no taxes and since there are no facilities for fishermen, they don't see any reason why they should pay levies because fish come from God and not the government.[46]

However, the restrictions and controls which stirred up so much opposition against the colonial administration are more tolerable after independence. The content of a message is often less important than the identity of the bearer and the instructions issued by, say, a District Governor have a legitimacy which the DC could never command. Also, UNIP officials who formerly attacked colonial regulations now defend the same regulations with new arguments. For example, before independence people were told that the administration issued hunting restrictions because the Europeans wanted to keep the game for themselves. After independence the argument is advanced that the game is the property of the nation and must be protected for the sake of 'our children'.

Some controls have been relaxed and not enforced effectively. For example, the amount of illegal hunting has risen dramatically since independence, and the government has been reluctant to assign a high priority to improved game controls, which would encounter local opposition. In Serenje District Norman Long found that in 1963 nearly two-thirds of the local farmers continued to use the traditional *chitemene* form of agriculture.[47] Since independence the minutes of the Serenje District Development Committee indicate that while civil servants would very much like to accelerate the change-over to more productive farming techniques, local UNIP officials are reluctant to associate themselves with such a locally controversial policy. Thus the party is regularly encouraged to denounce *chitemene* at political meetings, but local party officials are reluctant to risk their prestige and jeopardise their support by advocating a reform which over half the farmers in Serenje District regard as premature. The rewards a politician earns for advocating modernising schemes may not be commensurate with the risks he

46. District Local Government Officer, Kabwe Rural, to Provincial Local Government Officer, Central Province, 5 September 1967, Kabwe Rural Council estimates, file No. 102/49.
47. Long, *Social Change and the Individual, op. cit.*, p. 20.

runs of losing local support. This is a very important consideration in a district where factionalism within UNIP is an important feature of political life.

Let us now attempt to relate the growth of anti-colonial nationalism in Northern Rhodesia to the patterns of political support for the two major nationalist parties, UNIP and ANC. Congress remained the dominant party in a few areas, most notably in Southern Province and parts of Central Province, while UNIP established an unchallengeable position in the Luapula, Northern, Copperbelt and Eastern Provinces.

The continued allegiance of Southern Province voters to ANC was all the more interesting because the province participated fully in post-independence development despite its loyalty to ANC. UNIP, in its initial determination to achieve a one-party State in Zambia through the ballot box, made every effort to demonstrate that politically the province would have a strong voice within UNIP, and that the UNIP government would protect the economic interests of the province. UNIP's considerable efforts did achieve an 8·5 per cent increase in its vote in the 1968 general election, but this was a rather disappointing result given UNIP's advantage over ANC in terms of both organisation and ability to reward supporters.[48]

The social characteristics of the Southern Province are quite different from those of the provinces where UNIP has been strongest. The Southern Province is the most highly developed agriculturally, and is effectively isolated from the Copperbelt. Approximately 60 per cent of Southern Province wage-earners are employed within the province, mostly as farmers and farm labourers, and people of Southern Province origin constitute less than 2 per cent of the five largest Copperbelt towns.[49] By contrast, many of the people in the Luapula and Northern Provinces received their political education on the Copperbelt, and the economic and social interdependence of the Copperbelt towns and these labour reserves is very strong.

UNIP's failure to convert the Southern Province voter demonstrates that voters do not make their choices solely on grounds of material interest; their political education and historical experience must also be taken into account. People in the Southern Province still identified ANC as the legitimate party of African nationalism and Harry Nkumbula as its leader. Nkumbula continued to receive

48. As Molteno and Scott show, the UNIP government was able to apply considerable cross-pressures on the Southern Province voter, particularly in sizeable, cosmopolitan line-of-rail towns like Livingstone and Mazabuka. See p. 195 below.
49. Kay, *A Social Geography, op. cit.*, p. 103.

respect and support not so much because of his achievements or his policies as because he is the father of nationalism in Northern Rhodesia.[50] The voter's political preference for ANC was influenced by the political information and ideas that he acquired through the society in which he lived. The experience of colonial rule and the nationalist struggle, political influences from the family and locality, and work experiences instilled deep-seated political beliefs and orientations which were identified with ANC.

Furthermore, most ANC supporters were relatively free from cross-pressures which might incline them to change their political allegiance. The relative isolation of the Southern Province enabled local ANC political leaders to monopolise communication with the voters. Thus they were able to take credit for development projects in the province, denounce the UNIP government's propaganda as lies, and perhaps even to convince some voters that Harry Nkumbula was President of Zambia.

UNIP's initial dominance in Northern and Luapula Provinces, which supply most of the manpower for the Copperbelt, was continued in post-independence elections. Both the general election of 1968 and the 1969 referendum attested to a deep popular commitment to UNIP as the party of national independence. By contrast, the sudden and dramatic withdrawal of support from UNIP in the Western Province demonstrated that the ruling party had not sunk deep roots there.[51] The expressed political preferences of the province were clearly changeable to a degree that was not the case in the Southern, Northern and Luapula Provinces, where voters retained a strong allegiance to the political parties associated with the struggle against colonial rule. Western Province voters had little attachment to UNIP and even less to ANC, and they readily switched their political allegiance in response to changes in perceived interest. UNIP's eclipse in the December 1968 general election reflected local discontent over the defeat of prominent Western

50. Nkumbula traded heavily on his role as the leader of African nationalism during the 1950s. In November 1969 he responded to Kaunda's appeal to disband ANC and join UNIP by saying, 'UNIP are my children because they came from ANC. It is difficult for a son to write his father to join him.' See *Times of Zambia*, 10 November 1969.

51. Until 1962 the Litunga, paramount chief of the Lozi, refused to permit nationalist parties in Barotseland. See Mulford, *Zambia: the Politics of Independence, op. cit.*, pp. 211–28. The central position of the Zambezi river in the economic and social life of the Lozi and the relative physical and social isolation of Barotseland have in part insulated the Litunga and the Lozi aristocracy from forces which have broken down traditional loyalties elsewhere.

Province leaders in the UNIP central committee elections of August 1967, the prohibition of labour recruitment in Zambia for the South African mines, the high cost and slow pace of development in the province, and the government's delay in fulfilling its commitment to pave the main Lusaka–Mongu road.

Thus the African independence movement, in which many anonymous rural villagers played an important part, has had an impact upon post-independence political patterns as well. Historical experience and political tradition helped to determine whether Zambians considered UNIP or ANC to be the true party of African nationalism. Degree of contact with the Copperbelt seems to have been a particularly important determinant of political allegiance. The results of the post-independence elections suggested that voters were more changeable in their political preference where anti-colonial sentiment was weakest and where national political parties established themselves least effectively and at a late date.

# 3

# Cleavage and conflict in Zambian politics: a study in sectionalism

*Robert Molteno*

Since independence several political scientists and journalists[1] have used 'tribalism' as the touchstone to explain both electoral behaviour and leadership competition in Zambia, especially within the ruling United National Independence Party. During the independence struggle the African nationalist movement did not reflect significant 'tribal' divisions,[2] but conflict on sectional lines has increased sharply in the years since 1964.

The term 'sectionalism' is borrowed from Robert Rotberg, one of the pioneers in the study of Zambian politics.[3] It is used here in preference to 'tribalism' since its very vagueness forces the analyst—when talking, for example, of 'the Bemba' or 'the Lozi'—to ask in each case, and to answer empirically, the question: what kind of social group is being referred to? In contrast, the term 'tribalism' is a blanket word which does not distinguish between the different feelings of solidarity based on village, district, lineage, common language and culture. 'Tribalism', or even 'ethnicity' as used by Wallerstein,[4] also tends to assume that kinship links or long-standing political ties are the paramount solidary bond, when in fact geographical propinquity and linguistic unity may be more important factors

1. Mulford, 'Northern Rhodesia—some observations on the 1964 elections', *op. cit.*, p. 16; and J. A. Scarritt, 'The Zambian election—triumph or tragedy?', *Africa Today*, vol. 16, No. 1 (February–March 1969), pp. 4 and 5. For journalists, see Hall, *The High Price of Principles, op. cit.*, chapter 13, and references in B. V. Mtshali, 'South Africa and Zambia's 1968 election', *Kroniek van Afrika*, No. 2 (Leiden, 1970), p. 133.
2. R. Rotberg, 'Tribalism and politics in Zambia', *op. cit.*, p. 31, and Mulford, *Zambia: the Politics of Independence, op. cit., passim.*
3. Rotberg, *ibid.*, p. 32.
4. I. Wallerstein, 'Ethnicity and national integration in West Africa', in H. Eckstein and D. E. Apter (eds), *Comparative Politics* (New York, 1963), pp. 665–70.

in the formation of new sectional identifications. Thus Coleman and Rosberg[5] define tribalism as 'the persistence—indeed, the paramountcy—of "primordial attachments" ties; that is, individuals identify themselves much more strongly with historic groups defined in terms of kinship, religion, language or culture than with the civil order of the new States'. The term 'primordial attachments' suggests a long-standing, relatively immutable, even primitive emotional attachment.[6] It plays down the rational economic motivation which underlies the role of sectional groupings as interest groups in Zambia. Moreover, the reference to 'historic groups' assumes a coincidence in boundaries between pre-colonial polities and today's sectional groups which we shall see does not exist in Zambia.

The term 'tribalism' is open to further objections as a concept for the analysis of contemporary political behaviour. It has been used by social anthropologists in Zambia in at least two senses, when they argue that 'tribe' in town is a different social reality from 'tribe' in the rural areas.[7] It is for these kinds of reason that the late Melville Herskovitz stated that 'the concept "tribe" is difficult to define and of little utility' and ought to be avoided.[8] The final objection to the word 'tribalism' as a concept is its restriction largely to the Third World. Unlike the term 'sectionalism', 'tribalism' fosters the divorce between concepts and hypotheses developed to analyse political behaviour in the West and those evolved to study often essentially similar phenomena in Africa. It is entirely arbitrary to speak, for example, of the Flemings in Belgium as a nation but of the Lozi in Zambia as a tribe.[9] For both groups regard themselves as having their own language, cultural identity, and economic and political interests. For all these reasons the term 'tribalism' will be eschewed.

Sectional conflict in Zambia has increased since independence. 1966 saw the formation of the new United Party, which was largely Lozi-speaking in its leadership and support. 1967 saw bitter rivalry within UNIP over elections to the party's top organ, the central

5. J. S. Coleman and C. G. Rosberg (eds), *Political Parties and National Integration in Tropical Africa* (Berkeley and Los Angeles, 1966), p. 687.

6. *The Concise Oxford Dictionary* (fifth edition, 1964), p. 969.

7. M. Gluckman, 'Anthropological problems arising out of the African industrial revolution', in A. Southall (ed.), *Social Change in Modern Africa* (London, 1961).

8. M. Herskovitz, *The Human Factor in Changing Africa* (New York, 1962), pp. 69 and 70.

9. H. C. Kelman, 'Patterns of personal involvement in the national system —a social psychological analysis of political legitimacy', in J. N. Rosenau (ed.), *International Politics and Foreign Policy* (New York, 1969).

committee, with an electoral alliance of Bemba- and Tonga-speaking elements winning a disproportionate share of the eleven seats. In February 1968 President Kaunda threatened to resign because of his dismay at escalating sectional rivalries within the party. The same year saw the rise of new sectional groupings within UNIP—the 'Unity in the East' movement, combining Nyanja-speaking peoples in Eastern Province, and the Bantu Botatwe group uniting UNIP leaders in Southern and parts of Central Provinces. At the end of the year the opposition African National Congress fought the general election on an anti-'Bemba domination' platform. 1969 saw no abatement. Some political leaders from Luapula Province, hitherto a component of the Bemba-speaking bloc, alleged that Northern Province politicians (also Bemba) insulted Luapulans and were even taking over Luapula National Assembly seats. A climax in the discontent at the dominant position of Northern Province leaders came at the August 1969 meeting of the UNIP national council. President Kaunda was forced to send it home prematurely in order to avoid an attempt to unseat the Bemba-speaking Vice-president, Simon Kapwepwe. Soon afterwards he dissolved the central committee which had been elected in 1967 and nominated an interim executive committee, constituted to include prominent Eastern and North-western Province leaders. And a commission was set up specifically 'to determine ways and means of avoiding strife in the party' by reviewing the defects in UNIP's existing constitution.[10] This chapter will explore the nature of these conflicts, and will start by analysing the pre-independence situation.

When the African nationalist movement took organisational shape with the formation of the Northern Rhodesia African National Congress in 1948, its leaders came from several provinces.[11] Moreover, it stayed largely united for the first eleven years of its struggle. When in 1958–59 it split, the line of cleavage was not sectional; the issue was one of political strategy—how best to tackle the fact of continuing settler rule. Three groupings can be distinguished: the collaborators (a few chiefs and educated commoners) who joined white-controlled parties such as the ruling United Federal Party (UFP); the militants (originally ANC, but after 1959 UNIP) who were prepared to back their demands for majority rule and independence with tough action; and the moderates (the ANC from 1959 onwards) who were more disposed to compromise.[12] But when the 1962 elections

10. See chapter 4.
11. Mulford, *Zambia: the Politics of Independence, op. cit.*, pp. 16 and 17.
12. Mr Harry Nkumbula, president of ANC, even consented to become a member of the Legislative Council in 1959. *Ibid.*, pp. 88 and 90.

presented ANC with the choice of participating in a government dominated by the settler UFP or in one led by UNIP, it chose the second alternative in the interests of forming the first African government of Northern Rhodesia.

The nationalist movement also experienced non-ideological cleavages. From 1962 there was a division within UNIP between party activists of long standing and relatively little education and the new, professionally qualified men who were brought into the party in anticipation of UNIP's having to form its first government.[13] But the question arises: why, about the time of independence, was there a transition from a situation where the dominant party (UNIP) was relatively free from internal conflict—especially sectional conflict—and distinguishable from the opposition ANC in strategy and policy, to one where the ruling party has been both increasingly divided internally and separated from the opposition parties largely on sectional lines? This chapter will try to show why the lines of cleavage within and between the parties became sectional. But first we must examine three factors which help to explain the rise of conflict within UNIP.

## The rise of conflict in UNIP since independence

First, Northern Rhodesia was a British dependency, and a white settler dependency to boot. Almost all Africans were equally oppressed. Racial discrimination prevailed socially in the form of segregation, economically in the exclusion of Africans from skilled jobs, and politically in the very restricted franchise—until 1959 only eleven Africans had the vote.[14] The African nationalist movement therefore faced an external political enemy—Britain, as the ultimate imperial sovereign, and the settler-dominated governments of Northern Rhodesia and the Central African Federation. Two consequences followed: a great need for unity among the subject population, which ANC finally recognised in its 1962 decision to form a coalition government with UNIP; and, secondly, the manifest political irrelevance of linguistic and provincial differences in the face of a uniform blanket of racial oppression. But this situation changed drastically at independence. British overlordship and local settler rule both disappeared, and the need for unity apparently declined. The political enemy now became internal. There was competition between the two African parties, UNIP and ANC, and within the

13. *Ibid.*, pp. 190 and 191, and Kaunda, *A Humanist in Africa, op. cit.*, p. 102.

14. Mulford, *Zambia: the Politics of Independence, op. cit.*, p. 1.

ruling UNIP itself. Further, because ANC's electoral support was mainly in Tonga- and Ila-speaking areas, its political opponents could paint it as a sectional party.[15] Similarly, because the nationalist parties did not penetrate all the rural areas at the same time, much of UNIP's militant activity in the independence struggle was in the Bemba-speaking Northern and Luapula Provinces. A large proportion of its Youth Brigade was also Bemba-speaking.[16] This meant that UNIP itself could be portrayed as dominated by one section within the party and that other sections could feel their political positions endangered by this alleged dominance. Conversely, Bemba-speakers could, and before 1967 did, maintain that they were under-represented in the party's key organs relative to their contribution to the freedom struggle.[17]

Secondly, during that struggle it was not pleasant to be a political leader. Full-time activists suffered poverty, harassment by the police, occasional gaolings and restrictions, and acquired prestige only within the narrow circle of the party. One would therefore expect there to be less intense competition for top party posts during this period, and so less need for aspirant leaders to recruit support within the hierarchy of party activists on sectional, or any other, lines. But independence brings a revolution in the power, status, and income of many party leaders. A leadership position thus becomes more prized and competition can be expected to become more intense. So, as early as January 1964, when Dr Kaunda was constituting his first Cabinet, Lozi leaders used the ultimate threat of withdrawal from the party to insist on being given what they considered adequate ministerial representation. This growing competition for posts was also reflected in the bitterness which pervaded the 1967 central committee elections, and in the very early start (in mid-1969) to the intensive canvassing by UNIP leaders for the next elections, originally scheduled for August 1970. The news of the President's dissolution of the central committee in August 1969 greatly upset several of its members until the announcement next day of the re-constituted interim committee showed that very few had lost their positions. Nevertheless, one member wrote subsequently of his night-mares, which 'forecast doom and drastic reshuffles'.[18]

This trend towards increased competition for senior political posts was reinforced by two other factors. Before 1967 President Kaunda

15. Mulford, 'Northern Rhodesia—some observations on the 1964 elections', *op. cit.*, p. 16.
16. Rotberg, 'Tribalism and politics in Zambia', *op. cit.*, p. 31.
17. Hall, *The High Price of Principles, op. cit.*, pp. 197–9.
18. Mr Mainza Chona, *Zambia News*, 6 September 1969.

had promised that there would be a close correlation between UNIP central committee posts and Cabinet positions.[19] Since the latter carried not only great power but also salaries higher even than top civil service posts,[20] competition for party office was likely to increase. President Kaunda recognised this in 1969 and stated in August that 'in future, the composition of my Cabinet will not necessarily reflect the membership of the Central Committee'.[21] This intention was at once implemented, at least partially, since the reconstituted interim committee included for the first time two male members, A. B. Chikwanda and W. Chakulya, who were only ordinary backbenchers. The intensity of intra-party competition has also increased because many UNIP leaders lack sufficient education to be able to earn in non-political government posts salaries as high as those which they earn as MPs and District Governors.[22] Relative to politicians in developed countries, they have an unusually high personal interest in retaining their top political posts. They therefore fight for these posts with great determination and may be prepared to exploit sectional cleavages.

Thirdly, there was the fact of electoral institutions. These created a mechanism whereby politicians, in their striving for office, were forced to recruit support from the population at large.[23] Only at this stage did they have to differentiate themselves in the eyes of the electorate; and only at this stage did they have an interest in pointing out, playing upon, and even creating, new perceptions of social cleavages in the population. But in Northern Rhodesia it was only late in 1962 that a significant number of Africans gained the vote. Even then the main focus was on the 'national' seats, where the settler vote was essential to UNIP and ANC.[24] Universal franchise was conceded only a few months before independence. The general election of January 1964 was thus the first occasion when the main contest was between the two African parties fighting for the succession to a dying colonial government; and it was not until 1966 that local authority elections were held on a universal franchise. Only in 1967 did UNIP reintroduce contested elections for central

19. Hall, *The High Price of Principles, op. cit.*, p. 196.
20. In 1965 a Cabinet Minister received K7,720 p.a. (including a housing allowance), while a permanent secretary received K6,600.
21. The President's address to the nation on the occasion of his dissolution of the central committee, 25 August 1969. ZIS background paper No. 51/69.
22. In 1969 an MP and a District Governor earned respectively K3,700–K4,000 and K4,900 (omitting fringe benefits in both cases).
23. Rasmussen, 'Political competition', *op. cit.*, pp. 422–4.
24. Mulford, *The Northern Rhodesia General Election, 1962, op. cit.*, p. 85.

committee posts; since independence the practice had been for the
party president to present to delegates a single list of candidates for
unanimous endorsement.[25]

For these reasons political conflict increased in Zambia after independence and involved wider circles of people.[26] It is true that these
conflicts have tended to coincide with a variety of sectional cleavages
in the population. But it has been largely the increased competition
for top posts among leaders, and institutional factors such as elections
and the end of alien rule, which have prompted the increase in
conflict, rather than the enforced response of the politicians to deep-
seated emotional loyalties felt by the masses to sub-national groups.

Yet some writers have used this latter factor as the main explanation of political conflict in Zambia. Hall[27] analyses the tactical
electoral alliance between Bemba- and Tonga-speaking UNIP
leaders in the 1967 central committee elections on the following
lines. The real conflict was between Bemba and Lozi. The Lozi in
the nineteenth century had had some degree of hegemony over the
Tonga; the Tonga therefore hate the Lozi today; and so Tonga-
speaking UNIP leaders were willing to ally themselves with Bemba
leaders in order to bring down their historic enemies, the Lozi. Although it is correct that members of each of these categoric groups
do feel they have a certain collective identity, there are several flaws
in Hall's historical interpretation. It cannot explain why there should
have been such bitter conflict between Bemba- and Lozi-speaking
leaders in UNIP in the period 1967–71 when there is no record of
pre-colonial conflict between the two polities. It also cannot explain
the changing complexities of Zambian politics—why, in the 1968
National Assembly elections, many rural Lozi abandoned UNIP
and voted with their 'historic enemies', the Tonga, to back ANC; or
why in 1969 the alliance between Tonga- and Bemba-speaking
leaders in UNIP was clearly on the way out.

25. In order to reduce sectional conflict in the Uganda People's Congress,
President Obote in 1967 deliberately altered the UPC constitution to enable
national officials to be appointed by the party president, instead of being
elected. See N. Kasfir, 'The decline of cultural sub-nationalism in Uganda',
in V. A. Olorunsola (ed.), *The Politics of Cultural Sub-nationalism in Africa*
(New York, 1972).

26. Similar increases in conflict, often on sectional lines, have been noted
in other African States about the time of independence: for example, the
Ivory Coast, where even separatist movements grew up in the 1950s. See
Coleman and Rosberg, *Political Parties and National Integration, op. cit.*,
pp. 86 and 87. Also in the Congo (now Zaïre), where the 1957 elections saw
a rise in sectional rivalries. *Ibid.*, pp. 572 ff.

27. Hall, *The High Price of Principles, op. cit.*, pp. 197–8.

*The non-traditional nature of contemporary sectional political groups*

Other writers, including political scientists, have also analysed political conflict in Africa in terms of enmities between historic, pre-colonial polities.[28] We must examine the validity of such a view for Zambia more closely.

The first fact is that many States which existed on the eve of colonial rule in Northern Rhodesia were of recent origin and were still racked by internal conflicts.[29] One cannot assume too deeprooted a loyalty of their populations to either the boundaries or the rulers of these pre-colonial polities. Bemba-speaking polities were united for the first time only in the nineteenth century, and it was not until the middle of that century that they incorporated the Bisa by conquest. Likewise, many segments of the Lozi kingdom have mid- and late nineteenth-century origins—the Kalolo, who had a huge impact on the language and composition of the Lozi population, moved north over the Zambezi only in the 1840s; subsequent decades saw both the extension of the kingdom's population through wars of expansion and its division through frequent rebellions. The Ngoni are another example. They reached the Eastern Province in the 1840s and only settled in their present area (Chipata) a few years before the advent of the British South Africa Company. Moreover, the half-century of raiding and conquest from their first move northwards over the Zambezi to their conquest by the British in 1897 altered their original composition and language almost beyond recognition. One cannot, therefore, talk of 'primordial attachments' to these recently formed, fluid and divided polities.

The second point is that, while future surveys may show that many people still remember and identify with the pre-colonial polities of which their parents or grandparents were citizens, the boundaries of modern sectional groups often do not coincide with the boundaries of these pre-colonial polities.[30] There were scores of the latter. But in recent years there have been only a handful of major sections. Ila–Tonga-speakers, who live mainly in the Southern Province and the

28. Lewis has put this 'historical enmity' hypothesis in its bluntest form. W. A. Lewis, *Politics in West Africa* (London, 1965), p. 66.

29. A. Roberts, 'The nineteenth century in Zambia', *op. cit.*, p. 24; and J. Vansina, *Kingdoms of the Savanna* (Madison, 1966), pp. 209 ff., 212 ff, and 243.

30. The new boundaries of urban sectional groups elsewhere in Africa have been pointed out by Wallerstein, 'Ethnicity and national integration', *op. cit.*, and by S. K. Panter Brick, 'The right of self-determination: its application to Nigeria', *International Affairs*, vol. 44, No. 2 (1968), pp. 258–9.

western part of Central Province, remained in ANC consistently; those in UNIP allied with the Bemba leaders from 1967 to 1969. Bemba-speakers, living in Northern and Luapula Provinces and forming the largest part of the urban Copperbelt and Kabwe populations, have been overwhelmingly UNIP since 1960. The 'Unity in the East' movement, which intended to embrace all Nyanja-speakers (the Eastern Province population), formed a section in UNIP often acting in concert with leaders from the Western and North-western Provinces. There are also Lozi-speakers who were overwhelmingly UNIP until 1967, when many rural Lozi switched to the United Party, which, after being banned in August 1968, was incorporated into the ANC. There are other minor sectional groups— the Kaonde, Lunda and Luvale in the North-western Province; the Bantu Botatwe group of Southern and Central Province elements within UNIP; and, more recently, people who refer to themselves as 'Luapulans'.

What is more important is that there seems to be little or no coincidence between recent patterns of political conflict and the lines of pre-colonial conflict.[31] A group like the Bemba, which was internally divided in the last century, became solidly UNIP. Groups which clashed historically have acted in political concert—the Tonga were under periodic Lozi hegemony in the nineteenth century, yet from 1968 they were allied with the Lozi in one party. The Ngoni raided other States in what is now the Eastern Province, yet in 1968 they were allied with the rest of the province's population in the 'Unity in the East' movement. The Lozi clashed frequently with the Kaonde from 1885 to 1900, yet both groups voted UNIP in 1964. Finally, groups which did not clash in pre-colonial times, or indeed had no contact with one another, became political rivals. There was no Bemba–Tonga contact, yet most Tonga stayed in ANC, which was increasingly openly anti-Bemba. There was no contact between the Tonga and the polities of the Eastern Province, yet until recently they were ranged in opposing parties. There was no Bemba–Lozi contact, yet there has been intense political rivalry between these groups both inside and outside UNIP. These examples could be multiplied.

These historical data show that recent political alignments between UNIP and ANC, and within each party, were in no way 'historic groups'.[32] The boundaries of each political party's support, or of a

31. Rotberg, 'Tribalism and politics in Zambia', *op. cit.*, p. 30.
32. For a similar conclusion for Nigeria, see O. Oyediran, 'The role of ethnicity and partisanship in the politics of Nigerian students', *ODU— University of Ife Journal of African Studies*, vol. 4, No. 2 (January 1968).

section within each party, did not coincide with the boundaries of pre-colonial polities. For a process of aggregation had taken place, resulting in far fewer sectional groups than there were polities in the past. And in this process of aggregation both UNIP and ANC united individuals from polities which used to conflict with one another as well as from polities which had friendly relations, or no contact, with one another.

In addition to the empirical evidence there are logical objections to explaining contemporary cleavages in terms of historical conflicts. First, one cannot explain changing patterns of recent political behaviour in terms of a given historical fact. And patterns have changed in Zambia since independence. Mwinilunga (a largely Lunda constituency) swung to UNIP in the 1968 general election. In the same election eight seats in the Western Province switched from UNIP to ANC. In the June 1969 referendum, which was held to amend section 72 of the constitution, Solwezi constituency also swung away from UNIP. It is tempting to explain such changes in historical terms. For example, the two constituencies in Western Province which stayed UNIP in 1968 are inhabited by Nkoya whom the Lozi had conquered and incorporated within their kingdom in the 1870s. Can one explain the Nkoya's decision not to follow the 'true Lozi' into UP as a legacy of this conquest? But if so, how does one explain that in the early 1960s both the 'true Lozi' and the Nkoya supported UNIP? A sounder approach to explaining changes in the electorate's voting behaviour is to analyse contemporary forces acting on individuals; these include social pressures, economic interests and communications exposure.

There is a second objection to the historical explanation of sectionalism. Since it relies on a single variable, it cannot explain deviant cases. Thus in explaining why as many as 79 per cent of the Southern Province's electorate voted ANC in 1964, one might be tempted to argue that it was due to the Tonga-speakers' feeling of sectional solidarity, which in turn perhaps dated back to the pre-colonial period. But such an explanation based on historic solidarity cannot explain why 15 per cent of those same Tonga voted UNIP and why in the 1968 election there was an 8 per cent swing to UNIP. Again, only a multivariable model can throw light on these complexities. Indeed, there is an alternative explanation, theoretically more acceptable than the historical one, of the high degree of Tonga support for ANC. ANC had operated in the Southern Province for ten years before the Zambia African National Congress, the immediate forerunner of UNIP, broke away. By that time and even more so by the 1964 election, most people had been socialised into

an ANC party loyalty, as has happened in other countries with
parties of long standing. Socialisation may also explain why the
swing to UNIP in the Southern Province was so small in 1968 despite
the manifest cost of adhering to the opposition party. The constancy
of voters' party loyalties—in Southern Province, in the towns, and in
Northern and Luapula Provinces—in the country's only two general
elections, 1964 and 1968, can as easily be explained in terms of stable
identifications resulting from long political socialisation as in terms
of sectional solidarity with or without an historical origin. For ANC
and UNIP had operated in these areas for many years. This point
is reinforced by the fact that the only seats to have changed their
party allegiance—eight in the Western Province and Mwinilunga
and Solwezi in the North-western Province—are *all* situated in the
two provinces which were penetrated last by political parties[33] and
whose populations can therefore be expected to be least firmly
socialised into a party loyalty.

Another aspect of the irrelevance, by and large, of pre-colonial
polities to recent conflicts is the lack of continuity in goals between
these polities and modern sectional groups. If the latter are the
result of 'primordial attachments' to 'historic groups', one would
expect to find a continuing attachment to the political goals inherent
in pre-colonial polities. Yet whether we take the parties, or sectional
movements inside the parties, or chiefs, we find that they have all
been demanding the accelerated advent of modernity. This is not to
deny that there can be cultural conservatism, or that political demands for the protection of long-standing customs can be made.
1969 saw a prolonged row over a Copperbelt local authority's
attempt to move a circumcision camp further from the urban area
in order to avoid strangers blundering into it, and so being forcibly
circumcised. But such issues have not been the substance of Zambian
politics since 1964; instead, there have been demands for more rural
development, more jobs, better communications, and more modern
social services.

A few examples will illustrate this. There were policy differences
between the parties—for instance, on the importance of the private
sector. But both UNIP and the supposedly sectional ANC[34] agreed
on the need for rapid economic development. Similarly, sectional

33. G. L. Caplan, 'Barotseland: the secessionist challenge to Zambia',
*op. cit.*, pp. 343–60; and Mulford, *Zambia: the Politics of Independence*,
*op. cit.*, pp. 79, 117 and 122. See also pp. 59–61 above.

34. That ANC was a sectional party might be disputed in the light of its
spectrum of support: Tonga, Lozi and minority support in the North-western,
Eastern and Central Provinces.

movements in UNIP built their appeals partly on allegations of discrimination in the allocation of development funds, despite there
being no discernible factual basis for these allegations. Many Eastern
Province people felt that the Northern Province was getting more
than its fair share. They pointed to the tarring of the Great North
Road, the oil pipeline through that province, and the Tanzam railway, which will run through Northern Province.[35] These fears rose
with the ousting of the Eastern Province leader, Mr Reuben
Kamanga, from his central committee post in 1967. The 'Unity
in the East' movement in the next year was a response to the fear
that the reduction of Eastern Province leaders' influence in government would, *inter alia,* adversely affect the province's share of
development.

Another example was the feeling among some 'Luapulans' in 1969
that their province was not getting nearly as much development as
the neighbouring Northern Province. For example, the Minister of
State for Luapula pointed out that 'if we are realistic about developing all provinces in Zambia evenly, let us start at once working on
the Samfya–Serenje road. It is the feeling of everybody in the
province that the road is the only answer to overcome the geographical position of the province.'[36] And at least one new UNIP
Member from Luapula used parliamentary questions in 1969 to press
Ministers closely on development matters affecting the province.[37]
What is significant about this manifestation of sectionalism is that
it took place within the Bemba-speaking group along the line of the
modern administrative division of the area into two provinces.

The electoral consequences of a sectional movement using
economic grievances were most obvious in Western Province in
1968. When UNIP originally swept the province in the face of the
Litunga's hostility in the early 1960s, it made big promises of
economic development in this most neglected of all Northern
Rhodesian provinces. Partly because of atrocious communications,
very little development followed and cash incomes did not rise
significantly. The reaction was bitter, as was shown in a leaflet,
'Political Orbit', circulated in June 1969. The leaflet stated that the
Lozi had voted UNIP in 1963 and 1964 'and what did Sikota
[Sikota Wina, a Lozi Cabinet Minister] give us? What did we get?
Nothing. Instead we lost more and more, and we are going to lose

35. Letter to *Zambia Mail,* 9 May 1969.
36. M. Ngalande, 'Luapula Province: political report on the implementation of Humanism in Zambia', presented to the UNIP national council,
November 1968 (mimeo.), p. 2.
37. For example, *Nat. Ass. Deb.,* Hansard No. 18, 1 July 1969, cols 9–12.

more.' This bitterness was further increased by the fall in employment which resulted from the government's decision to show its
abhorrence of the South African regime by closing the Witwatersrand
Native Labour Association (WENELA). This association recruited
mainly rural Lozi to work on the South African gold mines as
migrants, thereby enabling several thousand families to earn cash
incomes. Mr Mundia's UP was able in 1967–68 to cash in electorally
on the disappointed hopes of modernity. The UP appeal was an
intricate combination which played on real economic grievances,
but which attributed their cause to the predominance of Bemba-
speakers within UNIP. Since that date MPs from the province
have pressed in the National Assembly their constituents' demands
for development. As the ANC Member for Sesheke (Mr S. Kakoma)
stated, in referring to allegations 'that some people in Barotse
Province are advocating secession', 'That is very untrue. What the
people in that part of the country wanted is development, full
stop.'[38]

Even chiefs have voiced the demands of their villagers for development. In June 1969 chiefs and UNIP leaders in Solwezi in
North-western Province combined in telling voters to abstain from
voting 'yes' in the constitutional referendum on the grounds that
the government had not done enough to develop the area.[39]

Parties, sectional movements and chiefs have all articulated
demands for modernity. This suggests that it is not primarily
historical loyalties which have fuelled the success of sectional appeals
but the escalation of the peasants' demands for the fruits of modernity. These demands arose in response to the promises of parties in the
independence struggle; but, inevitably, the capacity of the government was too limited to meet all these demands after independence.

There is one last respect in which the new and modern nature of
sectionalism in Zambia is revealed, and that is leadership. If contemporary sectionalism was a historical throw-back, one would
expect 'primordial attachments' to adhere to the descendants of the
traditional rulers of these once independent polities so that those
descendants would be looked to as the logical leaders of sectional
movements. In fact, although chiefs often retain a certain status and
respect, they have frequently not been able to influence significantly
the voting behaviour of their followers. In Western Province UNIP
swept the Katengo (local council) elections of August 1963 in the

38. *Ibid.*, Hansard No. 17, 4 February 1969, col. 298.
39. *Times of Zambia*, 4 June 1969.

teeth of hostility from the Litunga and his traditional lieutenants.[40] In Southern Province several chiefs publicly supported UNIP, and yet the province remained firmly ANC. In mid-1969 Senior Chief Shakumbila, of Mumbwa District in Central Province, and a life-long ANC supporter, switched to UNIP amid great publicity. Yet he failed to take his villagers with him in the referendum that followed. Conversely, the continued adherence to ANC of one of Eastern Province's two paramount chiefs did not prevent ANC from doing very badly in the 1964 elections and even worse in 1968. Chiefs have also occupied very few prominent leadership positions in either the political parties or sectional movements. The 'Unity in the East' movement was started by local UNIP officials in Chipata and, while several Eastern Province leaders secretly sympathised with it, neither they nor the chiefs came out publicly in support. The UP in Western Province was led by Mr Mundia, a university-educated former UNIP Minister of no high traditional status. Again, chiefs either refrained from committing themselves to UP publicly, or, like the Mulena Mukwae of Sesheke, continued to support UNIP. The only important UP leader with high traditional status was Mr H. Noyoo, a former Ngambela (Chief Minister).[41]

There are several reasons why chiefs rarely occupy prominent political positions. Many lack sufficient education for modern govern-ment posts. A chief's role requires his almost continuous presence at the local level, and where a chief has accepted national office it has meant the virtual abandonment of his role as chief. When the Mulena Mukwae of Sesheke became a UNIP Member of Parliament and Junior Minister in 1964, her people resented her prolonged absence from Mwandi so much that they voted her out of her parliamentary seat in 1968. Finally, a chief is supposed to be leader of all his people. Where his followers divided politically and he identified with one or other party, he undermined his authority with a segment of the villagers. Thus chiefs in politically divided areas, particularly Southern and Western Provinces and Mwinilunga District, often did not back either UNIP or ANC publicly, wheras chiefs in one-party (UNIP) areas, especially Northern, Luapula, Eastern, and parts of North-western Provinces, openly backed UNIP.

This non-participation of chiefs at the national level did not mean that sectional movements, and even national parties, were averse to trying to win them over. Modern nationalist parties in many parts of Africa have tried to recruit support by using chiefs and exploiting

40. Caplan, 'Barotseland: the secessionist challenge to Zambia', *op. cit.*, p. 353.
41. *Ibid.*

conflicts in the 'traditional'—or, more accurately, local—political
sub-systems.[42] The advantages of having two structures, the party
and the 'traditional' hierarchy, to communicate one's message to
the people are obvious. Chiefs can remain as one among several sets
of opinion leaders at the local level, although in Zambia their loss
of government roles and powers since 1964 has probably reduced
the extent to which they can influence villagers' behaviour. Nevertheless, it is true that even UNIP, particularly in areas where it was
weak, pressured chiefs to come out openly in its support in the hope
that they would lead their followers out of ANC. This was a
deliberate strategy in the 1968 general election.[43] And in at least one
case—that of Senior Chief Shakumbila of Mumbwa District, who
refused until June 1969 to abandon ANC—government recognition
was withdrawn and he lost his official position and allowances. But
the fact remains that this strategy was not successful, and at neither
national nor village level have chiefs been the main activists in
Zambian political organisations.

### The role of political leaders in fostering sectional identifications

It has been shown that there are no major points of resemblance between modern sectionalism and 'historic groups'. This fact and the
rise of acute political sectionalism only after independence show that
it is not the result of deeply felt popular loyalties to units, leaders or
goals which date from the pre-colonial era. This is not to say that
there were no sub-national group loyalties in the colonial period.
But often they were not conterminous with those that existed before
the advent of colonial rule. Moreover, the politicisation of these
sectional identifications—and in some cases, like the 'Luapulans' in
1969, even their creation—has taken place mainly since independence and on the initiative of national-level leaders themselves. It
may well be claimed that 'the creation of higher loyalties that
supersede parochial loyalties' is 'a universally acclaimed goal of the
African renaissance'.[44] Yet the Zambian lesson teaches that some
national-level leaders have deliberately set out to stimulate, and even
create, sectional identifications among the masses. This has happened

42. For example, the SLPP in Sierra Leone (Coleman and Rosberg,
*Political Parties and National Integration, op. cit.*, pp. 123–4), and the
CPP's strategy in the northern region of Ghana, where its structure was weak
(D. Austin, *Politics in Ghana, 1946–60*, London, 1964, pp. 359–62).

43. UNIP Election Strategy Committee, *Victory—Handbook for Party
Workers* (Lusaka, 1968), p. 8.

44. R. L. Sklar, 'Political science and national integration—a radical
approach', *Journal of Modern African Studies*, vol. 5, No. 1 (1967), p. 2.

elsewhere in Africa. 'Tribal movements may be created and instigated to action by the new men of power in furtherance of their own special interests.'[45] Motivated by their interest in retaining and advancing their political positions, they have to recruit support. And in appealing to people's interests on the basis of social divisions they have found sectional cleavages the easiest to use. Looking, therefore, at the rise of sectional loyalties in Zambia as they have affected political behaviour, it has not been in the first instance an upwelling of grass-roots mass emotion which in turn has compelled national-level leaders to react by submitting to its pressures and articulating sectional sentiments. While it may be true that mass sectional identifications have become increasingly a factor constraining politicians, the initiative seems to have been taken by the politicians themselves.

There is a good deal of evidence to support this hypothesis. Supporters of Simon Kapwepwe made it very clear in a letter to the press in November 1970:

I can assure you that you certainly cannot prove to be a national leader without sectional backing: to be a national leader usually you have got to start from the scratch, i.e. village, where you are born, district, and then province up to national level ... Mr Kapwepwe's political career started from his village in Chinsali district, just like Dr Kaunda, and Mr Nkumbula of Namwala, not to omit Mr N. Mundia: this is how politics start. Even if you can be well known here in Lusaka, without organising your village you would certainly stand to lose.[46]

President Kaunda, commenting on the 1967 central committee elections, also stressed the role of UNIP party leaders in fomenting sectional conflict:

We have canvassed so strongly along tribal, racial and provincial lines. I do not think we can blame the common man for this. The fault is ours, fellow leaders—we, the people (i.e. party leaders at all levels) here assembled. Was it really necessary to win votes by being tribal, racial, or provincial?[47]

The UNIP chairman of Solwezi rural council agreed with the President: 'Tribalism was hatched at Mulungushi by people from Lusaka—i.e. by those who were fighting for posts.'[48]

45. *Ibid.*, p. 6.     46. *Times of Zambia*, 7 November 1970.
47. President Kaunda's address to the UNIP national council in 'Mulungushi conference, 1967—proceedings of the annual general conference of UNIP, held 14 to 20 August 1967' (Lusaka, n.d., mimeo.), p. 52.
48. Minutes of extraordinary meeting of the North-western Provincial Development Committee, 14 February 1969 (mimeo.), p. 3; Office of the Minister, Solwezi.

What happened was that Bemba-speaking leaders, in wanting to increase their share of central committee posts,[49] canvassed for delegates' votes on sectional lines. Western and Eastern Province occupants of, or aspirants for, office did likewise. And, when defeated, they took the initiative in creating, or countenancing, an intensification of sectional movements within UNIP (with the secessionist threats inherent in them) as a way of pressuring the new UNIP leadership. So the 'Unity in the East' movement grew up in 1968 after the central committee elections. Similarly, UNIP Lozi leaders went to the local party apparatus in Western Province in late 1967 and told them not to campaign too vigorously against Mr Mundia's new UP.

Further evidence of how leaders took the initiative in spreading sectionalist awareness was provided by the campaign for the 1970 election, subsequently postponed, of UNIP's central committee. From mid-1969 politicians from Lusaka went out to the regions to influence the selection of delegates to the general conference which would elect the committee. Several prominent people publicly denounced unnamed UNIP politicians for slipping quietly out of Lusaka in order to whip up sectional support in the country. Mr Wilson Chakulya, general secretary of the Zambia Congress of Trade Unions, stated that ordinary villagers were contented until leaders from Lusaka came and poisoned their minds tribally. He alleged that tribal feeling was deeper in Lusaka than anywhere else.[50] The *Times of Zambia* commented that 'The main problem ... appears to be the existence ... of people who wish to exploit ethnic differences for their own benefit.' Mr B. Mufonka, president of the National Union of Commercial and Industrial Workers, agreed. 'There is tribalism in Lusaka and it is Lusaka which is tearing Zambia apart. We ask any political failure to remain quiet and not to involve people in his personal quarrel for personal gain.'[51]

That national-level leaders took the initiative in creating sectionalist perceptions is confirmed by statements made by UNIP leaders themselves. The Western Province Cabinet Minister in July 1969 condemned 'ambitious people ... who are hungry for positions'.[52] The District Governor for Lusaka, Mr B. Zulu, said that some UNIP officials were organising on a tribal basis for the 1970 central committee elections, and he attacked UNIP leaders who canvassed support in their constituencies on tribal lines.[53] In August

---

49. Hall, *The High Price of Principles*, *op. cit.*, pp. 196 ff.
50. *Times of Zambia*, 28 July 1969.
51. *Zambia News*, 17 July 1969.
52. *Times of Zambia*, 14 July 1969.
53. *Ibid.*, 29 July 1969.

1969 UNIP Youth in Chingola telegraphed Dr Kaunda requesting him to sack those Cabinet Ministers 'preaching tribalism and provincialism' in their provinces of origin.[54] And the District Governor for Mwense in Luapula warned Lusaka politicians and civil servants to stop sending 'tribalistic' circulars to the area.[55] A final example may be cited. The opposition to a Minister from Northern Province, Mr J. Mwanakatwe, standing in a Luapula Province constituency was alleged to have come not from local UNIP officials but from Luapula politicians in Lusaka who wanted to increase their parliamentary representation and so make claims to Cabinet seats.[56]

Of course, in recruiting support Zambian politicians not only differentiated themselves in the eyes of the public in terms of their sectional group membership. Some stressed their education and consequently superior ability to run a government; others their role in the freedom struggle. As Rotberg argues,[57] one line of cleavage in the Cabinet may have been between the university-educated 'new men' who played little role in the struggle for independence and the less educated party stalwarts, although this itself is an oversimplification. Some Ministers—such as S. Wina, N. Mundia, M. Sipalo and M. Chona—were both stalwarts and university-educated. Other stalwarts, like Dr Kaunda, may not have been to university but are intellectuals.

Secondly, some UNIP leaders distinguished themselves by taking up a particular ideological position. This was manifested early in 1969, when several Ministers publicly demanded the elimination of ANC,[58] thereby going against what had hitherto been UNIP policy on the creation of a one-party State only through the ballot box. Another example was former Vice-president Kapwepwe's campaign in 1970–71 to preserve traditional Zambian culture. In particular he wished to foster the use of Zambian languages in schools, although the policy of the Ministry of Education was to extend the use of English as the sole medium of instruction. There were also other, less publicised ideological divisions among UNIP leaders on such issues as foreign policy towards the white-ruled south and the meaning and implications of Zambian Humanism.

These divisions among political leaders in UNIP, on the basis of party record and ideology, both existed and cut across the third line

54. *Zambia Mail*, 12 August 1969.
55. *Times of Zambia*, 27 November 1969.
56. *Zambia News*, 23 July 1969, and *Times of Zambia*, 14 and 15 July 1969.
57. Rotberg, 'Tribalism and politics in Zambia', *op. cit.*, p. 32; and Mulford, *Zambia: the Politics of Independence*, *op. cit.*, p. 329.
58. For example, Mr Dingiswayo Banda. *Times of Zambia*, January 1969.

of cleavage, which was sectional. But what has to be explained is why, outside the secrecy of the Cabinet room, Zambian politicians appealed for support not mainly on the basis of their technical competence, party record or ideological position but on the basis of their sectional identification; and why, in their appeals for group support, sectional cleavage was relied on to the virtual exclusion of other social divisions such as class or religion.

Two sets of reasons suggest themselves. The first is minor: the tactical advantages of a sectional appeal. Many types of sectional appeal—for example, to a language group or to all villagers in one chief's area—resulted in a politician seeking the support of a group which had not merely a majority in a rural constituency but a near monopoly. This had the enormous electoral advantage for him of making the seat a 'safe' one. Secondly, a sectional appeal could have a communications advantage if it was made to, or within the boundaries of, a language group. Since in Zambia there is widespread ignorance of the official language (English), the politician who spoke the local language had a huge advantage over any rivals who did not. Finally, a sectional appeal, especially if directed at one's home area, could have an organisational pay-off. For the politician would have a network of kin permeating a significant part of the group to which he was appealing. His family might provide a useful and readily available body of activists on his behalf. For example, one aspirant UNIP candidate in the 1968 general election—the president of the Ideological Institute of Zambia—had for a long time kept up his links with his home area of Mporokoso and felt confident that, if he had stood as a UNIP Independent, he would have won the seat.

But the second and far more fundamental reason why Zambian politicians have tended to make sectional appeals is the relative absence of other major cleavages in the structure of Zambian society. In industrialised countries class has been the most common and dominant basis for interest-group appeals, and so for political cleavage. But in Zambia neither leaders nor followers have perceived class membership as a variable relevant to their political behaviour.[59] There has never been any socialist, let alone communist,

59. There are signs in some African States that class, sometimes in the unique rural form of chief versus commoner, is becoming a more significant variable in party appeals and electoral behaviour. See Sklar, 'Political science and national integration', op. cit., on Nigeria; J. Cartwright, 'Shifting forces in Sierre Leone', Africa Report, vol. 13, No. 9 (December 1968); and D. Koff, 'Notes on the Kenya general election: 1966—The contradiction of opposition', East Africa Journal, vol. III, No. 5 (August 1966).

party. UNIP itself must be classified as populist.[60] In 1967 it dropped even 'African democratic socialism' as its guiding ideology and substituted Zambian Humanism, a philosophy which denies the existence of classes in Zambia and 'welcomes [private] ownership of property'[61]—to which end, measures were taken in April 1968 to substitute a Zambian for a foreign capitalist class in commerce. A survey in 1968 of several hundred members of the Zambian elite revealed a remarkable ignorance of the meaning of socialism. When, in the 1968 elections, Mr J. Musole stood in a Lusaka seat on a socialist platform he polled only 5 per cent of the votes cast. The University of Zambia has very few students familiar with socialist ideas, which is not surprising in view of the small number of Marxists on the university staff[62] and a government ban on several socialist publications.[63]

It is this absence of a perception of class conflict that has very largely resulted in political competition following sectional lines. If it is conceded that classes with antagonistic interests do exist 'objectively' in Zambia, why have class identifications not yet emerged sufficiently to structure political conflict? First, several factors have prevented the Zambian masses from perceiving their social situation in class terms. The independence struggle was fought largely between groups defined by skin colour. The settlers were white and privileged, whereas all Africans were black and discriminated against. UNIP and ANC attracted almost as few whites as the settler UFP attracted Africans. The white working class on the mines, far from allying itself with the African workers, was the backbone of resistance to their demands. Both sides perceived the struggle as a colour conflict. And for UNIP this had the advantage of rallying all Africans, regardless of class, to the nationalist banner and so strengthening the movement.

After independence the perception of economic conflict in terms of colour continued. Most of the economy was still owned by whites and Asians. Most top jobs were still held by whites. The total number of white employees fell only from 31,700 in 1964 to 29,820 in June 1969. As late as the end of 1967 whites held two out of every three of the top 1,790 civil service posts, omitting vacancies. The income

60. P. Worsley, *The Third World* (London, 1964), chapter 4.

61. K. D. Kaunda, *Humanism in Zambia and a Guide to its Implementation, op. cit.*, pp. 3 and 49.

62. R. V. Molteno, 'Our university and our community', *Jewel of Africa*, vol. 2, Nos 3 and 4 (1970).

63. Statutory Instrument No. 51 of 1965 banned, *inter alia*, *World Marxist Review*, *The African Communist* and all publications of the World Federation of Trade Unions.

gap between Africans and whites remained very wide, with whites earning in 1968 on average ĸ4,875 and Africans ĸ789.[64] Measures to increase income equality therefore meant mainly a redistribution between whites and blacks, and so economic competition still appeared in colour terms. Similarly, the measures taken since 1968 to localise capital ownership involved, with the exception only of Mwaiseni Stores, the State taking over white-controlled foreign companies. No black-controlled Zambian company has been nationalised. Even high prices and the high-handedness of employers with workers can appear as the product of the selfishness and racialism of whites, and not as the typical behaviour of capitalists *per se*.

Since independence there has also been widespread and rapid upward mobility for indigenous Zambians. It has taken several forms. Rural emigration to the towns, together with a large growth in total employment, has enabled many to improve their economic position. Between 1963 and 1969 the urban population (Copperbelt, Kabwe and Lusaka) grew by 434,000, or 59 per cent; and between 1963 and 1968 employment rose by 97,000, or 38 per cent.[65] Moreover the shortage of trained Zambians has caused many who were under-educated and poorly paid to be promoted very fast and far.[66] School expansion is enabling many children to rise occupationally far above their parents.[67] The result is a relatively open society in which class barriers appear to be negligible.

Another possible factor which may have reduced class cleavage is the extended family, which can redistribute income so that the poor share in the income of their wealthier relatives.[68] However, one must remain sceptical of the importance of this factor in Zambia until it has been shown empirically that poor relatives do not resent their inferior position and that rich relatives do not try to escape this particular obligation.

A special factor, which has reduced class perceptions among the 70 per cent of the population which is rural, is the fact that most

64. *Monthly Digest of Statistics* (Lusaka), vol. VI, No. 9 (September 1970), tables 4 and 5.

65. ZIS press release No. 275/69, and *Monthly Digest of Statistics*, vol. V, No. 5 (May 1969), table 3.

66. V. Subramaniam, 'The social background of Zambia's higher civil servants and undergraduates' (University of East Africa Social Science Conference paper, Nairobi, 1969), tables 4 and 5.

67. *Ibid.*, table 3.

68. A. R. Zolberg, 'The structure of political conflict in the new States of tropical Africa', *American Political Science Review*, vol. LXII, No. 1 (March 1968), p. 74.

of the people are subsistence farmers with no landlords, money-lenders, or private marketing agencies battening on them. Even the chiefs are usually weak, especially with their loss of powers since independence. Rural Zambians cannot yet see themselves as an obviously or directly exploited class. Moreover, no leaders have come to either the rural farmers or the urban workers with an overtly class appeal. Members of the existing political elite have not done so, while President Kaunda has deliberately played down class conflict. Announcing the 51 per cent take-over of the mines in August 1969, he stated:

Now there is a clear identity of interests between workers and Government ... There is now no distinction between employer and employee, as is often the case in capitalist economies ... It is ridiculous for workers now in the light of these reforms to feel that they are a distinct class ... Now, the interests of ... any type of workers, indeed politicians, are all identical.[69]

As for the opposition ANC, it was to the right, not the left, of UNIP and refrained from any class appeal in the 1968 general election. Both parties agreed on the continuance of a mixed economy, private land ownership in several provinces, and income inequality.

The reason why present-day politicians have not recruited support on a class basis is that such an appeal would have undermined their own elite position. A class appeal would have had to attack not just foreign capitalists but the Zambian elite too[70]—its high income and propensity to consume, its increasing integration into the private sector and its failure to direct government investment mainly into productive facilities.[71] Zambian politicians are members of this elite and their social background is discontinuous with that of the masses. Almost no MPs have manual or peasant occupational backgrounds; they therefore neither feel an identity of class interests with the masses nor have appealed to them on that basis. On the contrary, they may seek to avoid a peasant or working-class challenge to their own position by diverting it into sectional rivalries between the masses themselves. Some writers argue that this is already happening elsewhere in Africa. 'Tribalism then becomes a

69. Kaunda, *Towards Complete Independence, op. cit.*, pp. 45 and 46.

70. The Kenya People's Union faced this same dilemma in the 1966 Kenya elections. Koff, 'Notes on the Kenya general election: 1966', *op. cit.*

71. Government spending has stressed recurrent and social service spending at the expense of capital and manufacturing and agricultural investment spending. Since 1968 capital spending has been a steadily shrinking proportion of government expenditure.

mask for class privilege' and 'an instrument of power politics in the hands of the ruling classes'.[72]

But why, finally, have farmers and urban workers in Zambia not produced a national-level leadership of their own willing to articulate class demands? The farmers have failed to do so partly because most of them lack sufficient English (which is essential for national roles in a multilingual society) and because they have no organisation capable of both generating a leadership and instituting collective political action. As for the urban workers, although nearly one-third of them are organised in trade unions, they have suffered from two difficulties. They have lost many union officials to more lucrative posts as civil servants and personnel managers; and, at the national level, their union leaders have tended to be more responsive to the wishes of government than to the grievances of workers.[73] For all these reasons, class is neither perceived yet as a major line of social stratification nor used by politicians as the basis on which to aggregate support.

But there does exist in Zambia one social cleavage which most people clearly perceive to exist, and which one might have thought could have become the basis of political competition. This is the cleavage between the urban and rural populations. There is a growing gap in the standard of living between the two. While average African wages (largely earned in the urban areas) rose from K272 in 1960 to K789 in 1969, the average value of subsistence production per family remained at about K50 per annum.[74] Some politicians, particularly President Kaunda, are aware of the potentially explosive nature of this gap.[75] Indeed, the only cases of swings of opinion away from UNIP—in the Western Province, where the party lost eight seats in 1968, and in Solwezi in 1969, where it failed to gain a 'yes' majority in the June referendum— were both in rural areas, and depressed ones at that. Why, then, in the period when inter-party competition was still permitted did no politician try to form a specifically agrarian party?

Several reasons can be advanced. First, as we have noted, the rural population has neither generated its own leaders nor been able to recruit leaders from the urban elite. One explanation of the

72. Sklar, 'Political science and national integration', *op. cit.*, p. 6; and B. Decke, 'What is tribalism?', *Africa and the World* (September 1970).

73. Bates, *Unions, Parties and Political Development, op cit.*, pp. 74–9, 216.

74. J. M. Mwanza, 'Towards income policy in Zambia' (University of East Africa Social Science Conference paper, Nairobi, 1969), p. 3.

75. For his analysis of the two Zambian nations, the one urban and the other rural, see Kaunda, *Towards Complete Independence, op. cit.*, p. 44; and Kaunda, *Zambia's Guidelines for the next Decade, op. cit.*, pp. 30 ff.

latter's aversion to leading specifically rural movements is that 'modern African leaders are creatures of the towns. Most of them grow up, live, and die in urban centres—even if they may be born in rural areas. They tend, therefore, to be more attracted to urban areas than to rural areas.'[76] Secondly, the conflict of interest between rural and urban dwellers is mitigated by the fact that many rural Zambians have shared in the increasing urban prosperity by going to town and either finding jobs or living off relatives there. Further, the rural areas are heavily subsidised by the urban areas. It is 'urban men' who staff the social services and development agencies which benefit the rural areas. It is the urban areas which produce the funds going into rural development. These factors reduce both the likelihood of the rural population perceiving their interests as clashing with those of the townsmen, and the extent to which they can afford to push their demands against the towns. The political result has been not rivalry between the three developed line-of-rail provinces (Copperbelt, Central and Southern) and the five outlying provinces, but a conflict over the distribution of funds among the five outlying provinces themselves. Thus local politicians in Western, North-western, Eastern and Luapula Provinces have all claimed that their areas have been neglected relative to Northern Province, the heartland of Bemba-speakers. Sectionalism has displaced an urban–rural cleavage.

There is one other cleavage which could form the social basis for political conflict but which has not done so, namely religious membership. The Christian Churches, many still heavily manned by expatriate priests, have abstained from political involvement. And pre-colonial religious beliefs have never taken large-scale organised form—they lack a professional priesthood and a set of precepts applicable to modern government. Only two religious movements have become involved in politics, and both in clashes with UNIP. The most serious was in 1964 when virtual warfare broke out between the Lumpa followers of Alice Lenshina and UNIP activists (and later the army) in Northern, Luapula, and parts of Eastern Province.[77] The second was the Watch Tower movement, whose refusal to participate in voting in the 1968 general election and the 1969 referendum provoked great resentment among UNIP activists and led to clashes and arson, especially in Luapula. It is significant that these, the most bloody and widespread political clashes which Zambia has seen, took place not between sectional

76. D. K. Chisiza, 'Africa—what lies ahead?', quoted in R. Dumont, *False Start in Africa* (London, 1968), p. 230.
77. J. W. Fernandez, 'The Lumpa uprising: why?', *op. cit.*

groups but within the Bemba and Eastern Province populations, on a religious–political line of division.[78] Nevertheless, these religious cleavages did not become an important basis for political appeals, despite ANC's proclaimed, but unfulfilled, intention of exploiting UNIP's aversion to Watch Tower.[79] The reasons are that Watch Tower and Lumpa together form less than 5 per cent of the population,[80] and both movements in any case reject political participation. Our conclusion must be that the major reason why Zambian politicians have turned to sectional social cleavages when recruiting support is the absence of other cleavages which could be used. The question then arises: what sectional identifications have they tried to create?

This question of the boundaries of sectional groups is an immensely difficult one and requires much more research. Only certain limited statements can be made here. Language is one factor which often defines the outer boundaries of the sectional group. It has been used in many countries, including Canada, India, South Africa and the United States, as a cleavage on which to build sectional perceptions of distinctive interests and so political support. This has happened in Zambia too. Most adults, particularly in the rural areas, speak only their home language. They rely on it entirely for communication, and their choice of social contacts is made within the limits set by language. Language thus separates most Zambians into several non-interacting groups, whose members perform their main roles within the social confines of their particular language group. It is obviously difficult for a sense of common identity to evolve among people who seldom interact across the boundary of language. It is not surprising, therefore, that in Zambia the main political sections have been linguistic groups—for example, all Bemba-speakers regardless of provincial boundaries; all who can understand Nyanja as a lingua franca (largely in Eastern Province); or the multitude of pre-colonial Ila–Tonga-speaking polities which now perceive themselves as having a common identity.

But while Zambia has no sectional group which embraces several very different language groups, within a single language group there can be sectional divisions whose boundaries are defined in

78. Lundazi regional report to the UNIP national council (mimeo., March 1969), p. 1.

79. Just after the clashes Mr Nkumbula announced that 'there was no difference between ANC and Watchtower'. *Zambia Mail*, 11 July 1969.

80. The largest estimate for the Lumpa was 60,000 in 1964. Fernandez, 'The Lumpa uprising: why?', *op. cit.* The leader of the Jehovah's Witnesses claimed 125,000 members in 1969. *Times of Zambia*, 15 January 1969.

terms of other factors. One example is the perception of 'we Luapulans', which first came to be articulated publicly in 1969. Here certain leaders from Luapula Province resorted to an administrative institutional variable to divide the Bemba-speaking bloc into separate, provincially defined perceptions of identity. A different kind of variable is reflected in the resentment among some in Eastern Province at the alleged predominance in the province's leadership of 'Tumbuka', notably Cabinet Ministers W. Nyirenda and A. J. Soko.

An important factor which influences a politician's choice of the kind of boundary he utilises to define a sectional group is the arena of competition within which he must recruit support. The arena is defined situationally, often by institutional factors—whether, for instance, access to a post depends on election, or not; and if so, who participates in the election. This arena influences the size of the group whose support a politician needs, and hence the criteria of cleavage he finds it convenient to exploit. The point can be readily illustrated. In the 1967 UNIP central committee elections Bemba leaders wanted to increase their share of key posts. Access to these posts depended on obtaining a majority of general conference delegates' votes. The first step was to create a feeling of solidarity among all Bemba-speaking delegates. Since, however, each party region sent an equal number of delegates, the number from each language group was roughly proportionate to the group's share in the total population, and so Bemba delegates were only a minority, albeit a large one. They needed an alliance. They could not choose Eastern or Lozi delegates because it was precisely the central committee posts held by leaders of those sections which the Bemba wished to acquire. So they turned mainly to Tonga-speaking delegates. This support had an obvious advantage: while Tonga delegates commanded many votes, their leaders had no electoral base because the province from which they came was solidly ANC. Their powerlessness would therefore reinforce Bemba dominance in the new central committee, since the two Tonga leaders, M. Chona and E. Mudenda, having been elected as a result of Bemba support, depended on the latter for keeping their positions. As for the Tonga delegates, the advantage to them of an alliance with the Bemba was that they doubled their representation on the central committee.[81]

This analysis suggests that the Bemba choice of the Tonga was

81. For details of the struggle over the central committee's composition, see Rotberg, 'Tribalism and politics in Zambia', *op. cit.*, and pp. 112–14 below.

influenced by the party constitution which laid down the composition of the general conference and the mode of electing the
central committee. The choice was a pragmatic decision of tactics.
Language boundaries were disregarded. Alleged Tonga dislike of
Bemba was no obstacle to the formation of the alliance, which shows
the relative unimportance of emotional factors in contemporary
sectional alignments. And the pragmatic basis of the alliance pointed
to there being nothing eternal about it. When circumstances
changed, as they did in 1970–71, the alliances—of Bemba and
Tonga and of the various segments of the Bemba section itself—
broke up.

Another aspect of the way in which the arena of competition has
influenced the politicians' choice of the boundaries of sectional
groups was shown by politics in the Eastern Province in 1967–68.
Having had their key leaders ousted from the central committee,
there was a great need for Eastern Province solidarity to ensure that
its maximum electoral strength would be forthcoming in future.
So 1968 saw the 'Unity in the East' movement. But simultaneously
there was competition within the province as to who should be its
main leaders and over the distribution of parliamentary candidates
among the province's own sections. In particular, there was resentment at alleged 'Tumbuka domination'. This showed that when the
arena of competition was the national level within UNIP, there
tended to be Eastern Province solidarity; but when the arena of
competition was within the province, further divisions and smaller
sectional loyalties developed. Politics in the other provinces can
probably be similarly analysed: solidarity at the level of national
competition; division at the level of intra-provincial politics.

This indicates a more general characteristic of political behaviour in Zambia: leaders and followers act situationally. Depend-
ing on how their social situation appears to them, they will act in
terms of nationalist norms and identifications or sectional norms and
identifications. Moreover, on different occasions they may act in
terms of different kinds of sectional ties. It is therefore an oversimplification of, at any rate, Zambian political experience to
assume that 'party leaders in African one-party-dominant States
have been basically committed to "national unity" as the supreme
value and goal'.[82] Consider the following hypothetical case. A
Zambian Minister flies to London to negotiate a loan. He acts
nationally as a 'Zambian', since domestic sectional cleavages are
irrelevant to his behaviour in the negotiations. On his return to

82. Coleman and Rosberg, *Political Parties and National Integration*,
*op. cit.*, p. 663.

Lusaka he may involve himself in a Cabinet dispute on the location of some development project—in which sectional splits follow linguistic or provincial lines. He may then tour his home province and discover that his leadership is being challenged. He then aligns himself with sections in the province which base themselves on dialectical differences,[83] or divisions among traditional leaders,[84] or geographical–historical cleavages,[85] or commoner–traditional ruler distinctions.

The same man can act successively in the various roles of 'Zambian', 'Eastern Province man', 'Tumbuka' or 'Tumbuka commoner'. He has a series of social ties, group loyalties, institutional environments. How he acts depends on his perception of what appears from his social situation to be most relevant at that moment. In other words, a loyal nationalist might also act as an ardent sectionalist politician.

*The response of the masses to sectional appeals*

The starting point for the success of sectional appeals, although in our view neither the only nor necessarily the most important variable, is the culture of the masses. In the absence of social survey research, little is known about the group identifications of Zambians, either of their boundaries or of the emotional intensity with which they are held. Clearly people do feel that they belong to a series of often concentric units: family, kin network, a particular area, a language group, and so on. These emotional orientations are not the same as 'primordial attachments', since the boundaries of this multitude of often categoric groups seldom relate to the boundaries of pre-colonial States. But their existence provides the politician with the initial building blocks for his sectionalist appeal. What he has to do is convince his potential followers of the political relevance of their existing group loyalties. Until he achieves this (and it is communications, economic situation, and other variables which facilitate his doing so, as we shall see), people feel group loyalties, but political sectionalism does not yet exist. However, once these loyalties are politicised and sectional perceptions come into existence, people will be socialised into them and social sanctions will be invoked to ensure behaviour in conformity with them. At this stage

83. As, for example, between Tumbuka and other groups in Eastern Province.
84. Clashes between the Litunga and his Ngambela in Western Province have been frequent.
85. For example, Sesheke versus Lealui in Western Province.

perceptions will become an independent variable influencing political behaviour. Not too much stress, however, must be placed on this cultural variable in explaining the masses' response to sectional appeals, since there are other variables which crucially influence their response: their communications exposure, economic interests and the inter-personal pressures resulting from their social situation.

That the cultural variable should not be placed in the forefront of any multivariable model explaining popular response is shown by the case of the Nkoya-inhabited seats in Western Province which stayed UNIP in the 1968 elections. It has been argued[86] that, since WENELA did not recruit there, its closure did not result in a fall in living standards as it did elsewhere in the province. There was no economic basis on which the UP's sectionalist appeal could capitalise. Thus when Mr Mundia tried to set up his new UP in Mankoya (now Kaoma) District, he received a rough reception. After the election UNIP was determined to keep the two Nkoya seats. Local UNIP leaders began to remind the population that they were not 'true Lozi', and indeed had been incorporated into the Lozi kingdom by conquest. But this emotional appeal to historic cleavages followed, and did not precede, the election, suggesting that it was not a major factor influencing the voters' behaviour. The motives of followers in responding to a sectionalist appeal which uses historical arguments and emotions must first be sought in contemporary variables of interests, social pressures, and consequent perceptions.

But sectionalist perceptions, once in existence, must have some independent influence on behaviour. In particular, they can become a parameter which limits a politician's choice of sectional identifications and alliances which he wishes to create, in addition to the influence of language boundaries and the arena of competition on his choice. Thus Lozi leaders in either UNIP or ANC might have had difficulty in leading their followers into an alliance with Bemba-speakers, given the degree of antipathy between the rank and file of the two groups. This may have been one reason why Mr Mundia rejected President Kaunda's call for the reunification of UNIP and ANC in November 1969.[87]

It follows that, while political leaders may take the initiative in creating sectional identifications, once there is a popular response there can be mass pressure on leaders to act sectionally. Sectionalism is a multi-stage phenomenon: the leader who fosters sectional identifications in stage one can be under pressure from his creation

86. Scott and Molteno, 'The Zambian general elections', *op. cit.*
87. *Times of Zambia*, 10 November 1969.

in stage two. This pressure can limit his choice in his future stimulation of sectional identities. It can also extend to those leaders who remain nationally oriented. The rise of UP provides an illustration. Its driving force, N. Mundia, had been sacked from the Cabinet in 1966. He pulled out of UNIP and built up an independent base through a sectionalist appeal in his home province. By mid-1968 sufficient rural Lozi had adopted the sectionalist political identification his party suggested for them to be able to put pressure on those Lozi leaders who had remained in UNIP.[88] The leaders did not give in to this pressure, and so went down to electoral defeat and temporary political obscurity in the general election.

Given the existence of a series of group identifications among the masses, their responsiveness to sectional appeals is influenced by other variables. One such variable is communications. People like to be consistently disposed, either favourably or unfavourably, both to the people who communicate a message and to its contents.[89] Where leaders in whom they already have confidence come, even if it is with a new message, they may respond positively to that message out of confidence in the communicator. In Zambia sectional messages have usually been communicated not by new politicians but by those very men who led the freedom struggle and used to articulate nationalist sentiments. Thus Mr Mundia was one of UNIP's main organisers in Western Province in the early 1960s and indeed the founder in 1960 of the Barotse Anti-secession Society.[90] Yet a few years later he came back with the sectional appeal of his new United Party. Several of his leading lieutenants in the UP were also experienced former UNIP politicians: D. Chikulo, UP national treasurer, had been a UNIP Member of Parliament, and W. Chipango, UP national secretary, was a former UNIP mayor of Livingstone.

Moreover, because of language barriers the independence struggle in each area was usually led by local men. In 1964 most UNIP and ANC Members of Parliament stood in their provinces of origin. Because of their successful leadership of the struggle, they gained much prestige; this is indicated, for example, by the praise songs for particular national leaders which are sometimes sung at UNIP rallies. When, in the years after independence, some of these same men returned to the people with sectional appeals, they were

---

88. The UP frequently alleged in public that M. Sipalo, A. Wina, and other Lozi-speaking UNIP leaders were secret UP members. ZIS *District News* No. 8/68, and ZIS press release No. 2624/67, 4 December 1967.
89. L. Festinger, *A Theory of Cognitive Dissonance* (London, 1957).
90. Mulford, *Zambia: the Politics of Independence, op. cit.*, p. 225.

returning to the very areas and language groups in which they had
first built their political reputations. In addition, their reputations
had probably not waned in the intervening period, since they had
often taken steps to benefit the people of their language group or
area. The UNIP national secretary, Mr M. Chona, stated that
most Zambians felt that they 'got better service' from leaders who
came from their own areas.[91] At one stage President Kaunda had to
forbid Ministers to recommend people for jobs. The result of this
patronage system was to reinforce a leader's standing among his
potentially sectionally aware followers and so to increase the likelihood of their responding favourably to his sectional appeal.

Communications variables can foster sectionalism in another way.
When eight out of eleven Western Province seats were captured by
the opposition ANC in 1968, many non-Lozi UNIP leaders interpreted the results as a 'tribal' defection by 'the Lozi', when it was
probably a reaction by a minority (34 per cent of the registered
electorate) of rural Lozi to a drop in their standard of living. These
leaders communicated their sectional interpretation to UNIP activists, some of whom then indiscriminately victimised Lozi living
outside Western Province.[92] So, owing to the communication of a
fallacious perception, the myth of discrimination put out by UP–
ANC became in part reality. This in turn made more Lozi perceive
their troubles as due to sectional discrimination.

Secondly, the economic position of the Zambian masses has
predisposed them to accept sectional appeals. Economic expectations
rose during the independence struggle. UNIP and ANC made
promises which stressed the immediate worthwhileness of independence rather than its necessity as a precondition to faster economic
growth.[93] Since 1964, however, expectations of a higher standard of
living in the rural areas have not been met, except indirectly
through the much wider availability of education and health
services. Rural Zambians want an explanation of their continuing
poverty. No leaders have come to them with a class explanation.
UNIP itself has not been effective in economic education, partly because its cadres know very little about economics and partly because
some UNIP leaders themselves have explained poverty in terms of
uneven income distribution between sectional groups. This happened in Solwezi District and in Western and Eastern Provinces.
UP and ANC leaders did the same. So the people, who know that

91. Quoted in Hall, *The High Price of Principles, op. cit.*, p. 198.
92. *Times of Zambia*, 24 December 1968.
93. 'The aims and objects of UNIP as set out in its pre-independence
constitution', quoted in Kaunda, *Humanism in Zambia, op. cit.*, p. 9.

they are at a disadvantage economically, have been led to perceive the cause as sectional discrimination.

There are several reasons why they accept such an explanation. They are not sufficiently versed in economics to realise that the real causes of their poverty are the underdeveloped state of the Zambian economy and the uneven income distribution between themselves and the economic elite, particularly the expatriate community. Three years after independence 38 per cent of the total wages and salaries bill was still going to non-Africans; the latter's share in the national income was in fact much greater, since income from rents, profits and dividends largely accrued to them.[94] Yet they comprised less than 2 per cent of the population.

Secondly, the fact that most rural Zambians speak only their home language, are too poor to buy radios, and are not sufficiently literate to read newspapers, renders them almost totally dependent for political information on politicians from their own section. When these politicians link the undoubted fact of continuing poverty with the alleged cause of sectional discrimination, most rural (and many urban) Zambians are unable to check the accuracy of that information. The District Governor of Choma made this point when reporting how easily ANC could mislead Southern Province people into accepting the idea that Mr Nkumbula was really the ruler of the province, since 'a villager who does not read the newspaper and who has no radio will not dismiss it'.[95]

Further, many sectional allegations cannot by their very nature be proved or disproved. Where a sectional motive is alleged—when, for example, some Eastern Province politicians stated that the tarring of the Great North Road was given priority because it ran through Northern Province—this cannot be disproved, even if there are obvious alternative explanations such as Rhodesia's UDI. Nor can a politician's prophecy of future sectional discrimination always be disproved. In 1968 ANC told Lozi voters that, if UNIP won, the Bemba would take away their cattle and their wives;[96] this did not happen, and ANC could claim that it was its victory in the province which averted the calamity! Or where it is alleged that one locality is worse off than others, as the Kaonde alleged in Solwezi in 1969, the fact that the rural population is tied by

94. Figures calculated from *Monthly Digest of Statistics* (May 1969), *op. cit.*, tables 3 and 4.

95. Choma District Governor's report to UNIP national council (mimeo., 19 March 1969), p. 1.

96. This propaganda was repeated in the June 1969 referendum. *Times of Zambia*, 4 June 1969.

poverty to a particular locality prevents people from travelling to rural areas in other provinces and seeing the falseness of the allegations.

In these cases sectionally defined parts of the population have been led incorrectly to perceive their poverty as greater than that of other sections. But it is possible for the level of economic development to coincide with sectional group boundaries. In such cases the masses have even more reason to accept a sectional explanation. One cause of such coincidence is the colonial legacy of geographically uneven economic development. In Northern Rhodesia the five outlying provinces, especially Western and North-western, were almost totally neglected. Sectional political behaviour has been particularly prevalent in these neglected areas—on the one hand we have had Bemba self-assertion,[97] and on the other, Eastern, Lozi and Kaonde discontent. In 1968–69 the Lamba alleged economic neglect, and it is noteworthy that although they are in Copperbelt Province they live in its rural and undeveloped areas.

There have been other reasons why, in the post-independence period, the level of economic development has coincided with section. The Zambian government has been opposed to white minority regimes in southern Africa and has reduced its links with them. One consequence was the closing of WENELA, which happened to operate almost exclusively in Western Province, whose inhabitants have been the sole sufferers from this policy. Another example is Northern Province, which has received more development funds than any of the other four outlying provinces, the cause being largely the impact of UDI and the pressing need to build new transport outlets to Tanzania; inevitably these outlets pass through Northern Province.[98]

In these cases where one sectional group is actually better, or worse, off than others the causes have been fortuitous. It is in principle possible that the cause can be sectional, and politicians' explanation of relative economic disadvantage in sectional terms can therefore be correct. While it must be stressed that there is no evidence of the distribution of development funds between provinces being influenced significantly by sectional considerations, the Zambian political elite has divided partly on sectional lines. The rivalry between these elite sections did result in the dominance at one time of Bemba-speakers over the UNIP central committee,

97. Hall, *The High Price of Principles*, *op. cit.*, pp. 197 and 199.
98. A contributory cause is that Northern Province has the largest population of the five provinces.

and to a lesser extent over the Cabinet and National Assembly.[99]
Since Bemba leaders depended on the support of their sectionally
identified followers, they could have used their preponderant political power to reward those followers by diverting public resources
disproportionately to the benefit of their own sectional base. So
many non-Bemba in and outside UNIP believed, anyway. The
UP organ, the *Mirror*,[100] pointed out that many top posts, including the President, Vice-president, Secretary to the Cabinet,
Commissioner of Police and chairman of the Public Service Commission were all held by Bemba. One Eastern Province intellectual
in UNIP tried to prove disproportionate Bemba respresentation
in the civil service which in fact does not exist.[101] These examples
could be multiplied.[102] Clearly, in the long run, one section could
have gradually achieved an average economic condition which was
better than that of other sections, although no Zambian politician
has ever proved that this has yet happened. Nevertheless, when
those elite sections who were 'out' made redoubled efforts in 1969
to get 'in' in the interests of their own political careers they could
whip up sectional support by putting a hard-headed, self-interest
argument to their followers: 'If you do not act cohesively, your
leaders won't get sufficient party and government posts. If your
leaders do not get sufficient posts, they will not be able to wield
sufficient power on your behalf in order to make sure that you
followers get your fair share of the jobs and development funds
going.' This argument, and the allegations of discrimination against
their followers by a government dominated by another section, can
increasingly have a basis in fact. And once sectional identifications
and economic status coincide for many people, it clearly becomes
rational to act politically in sectional terms; this, in turn, makes
it more difficult for nationalist leaders to reduce sectional perceptions.

99. 1969 and 1970 saw the step-by-step reduction of Bemba predominance. In January 1969 the President's new Cabinet included two additional
Easterners and one additional member from North-western. In August the
central committee was dissolved. The interim replacement committee included major Eastern and North-western leaders again. In September Vice-
president Kapwepwe was stripped of his major portfolios, and three additions
to the Cabinet were made from the relatively under-represented Central,
Luapula, and North-western Provinces. And in November 1970 the President
chose a new, Tonga-speaking Vice-president, Mr Mainza Chona.
    100. *The Mirror*, vol. 1, No. 1 (Lusaka, March 1968).
    101. See p. 286 below.
    102. For example, an ANC Member of Parliament alleged in 1969 that
Tonga-speakers were being excluded from the police and army. *Nat. Ass.
Deb.*, Hansard No. 17, 4 February 1969, col. 261.

It is very important to recognise the economic basis underlying apparently sectional politics in Zambia.

... the root causes of political competition [in Zambia] often lie in divergent economic and political interests, not in tribal differences... While tribe remains an important category of political analysis, it can be more usefully viewed as an aggregation of shared material interests rather than as an expression of traditional solidarity based on shared culture and historical experience and an innate hostility towards outsiders.[103]

When voters have supported a party, like the UP, or a sectional movement which does not hope for support from all parts of the population, this support may both appear to political actors, and be, rational. For where sections do differ in their average economic condition and where government is susceptible to collective sectional demands, a group may improve its economic and political position by closing its ranks and acting as an interest group to make demands on government. Sectionalist political behaviour, then, by leaders and followers is as rational as class-motivated behaviour.

The on-going strength of sectional solidarity is therefore not primarily the product of emotional and irrational loyalties. Rather, it derives from the role which sections play as interest groups which (like such groups everywhere) benefit their members by defending the latter's economic position and other interests through political action. This is why President Kaunda has been successful in containing sectionalism by political and economic compromise, thus bringing into question Arthur Lewis's assertion that sectional hostilities cannot be reduced by economic concessions.[104] In 1967 the President handled the strongly held feelings of Bemba UNIP activists that they were under-represented in the central committee both in relation to their proportion of the population and their role in the freedom struggle by allowing a free election to central committee posts.[105] When this subsequently led to discontent among ousted Eastern Province leaders, the President back-pedalled. 1968 showed these leaders still loyal to UNIP (although determined to regain their power in the party) and the province's population more solidly pro-UNIP than ever before—votes cast for ANC fell from 28,020 in 1964 to 4,951 in 1968. So Dr Kaunda moved to meet their demands. In January 1969 they received a large increase in Cabinet respresentation with the addition of two Eastern Province members. In August the President dissolved the offending central committee,

103. Rasmussen, 'Political competition', op. cit., p. 419.
104. Lewis, Politics in West Africa, op. cit.
105. Hall, The High Price of Principles, op. cit., p. 197.

and his reconstituted committee included their main leaders. The result was increased Eastern satisfaction. An example of the utility of economic, as opposed to political, concessions is Southern Province. In 1964 it voted overwhelmingly ANC. UNIP subsequently used various measures, including massive injections of development spending, to influence the electorate, and in 1968 it improved its position quite significantly. Not only was there a swing to UNIP of 8 per cent, but so many former ANC supporters abstained that the percentage of the registered electorate voting ANC fell from 79·0 per cent in 1964 to 55·8 per cent in 1968. At least one UNIP leader, the District Governor for Choma, concluded that if people were to be won over from ANC,

our government propaganda *must* be based on development, which the people can easily see and quote it, than political alone [*sic*] ... since we have already got our political independence; now we are fighting for economic independence.[106]

A further case of the utility of economic concessions in containing sectionalism was Solwezi in the North-western Province. The district's leaders had complained early in 1969 that their area lacked development, especially when compared with other provinces.[107] They put punch behind this view by successfully calling on UNIP voters to abstain in the 1969 referendum, thereby denying their own party a 'yes' majority in the district. But when development projects began subsequently to be implemented, the influential UNIP rural council chairman changed his stance and announced that 'no doubt people will change their attitude towards the government now that they are seeing fair play'.[108] And in fact in the 1970 local government elections UNIP candidates in Solwezi won easily.

Political culture, communications and economic variables affecting the Zambian population's response to sectional appeals have been examined. The last important variable is social structure. The rural population is a relatively undifferentiated mass. In each area everyone speaks the same language. Almost all are subsistence farmers with no big inequalities of income. Few belong to any voluntary associations. Each person's egocentric network is homogeneous in two senses: all his social contacts belong to his own language group; and these contacts are not stratified in terms of class, religion or other

106. Choma District Governor's report to UNIP national council, *op. cit.*, p. 2.
107. Minutes of extraordinary meeting of the North-western Provincial Development Committee, 14 February 1969, *op. cit.*, pp. 3 and 5.
108. *Zambia Mail*, 15 July 1969.

major cleavage. Most rural Zambians therefore have few social roles which can generate cross-pressures on them such that the contacts and interests involved in one set of roles generate pressure to act in one way, while other role sets generate counter-pressures to act in another way. Of course, social change is involving more rural people in more social roles, such as parents of schoolchildren, co-operative members, cash crop producers, and party activists. More people are therefore living in a potentially cross-pressured social situation.

An example is the Southern Province, where cash crop production has gone furthest. This involved many ANC supporters in interaction with the UNIP-controlled government, in their need for credit, technical assistance and marketing services. UNIP used public agencies to put ANC farmers under cross-pressures; thus, loans were often not given by the Credit Organisation of Zambia unless a UNIP card was produced. It was probably this kind of pressure which partly accounted for the swing to UNIP in this province. If, however, most rural Zambians are still free from cross-pressure, their favourable response to sectionalist appeals is not likely to be checked either by any social pressure or because any of their interests suffer as a result of their favourable response. Indeed, once some have responded, the pressure on the remainder is likely to be overwhelming, since each villager is so closely integrated economically and socially with his fellows that it is fool-hardy to antagonise them. The structure of rural society therefore poses few obstacles to the spread of sectionalism.

However, it may be objected that UNIP itself has a structure which is sufficiently dense on the ground to act as a source of social pressure on political actors, and that it would constitute a counter-pressure in favour of national unity in the event of any sectional appeal being made. Certainly UNIP is highly organised in many rural areas. In Luapula Province, for example, it had 463 branches, or one branch for every 350 adults, in 1968.[109] But despite its structural vigour, UNIP has often been a weak generator of cross-pressures in favour of national identification. In some cases the party itself has been the communicator of sectionalist perceptions at the local level. This has been facilitated by the fact that the President's policy of stationing provincial Cabinet Ministers outside their home provinces has not been followed to the same extent at District Governor level, and almost not at all at the lower levels of UNIP—regional officials and the part-time activists below them.

109. Ngalande, 'Luapula Province: political report on the implementation of Humanism in Zambia', *op. cit.*

The party's local personnel are linguistically and occupationally the same as the rural population, so that the party can easily articulate sectionalism at this key field-level. Examples are the 'Unity in the East' movement in 1968 and the Solwezi discontent in 1969. In both cases it was the local UNIP structure which articulated, and perhaps initiated, the popular discontent on sectionalist lines.

The Western Province afforded an example of UNIP merely acting as a weak generator of cross-pressures countering sectionalism. UNIP activists were not sure whether they really disagreed with the UP's message that the Lozi were discriminated against by the Bemba, for the UNIP Lozi leaders in Lusaka were precisely of this mind after August 1967. So the party did not act as a vigorous counter-pressure on the province's electorate. This was one factor in the massive swing away from UNIP in the 1968 elections.

The relative absence of cross-pressures in Zambian rural society has further consequences for the way in which the masses respond to sectionalist appeals. First, there may often be a high degree of unanimity in the popular response to such appeals. The Bemba, Lozi and Eastern Province sections in UNIP each seem to have maintained a high degree of cohesion at both leader and follower levels. This was indicated in the 1968 elections. A much higher proportion of rural Lozi swung away from UNIP than did urban Lozi.[110] The reason may be that urban Lozi were under far more cross-pressures than their rural counterparts.[111] The townsman lives in a multilingual environment. He is involved in a multitude of roles with people from other sectional groups, through his workplace, voluntary association memberships (especially the party), and because he lives in a linguistically mixed residential area. Many urban Lozi therefore had economic and social reasons for not abandoning UNIP and so for rejecting sectionalist appeals. On the other hand, townsmen may be even more predisposed to act sectionally than rural people. They are caught up in a desperate competition for jobs and houses. It is tempting for townsmen to categorise their competitors into sectional groups, for this can narrow the field of competition if they can then use the sectional identification of the person who controls access to resources and benefits to gain preferential access for themselves, or, conversely, to rationalise their exclusion. In this way, the townsman has a pre-eminent motive to act sectionally.[112]

110. See chapter 5.
111. Moreover, they were not suffering from the closure of WENELA.
112. In the Congo 'the need for a unified ethnic self-assertion was first felt in the city'. C. Young, *Politics in the Congo* (Princeton, 1965), p. 251.

The second consequence of the relative absence of cross-pressures in the rural areas is that sectionalist perceptions can spread very fast, helped by a common language and the extended kinship structure. In Western Province, Mr Mundia in late 1967 operated with almost no money or transport, few full-time helpers, and no existing party structure. Yet in little more than a year he captured the loyalty of one-third of the province's voters. Another example is Solwezi. In December 1968 it was solidly UNIP. Six months later, at the instigation of chiefs and local UNIP leaders, 92 per cent of the electorate refused to vote for UNIP in the referendum.

Our conclusions about sectionalism in Zambia can now be summarised. Sectionalism is a political phenomenon. It arises in the first place and primarily from competition for power among leaders. The latter choose to create sectionalist, instead of other, identifications because of the particular variety of social cleavages available in Zambia as a basis for recruiting political support. These cleavages include linguistic, regional and other social distinctions, but not class or religious ones. The people respond to leaders' appeals to act politically in terms of these sectionalist perceptions partly because they already feel they belong to a series of concentric sections (family, kin-group, chief's area, language group, and so on) and also because the leaders' struggle for power can affect the people's access to economic resources. Sectional groups are essentially interest groups competing for scarce resources. Their conflicts can therefore be contained by compromise. Sectional groups today clearly have little to do with pre-colonial polities and culture, either in their boundaries, goals or leadership. Moreover, they are only categoric groups—people perceive themselves and others as being members of groups, although the groups have no patterned structure resulting from actual social interaction. Identification with a sectional group only influences certain of an individual's roles—which roles depend on his own, and others', definition of his social situation. It is therefore possible for a person to behave successively in terms of national goals and sectional goals. Indeed, for one to hold a sectional identification is not the opposite of, and has nothing to do with, so-called acculturation into 'Western' norms. Sectional identifications in Zambia exist in the same way as in, say, the United States: in town and country, among the educated and the uneducated, among modernisers and 'traditionalists'. It must not be expected that economic growth or the spread of Western-type education will necessarily cause the decline of sectional identifications. For people always have interests which demand to be articulated and aggregated. These interests will continue to be defined in sectional terms until the social structure of Zambia becomes mainly stratified in terms of class, as has happened more or less in all industrialised States. Only when class divisions are perceived to be more relevant to the distribution of resources will sectionalism cease to be the main social base for political competition in Zambia.

## Sectionalism and national integration

Since sectionalism is likely to be an enduring phenomenon in Zambian politics, we must conclude by examining its consequences for national integration. Sectionalism has often been regarded as an especially grave danger to new States. For where other social bases to politics, like class, can at most result in internal revolution, sectional conflict can destroy the very boundaries of the State. How true is this for Zambia? We have seen that political conflict on sectional lines has increased since independence. But is it likely to increase further? There are several social processes which already seem to be increasing the number of sectional groups, the emotional intensity of sectional identifications, and the degree to which all potential members of a section conform to its dictates.

First, sectional political behaviour by one part of the population has tended to force other parts also to organise on sectional lines.[113] In the 1967 central committee elections, once one candidate for a post organised support for himself on sectional lines, it became difficult for other candidates to win votes on non-sectional bases such as ideology, personality or party record. They were forced to recruit support on sectional lines too. As President Kaunda stated after the elections:

It came as a complete shock to me when several times I was approached and told by this or that group about how the opposite team was canvassing along tribal, racial or provincial lines, only to hear that they—the accusers—were doing exactly the same.[114]

In this way sectional behaviour by one group compelled sectional reactions by others in self-defence, and all politics began to be permeated by sectionalist perceptions. The result was an increase in the number of sectionally defined groups. 1968–69 saw the rise of 'Lamba', 'Kaonde', 'Unity in the East', 'Bantu Botatwe', 'Lozi', and 'Luapula' perceptions and demands.

113. This 'spread effect' of sectionalism has been noted elsewhere in Africa—for example, Zaïre. Coleman and Rosberg, *Political Parties and National Integration, op. cit.*, pp. 572 ff.

114. 'Mulungushi conference, 1967', *op. cit.*, p. 52.

Secondly, once a sectional outlook has been adopted by some, political events have led more and more people to adopt such perceptions. When UP leaders tried to create sectional solidarity among Lozi-speakers they persuaded 34 per cent of the registered electorate in Western Province to vote for them in 1968. These electors outvoted the 21·5 per cent who remained loyal to UNIP, and so won eight seats for UP. The rest of UNIP was shocked at these losses, and on the line of rail some victimisation of Lozi followed, regardless of whether or not they belonged to UNIP. This victimisation in turn caused more Lozi to feel discriminated against and resulted in greater Lozi solidarity against UNIP. In the 1969 referendum UNIP votes dropped to 15·5 per cent.

Increasingly unanimous solidarity among the political adherents of sectional groups has also resulted at the leadership level. Once sectionalist perceptions are accepted by a large number of followers, the latter can put pressure on 'deviant' leaders who (they consider) should belong to the section but who have hitherto stood out against sectionalist feeling. This happened to Lozi leaders of UNIP in 1968. Another example was Mr Kapwepwe's resignation as Vice-president in August 1969. He said he was resigning in the interests of national unity since his vice-presidency had excited so much antagonism among non-Bemba sections in the party. But he was at once put under pressure from his own section in the party to revoke his resignation.[115] Clearly, once sectionalism gets a popular hold, it is difficult for a leader to act contrary to its pressures. But if leaders do succumb to such pressures, then all leaders in whom a particular section trusts start to articulate sectionalist interests, and this results in a further spread of sectionalist perceptions among all members of the potential group.

Finally, this trend towards sectional solidarity can be reinforced by the heightening of the emotional dimension. Once sectionalist identifications develop as fairly stable units of loyalty, they become part of each person's political culture. Others, particularly the younger generation, are then socialised into these identifications, and may internalise them as an emotional orientation. Sectionalism is transformed from being originally and primarily a pragmatic vehicle of interests into an embodiment of loyalties as well. This may partly account for the emotionalism which has increasingly characterised sectional conflicts. Examples are the angry reactions by Lozi Ministers to reports that a Bemba Minister of State had blamed 'the Lozi' for disturbances on the Copperbelt in August

115. ZIS background papers Nos 50/69 and 55/69, 25 and 27 August 1969.

1968,[116] Mr Kapwepwe's references in August 1969 to Bemba being persecuted and even threatening violence if he did not withdraw his resignation,[117] and the Eastern Province Provincial Development Committee meeting where civil servants came to blows after sectional insults had been made.[118] Another example was a vicious leaflet circulated in June 1969, attacking Cabinet Minister Sikota Wina and threatening to

fight in all corners of Zambia. Many bodies will be picked in the streets like bags of mealie meal ... But unlike other wars, we shall hunt for the guilty men first. Sikota, Nakatindi, and all their supporters.[119]

These are some of the processes which account for the rapid escalation of sectionalism since politics in Zambia first began to be perceived in these terms. This trend is likely to continue both because of the further operation of these processes, and because those institutions—the mass media, the educational system, the ruling party and the civil service—which might foster a countervailing sense of national unity tend not to be very effective.

In the first place, poverty often prevents these institutions from reaching all the population. The spread of the mass media is limited. Most of the 12,000 TV sets in 1970 were owned by foreigners. The daily sales of the major newspaper, the *Times of Zambia*, averaged 50,954 in June 1969, or just over 2 per cent of the adult population.[120] The number of radios is estimated to be roughly 200,000 for a population of some $4\frac{1}{2}$ million.

Lack of resources has also limited the impact of the educational system in fostering national integration. Owing to neglect during the Central African Federation, by 1964 only 379,000 children were in primary school out of a population of $3\frac{1}{2}$ million. The number rose to 609,000 in 1968,[121] but universal primary education has still not been achieved, and government can afford to take less than a quarter of primary school-leavers into secondary school.

Moreover, it must not be assumed that the school system automatically fosters national integration. In principle it can do so. For it socialises people into new norms and orientations; it does so with the young, who are still forming their attitudes; and it does so intensively over a number of years. But in Zambia most primary

116. *Nat. Ass. Deb.*, Hansard No. 15, 16 August 1968, cols 160 ff.
117. ZIS background paper No. 55/69, 27 August 1969.
118. *Times of Zambia*, 23 July 1969.
119. *Political Orbit* (mimeo.), June 1969.
120. *Times of Zambia*, 13 August 1969.
121. *Statistical Yearbook, 1968* (Lusaka, 1969), table 3.3.

schools are non-boarding. Each rural school therefore has a linguistically homogeneous and territorially adjacent pupil population.
School therefore does not end the lack of contact with other groups
which characterises village life. If the child has already been
socialised into sectional prejudices by his home, the school will not
break these down by promoting inter-sectional contact. The same
applies to most rural secondary schools. Although in 1969 the latter
were allowed to accept pupils from any part of Zambia, the
government does not pay pupils' transport costs from home to
school. For economic reasons most pupils are therefore forced to go
to their nearest secondary school, which thus retains its overwhelming linguistic homogeneity.

Moreover, the medium of instruction in most rural primary
schools is still the local language. This reduces the child's mastery
of the lingua franca, English, and so cuts him off from future easy
intercourse with Zambians of other language groups. It also means
that most teachers will belong to the same language group as the
community in which they teach. This makes it likely that they will
share any sectional identifications prevailing in the community, and
that their teaching may reinforce, and not reduce, any sectional
prejudices which children may absorb from their home backgrounds.

Even political parties in Zambia have not always been agencies
promoting national unity. We have analysed sectionalist movements
in UNIP and outside it, and we have seen how local party
activists deliberately spread sectionalist sentiments. UNIP headquarters has on occasion used a sectional appeal as a deliberate
act of electoral strategy. One case already noted was the party's
efforts in 1969 to keep the two Nkoya seats in Western Province
loyal by reminding villagers of their past conflicts with the 'true
Lozi' of the valley.

The civil service is another institution often assumed to contribute
to national unity. It may do so to some extent. But the increasing
interaction between civil servants and politicians at all levels since
1964 and the constant concern of civil servants both with their own
promotion and with the distribution of public resources between
areas and individuals have tended to transform the civil service from
an agency of national integration into yet another arena for
sectional competition. President Kaunda's action in making permanent secretaries members of the UNIP national council in 1969
reinforced this tendency.

It is clear that the institutions fostering a national identification
are often ineffective. Sectionalism is therefore likely to persist. This
fact has serious consequences for institutional stability because,

unlike other lines of cleavage, sectionalism has an inherent tendency towards secession. If a class feels oppressed by another class, it can try to overthrow it. If a section feels oppressed by another section, it can do likewise. But it can also conclude that an alternative solution is to set up a State of its own which will not have any other sections in it.

Secession as an alternative political strategy for an aggrieved sectional group is facilitated in Zambia by two factors. The first is that most of rural Zambia does not have a private land tenure system. It is not possible for anyone from any part of the country to move in, buy land, start farming, and so create a multilinguistic community. Access to land in the outlying provinces is determined not by the impersonal mechanism of money but by the personal mechanism of obtaining the permission of the chief who allocates land. The chief is usually reluctant to grant land to outsiders because of his own followers' pressure. So the linguistic homogeneity of most rural areas has been maintained by the land tenure system. Secession, then, appears relatively easy, since each sectional group monopolises a continuous stretch of the State's territory.

A second factor which renders secession feasible is the composition of the civil service. Civil servants at field level, such as crop demonstrators, literacy instructors, health assistants and teachers, must be able to communicate with the villagers. Most villagers do not know English, so that civil servants must know the language of the area. Since independence, however, the civil service has discontinued the practice of holding language examinations, which encouraged officers to learn several languages. Most officers at field level have therefore to come from the same language group as the villagers they serve. It follows that if sectionalism becomes strong in a region, the crucial field level of civil servants is likely to share these sentiments. Secession then becomes less disruptive administratively, since a large degree of staff continuity can be maintained.

A few Zambians do perceive secession as a possibility. Some supporters of the 'Unity in the East' movement talked vaguely of creating an independent Luangwa State. More frequent references to secession have emanated from Western Province, the most recent being after the 1968 elections.[122] However, a serious secessionist movement is not likely in Zambia. Secessionist attempts elsewhere in Africa, notably Biafra, have received widespread publicity. The lessons of prolonged warfare, terrible human cost, and manifest

122. Caplan, 'Barotseland: the secessionist challenge', *op. cit.*, pp. 357 and 359; *Times of Zambia*, 23 December 1968.

failure cannot have been lost. Moreover, a variety of factors—the outlying provinces' geographical isolation, their almost totally subsistence economies, and their complete dependence on copper revenues to finance the substantial social services and economic development they now enjoy—show all sections of the Zambian elite the personal economic price they would have to pay for leading a secessionist movement. If the main hypothesis of this chapter is accepted, that sectionalist movements are primarily an artifact of elite leaders who wish to improve their own positions, then the present nature of Zambia's economy makes it highly unlikely that they would initiate any movement to establish a separate State.

*Acknowledgement*

I should like to thank Professor William Tordoff for his detailed criticism of this chapter. His suggestions led to an important modification of its central thesis.

# 4
# Political parties: structures and policies

*William Tordoff and Ian Scott*

Classifications of African political parties have usually been based on the values and goals endorsed by party leaders, their perceptions of the roles performed by their parties and the nature of the political system within which the party operates. Coleman and Rosberg, for example, using these criteria, make the distinction between the revolutionary centralising party, defined in terms of its ideological, egalitarian, monolithic and coercive characteristics, and the pragmatic pluralist party, which is non-ideological, representative and more sympathetic to the continuing existence of traditional elites.[1] As Bienen has pointed out, however, the assumptions on which the classifications rest are open to question. 'The aspirations of certain elites... may or may not be significant' and the typologies themselves are 'not derived from the study of processes'.[2] As a consequence, they may have little relevance to an explanation of intra-party relationships. Moreover, the political elite's perception of the nature of its political party may not always correspond with the reality of that party's operation within the political system.

*The nature of the Zambian party system*

Zambian political leaders clearly believe that their parties display the characteristics which could be attributed to them by use of the Coleman and Rosberg typology. From its inception in 1959 the ruling United National Independence Party (UNIP) set out to establish permanent organisational contact with the population and

1. Coleman and Rosberg (eds), *Political Parties and National Integration, op. cit.* See also D. E. Apter, *The Politics of Modernization* (Chicago, 1965), and his similar distinction between the 'solidarity' and 'reconciliation' party.
2. H. Bienen, *Tanzania: Party Transformation and Economic Development* (Princeton, 1967), p. 5.

to enlist their support in its struggle against the Central African Federation. Its leaders depict it as both a mass party and, in President Kaunda's words, a 'revolutionary' party. Its constitution formally provides for a centralised machine, and in recent years it has shown a preoccupation with a collectivist ideology, Humanism, whose aim is 'to keep our society man-centred'[3] and which is linked with attempts to mobilise the nation for economic development.

Until it was given a legal monopoly of power in December 1972, UNIP was the dominant party in Zambia, its dominance 'co-existing with competition but without trace of alternation'.[4] Between 1964 and 1972 its ascendancy was so marked that, though an opposition party—the African National Congress (ANC)—existed throughout this period, there was never any prospect of power alternating between UNIP and its main rival, which had a sectional rather than a national appeal. Although the political system allowed opportunities for open dissent, the effectiveness of that dissent has been questionable. Zambia, in short, belonged to the 'world of snowballs, not pendulums—of dominance, not alternation'.[5]

There was periodic pressure from both the rank and file and some of UNIP's leaders to convert the party's position of dominance within the political system into one of legal monopoly through the establishment of a one-party State. Until February 1972, however, the party's official policy line was that, while it believed that the one-party State was desirable and inevitable, it did not believe in taking prohibitive legislative action against the opposition. Through effective organisation—in which its leadership places great faith—and ultimately through the ballot box, it was confident that the opposition would eventually be eliminated. Even if this objective was achieved, President Kaunda stated that UNIP did not intend to restrict the formation of opposition parties nor to prohibit them from entering the competition for power.[6] Despite this commitment to a policy of maintaining an open political system, the government banned the United Party (UP) in August 1968 and prohibited the organisation of the ANC in two of its areas of strength. Then in February 1972 President Kaunda banned the United Progressive Party (UPP), a new political party which had been formed by Simon Kapwepwe (a former vice-president of both UNIP and the

3. Kaunda, *Humanism in Zambia and a Guide to its Implementation*, *op. cit.*, p. 7.

4. W. H. Morris-Jones, 'Dominance and dissent: their interrelations in the Indian party system', *Government and Opposition*, vol. 1, No. 4 (July–September 1966), p. 454.

5. *Ibid.*, p. 460.

6. 'Mulungushi conference, 1967', *op. cit.*, pp. 10–11.

country) following his resignation from the ruling party the previous August. Soon afterwards, Kaunda announced that Zambia would become 'a one-party participatory democracy'. A twenty-one-member commission, drawn from a cross-section of the community and headed by Mainza Chona, the Vice-president since November 1970, was established to find the best way of implementing this decision, which (said the President) resulted directly from the 'irresistible demands' of the people throughout the country.[7] Even before the decision to institute a one-party State was taken, there were definite limits within which opposition parties in Zambia were required to operate. While the only formal requirement was that a party's method of organisation should exclude the use of violence,[8] the efforts of UNIP activists at the local level were often directed, by means of intimidation and the discriminatory use of the government machine, to turning their particular province or area into an exclusively UNIP domain.

Although the typologies were not specifically designed to apply to opposition parties, ANC leaders often expressed sentiments which would place their party firmly in the 'pragmatic pluralist' or 'reconciliation' mould. 'We are realists,' said Mr Edward Liso (then deputy leader of the party) in a National Assembly debate in which UNIP attempted to discover the philosophy of the ANC. 'The only philosophy we have in Congress is Christianity,' said the party's leader, Mr Harry Nkumbula.[9] The ANC could in no sense be described as a revolutionary party, although it did play a part, both before the 1958 split with UNIP's leaders and in the 1962 coalition government, in the movement for independence. It did not have a well developed party organisation, paid officials at the local level or the mass party's 'cradle-to-the-grave' perception of its relationship with the population. Yet, unlike most other opposition parties in Africa, the ANC proved resilient. Indeed, it not only maintained its position after independence but actually increased its representation in the National Assembly as a result of the December 1968 general election. In large measure its electoral success must be accounted for by its coalition, after August 1968, with the proscribed

7. *Africa Research Bulletin*: Political, Social and Cultural Series (Exeter), vol. 9, No. 2 (15 March 1972), pp. 2377–8.

8. The President released all political detainees on 6 November 1969 on the basis of a written guarantee from them that they would not organise violently. ZIS background papers Nos 77/69 and 81/69. The ANC was banned in the Mumbwa District in June 1969 on the grounds that it was intimidating the local population. Subsequently the party was also banned in the Livingstone District.

9. *Nat. Ass. Deb.*, Hansard No. 12, 12–19 December 1967, cols 218, 224.

United Party. That party, led by Mr Nalumino Mundia, a former UNIP Cabinet Minister and subsequently deputy leader of the ANC, in effect delivered much of the Barotse (now Western) Province to existing ANC strength in the Southern Province.

To summarise the nature of Zambian political parties in this way is not to say that they act, or can act, according to elite perceptions of the roles of their political parties. In the case of the ruling party, a variety of constraints results in only partial fulfilment of the party's aims to retain a centralised and disciplined machine and, through its structure, to mobilise the nation for economic development. Some of these constraints, such as poor communications of all kinds away from the line of rail and the lack of qualified personnel, are national problems. But they have political significance when related to the UNIP structure, for they work against control from the centre and increase the power of the local party official. That power may also be enhanced by the 'dilemma of scale' which operates when 'the boundaries of a political unit expand', making it 'more difficult to maintain effective control and to accommodate divergent interests successfully within it'.[10] Factionalism is not necessarily a constraint preventing the attainment of elite goals, and may merely indicate that the dominant party is subject to healthy internal competition. But intense factionalism, such as occurred in Zambia at both national and local levels, may serve to inhibit the operation of a centralised machine and obstruct development programmes which seek to utilise the party structure. Other constraints also affect the ability of the party to act in a manner calculated to achieve its policy objectives. The problems of transforming the party activist into a development-oriented leader and what President Kaunda describes as 'the falling off of momentum'[11] in the nationalist movement after independence are endemic to most new African countries. In Zambia, however, the very existence of the opposition prevented the UNIP structure from penetrating to any depth in two of the country's provinces and acted as a further brake on its efforts to realise its goals. Because its goals and its leaders' perception of its role were more limited, the ANC did not experience the same gap between aspirations and reality. Yet its leaders, too, faced constraints in the attempts which they made to construct an effective opposition party. The ANC was not the umbrella under which all groups opposed to UNIP could find shelter. Its organisation remained in a state of arrested develop-

10. Rasmussen, 'Political competition', *op. cit.*, p. 417. See also Morris-Jones, 'Dominance and dissent', *op. cit.*, p. 457.
11. Kaunda, *A Humanist in Africa, op. cit.*, p. 54.

ment following the split with UNIP's leaders and, partly through its own inactivity and partly through measures taken by local UNIP activists, it had neither a strong organisation nor electoral support in large areas of the country.

Although party performance, for the most part, does appear to have been dependent upon these constraints, the parties did on occasion succeed in acting in the way their leaders perceived. In this chapter we examine in greater detail the relationship of the constraints to policy implementation and party structures, and the conditions under which the parties sought to achieve their policy goals and structural objectives.

## The structure of UNIP

UNIP's early structure was modelled on that of the ANC. A president, other national office-holders, a national council and central committee at headquarters worked through seven (and subsequently—when the party extended its organisation to Barotseland—eight) provincial divisions. Each province was subdivided into constituencies and branches which often—and particularly in the Northern and Luapula Provinces and on the Copperbelt—enjoyed so much autonomy that they were impossible to control from the centre. Internal communication was ineffective and party policy was poorly co-ordinated, with serious results in the financial sphere.[12]

Kaunda, who had been elected president of UNIP in January 1960, therefore undertook a major reorganisation of the party preliminary to the 1962 general election. This reorganisation had three aspects. First, the party's eight provincial divisions were abolished and the provinces subdivided into twenty-four regions covering the whole country. Full-time regional organising secretaries were appointed by, and made responsible to, the party central committee. This step paralleled that taken in Tanganyika by the Tanganyika African National Union (TANU) between 1958 and 1960 and was adopted for the same reason—to secure tighter central control of the party's up-country organisation.[13] Secondly, steps were taken to integrate the youth and women's brigade more closely into the party; and thirdly, UNIP's national council was made larger and more representative of the regional organisation of the

12. Mulford, *Zambia: the Politics of Independence, op. cit.*, pp. 160–5.
13. Bienen, however, points out that officials appointed at regional and district levels in Tanganyika sometimes moved into elected posts. *Tanzania, op. cit.*, chapter IV.

party.[14] Subject to some revision (to accommodate, for example, an increased number of party regions) the 1962 constitution persisted until it was superseded by a new constitution, originally passed by a national council meeting in June 1966 and subsequently adopted, with minor alterations, by the general conference of the party in August 1967. The most recent constitution, adopted in May 1971, resulted in some changes to the central organisation but left the operation of the local levels substantially unchanged.

Throughout, UNIP's structure was based on two formal principles laid down in the party constitution. First, it was a party in which democracy was to be strictly maintained and, secondly, it was to be 'a militant organisation welded together by discipline which is obligatory on all its members'.[15] The difficulty of meeting the requirements of both discipline and democracy was one which had dogged UNIP from the outset and which the 1962 reorganisation had only partially solved. At the 1967 general conference of the party the President found it necessary to warn delegates that 'Party leaders at all levels must distinguish between Party discipline and suppressing the people's feelings on any subject'.[16] At the same time he took measures to foster intra-party democracy. The 1967 constitution retained the existing organs at national level—the central committee, the national council, and the general conference. Previously, members of the central committee—the most powerful party organ—ran for office on a balanced team ticket, endorsed by the conference delegates. For the 1967 party elections, however, the President announced that central committee posts would be contested on an individual basis. This decision produced intense and bitter competition for office. Although it was not necessarily the cause of factionalism within the party, it certainly accelerated its growth.[17] Divisions, perceived to be along 'tribal lines',[18] were accentuated by accusations and rumours grounded in ethnic prejudice and by the election results themselves.

The elections were held at Mulungushi (near Kabwe) in August 1967 in conjunction with the triennial general conference of the party. Of the seven contested seats, three were particularly important—those of the national vice-president, the national secretary

14. Mulford, *Zambia: the Politics of Independence, op. cit.*, pp. 234–9.

15. UNIP constitution, adopted on 9 May 1971 (n.d., mimeo.), preamble.

16. 'Mulungushi Conference, 1967', *op. cit.*, p. 9.

17. See Rasmussen, 'Political competition', *op. cit.*, pp. 421–3.

18. On the validity of this perception, see Molteno, chapter 3 above; Rotberg, 'Tribalism and politics in Zambia', *op. cit.*; Rasmussen, 'Political competition', *op. cit.* All three authors examine other dimensions of factionalism within UNIP.

and the national treasurer; Kaunda himself had been returned unopposed as national president. The contestants divided into two
main camps: a primarily Bemba–Tonga-speaking alliance under
the leadership of Kapwepwe, Foreign Minister and incumbent
UNIP national treasurer, and a Lozi–Nyanja-speaking alliance
which ranged behind Reuben Kamanga, the party and national
vice-president. In a bitter campaign the party was almost torn
apart by the intense sectionalism of its leaders (excluding, of course,
Kaunda himself) and their followers. The Kapwepwe group dubbed
their opponents 'intellectuals' and alleged that they were CIA
agents; the Kamanga group responded by accusing the Bemba–
Tonga alliance of having sold out to the communists. These
charges suggest that in 1967 the activist *v.* intelligentsia division
among UNIP leaders was now proving a source of friction;[19] it
was certainly true that the intelligentsia, fighting an election in
which delegates were almost entirely drawn from party activists,
were unsuccessful except where they contested seats against one
another. The attempt to play upon the fears of the activists *vis-à-
vis* the intelligentsia can perhaps be viewed as a shrewd political
tactic aimed at maintaining the position of dominance enjoyed by
the Bemba-speaking leaders in the party.[20]

The results of the central committee elections, as announced at
Mulungushi, showed that the Kapwepwe group had won all but
one of the contested seats. Leaders in the Eastern–Barotse camp
were incensed. They alleged both that the elections had been
framed and subsequently that the basis of representation at the conference (based mainly on 100 delegates from each of UNIP's forty-
seven regions)[21] had been unfair on the ground that it had given an
in-built advantage to the Bemba–Tonga alliance.[22] President Kaunda

19. See Kaunda, *A Humanist in Africa, op. cit.*, p. 102. Rotberg, 'Tribalism and politics in Zambia', *op. cit.*, p. 32, points to a 'pronounced division
within the party between the more recent recruits from the "intelligentsia"
and the pre-independence party activists'. But it is easy to exaggerate this
division. As Kaunda noted (*A Humanist in Africa, op. cit.*, p. 101), 'some
intellectuals were also freedom fighters'; good examples, apart from Kaunda
himself, are the Lozi Munukayumbwa Sipalo and Sikota Wina, both of
whom left university for political reasons without taking a degree and
joined the fight for independence.

20. During the struggle for independence the Bemba-speaking peoples
were the best organised in the country. On their part in the independence
movement and their dominance within it, see Mulford, *Zambia: the
Politics of Independence, op. cit.*, pp. 199–210, 229–39 and *passim*.

21. A further eighty-six delegates were members of the national council
and trade union leaders.

22. For example, it was pointed out that while the Eastern Province had

appointed a committee of enquiry under the Chief Justice, who reported that, while the votes had been miscounted at Mulungushi, none of the successful candidates was unseated by the recount.[23]

President Kaunda insisted that the election results should stand, and, in accordance with a previous intra-party agreement, he made Kapwepwe, his new deputy within UNIP, the national Vice-president.[24] His other Cabinet appointments reflected his respect for the elective principle, as expressed at Mulungushi. On the other hand, he sought to ensure a balanced central committee by appointing to it four national trustees from areas which would otherwise have been under-represented as a result of the elections.

After August 1967, however, the split within UNIP went too deep to be healed by what had become a familiar balancing device, by which President Kaunda had successfully balanced the various factions within his party in making appointments to both the central committee and the Cabinet.[25] The central committee lacked internal unity and its effectiveness was reduced. Personal recriminations within UNIP, with their tribal and provincial overtones, had not abated by February 1968, when the national council held a stormy meeting in Lusaka. On 5 February a disgusted Kaunda announced his resignation as national President.[26] He had not, however, taken the constitutional step of submitting his resignation in writing to the Chief Justice when he was prevailed upon by all sections of the party to remain in office.

In the months which followed, Kaunda temporarily reunited UNIP behind his leadership as the party geared itself to fight the

only five party regions (and was therefore represented at Mulungushi by 500 voters), the Northern and Southern Provinces had seven regions each; yet, whereas UNIP was dominant in the Eastern Province and unchallenged in the Northern Province, it had only minority support in the Ila–Tonga-speaking Southern Province.

23. 'Report of body of public persons appointed to examine and report on the elections of the United National Independence Party offices, held at Mulungushi on 19th August 1967', 24 August 1967. This was one of several reports submitted by the committee of enquiry to the President and subsequently released by the Zambia Information Services.

24. Cf. the government newspaper *Zambia Mail*, 1 September 1967, which referred to 'the President's promise to UNIP that he would appoint as the country's Vice-president the man chosen as the party Vice-president'. The promise had probably been made following discussion in the UNIP national council in April 1967.

25. See Mulford, *Zambia: the Politics of Independence, op. cit.*, pp. 300, 329–30.

26. *The Times* (London), 15 February 1968; *Zambia Mail*, 16 and 23 February 1968.

first general election after independence. But clashes during the election campaign between UNIP and the UP on the Copperbelt, with Lozi immigrants accused of supporting the opposition, increased Lozi-speaking fears of Bemba domination.[27] Once the elections were over, the faction-fighting within UNIP was resumed, with the antagonists mustering support in anticipation of fresh central committee elections in August 1970.[28] This competition continued despite the government campaign for a national referendum in June 1969. The anti-Bemba-speaking group was convinced, with some justification, that Kapwepwe's position was weakened—his 1969 budget had been unpopular on the Copperbelt; the (Bemba-speaking) Luapulans were reacting against northern Bemba dominance;[29] and there were signs of division even within the northern Bemba group.[30] Leaders of this (anti-Bemba-speaking) group therefore expressed confidence in the outcome of the 1970 elections. But they were afraid of what might happen in the interim, given what they believed to be a threat to Kaunda's position from Kapwepwe and his associates. With the judiciary crisis of July 1969 and the storming of the High Court by the UNIP-recruited Zambia

27. The most serious incident took place in August 1968 at Chililabombwe, when two UNIP officials were killed. It was reported in the press that Mr Peter Chanda, the Minister of State for the Copperbelt Province, held a Lozi group responsible. His alleged statement led not only to an angry retort by five Barotse Ministers and to sharp exchanges in the National Assembly but, more important, to pressure by Lozi leaders on the Copperbelt and in Lusaka that Ministers from the Western Province should withdraw from the government. *Times of Zambia*, 14, 15, 17 and 21 August 1968.

28. The UNIP constitution (1967) laid down that members of the central committee should hold office for a period of three years. Constitution of the United National Independence Party, Zambia, adopted on 15 August 1967 (n.d., mimeo.), clause XVII, 4.

29. In July 1969, for example, a group of Luapula MPs complained that top-ranking politicians from the Northern Province had labelled Luapulans 'batubulu' (foolish fishermen) who were destined to be ruled by others. *Zambia News*, 13 July 1969. In a by-election at Kawambwa in July 1969 there was some feeling among constituents that a Luapulan should have been nominated for the seat rather than the Northern Province Secretary General to the Government, John Mwanakatwe. *Ibid.* In the event, Mwanakatwe was accepted as UNIP candidate and was returned to Parliament unopposed.

30. This had two aspects. First, there were signs of restiveness in the Northern Province among the Namwanga and Mambwe of Isoka and Mbala, as well as at Mkushi. Secondly, some of the more recent recruits to the Bemba-speaking leadership—such as Valentine Musakanya, former head of the civil service and a Minister of State from February 1969—wanted UNIP to emerge as a progressive party, shorn of its freedom-fighting image.

Youth Service,[31] UNIP seemed to be subject to a policy of drift rather than of direction.

In August 1969 the crisis finally came to a head. That month a meeting of the national council of the party was closed by the President before it was able to complete its business. Allegedly, the reason was the tabling of a resolution, which was reported to have the support of politicians from seven out of Zambia's eight provinces,[32] to oust Vice-president Kapwepwe. Two weeks later Kapwepwe announced his resignation from the vice-presidency of the republic and the party and made it clear that he did not intend to contest the next central committee elections. He gave as the reason for his resignation (which was subsequently withdrawn)[33] the fact that some of his colleagues had been rude and abusive to him and had never recognised him as a 'popularly elected Vice-president'. In addition, he said that the Bemba-speaking people had suffered, both physically and materially, because of his position as Vice-president.[34] A few hours after the resignation (though not, apparently, on account of it) the President dissolved the central committee and assumed direct power over the party as its secretary general.[35] Three Ministers of State were made responsible to him for party administration, finance and publicity. None of them had been a member of the previous central committee or served on the interim executive committee which Dr Kaunda established soon afterwards. Six of the eleven members of the latter committee had served on the central committee, but three party leaders who had been defeated at Mulungushi in 1967 were also included; these were Reuben Kamanga and Wesley Nyirenda from the Eastern Province and Humphrey Mulemba from the North-western Province. The new committee, however, had virtually none of the formidable powers possessed by its predecessor.

Although, in his statement dissolving the central committee, President Kaunda condemned factionalism and pointed to its dele-

31. See *Times of Zambia*, 17 July 1969; *Zambia Mail*, 17 July 1969. Recruitment to the Youth Service was primarily in the hands of UNIP regional secretaries but the service itself was a statutory body.

32. *The Guardian* (London), 28 August 1969. If this report is accurate the suggestion that Kapwepwe was losing support among Bemba-speaking politicians outside the Northern Province is confirmed.

33. At the request of the President, Mr Kapwepwe agreed to remain in office until the next party elections; his portfolio was reduced and initially he was responsible only for culture.

34. ZIS background paper No. 50/69, 25 August 1969.

35. He did so, not under powers conferred on him by the party constitution, but under emergency powers vested in him by the general conference. See 'Mulungushi conference, 1967', *op. cit.*, p. 42.

terious effects on the implementation of party policy, he clearly saw UNIP's troubles as stemming from structural failure:

Unfortunately, it is quite evident that the present Party constitution has failed to provide stability and efficiency in the Party machinery.... A constitution which fails to bring about stability and efficiency and which instead promotes strife in the party cannot be an instrument for nation-building.... Since the election of the central committee, which I have just dissolved, the nation has witnessed the rise of strange phenomena on our political scene.... Parochialism among certain sections of our community has been on the increase and has tended to throw dust into the eyes of leaders and followers alike.... Instead of devoting our efforts to nation-building there have been people among us who have been engaged in fostering purely sectional interests. The result has been to sap the energy from this nation necessary to make national unity and economic development a real success.[36]

The belief that the party's structure was responsible for its problems led to a decision to review its constitution. A commission, composed of prominent party and public figures, was set up under the chairmanship of the Attorney General (Mr F. Chuula) and given wide terms of reference which included the relationship between the party and the government, the question of discipline, and 'ways and means of avoiding strife in the party'.[37]

In its report of March 1970 the Chuula Commission issued a complete draft for a new UNIP constitution. Its most significant proposals, and the ones which aroused most controversy, were designed to reduce the intensity of competition for posts on the party's central committee, and the likelihood of this competition following sectional lines. When made public in September 1970,[38] the proposals were criticised fiercely, particularly by Bemba-speaking activists, some of whom belonged to a dissident group within the party of self-styled 'UNIP militants'.[39]

The Chuula proposals were substantially modified by the UNIP national council, meeting early in November. After three days of heated debate the council claimed to have reached agreement on a new constitution, to be ratified by the general conference in the following May. But the new constitution was never published. It was merely leaked to the press that the key Chuula proposals on the composition of, and mode of election to, the central committee

36. Broadcast to the nation on radio and television, 25 August 1969.
37. *Times of Zambia*, 26 and 27 August 1969.
38. See *Zambia Daily Mail*, 23 September 1970.
39. The 'UNIP militants' were a small clique of former UNIP office-holders, mainly at constituency and branch levels in Lusaka and the Copperbelt.

were rejected. Instead, the committee would consist of twenty-five members—the secretary general and twenty other members elected by the general conference, and four nominated members.[40] This particular provision was upheld during the vicissitudes which followed, but it quickly became clear that top UNIP leaders were still not agreed on certain key issues: for example, whether there would be a deputy to the secretary general; whether, in the slate of candidates presented to the conference by the interim committee, each of Zambia's eight provinces would be given two representatives; and whether the basis of representation at future general conferences ought still to be 100 delegates from each party region in a province[41] (which would favour those provinces, like the Bemba-speaking Northern Province, with a large number of regions) or should be provincial equality (which would favour those provinces, such as Western, with relatively few UNIP members, and work to the disadvantage of those provinces monopolised by UNIP).

In the event, the differences within the party were temporarily contained. In May 1971 the general conference convened at Mulungushi on the 1967 basis of 100 delegates for each party region and both approved a new constitution for the party and endorsed the list of new central committee members submitted to it by the national council. Though there was nothing in the constitution about the provincial equality of representation on the central committee, to which Kapwepwe had objected vigorously, the provision that delegates to future conferences should be returned on the basis of 600 members from each province[42] and the absence of any provision for a deputy secretary general were a setback for the Bemba-speaking group within UNIP.

This group was already discomfited on other grounds. As we have seen, in August 1967 the political pendulum had swung in favour of the Bemba-speaking group, led by Kapwepwe, when he ousted Kamanga as Vice-president. But by August 1969, when President Kaunda scrapped the central committee elected at Mulun-

40. *Zambia Daily Mail*, 9 November 1970.
41. The province is an administrative unit and has been under a resident Cabinet Minister since early 1969. Each province is broken down into administrative districts and the area of the district normally coincides with that of the UNIP region. The latter is divided into party constituencies, branches and villages (sections in the towns).
42. The UNIP constitution, as approved at Mulungushi in May 1971, prescribed that these provincial members should be selected from branches of the party by regional annual conferences. The general conference should at other times also include all members of the national council, and trade union and farmers' representatives. Articles 6 and 34(3).

gushi two years earlier, it had swung away from them towards the Nyanja-speaking group. (The Lozi-speaking group had also 'lost out', since Arthur Wina and Munukayumbwa Sipalo had been defeated in the 1968 general election; they had been highly efficient Cabinet Ministers who had failed in their bid to secure party office and central committee membership in 1967.) From 1969 onwards, members of the Bemba-speaking Northern Province section in the party voiced their discontent and even subjected President Kaunda to criticism, although it was usually private or indirect. This criticism came to a peak early in 1971. In the debate following the President's address to the National Assembly, one Northern Province MP after another attacked the President's policy on citizenship and the economic reforms.[43] Early in 1971 also allegations were made by two Northerners—Justin Chimba, a Cabinet Minister, and John Chisata, a former Minister of State—that the reason for not prosecuting certain Ministers suspected of misappropriating funds was not lack of evidence but tribalism and corruption in the government, leading to cover-up action in favour of non-Bemba politicians. The President appointed a Commission of Judges to enquire into the truth of these and their other allegations. No confirmatory evidence was produced,[44] and Chimba and Chisata were discredited. Chimba, who belonged to the militant old guard of Bemba-speaking politicians, was subsequently dropped from the Cabinet. Predictably, both men followed Kapwepwe into the United Progressive Party in August 1971. The formation of the UPP was a sign that the sectionalism within UNIP had become so intense that it could no longer be contained.

Intra-party competition has clearly played a major role in stimulating the factionalism which has led to the successive crises which have beset UNIP since 1967. But it is only one dimension of the problem of factionalism. The composition of a faction and the methods it uses to achieve its ends are separate, if related, issues which could nonetheless have a bearing on relations between the party centre and the local level. Our concern here is not to explore these other dimensions[45] but simply to point to intense intra-party competition as a general limiting factor working against the party ideal of a united political elite which could, through the use of a centralised machine, issue directives to the local level and expect to see them carried out. Competition for national office, where those

43. See pp. 224–5 below.
44. *Report of the Commission of Inquiry into the Allegations made by Mr Justin Chimba and Mr John Chisata* (Lusaka, May 1971).
45. See chapter 3.

returned are not accepted by those who opposed them, not only (as
the President implied[46]) precludes co-operation for party policy
objectives but also affects the way the party machine operates.
A relatively weak centre increases the power of the local man and,
since the national leaders are aware that their power largely depends
upon their geographical base of support, the local politician may
have some insurance that his actions will be viewed sympathetically
by at least some of the elite.

Intense and bitter intra-party competition, however, is by no
means the only constraint limiting control over the local levels. As
we shall seek to show, even prior to the overt appearance of
factionalism the party's centre was not able to exercise to the fullest
extent the powers vested in it by the party constitution. The central
committee is the party's most important administrative organ,
though it wields less power under the constitution of 1971 than it
did under that of 1967.[47] Kaunda's position as secretary general
of UNIP was strengthened, and only if he could not attend the
central committee was the latter to choose one of its members to
'discharge the functions of the secretary general'.[48] The new constitution does not formally embody the Chuula proposal for strict
equality of representation in the central committee between the
provinces, to which Kapwepwe had objected vigorously, but merely
states that 'regard will be paid to the merit of the candidates as
well as the need to get candidates from all parts of the country'.[49]
The central committee was to comprise the secretary general
and twenty other members elected by all the party delegates at a
general conference every five years, and four members appointed by
the secretary general.[50] To ensure fair representation and to reduce
dissension among the delegates, the constitution provides for the
outgoing central committee to draw up an official slate of candidates for approval by the national council and subsequent presentation to the general conference. This had been the procedure
prior to the 1967 elections and was followed again at the May 1971
conference. The twenty candidates put before it, and elected unopposed, comprised two from each province, with Northern and

46. See p. 117 above.
47. The position may change again when the government's one-party
State proposals are implemented. In general, however, major changes in the
May 1971 UNIP constitution are not envisaged.
48. UNIP constitution, May 1971, art. 9.
49. *Ibid.*, art. 6.
50. *Ibid.*, art. 5. Under the government's one-party State proposals, the
President will nominate three members, and the Prime Minister (appointed by
him) will serve *ex officio*. See p. 153 below.

Eastern, because of their size, getting additional representation.[51]
None of the central committee members was entitled to be appointed
by the secretary general as one of the five named executive officers
of the central committee—the administrative secretary, financial
secretary, publicity secretary, youth secretary, and women's
secretary.[52] Members could however be appointed to serve on one of
the central committee's four sub-committees.[53]

Although the national council retains the formal right to determine party policy, the central committee is responsible for its formulation and implementation. The committee also has complete control over all officials at party headquarters and in the party regions,
and it appoints regional officials. It selects parliamentary candidates
and is also required to approve UNIP local government candidates
selected by a regional conference. Finally, the committee has the
right to summon meetings of the national council and general
conference of the party—bodies which, in theory, exercise a limited
amount of control over its activities.[54]

The general conference was given the power to review party
policy, elect the central committee, and amend the party's constitution. Delegates to future conferences were to be returned on the
basis of 600 members from each province, selected from branches of
the party by regional annual conferences. The general conference
was also to include trade union and farmers' representatives, as
well as all members of the national council.[55] The latter now became a somewhat unwieldy body,[56] meeting at least twice a year.
It was charged with the responsibility of reviewing the decisions of
the central committee and of lower levels of the party and of
deciding on proposals for inclusion in the party programme, although this must have a two-thirds majority of the council.[57]

51. *Times of Zambia*, 11 May 1971.
52. UNIP constitution, May 1971, art. 10(1).
53. *Ibid.*, art. 13.                          54. *Ibid.*, art. 12(5).
55. *Ibid.*, arts 6 and 34(3.)
56. Under the 1971 constitution the composition of the national council is:
(a) members of the central committee; (b) UNIP MPs; (c) District Governors;
(d) three officials, inclusive of the regional secretary, from each party region;
(e) six representatives elected by the Zambia Congress of Trade Unions;
(f) two representatives elected by the Farmers' Union; (g) heads of Zambian
Missions abroad; and (h) executive officers at national headquarters.
57. Under the government's 1972 proposals the general conference will
lose to the national council its power to amend the party constitution and
'up to' 600 members from each province will be selected by the provincial
party conference. The *ex officio* membership of the national council will
remain unchanged, but the affiliated membership is likely to be broadened.
Government Paper No. 1 of 1972, *op. cit.*, pp. 28–9.

In practice, the central organs of the party have not been able to fulfil their constitutional obligations. Normally, it has been the central committee that has controlled the national council in terms of national policy formulation. Except in times of crisis (for example, in February 1968 and August 1969), the national council has been a less important party organ than its Tanzanian counterpart, the national executive committee. One reason for this is that while both bodies are strongly representative of regional interests, the three representatives from each region are appointed by the central committee in Zambia, whereas two out of three of them were elected in Tanzania. Secondly, whereas under the provisions governing the UNIP elections of 1967, eleven out of fifteen members of the central committee were elected on an individual basis, only key TANU office-holders were elected, the rest (before 1969) being nominated by the party president. Again—though here there was no significant difference from the Tanganyikan practice[58]—the weakness of the national council in relation to the central committee, before that body was dissolved in 1969, was partly to be explained by the fact that from September 1967 all except one of the central committee members held a government post, and eleven out of fifteen of them were Cabinet Ministers.[59] It was not accidental that the period (August 1967 to February 1968) when—following the elections at Mulungushi—the central committee lacked internal unity and met infrequently coincided with a period of outspokenness in the national council. Regional members of the latter were, after all, merely echoing the views expressed both outside and inside the council by the national party leaders.

The national council has been used mainly as a platform for the announcement of policy by the party leader. For example, at national council meetings President Kaunda launched Humanism (April 1967), announced the intention of his government to acquire a controlling interest in twenty-six manufacturing and retailing concerns (April 1968), outlined proposals for the decentralisation of government (November 1968), requested the mining companies to provide government with a 51 per cent share in the industry (August 1969), and announced reforms in the financial sector (November 1970). But the announcement of policy intentions has not sparked intense or informed debate in the council. Rather,

58. See W. Tordoff, *Government and Politics in Tanzania* (Nairobi, 1967), pp. 78–9. The structure of TANU was changed substantially in 1969.

59. Including the President and Vice-president. Under the government's 1972 proposals the central committee and Cabinet are to be established as separate bodies. See p. 153 below.

the tendency has been for the policy statement to be adopted unanimously and for the council to pass on to discuss the provincial reports on the strength and activities of the party and to consider more parochial matters. Given the composition of the national council, this is not altogether surprising. As the Bemba proverb says, 'Akachila kambushi kasengula apo kalele.'[60] Issues such as the relationship between party and police, communications in particular areas, or problems created by the Watch Tower sect, may have more relevance to the local official than broad policy considerations. The council thus provides an important opportunity for regional officials to draw the national leaders' attention to local problems and grievances. It is when such matters are being ventilated or when, as in early 1968 and early 1971, sectional divisions in the party are particularly acute that there is some truth in the claim made by a number of regional secretaries that ministerial rank is set at a discount in the national council and its members are critical of departmental policy. With rare exceptions, however, the council's constitutional function of reviewing central committee decisions does not appear to have been of any practical significance.[61] The agenda of the meeting is controlled by the central committee and the drafting of its resolutions is normally in the hands of a small group of important politicians. Of the six-man committee, for example, who drafted the resolutions of the March 1969 national council meeting, three were members of the central committee and two were Ministers of State. Moreover, all the indications are that under the 1971 constitution the national council has, if anything, decreased rather than increased in importance and effectiveness. For its part, the general conference is too large and does not convene often enough to exercise any sort of control over party policy.

If these two national organs have not used their few means of control over the central committee, it is equally true that the committee itself was able to exercise only limited control over the regional and sub-regional levels. There were a number of reasons for this. After the 1967 conference the central committee did not meet regularly again until well into 1968; two of the nominated members of the committee failed to take their seats because of the

60. 'The goat's tail sweeps where it sleeps.' A regional representative of the national council might express the point as follows: 'Though we realise that the country faces many problems, we can only concern ourselves with our own local problems.'

61. One exception was at the end of 1963, when the national council refused to accept a number of the candidates nominated by the central committee for the January 1964 general election.

strength of local pressure against their doing so;[62] and the committee
instructed top party leaders to discontinue for the time being the
practice of touring the rural areas in order to meet the people and
address public meetings. Two of the elected members of the central
committee—Mainza Chona, the national secretary, and Maria
Nankalongo, the director of the women's brigade—were full-time
party officials. But Chona lacked dynamism and the capacity for
effective organisation; he had lost face with some of his colleagues
in 1967 when, at the eleventh hour, he had gone back on his
former declaration not to seek re-election as national secretary;[63]
and he lacked a power base in his own area (the Southern Province).
Chona and Mrs Nankalongo apart, the remaining nine elected
members of the central committee were Cabinet Ministers with
departmental responsibilities and could not afford to devote a
great deal of time to their party office. Moreover, the headquarters
staff was small, consisting of an administrative secretary as well as
an under-secretary for each of the party office-bearers. With the
expansion of the party after independence, the staff was unable to
supervise in any detail the activities of the local organisations.

One indication of the administrative difficulties faced by the
central committee is contained in the national treasurer's report
to the 1967 conference. In this report it was revealed that the party,
owing to the demands placed upon it and the poor response to
fund-raising drives, had very nearly gone bankrupt in the immediate years after independence. Two reasons were given for this:

62. These were Mr C. H. Thornicroft, MP for the Katete constituency in
the Eastern Province and a Minister of State, and Mr Fine Liboma, political
assistant for Sesheke and Mankoya in the Western Province (from December
1967) and subsequently a District Governor. Mr Liboma attended one
meeting of the central committee following his nomination in September
1967, but then withdrew for several months. It was not until mid-1968 that
Mr Thornicroft could be prevailed upon to take his seat on the central
committee.

63. It is alleged that Chona had been unhappy at the decision taken by the
national council in April 1967 that the national secretary should be Minister
without Portfolio. Aaron Milner, the able deputy national secretary, decided
to contest the national secretaryship when Chona made it known that he
was not seeking re-election. Since Chona allowed his candidature to go
forward only some five minutes before nominations closed, there was no time
for Milner to withdraw and seek re-election as deputy national secretary.
But for Chona's tactics, Milner would probably have observed the convention
of the central committee (endorsed by the national council in April 1967) that
members of the committee should not contest office with each other. This
convention was first broken by Kapwepwe when he decided to challenge
Kamanga for the party vice-presidency.

Before Independence we got some help from some friendly countries and indeed our own subscription and membership fees including donations. But after Independence the Party suffered from two things: one, the aforesaid friendly countries stopped sending up any donations as a Party, they moved with the formation of the government.... Secondly, our people, most of them took it for granted that after Independence there was no need for further contributions to the Party.[64]

The treasurer was required to submit a detailed report on the party's finances but he was unable to do so because receipt books had been lost, no accountant had been found for the party, and financial reports had not been submitted by regional and constituency officials. In succeeding years financial problems continued to plague the party. In 1969, for example, the auditors found that UNIP had an excess of current liabilities over current assets of K138,638 and that 'the control of Income and Expenditure remain[ed] completely inadequate'.[65]

Nevertheless, after 1966 the sheer scale of the party's income and expenditure increased dramatically. Amounts remitted from the regions rose from K5,274 in 1966 to K32,686 in the first six months of 1967.[66] And in the first ten months of 1968 the Copperbelt remitted from the sale of party cards alone an amount more than double that collected from the entire country between April 1965 and December 1966.[67] There were two major reasons for the startling improvements in the amount of money received from the regions. First, in 1967 the government increased the number of politicians holding government appointments (as Public Relations Assistants[68] and political assistants) on the staff of the provincial Ministers of State. Greater use could therefore be made of government machinery to buttress the party organisation and, in particular, to tighten party financial regulations. Secondly, at a UNIP national council meeting in October 1966 a resolution had been passed laying down certain principles for the conduct of financial affairs. The resolution was brought into effect by a handbook issued

64. 'General financial report to the Mulungushi conference of 15 August 1967' (mimeo., n.d.).
65. 'Report of the auditors upon the accounts for the year ended 31 December 1969' (mimeo., n.d.).
66. 'General financial report', *op. cit.*
67. 'Western Province report to the national council of UNIP, 9–11 November 1968' (mimeo, n.d.). See table 4.1.
68. The full title of this officer was 'Special Presidential Public Relations Assistant to the Minister of State'. He was usually called Assistant to the Minister and sometimes 'Assistant Minister'.

to party officials in December of that year.[69] Under the regulations party regions were no longer allowed to retain membership subscriptions, donations and funds raised through dances and other social functions. They had now to remit all money received in the region to party headquarters in Lusaka either directly or through the Minister of State. They had to submit, usually through the Minister, their estimate of annual regional expenditure, and the amount approved by headquarters for each region was then forwarded to the region concerned.[70] The Minister of State instituted a regular check of regional account books, with a Public Relations Assistant serving as provincial accounting officer. Moreover, UNIP regional and provincial financial committees were widely established, members of the provincial committees being nominated by the Minister of State. Among the advantages of the new system over the old one were the better utilisation of the scarce resources of the party and a more equitable distribution of funds among the various party regions—the former system had benefited the richer regions, notably those on the Copperbelt.

This introduction of greater central control, coupled with a vigorous (and sometimes injudicious) card-checking campaign, paid substantial financial dividends for the party. It was matched, and eventually surpassed, by income derived from investments; these included UNIP House, an imposing, multi-storey building in Cairo Road, Lusaka.[71] By 1969 only one-sixth of the party's income of K636,928 was collected from the regions, while over three-quarters came from investments.[72] With this improvement in its financial state the party was able to indulge in large spending. Its budget for the 1968 election was K250,000, and it has subsequently spent large amounts on transport (over K200,000 in 1968–69) and has increased the salaries of its regional officials.

Though UNIP has had no formal provincial organisation since 1962, the Ministers of State—supported by Public Relations

69. 'United National Independence Party: handbook for financial organisation' (Lusaka, December 1966). This, and the following, section is based on discussions with Ministers of State and regional secretaries of UNIP.

70. A party region could apply to national headquarters for additional financial assistance in order to meet unforeseen expenditure, such as major repairs to the party Land-Rover(s). The regional secretary of Petauke in the Eastern Province said (August 1967) that the average monthly expenditure of his region varied between K30 and K100, most money being spent on travelling.

71. Party headquarters are established in Freedom House, an older and much more modest building in Freedom Road, Lusaka.

72. 'Report of the auditors upon the accounts for the year ended 31 December 1969', *op. cit.*

Assistants and political assistants—helped to bridge the gap between the national headquarters of the party and the regions. By early 1968 there were four Public Relations Assistants in the Copperbelt Province (first appointed in October 1966), two in the Central Province, and one each in the six other provinces, while the number of the (twenty-two) political assistants varied between one in the Copperbelt Province to four in the Northern Province. Each political assistant supervised the affairs of one or more party region and helped to interpret government policy. As with the Public Relations Assistant, the main criterion for appointment as political assistant was long service to the party—most appointees were former regional secretaries. The political assistant was in effect a senior regional secretary paid out of government rather than party funds. His functions duplicated those of the regional secretary and, inevitably, the two officials sometimes clashed with each other. The fact that the post of political assistant was created in the first place and retained for so long despite both duplication and conflict reflected the increasing importance attached to central control by the party leadership.

In January 1969 a Cabinet Minister was appointed to each province. Though the Minister of State was retained, the subordinate posts of Public Relations Assistant and political assistant were abolished. Most of the politicians who had held the latter posts were appointed by the President as District Governors, each of whom became head of an administrative district. In politicising the district administration, Zambia followed the precedents set in English-speaking Africa by Ghana in 1957 and Tanganyika in 1962–63. As far as relations with the ruling party were concerned, she followed the Ghanaian rather than the Tanganyikan model. Though the boundaries of the party region coincided with those of the administrative district,[73] the District Governor was not made the *ex officio* regional secretary of UNIP. He was, however, recognised by President Kaunda as the senior party representative in his district—an arrangement sometimes disliked in party regions where the Governor was heavy-handed and clashed with local politicians.[74]

73. Fifty-three District Governors were appointed, and the number of party regions was increased from forty-seven to fifty-three.

74. This was the case, for example, at Mwinilunga in the North-western Province in 1969, and at Chililabombwe on the Copperbelt. Sometimes, too, the District Governor sought to win favour with UNIP regional office-holders by taking a tough line with the District Secretary and other civil servants; this occurred in 1969 at Mumbwa (Central Province), where the Governor was new to political office.

Among the latter, the three regional officials—the regional secretary, the regional youth and publicity secretary, and the regional women's secretary—are appointed and paid by the centre.[75] In making appointments, the central committee takes into account the recommendation of the provincial Minister (formerly Minister of State) as well as local party wishes. The regional women's secretary is occasionally elected by the regional conference of the party, although this is not formally recognised in the constitution. Unlike some of the District Governors, regional secretaries are usually either from the local area or are at least able to speak the local vernacular language. The plethora of tasks performed by the regional secretary ensures that he is in close contact with the feelings of the population and he was, before January 1969, the focal point for local requests and grievances, especially in regions where UNIP was dominant. Though this mantle has in part been assumed by the District Governor, the regional secretary still heads a local pressure group which seeks to satisfy people's needs by appeals to the rural council, the district development committee, visiting Ministers and, of course, the District Governor himself. Thus a strong local base, which may have been cultivated over a period of several years in junior party offices in the region, often gives the regional secretary a greater degree of independence of the centre than the method of his appointment might suggest.

The responsibility for youth in the region is entrusted to the youth and publicity secretary, who also serves as deputy regional secretary. His position is a rung on the party promotion ladder rather than that of the direct representative of youth, and he will, under normal circumstances, expect to succeed to the position of regional secretary. Party youth have been a special cause for concern among party leaders, since they have often acted in an irresponsible and, occasionally, a lawless fashion.[76] One example out

75. The salaries of regional officials were doubled in October 1971. A regional secretary now receives K120, a regional youth secretary K110, and a regional women's secretary K80 per month; free accommodation for the regional and youth secretaries is provided by the party.

76. Angi and Coombe observe that 'The ruling party has found it difficult to re-orient youth activism toward the constructive effort of nation-building. Organised youth have increasingly been involved in provocative undertakings such as demonstrations against the judiciary, political card checks, mini-skirt bans, requests for powers of arrest, campaigns against hooliganism, and road patrols. Government and party have attempted to enforce strict discipline, without notable success.' C. Angi and T. Coombe, 'Training programmes and employment opportunities for primary school leavers in Zambia' in *Manpower and Unemployment Research in Africa* (Lusaka, November 1969).

of many which could be quoted is taken from the Luapula Province in the registration period preceding the local government elections of September 1966. In a report on the elections, the acting Provincial Local Government Officer stated:

On the political side, troubles only brewed in the Kawambwa District where U.N.I.P. youths had begun beating people who had not registered as Local Government Electors. At first, the local U.N.I.P. Officials declared the spirit of non-cooperation in the registration of voters for these very elections, because they were not employed as registration officers themselves.... In Chief Milambo's area in the Fort Rosebery District, U.N.I.P. youths began beating Congress people prior to the Local Government elections.[77]

Although the party youth can usually be mobilised for specific purposes by regional officials, control over them has been spasmodic. Throughout the country they have retained an informal and slightly separate position within the main body of the party.[78] In strong UNIP areas youth are well represented at both the branch and the constituency level.

The third regional official, the regional women's secretary, has been mainly employed in establishing and organising women's clubs for development purposes. In some parts of the Northern Province women party officials at the sub-regional level have been culled from the clubs themselves. Women's activities, however, are strictly controlled by the top-ranking male officials in the region.

The independence of the party region from central control appears to vary according to its strength and location. In the rural areas, where communications with Lusaka are poor, the region may enjoy substantial *de facto* independence. In the North-western Province, for example, a participant in a provincial development committee meeting complained that 'Headquarters in Lusaka did not know what Regional Headquarters were doing and saying...'[79] Since communications with the province are very limited during the wet season, this sort of problem is perhaps to be expected. There are, however, cases in which local party officials, owing primarily to their distance from the centre, have been able to ignore directives

77. Acting Provincial Local Government Officer, Luapula Province, to Permanent Secretary, Ministry of Local Government and Housing, No. MG/LP/5718/2, 6 January 1967; Ministry of Local Government and Housing file No. LGH 5010, part V: 'Local government policy elections'.

78. Despite the strictures of the One-party Commission, the government has decided that the UNIP youth wing should be maintained. Government Paper No. 1 of 1972, *op. cit.*, p. 27.

79. Minutes of extraordinary meeting of the North-western Provincial Development Committee, 14 February 1969, *op. cit.*

from Lusaka. In the 1968 elections, in some rural areas, the party prevented ANC candidates from lodging their nomination papers despite specific instructions to the contrary from the centre. Local independence does not depend solely on poor communications. The strength of the local organisation, particularly on the Copperbelt, has sometimes deterred any detailed examination of its affairs by party headquarters. One Copperbelt regional official allegedly warned that he would brook no interference from Cabinet Ministers or other politicians in the running of his region. The regional secretary's position is also dependent upon his responses to parochial pressures. In the Northern Province a regional secretary refused to apologise for the hostile reception given to a visiting Cabinet Minister, claiming that this reflected the feeling of his people. No subsequent action was taken against him, and he eventually became a Member of Parliament.[80] Despite these examples of regional independence, the central committee was able to enforce a number of disciplinary actions against regional officials. Its greatest latitude in this respect was when it was in total agreement on a particular line of action and when it was dealing with the weaker organisations of the Southern, Western, and North-western Provinces.

Below the regional level the party is organised into constituencies, branches, sections in the urban areas and villages in the rural areas. The party constituency, whose numbers vary in relation to the geographical size of the region, does not correspond with the parliamentary constituency. In 1968 the Copperbelt towns had an average of two party constituencies each, while the rural Copperbelt, which is one party region, had fourteen. The UNIP constitution prescribes that constituency officials shall be elected every three years. In fact the element of genuine free choice may sometimes be limited, and the regional officials may determine who has the strongest claim for election to a particular office. Nevertheless, in many areas—and notably in the Northern and Luapula Provinces—there is considerable competition for office, probably because the holder thereby establishes a claim to party patronage. Constituency officials usually become city, municipal or rural councillors, a fact which—with their length of tenure as party officials—tends to make them important local political figures. This is particularly true of the constituency official who becomes rural council chairman. Constituency

80. Nor was disciplinary action taken against the Public Relations Assistant, who was mainly responsible for the incident; he was subsequently made a Minister of State. The Minister concerned was the Lozi-speaking Munukayumbwa Sipalo, who was unpopular with the Bemba-speaking wing of UNIP. *Times of Zambia*, 30 April 1968.

secretaries, who are often full-time party officials, quite frequently succeed to the position of regional youth secretary. Party office may also pave the way to the post of secretary of a co-operative society[81] or to paid employment with the government. But party patronage is limited, and local officials must create their own opportunities for employment—as, for example, they sought to do when they pressed to be made registering officers for the 1966 local government elections.[82]

At the branch level, officials are elected annually. Some of them, too, serve as local government councillors. Those who are not council members (as well as some of those who are) look to the party to provide them with employment in return for their voluntary service. In an area such as the Luapula Province, which in 1967 had as many as 425 branches distributed between four party regions and seven constituencies, this poses an impossible task for regional officials as well as the provincial Cabinet Minister.[83] It also adds to the organisational difficulties of UNIP because, as one regional secretary in the province explained, unemployed branch officials who are not councillors cannot be trusted to issue party membership cards at 20 ngwee a time. On the other hand, branch officials are so dependent on the good graces of their seniors that they are not normally able to exercise great influence on regional and national figures. The regional and constituency officials usually have enough sanctions at their disposal to keep branch, section and village leaders in line. However, since these leaders operate in what is essentially a local political arena and have limited opportunity for upward mobility within the party, it may prove difficult to prod them into taking effective action—for example, in helping to enforce unpopular agricultural regulations.

The critical test of a centralised structure is the ability of its leadership to mobilise the whole structure in pursuance of elite-formulated objectives. The extent to which UNIP's structure has

81. This post became less attractive when the Co-operative Department insisted that its holder was not a salaried manager but a worker who should receive only the same benefits as the other members of the co-operative society.

82. UNIP officials at Kawambwa in the Luapula Province threatened to boycott the elections unless they were appointed registering officers, while party officials along the line of rail were even reported to be persuading the people not to register. CAB(66) 130, 14 April 1966; Ministry of Local Government and Housing file No. LGH 5010, vol III, 'Local government elections policy'. See also p. 129 above.

83. The problem is similar in the Northern Province, where one regional secretary described his office as 'an employment agency'. When labourers are required for (say) road work, he informs his constituency officials and the latter recommend who should be employed.

been centrally controlled and directed thus affects not only the nature of the party but also the use to which it can be put to achieve the development goals of the leadership. In their attempts to mobilise the party, UNIP's leaders can claim only partial success. They have been able to mobilise it at times of elections where the presence of national leaders, the sense of political participation and the prospect of competition has meaning for the local activist. Even at such times, however, the local organisation has not always fulfilled the directives of national leaders. During the 1968 election campaign the elaborate set of instructions prepared by the central committee[84] was not followed to the letter by party organisers.

Nonetheless, the frequency of elections themselves—parliamentary, local government and party—has been an important means of instilling a sense of unity and purpose in the party. In this respect the performance of UNIP's structure has been impressive but has not been matched by corresponding party activity in attempts to realise the development-oriented policy objectives of its leadership. While party officials at regional and sub-regional levels lose few opportunities to press both the local and central governments to develop their areas, they have, with few exceptions, signally failed to use the party itself as an instrument of development. The following comment on the primary school building programme in the Provincial Progress Report for the Northern Province in October 1967 was not at all atypical: 'Self-help is at a slow pace, it is not as it used to be in the past.'[85]

The reasons for UNIP's failure to transform itself into an economic mobilisation agency therefore go well beyond the preoccupation of its cadres with competition among themselves. From 1964 the party was weakened by a large-scale loss of manpower as party activists at all levels became MPs, joined the civil service or were absorbed into parastatal bodies. UNIP has made no attempt to train its remaining cadres in agricultural policy, techniques and mobilisation methods, and therefore lacks a network of activists in the villages capable of leading the population. Moreover, because of lack of funds, it employs fewer than 200 full-time, and usually under-educated, officials. Each of the party's fifty-three regions has three of these officials—clearly insufficient to mobilise an average of 80,000 people per region, even if they had adequate transport and office facilities, which they do not. One must also remain sceptical

84. 'General elections victory handbook for party workers' (Lusaka, n.d.).
85. 'Northern Development Plan: Provincial Progress Report', 18 October 1967, ADM. 5/1; Northern Province: Provincial Development Committee minutes, ADM. 5/1/1, Minister's Office, Kasama.

of the effectiveness of UNIP's reliance on periodic exhortation as a
mobilisation strategy, especially when such appeals come from
District Governors and Ministers whose standard of living and way
of life set them apart from the ordinary people. Again, the task
of mobilising villagers for economic development is much more formidable than the political mobilisation which the party engaged
in before independence, since it requires the person being mobilised
to engage in continuous effort involving new skills. Yet Zambia has
experienced a heavy drain to the towns of those villagers with
initiative.[86] Of those who remain, very few are literate: in the whole
country in 1969, only 35 per cent of males and 19 per cent of
females were literate, and these were mainly concentrated in the
urban areas.[87] As a sample survey in Katete and Mumbwa Districts
showed, very few parents of primary school leavers in the country
want their children to take up farming;[88] in any case, the Zambian
school system does not equip its children with most of the skills
necessary to be a successful farmer.[89]

We have pointed to a number of constraints which limit the use
of UNIP's structure as an instrument for achieving the development
objectives of the party. But it should also be emphasised that there
are centralising features in the party's structural framework which
could conceivably become important for the effective establishment
of central control in the future. Even if the 1967 constitution did
not operate in its intended manner, formal power still lay with the
centre, and one of the immediate results of the August 1969 crisis
was the centralisation of the party machinery to an even greater
degree. This commitment of the leadership to the principle of
central control is reflected in the new party constitution, as well as
in the government's one-party State proposals.[90] The introduction
of Cabinet Ministers in the provinces and District Governors in the
regions, as well as the proposed construction of direct communications links between the President's Office and regional headquarters,
may also be interpreted as attempts to establish stricter control

86. Mwanza, 'Towards income policy in Zambia', *op. cit.*, p. 6.

87. *Zambia: Six Years After* (Lusaka, 1970), p. 8.

88. C. Elliott *et al.*, *Some Determinants of Agricultural Labour Productivity in Zambia* (Lusaka, November 1970, mimeo.).

89. We are indebted to Robert Molteno for providing the substance of this
paragraph.

90. Thus regional officials are not to be elected by members of the party
within the region (as suggested by a number of petitioners), but will continue
to be appointed by the central committee. Government Paper No. 1 of 1972,
*op. cit.*, p. 25.

over local party organisations. The extent to which these measures can bridge the gap between leadership aspirations and party performance will help to determine the future evolution of UNIP now that a one-party State has been legally established.

## The structure of ANC

The ANC was never faced with the sort of structural problems which UNIP encountered. In the 1958–59 split with UNIP's leaders the party lost most of its organisational talent and did not subsequently develop an organisation of any substance. Although its leaders often paid lip service to the need for a strong organisation, they did little to build one.

Power within the party was almost entirely vested in the national president, Harry Nkumbula, and the ANC constitution simply formalised this fact. As national president, Nkumbula appointed the twelve party officials at headquarters. He was also given the power 'to appoint and re-shuffle the Central Executive Committee, Provincial Officers, District Officers and Constituency Secretaries from their posts if and when he shall find it necessary to do so'.[91] The national assembly of the party, which had the power to suspend or expel party members and office-bearers, was also controlled by the national president, since he was responsible for appointing a majority of its members. According to the party constitution, the national president was to be elected every three years by the general conference. The conference itself, however, was largely composed of members of the central executive committee and the national assembly, although branches with over sixty members were entitled to send one or two delegates at the discretion of the central executive committee.

The ANC, despite its lack of support in most of the country, claimed to be a national party, and its headquarters officials normally included representatives of the major ethnic groups. This was not necessarily official party policy. At a post-mortem on the 1968 election Nkumbula raised objections to the suggestion that headquarters staff should be appointed on a provincial basis. 'To appoint officers on the Provincial level would be tribalistic,' he said. 'Appointments should be done on merit. . . .'[92] He also mentioned the problem of salaries and housing for the proposed provincial representatives. The party suffered from a chronic shortage of

91. ANC approved constitution (1968), clause 10(c).
92. Minutes of the ANC post-election conference, 4 January 1969 (mimeo.).

funds and transport; at one stage the ANC did not have sufficient funds to print its party cards. The headquarters staff were the only paid officials which Congress possessed, and even they, with the exception of those MPs who had been appointed office-bearers, were willing to give up their posts if they could find more remunerative employment elsewhere. The MPs provided the hard core of party administrators and the main means of contact, such as it was, between headquarters and the local level.

Since independence ANC's organisation has hardly existed outside the Southern Province, the Mumbwa District and the Copperbelt town of Mufulira; the party owed its success in the 1968 general election in Western Province to a few prominent individuals who had belonged to the United Party. The predominance of UNIP and difficulties in organising in its areas of support were important reasons for the restricted scope of the ANC. But the defection of most of the Western Province from UNIP and the 'no' vote in Solwezi in the June 1969 referendum showed that political allegiance could change in relatively short periods of time. The failure of the ANC to expand into areas where there were significant grievances was partly connected with the nature of the party and its organisation. For even in its areas of strength the ANC was quiescent. Before its merger with the UP its organisation did not attract in large numbers the mobile, lower-level militants, and it was content, for the most part, to try to retain existing support for the party rather than to woo UNIP supporters. Its methods were rudimentary. It sought to depict ANC's strength as greater than it actually was and to play upon the latent fears of the population by spreading highly coloured versions of UNIP's iniquities.[93] Rumour seemed to be one of the few political weapons at the disposal of the party's weak local organisations. They had limited funds, no full-time officials, no largesse to distribute among their supporters, and virtually no transport. A former UP member, who became an ANC Member of Parliament, suggested further difficulties:

He spoke of the ANC officers who were appointed to certain posts, but did not follow the constitution. He had traced out how in certain areas Provincial Officers collected dues and used it without the knowledge of National Headquarters ... Communication is needed between Headquarters, Provincial Districts, Constituencies and branches.[94]

The weakness of the ANC local organisations and their poor communications with headquarters meant that their interests did

93. See chapter 3, above.
94. Minutes of the ANC post-election conference, *op. cit.*

not serve as a basis for factions within the party. Nor did national
policy issues polarise party leaders. Rather, it was the concentration of power in the hands of Nkumbula which focused intra-party
disputes on the nature of his political tactics and leadership.
Frequent attempts were made to remove him during the period
1958–60, when UNIP's leaders attacked both his tactics towards the
colonial regime and his alleged personality defects.[95] In 1963 Job
Michello broke away from the ANC to form the People's Democratic
Party (PDC). Two years later a further revolt took place, led,
according to Nkumbula, by five headquarters officials, four ANC
MPs, and former members of the PDC who attempted to oust
the ANC president. Allegations were apparently made that he had
failed to visit the Northern, Eastern and Luapula Provinces.[96] In
May 1969 the formation of the Zambia African National Democratic Union (ZANDU) was announced. Although this party was an
offshoot of the UP, two of its leaders had unsuccessfully attempted to
win ANC nominations in the 1968 general election.[97] Thus the
ANC was not only racked by political in-fighting but also failed to
accommodate new opposition parties. Even though the policies
of the PDC, ZANDU and the UP were close to those of the ANC,
they, for the most part, chose to lead an entirely separate existence.
The autocratic manner in which Nkumbula ran the ANC may
have been a reason for the failure of the party to retain the loyalty
of all groups within it, and also goes some way to explain its inability to induce, with the exception of the artificial circumstances
of the merger with the UP, new political parties to join forces with
it. In the case of the UPP, however, it seems to have been the ANC
which rejected the proposed alliance between the two parties.

Of the newer political parties, both the UP and UPP temporarily
gained positions of political prominence, though the UPP was too
short-lived to develop any strong organisational roots. The UP
was formed in 1966 by an ex-ANC politician, Mr M. Mumbuna,
but he relinquished the leadership to Mundia in the following
year.[98] The effects of the closure of the system of recruiting Lozis to
the South African gold mines, coupled with the perception of discrimination against the Lozi at the UNIP party conference in

95. See Mulford, *Zambia: the Politics of Independence, op. cit.*, chapters
II–III.

96. Address by the National President of Congress at the sixteenth annual
conference, November 1965 (mimeo.).

97. ANC files (applications for ANC candidature in the 1968 general
election).

98. We are indebted to Robert Molteno for information on the formation
and organisational strength of the UP.

1967, enabled the party to pick up momentum. According to the Registrar of Societies' records, only seven branches of the party were registered between June 1966 and June 1967. In the next year, however, twenty-five were registered. Even this increase did not reflect the influence of the party, since the grievances it articulated grew faster than the party's formal structure. Although its leadership and support were mainly drawn from the Western Province, the party did attempt to expand into other areas, and by 1968 it had branches in all but the Northern, Eastern and Luapula Provinces. On the Copperbelt its organisational efforts brought it into direct competition with UNIP, and violent clashes occurred between the supporters of the two parties. After the murder of two UNIP officials in August 1968 the party was proscribed and its leaders were restricted.

For the immediate purpose of contesting the 1968 general election, the remaining leaders of the banned party took their supporters into the ANC. The UP had apparently suggested an electoral alliance to the ANC prior to its proscription but this had been rejected because the ANC felt that the proposed allocation of seats did not adequately reflect the relative strength of the two parties. As it was, former UP members contested a number of seats in the election and won eight of the eleven seats in the Western Province. In January 1969 Mundia was appointed deputy leader of the ANC, but he was not released from restriction until November of that year. Though the merger had the effect of strengthening slightly ANC's organisation and, especially through Mundia, of increasing the party's effectiveness in the National Assembly, it did not result in any substantial change in the nature of inter-party competition in Zambia. In this respect the UPP—until the party was banned in February 1972—promised to be much more important.

## The structure of UPP

The precipitant event leading to the formation of the UPP in August 1971 was President Kaunda's dismissal, earlier that month, of four Bemba-speaking Ministers. The real cause, however, was that by 1971 the balance of power within UNIP had swung away from the Bemba-speaking section, of which Kapwepwe was the leader and Chimba (one of the Ministers dismissed) his principal lieutenant. These two were followed into the new party by four other (Bemba-speaking) MPs, as well as former government and party office-holders (including a few ex-District Governors, ex-UNIP regional secretaries and ex-mayors) who had been removed from their posts for various offences. A few other prominent Zambians, such as the president and secretary general of the Zambia National Council for Commerce and Industry, also joined the party.[99] So too did nine university students who abandoned their studies to become full-time UPP organisers following the detention of most of the leading UPP officials (but not Kapwepwe himself) in September 1971.[100] UNIP's intra-party struggle, therefore, 'now entered a new phase with the transformation of one faction into an opposition party, which explicitly challenged Kaunda's leadership'.[101]

Though the defections from UNIP were not on the scale at one time feared, it was suspected that many who remained within the ruling party, particularly those from the Northern Province, secretly supported the UPP. The latter deliberately fanned such suspicions.[102] It appeared to be well financed and quickly showed considerable organisational competence, especially on the Copperbelt, where it sought support among the urban population, who were believed to respect Kapwepwe and to be disgruntled at the decline in their real standard of living.[103] Posters and wall slogans appeared in every Copperbelt town, while UPP activists sought to swell their party's membership by door-to-door campaigns and through the sale of party cards. A working relationship (including the sharing of offices) was established with the ANC, though the latter fought shy of a formal merger when it realised the extent to which the new party's leadership was dominated by Bemba-speakers.[104] This dominance was reflected in the fact that five of the eight members of the UPP's interim executive committee, its entire Copperbelt provincial committee, as well as the six MPs who left UNIP to join the new party, all belonged to the Bemba-speaking group.[105] The committee arrangements, however, may have been temporary—thus it was intended that the interim executive com-

99. Molteno, 'Zambia and the one-party State', *op. cit.*, pp. 6 and 8.

100. By early October 1971 116 UPP leaders and organisers had been detained. *Zambia Daily Mail*, 12 October 1971.

101. Gertzel *et al.*, 'Zambia's final experience of inter-party elections', *op. cit.*, p. 58.

102. *Times of Zambia*, 7 September 1971; *Zambia Daily Mail*, 23 October 1971.

103. In recent years, prices had risen faster than wages, which, under the government's anti-inflation policy introduced early in 1970, could not increase by more than 5 per cent a year.

104. *Times of Zambia*, 24 August 1971; *Zambia Daily Mail*, 31 August and 18 September 1971.

105. *Zambia Daily Mail*, 3 September 1971.

mittee should eventually have twenty members.[106] The evidence of UPP activities suggested that the party was fully aware that it had to make a broad appeal if it was to realise its potential of becoming a Copperbelt party, drawing support from all linguistic groups resident in the urban areas of the Copperbelt Province.

The emergence of the UPP presented UNIP with a dual problem. On the one hand, Kapwepwe and the new party were 'implicitly a major element in the whole issue of Copperbelt politics, and the recurring conflict between miners and Government over issues such as job evaluation'.[107] On the other hand, the sectional identification of the UPP—which, if too closely drawn, would work against the party on the Copperbelt—threatened UNIP's hold in other parts of the country. For Bemba-speakers—that is, the Bemba proper and their allied linguistic groups (numbering about seventeen)—are the largest section in Zambia, making up approximately 34 per cent of the population.[108] They not only form the single biggest group on the Copperbelt, but also dominate the Northern and Luapula Provinces, as well as parts of the Central Province. Historically the Bemba constituted the political backbone of UNIP, and Kapwepwe and Chimba, who are both from the Northern Province, were foundation members possessing considerable organisational ability. The danger to UNIP and the government, for which 1971 was economically and in other respects a difficult year, was that the new party might extend its appeal among the rural Bemba, thereby further increasing the sectionalism of political competition in Zambia. Even though the UPP's proposed merger with the ANC came to nothing, the awful prospect for UNIP was that at the general election due to be held by December 1973 ANC would retain its hold over the Southern and Western Provinces and that the UPP might wrest control from UNIP of the Northern, Luapula and Copperbelt Provinces.

Objectively, it is questionable whether the threat which the UPP posed to UNIP was as great as the leaders of the ruling party feared. But their perception of the threat was very real and led them to over-react to the situation. UPP supporters were suspended, dismissed and threatened with dismissal and eviction from their houses by either the government itself or agencies answerable to it;[109] leaders

106. Constitution of the United Progressive Party (mimeo., n.d.), art. 7.

107. Gertzel *et al.*, 'Zambia's final experience of inter-party elections', *op. cit.*, p. 74.

108. The Bemba proper represent approximately 18 per cent of the total population. *Ibid.* (The figures are calculated from the 1969 census.)

109. The local authorities were one such agency. For the case of Kafue township council, see *Zambia Daily Mail*, 7 September 1971.

and organisers of the new party were detained; UPP applications for the registration of its branches were not accepted and permits for party meetings were withheld; inducements to remain loyal were offered to officials of the ruling party, chiefs and students.[110] Initially, too, the UNIP leadership may not have taken adequate steps to restrain the party faithful, as a result of whose efforts shops belonging to UPP men were closed or boycotted[111] and a number of people were assaulted and houses stoned, particularly on the Copperbelt. On the other hand, in 1971 President Kaunda and his colleagues resisted mounting pressure for the banning of the UPP[112] and the new party was allowed to contest important parliamentary by-elections held in December of that year.

The withdrawal from UNIP of six MPs who joined the UPP and the defection (this time *to* UNIP) of five ANC Members meant that eleven seats were vacant under the constitutional provision which requires the resignation of an MP who transfers his allegiance from the party on whose ticket he won his seat;[113] a twelfth seat fell vacant when Mr Mungoni Liso, the ANC secretary general, was suspended from the National Assembly. Of the twelve seats that were subject to election, Mkushi North went to an unopposed UNIP candidate, while the other seats (which were distributed over five of the country's eight provinces) were contested by UNIP and either the UPP or the ANC.[114] Under an electoral pact, the two opposition parties did not compete against each other in any constituency, but were outmatched by UNIP in terms of transport and funds, and were restricted in their access to the mass media and in the number of meetings which each was allowed to hold. In the five constituencies contested with the UPP, the ruling party sought to discredit and destroy Kapwepwe as a credible alternative to Kaunda. This tactic meant that the key constituency in the election was the Copperbelt seat of Mufulira West, where Kapwepwe (former MP for Kitwe) had chosen to stand. UNIP made a direct

110. UNIP officials were provided with new transport and President Kaunda raised their salaries. *Times of Zambia*, 2 and 4 October 1971. Chiefs were told that their allowances would be increased and students that they would no longer be bonded to work for government.

111. One of those who suffered in this respect was Mr Ray Banda, UPP's secretary for publicity and a former UNIP regional secretary for Chipata in the Eastern Province. *Ibid.*, 26 August 1971.

112. Early in September 1971 UNIP headquarters claimed to be receiving an average of twenty telegrams a day calling for the banning of the UPP. *Ibid.*, 7 September 1971.

113. Constitution of Zambia, s. 65: appendix 3 to the *Laws* (Lusaka, 1965).

114. The account which follows is based on Gertzel *et al.*, 'Zambia's final experience of inter-party elections', *op. cit.*, pp. 58–77.

appeal for the support of the miners, who were predominantly Bemba-speakers and who, with their wives, comprised the vast majority of the voters in the constituency; it also sought to capture the vote of the people in the constituency who came from Luapula Province and whom the Kapwepwe faction was believed to have alienated.

In the event Kapwepwe won his seat in Mufulira West—on a gross percentage poll of only 46·93—despite the fact that he had not campaigned personally. UNIP candidates were successful in the other four UNIP–UPP contested seats and the ruling party won back from the ANC two of the Western Province constituencies which it had lost in December 1968. Predictably, UNIP leaders claimed publicly that these results indicated the party's strength. But privately they could draw only cold comfort from results which meant that the ANC retained control of its traditional stronghold, the Southern Province, and that Kapwepwe had not been removed as a challenger to Kaunda's leadership.

In February 1972, six weeks after the by-elections, the UPP was banned and its leaders who were still at large (including Kapwepwe, the party president) were detained.[115] Three weeks later President Kaunda announced the Cabinet's decision to establish a one-party democracy. The ANC protested vigorously, and in March 1972 a new party—the Democratic People's Party (DPP), led by Mr Foustino Lombe and largely made up of former UPP members— was formed to oppose the establishment of a one-party State.

The President's announcement was a tacit admission that the UPP had served as the catalyst which had prompted him to reverse his previous stand that the one-party State would be created only through the ballot-box. It also signalled the approaching end of the inter-party competition which had been a notable feature of Zambian political life since independence.

### Inter-party competition

As far as it affected the achievement of party objectives, perhaps the most important single feature of inter-party competition was the allegiance of the political parties' geographical bases of support.

115. In announcing (on 4 February 1972) that he had banned the UPP and authorised the detention of 123 of its leading members, including Kapwepwe, President Kaunda described the UPP as a party 'bent on violence and destruction'. *Africa Research Bulletin*, Political, Social and Cultural Series (Exeter), vol. 9, No. 2 (15 March 1972), p. 2377A. A large number of detainees, including Kapwepwe, have subsequently been released following their 'rehabilitation'.

Until the emergence of the UP in 1966, UNIP was virtually unchallenged in most of the country. Nonetheless, the rural areas of
the Southern Province withstood all attempts to win them over to
the ruling party. UNIP did have some limited success in the small
towns of the province. It controlled many of the local councils and,
in a 1967 by-election, it won the Mazabuka constituency, only to
lose it again in the general election of the following year. That
election saw an 8·2 per cent swing to UNIP in the province but,
although the party retained the Livingstone constituency, it made no
new gains. Confined mainly to its Southern Province base, the ANC
did not pose a threat to UNIP's tenure as the governing party,
and until 1968 the latter looked forward to the gradual eclipse
of the opposition.[116] The defection of most of the Western Province
and the continued strength of the ANC in the Southern Province
in the 1968 elections changed UNIP's attitude to the opposition
but did not alter the division of the country into substantial contiguous areas on opposite sides of the political fence.

The failure of UNIP to penetrate the Southern Province (which
was confirmed in the by-elections of December 1971) and the
fragility of its structure in the Western Province[117] have prevented
attempts to use the party as an instrument for development in
those provinces. The party clearly saw its priority as that of political organisation. The Minister of State for the Southern Province
said in November 1968 that 'Any committees . . . now being formed
are primarily for party organisation and productivity committees
[on which grass-roots party officials are represented] are at the
moment premature in the Province.'[118] But the dispersion of party
support in the rural areas makes organisation difficult. Membership
in the rural branches of the party in the Southern Province is
sometimes little more than the requisite eight office-bearers, and
this has the effect of making the party region or constituency the
party's basic unit, a unit which has few personnel and which is too
large in size to engage in effective mobilisation of the whole population. By way of contrast, branches and sections on the Copperbelt
are effective party units and the level of penetration of the party
into the community's affairs is much greater. Some indication of
the great variation in party organisational strength—and, by im-

116. For greater detail on UNIP's differing attitudes towards the opposition parties, see Rasmussen, 'Political competition', *op. cit.*

117. As we noted above, however, UNIP regained two Western Province
seats in the by-elections of December 1971.

118. 'Road to Humanism in the Southern Province', 5 November 1968
(mimeo.).

plication, UNIP's potential for achieving development goals through its structure—is contained in table 4.1.

*Table 4.1*
Registered UNIP organisations in the Southern and Copperbelt Provinces, November 1968

|  | Southern | Copperbelt |
|---|---|---|
| Regions | 7 | 8 |
| Party constituencies | 60 | 25 |
| Branches | 259 | 189 |
| Average membership per branch | 29[a] | 704[a] |
| Sections/villages | 333 | Over 650[b] |
| Card-carrying members } Jan.–Nov. 1968 | 7,405 | 133,000[c] |
| Subscriptions from cards } | K1,600[a] | K26,658[a] |
| Population, November 1968 estimate | 495,000 | 779,000 |

*Notes*

a Figures rounded.
b 1969 figure.
c An estimate based on the sale of party cards. In August 1968 the party provincial treasurer said that more than 100,000 cards had been sold during the year. (*Times of Zambia*, 6 August 1968.) Some cards were sold to children on the Copperbelt and the average adult membership of the branch is likely to have been somewhat lower than the figure given.

*Source.* Provincial reports of the national council, November 1968.

The nature of party support also exacerbates the problems of national unity,[119] on which UNIP's leaders lay great stress. But these leaders are themselves mainly drawn from the areas in which the party's strength is greatest. As we have noted, the President sought to balance his Cabinet and his party committees very carefully in order to obtain a nationally representative leadership. For the ANC, the limited geographical distribution of its support seriously affected its credibility as an alternative government and exposed it to UNIP charges that it only maintained its position by preaching tribalism. ANC leaders talked vaguely of the possibility of secession for the Southern and Western Provinces.[120] Though such talk was unrealistic, it underlined the fact that large contiguous areas provided the bases of support for Zambian political parties.

119. See chapters 3 and 5.
120. Minutes of the ANC post-election conference, *op. cit.*

*Party policies and ideology*

The types of policy goal articulated by the party leadership have been one of the criteria used to build classifications of African political parties. In Zambia the formulation of these goals has been almost exclusively the prerogative of national party leaders. The great majority of local officials have not been involved or even appeared anxious to be consulted; yet it is upon them that the party ultimately depends to mobilise the people (which has not so far occurred) and achieve the goals which it has adopted. In Bienen's terms, 'the aspirations of certain elites ... may or may not be significant' in assessing the extent to which the parties in Zambia have been able to implement their respective policies.

UNIP's leaders are unequivocably committed to the rapid economic development of the country. In a pamphlet[121] distributed before the January 1964 general election they laid down the party's general policy programme. Its economic policy was to provide a 'conducive climate for investment ... not only for a take-off into sustained growth but also to create more avenues for employment'. At the same time it would seek to 'eliminate inequalities in income and wealth'. Greater emphasis was to be placed on agriculture in an effort to diversify the economy. In the field of social services, the party called for vastly increased spending on education, housing, health facilities and training opportunities for unemployed youth. In foreign policy the new nation was to be non-aligned and was to strengthen its communication links with East Africa. Five years later, during the 1968 election campaign, the party looked back with some satisfaction at the results of this programme. 'Not even UNIP's political enemies can deny the fact that the past five years under our rule have seen an unprecedented expansion in all fields....'[122]

While UNIP had some cause for satisfaction with the progress made, attempts to put the basic programme into effective operation have met with many setbacks. The strains created by Rhodesia's UDI adversely affected the implementation of the first National Development Plan. Urban migration has checked efforts to develop the rural areas and has overloaded existing social services in the towns. The government's stress on the need for increased agricultural production and development has had disappointing results. The Zambia Youth Service, set up to train unemployed youth, was not particularly successful and has been abolished. The high expectations of party leaders have not always been fulfilled.

121. 'When UNIP becomes government' (Lusaka, n.d.).
122. 'A promise fulfilled' (Lusaka, 1968).

Many new policy initiatives, particularly in the economic field, have been taken since independence. The government has sought to play a more active role in the economy by gaining controlling interests in the copper mines and some of the country's manufacturing and retailing concerns. Since UDI steps have been taken to reduce the importance of the country's trade and communication links with the minority regime. In addition, the formal introduction of the ideology of Humanism in April 1967 contained a number of specific proposals for development.[123] Even before independence the President had expressed his belief in the importance of traditional values, a classless society, and the need for self-reliance. Although these beliefs were incorporated in the new ideology, an attempt was made to relate them to the modernising process. Co-operatives, for example, were regarded not only as an important means of development but also as a method of retaining the traditional way of life. A new departure was the emphasis on the role of the party structure in development. Party officials were to be involved in such projects as village regrouping, the young farmers' clubs and the co-operative movement,[124] and they were to participate in decision-making through the provincial, district, ward and village development committees. The provincial and district development committees are now chaired by the provincial Cabinet Minister and District Governor respectively.[125] At lower levels, the ward development committee normally includes party constituency chairmen or secretaries, and the party village chairman is a member of the village productivity committee. In practice, the establishment of these committees often proved difficult, and no one seemed certain what they were meant to do. In April 1971, therefore, a pocket manual was published, on the President's initiative, to guide village productivity and ward development committees as to their functions.[126]

Humanism, President Kaunda has said, is 'not only a guiding light in the future development of this nation but also a way of life'. It aspires to relate a recognition of the importance and centrality of man to the whole field of human endeavour. It is portrayed as a national philosophy and, as such, efforts have been made to spread its message to all parts of the country. In March 1969 a

---

123. *Humanism and a Guide to its Implementation, op. cit.*
124. After November 1968 every UNIP Member of Parliament was required to belong to a co-operative society.
125. Before January 1969 by the provincial Minister of State and the UNIP regional secretary respectively.
126. *Village Productivity and Ward Development Committees, op. cit.*

Ministry of National Guidance was established for this purpose. Within the party, committees and seminars have discussed its implementation. Within the civil service and, to some extent, industry, workers' committees have been formed to consider its applicability to their tasks. The fruits of this activity have still to be realised, and the impact of the doctrine as a means of mobilisation has yet to be effectively felt.

Relationships between the party and other institutions, which play a part in the development process, have not been as close as party leaders have desired. President Kaunda perhaps best expressed the party's view of the ideal relationship between the party and the civil service when he said, 'Government is a mere instrument of the Party. Government is a mere servant of the Party. Government must do what the Party wants.'[127] In practice the relationship appears to have been somewhat different. In December 1969 the Minister of National Guidance said, 'There is no co-operation between civil servants and party leaders.'[128] Earlier in the year the civil service had been assured that the introduction of the workers' committees would not lead to the politicisation of the whole structure.[129] The possible fear of political interference has not, however, been the only impediment to close relations. One civil service committee pointed out after a meeting of the party's national council that 'The only Ministry which appears to have been made aware of the UNIP resolutions ... was the Ministry of Rural Development. There is no recognised machinery for Government ministries to make their comments on UNIP resolutions before they are submitted to Cabinet.'[130] Trade unions, too, have had uneasy relations with the party. Having played a prominent part in the nationalist movement, many of their leaders left the unions after

127. Dr Kaunda's address at a mass rally in Lusaka, marking the tenth anniversary of UNIP, 25 October 1969; ZIS background paper No. 81/69. In this context the word 'government' can be taken to apply to the civil service. Further evidence of the desire for close relations between the party and the civil service is contained in Zambia's guidelines for the next decade: President Kaunda's speech to the UNIP national council, 9 November 1968. 'Time is now when we should integrate more the party and government' (p. 19); 'certain posts within the party and within the government may become interchangeable' (p. 20); and, speaking of District Governors, 'This is another one of those posts that might be interchangeable, that is, between politicians and civil servants' (p. 23).

128. *Zambia Mail*, 13 December 1969.

129. Cabinet circular No. 60 of 1969, August 1969.

130. Draft recommendations of an *ad hoc* committee called by the Ministry of Rural Development to consider a proposal of the UNIP national council to establish three primary service centres in each district.

independence for management, party and government employment. On the Copperbelt the strength of the party machine has led to incidents where the party has either intervened or created disputes without reference to the unions. Although UNIP is conscious of the importance of working with the latter, the autonomy of the unions has been curtailed, and this has caused some resentment among their leaders. In a third institution, the University of Zambia—the future source of the nation's high-level manpower— the governing party has not been able to establish an effective party branch on the campus, and student alienation from the government increased sharply in July 1971 when the government closed the University for six weeks after student demonstrations against the French sale of arms to South Africa.

The difficulties which UNIP has faced in its efforts to participate constructively in development policies appear to stem from the constraints under which it operates. The problems of mobilising the party machine, ineffective communication and co-ordination with government, and the unskilled activist at the local level have all affected the ability of the party to change from an organisation striving for independence into a development-oriented institution. There has been an awareness of these problems,[131] and some attempts have been made to overcome them. With the concept of 'decentralisation in centralism',[132] the party seeks to maintain central control and direction by placing senior party officials in the provinces and regions. Specific instructions have been given to these officials 'as to what [they are] supposed to be doing as well as what [they are] not supposed to do'.[133] President Kaunda is still confident that, as he said in 1969, UNIP 'is going to be an instrument for development'.[134]

With the coming of independence the ANC achieved its major objective.[135] Since that time policy considerations appear to have been subsidiary to the party's belief that, in order to retain its support and ward off the introduction of a one-party State, it must

131. See Kaunda, *A Humanist in Africa, op. cit.,* chapters 3 and 5.
132. 'I define this decentralisation in centralism as a measure whereby through the Party and Government machinery, we will decentralise most of our Party and Government activities while retaining effective control of the Party and Government machinery at the centre in the interests of unity. In short, we will decentralise but avoid regionalism.' Kaunda, *Zambia's Guidelines for the next Decade, op. cit.,* p. 19.
133. ZIS background paper No. 91/69.
134. *Ibid.,* No. 81/69.
135. Five years after the achievement of universal suffrage the ANC still occasionally used the slogan 'One man, one vote' at party rallies.

oppose UNIP at every turn. The ANC's policy proposals generally lacked substance and were often simply the reverse of those advocated by the ruling party. However, policy differences did exist. The ANC was more pragmatic than UNIP in both domestic and foreign policy. It believed in private enterprise, was opposed to government participation in the economy and was less concerned with the mobilisation of the population. Partly because it believed that they were used for political purposes, it proposed greater independence for traditional rulers and trade unions and advocated training programmes for Zambia's youth. In foreign policy it favoured the establishment of trading links with Rhodesia and questioned the benefit to Zambia of entry into the East African Common Market. The Zambia–Tanzania railway was criticised on the grounds that it would be mainly to Tanzania's advantage and dangerous to Zambia's internal security because of Chinese involvement in the scheme. It regarded the concept of non-alignment as too vague to be practical and believed in some disengagement from the socialist countries. But the ANC was not primarily concerned with producing a constructive alternative policy, and failed to attract the support of groups which became alienated from the ruling party.

The United Party grew in strength because of its ability to articulate grievances held in the Western Province. The closure of the WENELA recruiting system (resulting in at least temporary unemployment for large numbers of Lozis), dissatisfaction with the pace of economic development in the province, and the results of the 1967 UNIP elections at Mulungushi were all grist for the party's mill. It was also willing to supplement these real or perceived grievances by playing upon tribalistic sentiments. It alleged, for example, that Lozis were discriminated against in the allocation of civil service jobs and loans, and it circulated the rumour that the Bemba wanted to take over Lozi cattle and farms.[136] In its short period of existence it scarcely had time to develop more positive policies. Its reactions to UNIP policies, however, suggest that the party was fairly close to the ANC. In its publication the *Mirror* the UP expressed its dislike of the economic measures announced at Mulungushi in April 1968.[137] It was also opposed to Humanism, believing that the ideology was too vague to be useful. And it favoured closer links with the minority regimes of the south. Its merger with the ANC did not, therefore, involve the two parties

136. For the effects on voting patterns of the UP's ethnic appeal, see chapter 5.

137. The *Mirror*, vol. 1, No. 1 (March 1968), and No. 3 (May 1968).

in any protracted debate over policy. Rather, the question they faced was the nature, in terms of political tactics and organisation, of the marriage of a dynamic party to one which had previously accepted a somewhat passive political role.

Since the UPP existed for an even shorter period than the UP, it becomes largely a matter of surmise to determine where the party stood on policy issues. Initially, UPP leaders accused the UNIP government of pursuing poor agricultural policies, of financial mismanagement and dictatorial tendencies,[138] but offered no detailed critique of UNIP policies nor put forward any alternatives. Mr Kapwepwe, the party president, was equivocal over the government's policy of political confrontation with, and economic disengagement from, white-controlled southern Africa, and merely said that this was a policy area to be decided after agreement had been reached with ANC (which advocated a Malawi-type approach).[139] The UPP constitution[140] stated that it was a socialist party, but in a subsequent television interview Kapwepwe refused to say what his party meant by socialism or what its attitude was to the place of foreigners in the economic life of the country.

Elections often serve as a mirror which reflects the stand of competing parties in a country's politics. Unfortunately, the Zambian by-elections of December 1971 serve as a poor guide to UPP policies. Virtually all that can be gleaned from Mr Kapwepwe's press statements and such scanty information as is available was that the UPP would maintain the same basic policies as the UNIP government but would implement them more efficiently and effectively.[141] UPP leaders were true to their origin as a faction which had split away from a ruling party whose policies they had themselves helped to shape. 'By offering more effective government, they justified their claim to be more truly nationalistic than UNIP.'[142] But they had nothing new to offer to the very poor, the unemployed and the slum-dweller and therefore, as Robert Molteno has pointed out, 'the UPP's pretensions to radicalism must be viewed with the gravest caution'. [143]

With rare exceptions, prominent trade unionists held aloof from

138. *Times of Zambia*, 23 August 1971.

139. *Sunday Times* (Johannesburg), 29 August 1971, quoted by Molteno, 'Zambia and the one-party State', *op. cit.*, p. 8.

140. Reproduced in *Zambia Daily Mail*, 25 August 1971.

141. *Sunday Times* (Ndola), 22 August 1971; *Times of Zambia* and *Zambia Mail*, 23 August 1971.

142. Gertzel *et al.*, 'Zambia's final experience of inter-party elections', *op. cit.*, pp. 73 and 77.

143. 'Zambia and the one-party State', *op. cit.*, p. 8.

the new party,[144] whose leaders at all levels tended to be drawn
from the ranks of Zambian businessmen.[145] Again, it was businessmen who, according to Kapwepwe, provided most of the party's
funds.[146] UNIP leaders were convinced, however, that the UPP also
received financial assistance from external sources, including East
Germany and South Africa.[147]

The way in which Zambian political parties have operated does
not, therefore, seem to have been determined by the policy objectives
of their leaders. UNIP's organisation has fulfilled important functions—for example, as an electoral machine and as a structure
which receives and solves the problems and grievances of local communities—but, partly because it has concentrated on these roles, it
has not served as an institution for the implementation of the
leaders' highest priority, that of development. The ANC, for its
part, did not actively promote or publicise its policies. Its pragmatism was the pragmatism of a desire to survive, with tactics dictated
from the top, rather than that of a will to provide a framework for
formulating constructive policy proposals out of conflicting interests.

## Conclusions: the one-party State

Zambia's first eight years of independence have witnessed attempts
by political leaders to change the roles played by their political
parties, which were originally designed for agitational purposes.
UNIP's leaders have laid emphasis on new objectives and have
sought to imbue their followers with the principles of a development
ideology that will spur them to new efforts and so make possible
the achievement of long-range national goals. The monumental
task of redirecting the energies of the party towards development
has inevitably produced strains. For example, the Bemba-speaking
activists in the Northern and Luapula Provinces have been reluctant
to forego the position of dominance with UNIP which they
enjoyed at the height of the independence struggle, and this has
made more difficult the task of creating a progressive, forward-look-

144. One exception was the president of the National Union of Commercial and Industrial Workers.
145. Molteno, 'Zambia and the one-party State', *op. cit.* See also *Zambia
Daily Mail*, 14 September 1971, and *Times of Zambia*, 15 September 1971.
146. See *Times of Zambia*, 8 September 1971.
147. For the grave, but unsubstantiated, allegations made by President
Kaunda and other UNIP leaders against the UPP, see *Zambia Daily Mail*,
28 August and 21 September 1971, and *Times of Zambia*, 13 September
1971.

ing party shorn of its freedom-fighting image. The 1967 attempt to make UNIP a more open party by introducing elections to the central committee on an individual basis initiated a period of intense competition within the ruling party, and eventually resulted in the withdrawal from UNIP of a Bemba-speaking faction led by Simon Kapwepwe. If we take political competition to mean the 'measure of the presence in a political system of opportunities for open and effective dissent'[148] and apply that definition to the intra-party struggle, it is evident that UNIP was too weak both institutionally and organisationally to allow the unchecked interplay between factions.

Other conclusions follow. First, the party could not have weathered the succession crisis with which President Kaunda threatened it in February 1968, since its cohesion was still unduly dependent on the party president. Indeed, there is little doubt that the whole Zambian political system would have collapsed if that particular crisis had occurred. Kaunda did not seek at this juncture to turn his personal ascendancy over UNIP into one-man rule after the Nkrumah model—he had already turned down the life presidency of the party and discouraged exaggerated attempts to exploit his charisma.[149] The second conclusion is that some action to check the faction-fighting within UNIP was urgently required by August 1969, and that the initiative could have come only from President Kaunda. Thirdly, the struggle for power in Lusaka has had the effect of reducing further the ability of the party's central committee and secretariat to control the party's up-country organisation. Finally, the new constitution adopted by UNIP in May 1971 served only to convince Kapwepwe and his lieutenants that the balance of power within UNIP had swung firmly away from themselves. When, in August 1971, President Kaunda removed Chimba and other leaders of the Kapwepwe faction from his Cabinet, this faction left UNIP and launched the UPP. Unwittingly they thereby paved the way for the legal establishment of a one-party State.

For the new emphasis upon the one-party State in the latter part of 1971 was 'directly related to the changed situation in the factional struggle within UNIP'.[150] It was claimed on the Copper-belt that a one-party State would overcome the confusion resulting

148. Morris-Jones, 'Dominance and dissent', *op. cit.*, p. 454.

149. Cf. *The Voice of UNIP* (Lusaka, May 1965), which described Kaunda as 'the Son of God . . . conceived as not only enjoying the presence of the Lord at his birthday, but also living in the presence and favour of the Lord'.

150. Gertzel, *et al.*, 'Zambia's final experience of inter-party elections', *op. cit.*, p. 70.

from the creation of the UPP, and bring an end to card checks and violence. The emergence of the UPP had meant the further sectionalisation of political competition in Zambia. Intense and bitter sectionalism had nearly destroyed UNIP and now threatened the very fabric of Zambian society. Fears on this score may be accepted as one reason which led President Kaunda to agree that the time had now come for his party to be given a legal monopoly of power.[151]

There were, however, probably also other reasons for this reversal of previous policy. One may have related to the survival of UNIP as Zambia's ruling party. The strongly repressive measures taken against the UPP, culminating in its banning, reflected the belief that the UPP constituted a clear threat to UNIP's continued tenure of power. The UP precedent was not encouraging: though banned, it had survived organisationally within the ANC and had enabled that party to win control of the Western Province in December 1968. Another reason may have been socio-economic: the conviction that increased sectionalism would discourage further the already negligible inflow of private foreign investment and would throw into jeopardy the whole of the government's rural development programmes.[152] Again, there may have been considerations relating to defence and security: the fear that internal political and economic difficulties, such as faced Zambia in 1971, might be exploited by the white minority regimes of the south. There were some grounds for believing that these regimes might seek to topple President Kaunda's government through the agency of one or more of Zambia's opposition parties which, if returned to power, would adopt a less intransigent attitude towards them.[153] To these possible reasons might be added two others: the conviction that only a united Zambia could help to achieve the liberation of Africa, and Tanzania's example of operating successfully a legally established one-party State for seven years. Kaunda is particularly close to President Nyerere and has followed his lead in other matters. Significantly, the method of enquiring how best to establish a democratic

151. The one-party State was a key issue at the emergency session of the UNIP national council held in Lusaka between 1 and 3 October 1971.

152. Thus if UNIP became preoccupied with combating the political power of the UPP, its chances of initiating rural mobilisation through the Registration and Development of Villages Act, 1971, would be reduced. See Molteno, 'Zambia and the one-party State', *op. cit.*, pp. 16–17.

153. Molteno, *ibid.*, p. 17, n. 24, points out that the Afrikaans' pro-government press in South Africa came out in strong support of Mr Kap-wepwe, arguing that he, unlike Dr Kaunda, was a man with whom South Africa could do a deal. See *Zambia Daily Mail*, 8 October 1971.

one-party State—by means of a National Commission sitting publicly under the chairmanship of the Vice-president—was based on the Tanzanian rather than the Ghanaian model. Clearly, too, in making its recommendations the Commission took account of Tanzanian experience, as did the government in deciding which of those recommendations it would accept.

The National Commission submitted its report to the President on 15 October 1972, and the government issued its paper (No. 1 of 1972) on the report a month later.[154] The most fundamental change resulting from these steps—and given legislative effect by the National Assembly in December 1972—is that UNIP now enjoys a legal monopoly of power. In most respects, however, the provisions of the May 1971 party constitution will still operate, though they are to be amended to accommodate a Prime Minister and a secretary general of the party, and to establish the central committee and Cabinet as separate bodies.

According to government paper No. 1 of 1972, the central committee of UNIP will comprise: the president of the party, who, in his capacity as President of the Republic, will have full executive powers and be supported by a Prime Minister responsible for government administration; the Prime Minister, *ex officio*; three members nominated by the President; and twenty other members elected by the party's general conference. The President will appoint a secretary general of the party from among members of the central committee: the secretary general will be an *ex officio* member of the Cabinet and will act for the President when the latter is absent from the country or otherwise directs. The party is declared to be 'supreme', and members of the central committee, who will be full-time, are to take precedence over members of the Cabinet. Except for the Prime Minister, no Minister will be a member of the central committee.

It is, of course, far too early to determine how much political competition will be allowed in Zambia. But the presidential intention seems clear: 'There shall ... be complete freedom among the people to participate fully in the running of their affairs at local and national level through institutions under people's own control.'[155] As far as the centre is concerned, we have seen that when, in 1967, UNIP allowed the democratic election of central committee members, the result was an alarming increase in the

154. *Report of the National Commission, op. cit.*, pp. i–x and 1–72, and Government Paper No. 1 of 1972, *op. cit.*, pp. 1–31.

155. *Report of the National Commission, op. cit.*, p. ix: schedule to Statutory Instrument No. 46 of 1972.

sectional alignments of the politicians. Is it likely under the new
proposals, which provide for twenty members of the central committee to be elected, that competition will have to be reduced if
intense factionalism is to be contained? The establishment of the
central committee and Cabinet as separate bodies reduces this
danger considerably. An intriguing question for the future is where
the locus of power will lie in Zambia: with the President and
Cabinet or with the President and central committee? On the
answer to that question will depend the answer to another: will
Zambia's present Ministers prefer to remain in the Cabinet or
seek instead election to the central committee? The offices of
secretary general of UNIP and Prime Minister may well become
the target of political ambition, since, with the President, these are
the only office-holders who are to be members of both bodies.
Appointment to these key posts is in the gift of the President. Somewhat contrary to the intentions of the National Commission,[156] it
is above all his powers which are increased under the government
paper.

The problem facing President Kaunda is infinitely greater than
that which confronted President Nyerere in 1965. Zambia is not, as
Tanzania was, a predominantly rural, pre-industrial and largely
homogeneous society. On the contrary, it is one of the most
urbanised and industrialised countries in black Africa, with a fairly
high level of social stratification: it has sharp sectional divisions
and quite strong interest groups (notably the Mineworkers' Union of
Zambia). Already, before legalisation Tanzania (more strictly, Tanganyika) was a *de facto* one-party State; there was virtually no opposition to TANU. This is not the case in Zambia, where from
December 1968 until December 1972 the ANC controlled two of the
country's eight provinces and the UPP, until it was banned in
February 1972, threatened UNIP's hold among at least the urban
population of Copperbelt Province. While appreciating the magnitude of the problems facing President Kaunda, one cannot be
confident that sectionalism will be reduced or political stability
increased by the legal establishment of a one-party State.

156. For example, the Commission had suggested a limit to the tenure of
office of the President and had proposed to curtail his veto powers. These
proposals were rejected by the government. *Report of the National Commission, op. cit.*, p. 13, para. 48(2), and p. 23, para. 86; Government Paper
No. 1 of 1972, *op. cit.*, pp. 5 and 11–12.

# 5

# The 1968 general election and the political system

*Robert Molteno and Ian Scott*[1]

## Background to the election

Zambia's first post-independence general election for both the National Assembly and the presidency was held some four years after independence, on 19 December 1968. It took place at a time when the nation had experienced great economic expansion and change.[2]

UNIP had been returned to power in 1964 on a manifesto which had promised the electorate increased economic benefits. Thereafter, rapid advances were made: employment and wages rose rapidly; social services were expanded and money was poured into the agricultural sector in the form of credits for farmers and to assist the establishment of co-operative societies. In April 1968 the government took the first of what proved to be a series of economic reforms by buying a controlling interest in twenty-six major companies. The implementation of UNIP's 1964 election promises brought increases in real income to many Zambians. But it also brought many problems. It did not immediately relieve the poverty of the majority of the population, particularly in the rural areas, and people flocked from the countryside to the towns in search of better living conditions. On the Copperbelt, the backbone of the nation's economy, there was considerable industrial unrest (especially in 1966) and, partly as a result of the Rhodesian UDI, inflation was cutting into the monetary gains made by the

1. In conducting the research for this study the authors relied mainly on extensive field trips in most provinces; interviews with officials at all levels in the electoral administration, as well as with candidates and election workers of both parties; documentary sources, including Zambia Information Service press releases; the mass media, and Hansard. Material collected in interviews is not usually referred to in footnotes.

2. For an analysis of the UNIP government's achievements after 1964, see chapter 10.

urban dweller since independence. Nevertheless, with an election
pending, the government justifiably decided to stand on its record
and rely on the high level of popular consent which rapid economic
growth had helped maintain since 1964.

But economic development was not the only change to have taken
place since 1964: the political context was also very different and
indeed less optimistic. The atmosphere was no longer the euphoria
of treading the final steps on the road to independence. The country
had been independent for four years, and these years had not been
entirely free of political troubles. There were considerable strains
within the ruling party. At the first post-independence UNIP
general conference, held in August 1967, campaigning for party
office had been conducted on openly sectional lines.[3] The defeat of
most of the party's Lozi and Eastern Province leaders, in conjunction with the discovery that on the first count there were more
votes cast than accredited delegates, caused bitter recriminations.
In February 1968, as a result of continuing strife between top party
leaders, Dr Kaunda resigned briefly.[4] Thus while UNIP went into
the election later in the year outwardly unified, the solution to its
factional problems had not been found. Secondly, a new opposition
party, the United Party (UP), had been formed in the middle of
1966. Based primarily on Lozi grievances and fuelled by the results
of the UNIP elections of 1967, the party expanded rapidly and
threatened to upset the hitherto stable political balance between
UNIP and ANC. Moreover, many UNIP supporters suspected
that Lozi leaders within UNIP were secretly attracted to the new
party. The UP was proscribed in August 1968, a few months before
the election, allegedly for using violence, and a handful of its
leaders were first detained and then restricted.

As for ANC, it entered the election a victim of its own organisational, financial and leadership weaknesses and of harassment from
local-level UNIP officials. ANC confidence for the forthcoming
contest was bolstered, however, by several factors. In March 1968 it
retained four Southern Province seats in by-elections. The *de facto*
merger with UP in the middle of the year brought the party an
enormous access of strength; Nkumbula, the party leader, showed
renewed vitality; and the party was convinced that there was
widespread discontent with the UNIP administration. Indeed,
ANC's optimism did not decline until after nomination day, when
it became clear that local-level UNIP officials were determined to

3. 'Mulungushi conference, 1967', *op. cit.*, p. 52.
4. For greater detail on these developments, see chapter 4, especially pp.
112–14.

bend the electoral rules to UNIP's advantage, and that the Parliamentary Elections Office (PEO) was unable, and the police were often unwilling, to prevent this happening.

Both parties approached the campaign with clear priorities. First, the ruling party wanted a peaceful, fair and speedily concluded election with a high turn-out and overwhelming victory for its own candidates. ANC, in contrast, saw the election not as a constitutionally required formality which would enhance the reputation of the government but as a genuine contest for office, albeit with the odds heavily weighted against it. Secondly, because of the potentially disruptive consequences of factionalism, UNIP could not afford to make particularistic appeals to individual constituencies or sections of the population, but had to campaign in terms of the advantages which its rule had brought to the nation as a whole. This was different from the attitude of ANC, which, knowing that it had no chance of winning seats in Northern and Luapula Provinces, felt free to try and increase its appeal to other Zambian sections by playing up alleged Bemba domination. This was helped by the fact that Bemba-speakers from Northern Province did at that time hold the top offices of President, Vice-president, Secretary to the Cabinet, Commissioner of Police and chairman of the Public Service Commission. Thirdly, as a matter of political tactics UNIP had to emphasise its past achievements and divert attention from the country's difficult economic future. ANC, as was to be expected, tried to circumvent this ploy by concentrating on the policy failures of the UNIP government, but was unable to put forward substantive alternative policies of its own. Finally, UNIP saw the election as providing the possibility for an advance towards its goal of a one-party State through the ballot box. Naturally, ANC vehemently opposed this objective and was determined to win enough seats to frustrate it.

*Electoral administration*

To institutionalise competition for office, it was necessary to have an election which was manifestly fair. To have done otherwise would have led to permanent disenchantment with the political process among opposition supporters and possibly also among certain elements in UNIP. The potential for more immediate disruption would also have been present. As President Kaunda put it, 'Examples abound in Africa...of the chaos which can result from either incompetently or dishonestly run elections.'[5] Accordingly, he instructed the civil servants administering the election to carry

5. PEO 101/5/48/S, 2 October 1968.

out their duties 'absolutely free of any political interferences or
pressures either from Ministers of my Government or from officials
of any political party, either at national, regional or district level'.[6]
Despite this firm presidential commitment to the principle of a
fair election, a major problem lay, first, in convincing the opposition
that the government was sincere and, secondly, in persuading local
UNIP activists that a free election was desirable. As we shall see, the
President in the end failed in both these objectives.

The electoral administration differed considerably from that
which had run the 1964 election.[7] In 1964 the election had been
administered mainly by the District Commissioners. This decentralised system was replaced, in mid-1967, by one which provided for
much greater central control. A Director of Elections with direct
access to the President headed a Parliamentary Elections Office,
which was staffed mainly by expatriates from the former provincial
administration. These officers were firmly committed to the value of
a free multi-party election. The PEO in turn was responsible only to
a three-man Electoral Commission which existed by virtue of the
constitution[8] and was appointed in December 1967, one year before
the general election took place.

The membership of the Commission reflected the executive's
intention to hold a fair election. It consisted of Mr Justice Pickett, a
High Court Judge; Sir John Moffat, former leader of the defunct
Central African and Liberal Parties; and Mr Edward Shamwana,
a Lusaka lawyer. None of them had close connections with the
ruling party, although Sir John had unsuccessfully contested a
reserved roll seat for UNIP in the 1964 general election. The ANC
did not challenge his impartiality, but it did object to his appointment on the grounds that he was not a lawyer.[9] It also put forward
the suggestion that the Delimitation Commission (a constitutionally
separate body which had the infrequent task of delimiting constituency boundaries) should be composed of representatives from
each of Zambia's eight provinces in order to avoid bias in favour
of any one area.[10] The government rejected this proposal, and the
Delimitation Commission's membership in 1968 was in fact the
same as that of the Electoral Commission.

The Delimitation Commission came into existence because the

6. *Ibid.*

7. Mulford, 'Some observations on the 1964 election', *op. cit.*

8. Constitution of Zambia, s. 67.

9. *Nat. Ass. Deb.*, Hansard No. 12, 15 December 1967, col. 220; and
Hansard No. 13, 28 March 1968, col. 1570.

10. *Ibid.*, Hansard No. 12, 13 December 1967, cols 78–9. Section 67 of the
constitution limits the membership of an Electoral Commission to three.

*Table 5.1*
The 1968 general election—a chronology

| Date | Event |
| --- | --- |
| Mid-1967 | Parliamentary Elections Office created as a department in the Cabinet Office. |
| Late 1967 | PEO staff built up (largely from former members of the Provincial Administration). |
| 10 December 1967 | Electoral Commission (Supervisory) appointed by the President. |
| February 1968 | Delimitation Commission set up. |
| May 1968 | Electoral Act passed in which Parliament delegated its powers to make electoral regulations to the Electoral Commission. |
| 11 May 1968 | Delimitation of 105 constituencies completed by the Delimitation Commission (consisting of the same persons as the Electoral Commission). |
| June–July 1968 | Registration of voters. |
| 14 August 1968 | United Party banned and its six top officeholders detained. |
| 16 August 1968 | Electoral (National Assembly Election) Regulations and Electoral (Presidential Election) Regulations published. |
| August–October 1968 | Selection and training of returning officers. |
| August–December 1968 | Campaign by PEO and political parties to teach voters new method of casting ballot. |
| 2 November 1968 | President dissolves first National Assembly; date of election announced. |
| 16 November 1968 | Nomination day for presidential candidates. |
| 23 November 1968 | President Kaunda announces names of UNIP National Assembly candidates. |
| 26 November 1968 | Nomination day for National Assembly candidates. |
| 19 December 1968 | **Polling day**. |
| Late December 1968 | President Kaunda's press conference at which post-election discrimination against ANC was launched, including calls for a one-party State by some UNIP leaders. |
| 4 January 1969 | ANC holds election post-mortem conference. |
| 30 January 1969 | Climb-down on anti-ANC measures; wave of violence declines. |

Constitution (Amendment) (No. 3) Act of 1967 had increased the number of elected MPs from 75 to 105, thereby making a new delimitation necessary.[11] Appointed in February 1968, the commission completed its work in May. The constitution required the delimitation to be carried out on the basis of a population quota, which was calculated by dividing the population of the country (in this case projected from the 1963 census) by the number of constituencies. This principle of delimitation immediately became an issue in the election—not merely between the parties, but within UNIP itself. So long as the latter gave most seats in a province to 'local' men (i.e. from that province), any change in the allocation of seats between provinces would affect the distribution of power within the party. Several MPs, including UNIP Members particularly from North-western and Eastern Provinces, saw advantages, therefore, in challenging the population quota as the basis for delimitation. Some felt that a more equitable or politically acceptable distribution of seats would result from the use of the voters' roll to establish a quota of registered voters for each constituency,[12] as had been done in 1963.[13] Other MPs took a different line. Of the many Members who criticised the use of population projections from the 1963 census, one called for a new census before the election,[14] while the UNIP Member for Petauke argued that the forty new seats should be divided equally among the provinces.[15]

None of these objections carried weight with the government, which pointed out that the constitution required the use of a population quota and that, if a census was to be held before the election, it would be necessary to extend the life of Parliament beyond its constitutional time limit.[16]

11. The Electoral Commission (Supervisory) was established on 10 December 1967 and has not yet been dissolved. The Electoral Commission to delimit constituency boundaries (herein referred to as the Delimitation Commission) was set up on 2 February 1968 and was automatically dissolved after the presentation of its report on 11 May 1968.

12. *Nat. Ass. Deb.*, Hansard No. 12, 13 December 1967, col. 81; Hansard No. 14, 25 April 1968, col. 101. See also *Report of the Electoral Commission (Delimitation of Constituency Boundaries)* (Lusaka, 1968).

13. *Report of the Delimitation Commission* (Lusaka, 1963). The quota for the main roll constituencies was 21,298, and for the reserved constituencies, 2,398.

14. *Nat. Ass. Deb.*, Hansard No. 14, 25 April 1968, cols 124, 142–9, 161.

15. *Ibid.*, col. 125. The ten reserved roll seats were abolished and the number of parliamentary constituencies was increased from seventy-five (sixty-five main roll and ten reserved roll) to 105 by the Constitution (Amendment) (No. 3) Act of 1967. Only one voters' roll, based on universal franchise, remained.

16. *Ibid.*, 25 and 26 April 1968, cols 133–4, 176, 185.

In the event, the delimitation was not entirely fair and there was some unintentional inequity in the distribution of seats between provinces. The projections from the 1963 census figures did not indicate the extent of the urban migration which had occurred since 1963,[17] with the result that the Northern and Luapula Provinces were over-represented and the heavily urbanised Central and Copperbelt Provinces were under-represented. There were also big discrepancies in the number of voters in different constituencies.

Yet another cause for controversy before the campaign proper, and again within the ruling party, was the Delimitation Commission's procedure in delimiting constituency boundaries. The commission, sitting in Lusaka, apparently first delimited the constituencies on *a priori* grounds, using chiefs' areas and district boundaries for this purpose; it then travelled to the provincial centres to hear local evidence and presumably, in some cases, to make consequent adjustments. These methods were criticised as unfair by the UNIP Member for Kasempa in North-western Province,[18] where dissatisfaction with the small number of seats allocated to the province by the Commission led to talk of putting up independent candidates.[19] However, even if the constitution had permitted delimitation on the (1963) basis of the number of registered voters, the province would have benefited only slightly, and this despite the 'sympathetic consideration' given by the commission to the rural areas (see table 5.2).

Following the delimitation of constituencies in May, each district had been divided into a number of polling districts. During the next two months voters, who had to be Zambian citizens and at least eighteen years of age (compared to twenty-one in 1964), were registered in the polling districts in which they resided.[20] The final registration figures were fed into a computer which produced the electoral registers for individual polling districts.

The number of registered voters increased by 15 per cent over the 1964 figure. This was less than expected in view of the reduced voting age and the fact that the population had increased by 16·5 per cent between June 1963 and August 1969.[21] Though the initial

17. *Census of Population and Housing, 1969—First Report* (Lusaka, 1970).

18. *Nat. Ass. Deb.*, Hansard No. 14, 25 April 1968, col. 114.

19. *Zambia Mail*, 2 August 1968.

20. An applicant for registration had to furnish, *inter alia*, proof of his Zambian citizenship. When accepted, he was issued with a voter's registration card. Electoral (Registration of Voters) Regulations, 1968, s. 12.

21. Calculated from the number of eligible voters on the basis of the 1963 and 1969 censuses, *op. cit.* These figures should be treated with some

*Table 5.2*
Allocation of seats and registration of voters by province

| Province | Seats | No. of registered voters | Average per seat | Population |
|---|---|---|---|---|
| *1964* | | | | In 1963[a] |
| Western (Barotse)[d] | 7 | 144,186 | 20,598 | 363,000 |
| Central | 9 | 186,415 | 20,713 | 505,000 |
| Eastern | 10 | 207,386 | 20,738 | 480,000 |
| Luapula | 6 | 125,645 | 20,941 | 357,000 |
| Northern | 9 | 201,095 | 22,344 | 564,000 |
| North-western | 5[b] | 90,853 | 18,171 | 211,000 |
| Southern | 8 | 179,447 | 17,431 | 466,000 |
| Copperbelt (Western)[d] | 11 | 244,777 | 22,252 | 544,000 |
| Total | 65 | 1,379,804 | 21,228 | 3,490,000 |
| *1968* | | | | *1969*[a] |
| Western (Barotse)[d] | 11 (11)[c] | 163,290 | 14,845 | 417,000 |
| Central | 16 (17) | 259,494 | 16,218 | 708,000 |
| Eastern | 14 (15) | 227,753 | 16,268 | 509,000 |
| Luapula | 10 (9) | 134,893 | 13,489 | 338,000 |
| Northern | 16 (13) | 202,725 | 12,670 | 541,000 |
| North-western | 6 (7) | 103,184 | 17,197 | 227,000 |
| Southern | 14 (13) | 190,673 | 13,620 | 499,000 |
| Copperbelt (Western)[d] | 18 (20) | 305,954 | 16,997 | 815,000 |
| Total | 105 | 1,587,966 | 15,123 | 4,054,000 |

*Notes*

*a* *Monthly Digest of Statistics* (Lusaka, 1970), vol. v, No. 12, December 1969. Figures are based on the June 1963 census and the August 1969 census.

*b* Includes one constituency which covers part of both the North-western and Western Provinces.

*c* The figures in brackets represent a possible allocation of seats on the basis of the number of registered voters. The figures are obtained by dividing the number of registered voters in each province by the average number of registered voters per constituency and allocating an extra seat to those with the highest remainders.

*d* In 1969 Barotse Province's name was changed to Western Province, and Western to Copperbelt Province. The 1969 nomenclature is followed in this chapter, as elsewhere in the book.

registration period of three weeks was extended in some areas because of the poor response of the population, the percentage of
eligible persons who registered as voters fell from 92 per cent in
1964 to 83 per cent in 1968.

The stage was now set for the next phase in the setting up of a
viable electoral administration: the education of the electorate and
preparations for polling. The District Secretaries, who had usually
been responsible for supervising the registration of voters in their
districts, were normally also appointed electoral officers. They had
to distribute equipment for the polling stations, provide transport
and generally supervise the election in the constituencies within
their districts. They also appointed and trained over 8,000 presiding
officers and polling assistants to run the polling stations. In addition,
returning officers for the individual constituencies were appointed:
they were responsible mainly for determining the validity of nomination papers on nomination day and for the count at the end of
polling day.[22] Both electoral officers and returning officers under-
went a training course run by the Parliamentary Elections Office
immediately after the registration of voters had been completed in
July. Forty-three of the 105 returning officers were expatriates, and
the Electoral Commission relied heavily on the civil service in
seeking the best qualified people for the task. Similarly, presiding
officers and polling assistants were recruited from amongst the
most able and educated men in the area. In rural constituencies
they were drawn mainly from primary school teachers and clerks.

The establishment of a competent and impartial electoral administration was particularly important in view of the introduction
of a new voting system, whereby the voter marked his ballot paper
and deposited it in a single box which was in full view of the presiding officer. The ballot paper itself contained the candidate's
name, his symbol or that of the political party under whose banner
he was standing, and the name of the candidate whom he was
backing for the presidency.[23] No parliamentary candidate could be
validly nominated unless he supported a presidential candidate.
This was because the constitution required the presidential and
parliamentary elections to be held simultaneously, with each voter

caution. There are doubts about the accuracy of the 1963 census, and the
system of registration in 1964 may have allowed for multiple registration.

22. The Electoral (National Assembly Elections) Regulations, 1968 (Statutory Instrument No. 316 of 1968), ss. 16(1), 46(1).

23. The symbols for the political parties were the hoe (UNIP) and the
lion (ANC). The three independent candidates adopted oxen, a cock and a
fish as their symbols.

receiving only one ballot paper on which his vote for a parliamentary candidate automatically counted towards the total vote of that presidential candidate who was supported by the parliamentary candidate.

Nomination day for presidential candidates was 16 November. Earlier in the month a UNIP national council meeting unanimously approved Dr Kaunda as the party's candidate. The ANC contestant was also its party leader, Mr Nkumbula, who, unlike Kaunda, was subsequently nominated as a parliamentary candidate as well. Each presidential candidate deposited κ400 and was required to have the signatures of at least 1,000 registered voters in support of his candidature. Parliamentary candidates needed only a proposer and a seconder resident in the constituency, and a deposit of κ50, recoverable if the candidate obtained more than 10 per cent of the vote; unlike voters, candidates had to be at least twenty-one years of age.

Nomination day for parliamentary candidates was held ten days later. A weakness in the system of electoral administration was revealed when ANC candidates attempted to lodge their nomination papers. UNIP local activists successfully prevented some opposition candidates from reaching the returning officers in the Northern, Luapula, Eastern and North-western Provinces. Similar but unsuccessful attempts were made in some Western Province seats (where the ruling party was by this time much weaker) and even on the Copperbelt. ANC candidates for constituencies in the Northern and Luapula Provinces attempted to travel through the Luapula Province to reach their constituencies. UNIP supporters, however, in the words of the court which subsequently ruled in favour of fifteen of ANC's twenty-two electoral petitions, 'intentionally impeded the progress into the Luapula province of the ANC men . . . and intimidated them . . .'.[24] The candidates were forced to return to the Copperbelt. Although the President gave them police protection and had them flown back to the provinces at the eleventh hour, they did not arrive in time to lodge their nomination papers. In Eastern Province several ANC candidates successfully evaded or broke through the UNIP road-blocks, which were manned twenty-four hours a day. Other candidates, however, were physically prevented from presenting their papers by threatening crowds of yellow-shirted UNIP activists gathered outside the very offices of the returning officers. As a result, thirty seats went to UNIP unopposed on nomination day, although (as we have noted) fifteen

24. 'Judgement of the High Court in the matter of ten consolidated election petitions on diverse days in April, May and June 1969' (mimeo.).

were subsequently invalidated by the High Court after ANC election petitions.[25] Since UNIP successfully nominated candidates in all 105 constituencies, while ANC was able to contest only seventy-three seats (with three independents contesting two more seats), UNIP went to the polls with the immense advantage of thirty uncontested seats.

Despite these distressing events, the PEO did an extremely thorough job in so far as lay within its powers. The blatant forms of rigging which have abounded in certain other African States did not take place. There was no gerrymandering of constituency boundaries; opposition areas did not receive fewer polling stations; there were extremely tight security precautions in the distribution of ballot papers; polling (surprisingly, in view of the violence of nomination day and the frequent violence of the campaign) took place peacefully; and the counting was fair. Nevertheless, not all the assumptions on which the PEO's successful operation depended were met. While the Electoral Commission was independent, the legitimacy of multi-party electoral competition was not universally accepted in the ruling party. Indeed, the rhetoric of the party often implied that the ANC had no right to exist. Thus UNIP's director of elections said early in the campaign, 'Their work [that of UNIP activists] will be aimed at wiping out the ANC,' while Mr Daniel Munkombwe, political assistant for the Southern Province, added more graphically that the opposition would be 'bulldozed and crushed'.[26] Such statements encouraged local UNIP activists to circumvent the intentions of an impartial electoral administration. This was particularly easy where ANC was almost totally lacking in popular support since the 440-yard rule (which forbade uniformed party workers to approach polling stations on election day) was not extended to nomination day; UNIP activists could therefore completely surround the returning officers. Secondly, the Elections Office had virtually no full-time civil servants directly under its control. While it depended on the civil servants who acted as its *ad hoc* agents and the police, it was not always successful in controlling the actions of these officers in areas where they were subject to considerable pressure from local UNIP supporters to

25. ANC challenged twenty-two of the thirty uncontested seats in the High Court and won fifteen of its petitions. In the event, it fought only three of the subsequent by-elections (all in the Chipata area of Eastern Province) and won only 7 per cent of the votes cast.

26. Cf. also the statement of Mr Wesley Nyirenda, Speaker of the National Assembly, who said that UNIP would reconsider the whole position of opposition parties after the election. *Times of Zambia*, 3 and 7 December 1968; *Zambia Mail*, 6 December 1968.

play a partisan role. Thirdly, local UNIP officials shared neither the values nor the assumptions on which the system of electoral administration rested.[27] Many of them disliked the idea of competition for office within a multi-party system, and did not view the ANC as a legitimate alternative government. On the contrary, some were openly committed to the notion that the election was an opportunity for the establishment of a one-pary State. 'Eastern Province will be a one-party province,' thundered one such official outside the Chipata returning offices on nomination day.

The electoral system's lack of legitimacy became even clearer after the general election. In 1969 the law was altered in various ways to make life more difficult for opposition parties: a National Assembly candidate now required seven, instead of two, nominators; a person who was restricted could no longer stand for election (which prevented a repetition of Mr Mundia's victory in Libonda while he was restricted in Northern Province); a restricted MP lost his seat after six months; and an Assembly candidate could no longer simultaneously be a candidate for the presidency, as Mr Nkumbula was in 1968. Moreover, the basic predilection of UNIP leaders at all levels for a one-party State also became obvious in the wake of their disappointment at ANC's electoral gains. There was an upsurge in demands for the statutory abolition of opposition parties. A wave of discriminatory action against ANC supporters was initiated by the President himself with the slogan 'It pays to belong to UNIP'. Measures included the closing of ANC shops[28] and the refusal of the new Speaker of the National Assembly to continue recognising the ANC as the official opposition.

Nevertheless, during the election some of UNIP's top leaders, particularly the President, took steps to ensure the independent and impartial operation of the electoral system. These steps were effective except in certain areas on nomination day itself. Dr Kaunda lent both material and moral support to the establishment and operation of a system which would ensure multi-party competition and choice at the polls. The Electoral Commission functioned independently of political influence and the new voting safeguards were accepted. Fifteen ANC candidates were flown in a Zambia Air Force plane to Northern and Luapula Provinces so that they could lodge their nomination papers;[29] ANC meetings were permit-

---

27. These assumptions were set out in the *Candidates' Guide* issued by the PEO. *Candidates' Guide* (Lusaka, 1968), p. 29.

28. This action was subsequently reversed on the ground that it was unconstitutional and under pressure from a deputation of the House of Chiefs.

29. ZIS press release No. 2068/68, 26 November 1968.

ted; and there were no instances of executive interference when the votes were counted. Indeed, the PEO designed an elaborate counting procedure which not only allowed each party to have its candidate and two polling agents present but also made rigging in the counting impossible without the collusion of at least three counting assistants. On a cynical view, it can be argued that the UNIP leadership was willing to have a fair election because it was confident that it would receive overwhelming support at the polls. But it was also concerned to demonstrate its own legitimacy. The winning of mass support might cause any group of army officers who contemplated a coup to think twice about overthrowing a genuinely popular government.

As for ANC's attitude towards the administration of the election, three stages can be distinguished. Initially, the party was suspicious of the powers granted to the Electoral Commission and the possibility of gerrymandering by the Delimitation Commission. Unlike UNIP Members, ANC parliamentarians showed concern over the methods of conducting the election but, again unlike their counterparts in the ruling party, were little troubled by the provincial distribution of seats. After April 1968 ANC fears were, to some extent, allayed by the actions of the President, the Electoral Commission and the PEO. In addition, ANC's perception of its growing strength led it to believe that it would win regardless of the method of election. After nomination day this belief was no longer tenable, and the ANC reverted to its original suspicious attitude towards the President and the Elections Office. When it became clear that the safety of ANC candidates could not be guaranteed, Nkumbula demanded the resignation of the Commissioner of Police.[30] In an act of desperation a few days before polling, he alleged that the ballot boxes had already been filled with forged papers.[31] Again, after the election and as a rationalisation of defeat, individual ANC candidates claimed that ballot box seals had been broken illegally. The party did lodge a few election petitions on the counting of the vote, but these were all rejected by the High Court.

Neither party, then, regarded the electoral mechanism as fully legitimate. The electoral administration was a borrowed institution, run by expatriates and too new to have gained wide acceptance from party workers. For tactical reasons, however, it was important to both sides to subscribe, at varying times, to the ideal of an election run on multi-party lines. The legal arrangements benefited the ANC, and the party was willing to extract whatever protection the

30. *Times of Zambia*, 26 November 1968.
31. ZIS press release No. 2159/68, 16 December 1968.

law afforded its candidates. For UNIP's leaders the election could serve as part of a long-term plan to institutionalise its rule and to show that it enjoyed mass support. It was these factors which, despite the events in certain areas on nomination day, enabled the system to work successfully and allowed a relatively fair election to be held.

## The recruitment of candidates

Before looking at the course and pattern of the short, three-week campaign after nomination day, we examine the contrasting ways in which the two parties selected their candidates. This reveals a great deal about the nature of the parties and also had some effect on the composition of the executive after the election, as well as on the operations of the National Assembly.

Procedures for the selection of parliamentary candidates differed markedly between the two political parties. According to the 1967 UNIP constitution (since replaced), parliamentary candidates were to be selected by the central committee and approved by the party president.[32] Probably because of the intense factionalism within the committee, the procedure was in practice reversed. The power of selection was delegated to the President at a meeting of the national council in November 1968, and his choice was merely approved by the central committee. While the final choice did not have to be submitted to the party's national council, party officials (including existing MPs) in several of the eight provinces drew up lists of people whom they considered to be suitable candidates and sent them to the President. This procedure illustrated the intricate combination that has long characterised UNIP between provincial power groups which wield great influence in party deliberations and the formally all-powerful and impartial personal leader, Dr Kaunda. In addition, in this case many individual aspirants applied to the President personally to be nominated as candidates,[33] and some were interviewed by senior party officials in Lusaka. One MP later estimated that there had been as many as 800 applicants, although very few were nominated and then only in hopeless seats.

President Kaunda did not announce the names of the UNIP candidates until 23 November, three days before nomination day. The party leadership was concerned that independent candidates from within the party ranks might stand; they would name Kaunda as their presidential choice, but would cut into the votes of the

32. UNIP constitution (1967), clause XXII.
33. *Times of Zambia*, 25 November 1968.

official UNIP candidates. Throughout October and November the leadership, under Dr Kaunda, used repeated threats to discourage such candidates.[34] The late announcement of the party slate was designed as an additional measure to check individuals who had not won the party nomination but who, given time, might have been tempted to run as independents; among them were nine of UNIP's sitting MPs who were not renominated. This combination of methods was successful and only one rebel candidate stood against an official party candidate.

The ANC constitution did not specify any procedure for the selection of parliamentary candidates, and in compiling the party's slate for the election a variety of methods was used. First, the nine sitting MPs were all chosen to run again.[35] Secondly, the UP—most of whose members had joined the ANC after its proscription in August 1968—put up candidates under the ANC banner in eight of the eleven Barotse seats and in several constituencies in the North-western, Copperbelt and Central Provinces. There were about twenty of these candidates: at least in Western Province, they were all selected by the former UP officials, and ANC headquarters in Lusaka played no role in their choice. Thirdly, two white independents, former members of the National Progress Party (originally called the United Federal Party) and independents in the previous Parliament, contested the election with ANC support. This support was given on direct instructions from the ANC leader, who provided Mr Hugh Mitchley with a safe party seat (Gwembe North in the Southern Province) and toured the constituency with him during the campaign. The fourth method, which applied to all new ANC candidates, was the most complex and took place over a period of some months. Initially applicants, of whom there were more than 1,000, wrote to the party's headquarters expressing their willingness to stand as candidates. Most gave some biographical information and their reasons for supporting the party.[36] If this information met the standards of a committee composed of the party's national office-bearers the prospective candidate was short-listed and interviewed. The main criteria appeared to be educational achievement and length of party membership. However, in

34. *Ibid.*, 11 November 1968; and ZIS press releases Nos 1826/68, 13 October 1968, 2000/68, 10 November 1968, and 2007/68, 13 November 1968.

35. One ANC member, Mr E. M. Liso, was not a sitting MP in November 1968, but the courts later decided that he had held the seat for Namwala at that time. There were four vacant seats when the National Assembly was dissolved.

36. ANC files.

*Table 5.3*
New UNIP candidates: occupational background[a]

|  | *No. of candidates* | *No. of elected candidates* |
|---|---|---|
| (a) *Candidates holding party office* [b] |  |  |
| Assistants to Ministers of State, political assistants, former regional secretaries | 17 | 12 |
| Current regional secretaries | 9 | 7 |
| Constituency officials [b] | 2 | 1 |
| Other (regional trustees, regional women's secretaries) | 5 | 4 |
| *Total* | 33 | 24 |
| (b) *Candidates holding no formal party office* |  |  |
| Civil servants and diplomats | 8 | 6 |
| Teachers/lecturers | 4 | 2 |
| Journalists | 1 | 1 |
| Lawyers | 1 | 1 |
| Trade unionists | 1 | 1 |
| Ministers of religion | 1 | — |
| *Total* | 16 | 11 |
| (c) *Information not available* | 3 | 2 |
| *Total* | 52 [c] | 37 |

*Notes*

a This table excludes sitting UNIP MPs who stood for re-election. Data are drawn from K. Mlenga (ed.), *Who's Who in Zambia* (Lusaka, 1965), National Assembly records, Zambia Information Service press releases, and interviews with candidates. In most cases the criterion is the full-time, paid party office (subject to the exception in note *b*) held by the candidate at the time of his election. For those who did not hold party office, primary occupation is used.

b These officials differed from one another in status and source of income. The most senior, Assistants to the Minister of State (originally called Special Presidential Public Relations Assistants) and political assistants, were paid out of public funds, although they were not civil servants and were usually promoted regional secretaries. The regional secretaries were also full-time office-holders but were

some areas where the party's support was limited it had little choice but to adopt any candidates who put themselves forward.

The expansion in the number of parliamentary seats made possible a change in patterns of recruitment to the National Assembly and therefore in the concerns and attitudes of MPs, with Parliament emerging perhaps as a different kind of institution. The 105 seats were contested by sixty-two sitting MPs—fifty-one UNIP,[37] nine ANC and two independents. Because in two constituencies there were contests between sitting Members, at least forty-five seats had to be filled by candidates who had not been members of the Assembly in November 1968. Yet despite this opportunity to provide a broader representation of social groups than in the past, both parties continued to rely on virtually the same sources from which to draw their candidates.

As in 1964, UNIP recruited primarily from its full-time, local-level party workers (see table 5.3). Thirty-three of its fifty-two new candidates had held party office at the sub-national level. Of the total 105 UNIP candidates, fifty-one had at some earlier stage in their careers served in local party posts, and a further sixteen had been national organisers. Only twenty-seven candidates had no formal experience in the organisation.[38] Of those who had not held party office, civil servants and diplomats were by far the next largest group of candidates; but many of them and the sprinkling of candidates from other occupational groups had long-standing, if informal, connections with the ruling party. Clearly, loyalty and service to the party were the dominant criteria in the selection of UNIP's candidates.

Another important dimension of UNIP's selection process was

37. This includes MPs nominated by the President. Four of the five nominated MPs ran as UNIP candidates, and the other was subsequently renominated to the new Parliament.
38. No information was available for eleven candidates.

---

*Table 5.3—Notes—cont.*

paid out of party funds. Regional trustees and constituency officials were part-time, unpaid party office-bearers.

c There were in fact fifty-four UNIP candidates who were not members of the National Assembly in November 1968; but two of these had been elected to the Assembly in 1964 and had subsequently resigned. They are not, therefore, included in this table. Five candidates, included in the table, had unsuccessfully contested seats in the 1964 election.

the party's decision as to where its candidates should stand. President Kaunda had announced before the election that, in order to foster national unity and to remind party followers that their first loyalty ought to be to the party and not to particular leaders from particular areas, UNIP candidates would stand largely outside their provinces of origin. In fact, as already noted, local-level UNIP activists played a considerable part in suggesting the names of acceptable candidates to the President and in pressuring him over

*Table 5.4*
UNIP candidates by province of birth and provincial location of constituency contested

| Province | Candidates standing in province of birth | | Candidates standing outside province of birth | | Total No. of candidates by province | |
|---|---|---|---|---|---|---|
| | Total con-testants | Success-ful con-testants | Total con-testants | Success-ful con-testants | Total con-testants | Success-ful con-testants |
| Western | 10 | 2 | 2 | 2 | 12 | 4 |
| Central | 12 | 10 | – | – | 12 | 10 |
| Eastern | 12 | 12 | 4 | 4 | 16 | 16 |
| Luapula | 8 | 8 | 1 | 1 | 9 | 9 |
| Northern | 13 | 13 | 9 | 9 | 22 | 22 |
| North-western | 6 | 6 | 3 | 3 | 9 | 9 |
| Southern | 13 | – | 3 | 3 | 16 | 3 |
| Copperbelt | 5 | 5 | 1 | 1 | 6 | 6 |
| *Total* | 79 | 56 | 23 | 23 | 102[a] | 79 |

*Note*

[a] Information not available on two UNIP candidates. One other candidate was born outside Zambia.

the number of candidates from each province. Moreover they successfully persuaded him that it would be politically unrealistic to run candidates outside their province of origin (see table 5.4). In the event, only twenty-three UNIP candidates stood outside their 'home' province, and most of these contested urban seats with ethnically heterogeneous populations. Indeed, in those rural areas where UNIP was relatively weak, such as Southern, Western and even North-western Provinces, all but two of its candidates were local men; and even in strong UNIP rural areas like Northern,

Luapula and Eastern Provinces only one or two seats were contested (and won) by UNIP candidates from outside their provinces of origin. This reversal of the President's intentions indicates that one major limitation on his power stems from the lack of a sense of national identification within UNIP; first manifested in the tensions surrounding the construction of the first all-UNIP Cabinet in 1964, it became obvious at the time of the party's 1967 central committee elections and the National Assembly debates on the Delimitation Commission's report, and has been a notable feature since the 1968 general election.

*Table 5.5*
ANC candidates by occupation[a]

|  | No. of candidates | No. of elected candidates |
|---|---|---|
| Professional politicians[b] | 19 | 9 |
| Traders[c] | 9 | 5 |
| Teachers | 7 | 3 |
| Farmers[c] | 5 | 3 |
| Civil servants | 4 | 1 |
| Mine employees | 4 | – |
| Railway employees | 2 | 1 |
| Clerks | 2 | – |
| Other company employees | 4 | 1 |
| Information not available | 17 | – |
| Total | 73 | 23 |

*Notes*

a The candidates' occupations were those they held immediately before their selection by the party.

b This includes the nine ANC MPs at the time of dissolution, one former MP and nine full-time party workers.

c Some candidates were both farmers and traders.

*Source.* As table 5.3.

The diverse ways in which ANC candidates were selected resulted in different limitations on its choice in different areas. In Northern and Luapula Provinces, in particular, the party leadership had little option because of the party's minuscule support (see table 5.8) and the consequent scarcity of would-be candidates. Another restriction was the possibility of job discrimination after the election, a factor which may well have discouraged aspirants for the ANC nomination and compelled the party leadership to rely heavily, as in 1964, on self-employed persons and professional politicians (see table 5.5). Thus in Barotse several of the ANC candidates were relatively well-to-do traders, and this gave them a financial and hence organisational edge over many ANC candidates elsewhere. In Eastern Province many of the party's candidates were headquarters officials of the party who, though often born in the constituency where they were standing, had been away

Table 5.6
Parliamentary candidates by age[a]

|  | UNIP | | ANC | |
| Age | No. of candidates | No. of elected candidates | No. of candidates | No. of elected candidates |
|---|---|---|---|---|
| Under 30 | 6 | 5 | 10 | 3 |
| 30–35 | 13 | 9 | 12 | 1 |
| 36–40 | 35 | 23 | 12 | 3 |
| 41–45 | 21 | 20 | 15 | 6 |
| 46–50 | 14 | 12 | 8 | 4 |
| Over 50 | 3 | 2 | 3 | 3 |
| Not available | 13 | 10 | 13 | 3 |
| Total | 105 | 81 | 73 | 23 |

Note

a  As of 19 December 1968.

Source. As table 5.3. The three independent candidates are excluded.

from the province for some time. Nevertheless, a few ANC candidates did come from the civil service, the teaching profession and the mining companies. But, as with UNIP, party loyalty was in all cases the yardstick of recruitment and the one which the selection process was mainly designed to test.

The social background of both parties' candidates did not differ markedly from 1964.[39] In terms of age, however, candidates—in view of the large number of MPs standing for re-election—were older, on average, than in the previous election. Over half

39. Mulford, 'Some observations on the 1964 elections,' op. cit.; and chapter 6.

UNIP's candidates were between the ages of thirty-six and forty-five and few were over the age of fifty or under thirty (see table 5.6). Of the nineteen UNIP candidates under thirty-five, fourteen had served as party officials and, of these, twelve were elected. In contrast, only two of those under thirty-five who had not served as party officials were elected. Service in the party organisation thus emerges as the most effective avenue of recruitment for young, aspiring national-level politicians.

As for ANC, a significantly higher proportion of its candidates were younger men, but they stood far less chance of success than

*Table 5.7*
UNIP candidates by education

| Educational level[a] | No. of candidates | No. of elected candidates |
| --- | --- | --- |
| Primary schooling only | 29 | 25 |
| Some secondary schooling | 38 | 31 |
| Full secondary schooling | 5 | 3 |
| Some university | 5 | 5 |
| University degree (or equivalent) | 15 | 9 |
| Information not available | 13 | 8 |
| *Total* | 105 | 81 |

*Note*

a These are academic educational attainments. Many party officials have some additional training, usually in the field of artisan skills.

*Source.* As table 5.3.

their older colleagues. Over 50 per cent of ANC's successful candidates were over the age of forty. As with UNIP, the chance of electoral success tended to increase with the age of the candidate. This reflects the number of established politicians who were re-nominated in safe seats, and cannot be interpreted as evidence of the intrinsic voter appeal of older candidates.

The educational attainments of candidates in the 1968 elections were similar to those of their predecessors in 1964. UNIP ran twenty candidates who had either obtained a university degree or who had attended university (see table 5.7). A direct correlation existed, however, between lack of formal education and those who had held local-level party office. The vast majority of UNIP candidates who

had been party officials had less than full secondary education.
Moreover the minority of more educated candidates did not fare
so well electorally, although this is largely accounted for by the
unexpected defeat of several university-educated leaders in the
hitherto safe UNIP seats in Western Province. ANC candidates
tended to have less education than UNIP. Only three had university
degrees, and two of these were defeated. Six other successful ANC
candidates had completed secondary education, but the majority
(sixteen) had not. The result was a National Assembly dominated by
members with little formal education but who had demonstrated
their party loyalty.

Several significant consequences for Zambia's political system
stand out from the candidate selection process. In the first place, the
similar backgrounds of elected members, compared to the 1964
elections, made likely the continuance during the second Parliament
of existing institutional patterns established during the life of the
first Parliament[40]—in particular, a rigid acceptance of party discipline by UNIP Members; a reluctance by UNIP back-benchers
to participate in debate; and an inability on the part of ANC to
mount very skilful and prolonged opposition or to put forward a
wide-ranging and coherent set of policy alternatives. Thus the
new National Assembly was not likely to experience much livelier
debates or to become a forum for controlling the executive and
modifying its policy proposals. This likelihood was reinforced by the
almost immediate absorption into the executive of every UNIP
Member with a university education. Moreover the President's
appointment as Ministers of four well educated civil servants (whom
he first nominated to the Assembly) strengthened an executive that
was already dominant. While these appointments highlighted the
considerable stress placed by Dr Kaunda on educational qualifications for ministerial office, it also reduced the number of well
informed, articulate back-benchers, who alone could begin to change
the Assembly's existing rubber-stamp image. Though in 1969 there
were over forty UNIP back-benchers, they tended to be the less
educated MPs, and only half of them were even prepared to put
parliamentary questions. Furthermore, their numbers declined
steadily throughout the second Parliament.

Secondly, since only fourteen candidates with a university training were elected (together with three others who had completed
secondary schooling), President Kaunda has not been able during
the second Parliament to choose either a Cabinet or Ministers of

40. This did happen, by and large. See chapter 6.

State with as high an average level of formal education as before. Moreover, not even the President's appointment to office of educated nominated MPs could make much difference to a body of Ministers which by 1972 was over fifty strong.

Thirdly, the recruitment process confirmed the mounting importance of the ruling party's bureaucracy, and in particular of its full-time local-level officials. In the 1962 elections not one of UNIP's loyal organisers below the headquarters level had been selected as a candidate.[41] Yet in the 1964 and 1968 elections the party recruited primarily from this source. It did so for a variety of reasons. The party regards the parliamentary constituency as party property rather than as the domain of the MP representing it in the Assembly, and the interests of constituents are usually handled by the full-time party officials in the area. MPs do not visit their constituencies frequently and, where they have not emerged through the local organisation, may have little or no personal political base. Furthermore, President Kaunda's attempts since 1964 to give his party an economic mobilisation role and a political control function over the civil service at field level meant that UNIP, unlike many ruling parties in Africa, did not neglect its own organisation. The national leadership also, of course, required the full co-operation of party officials to communicate the party's message to the voters and to ensure a high turn-out at the polls in the frequent elections which punctuated Zambia's multi-party political history between 1962 and 1972. The solidarity of the party and the efficient functioning of its machinery clearly depended on contented local officials. Their promotion to the much more highly paid rank of MP, with the consequent additional possibility of acquiring ministerial office, is one major way in which UNIP's national leadership has kept alive the active loyalty and enthusiasm of the party's field-level organisers.

One deleterious result of UNIP's heavy reliance on its own cadres as parliamentary candidates has been a reinforcing of certain reactionary tendencies in the party and legislature. Not only is the new intelligentsia excluded, but so are other people who, though less educated, are also not professional politicians and may therefore be less inclined both to toe the party line and make sectional appeals. Non-professional politicians in the National Assembly might also have been less prone than the present parliamentary wing of the party to consent to legislation which has increasingly circumscribed political competition and popular control. The main instances of this tendency during the second Parliament were the amendment to

41. Mulford, *Zambia: the Politics of Independence, op. cit.,* p. 323.

the constitution in mid-1969 to eliminate the people from participating through referenda in the process of constitutional amendment, and the rejection by the Cabinet and UNIP central committee in 1972 of the proposals of the 'one-party participatory
democracy' commission to ensure almost unfettered competition
for office.

Another harmful effect has been a less than fully representative legislature, thereby reducing its effectiveness as a major
forum for the articulation of interests. The party has remained a
relatively closed system and has not found it easy to recruit new personnel from the growing number of younger and more educated
Zambians. Important occupational groups are also surprisingly
under-represented. No small-scale farmers, who comprise the bulk
of the country's population, exist in the ranks of UNIP Members
of the second Parliament. The nearest that agricultural interests
come to representation in the National Assembly is through some
UNIP Ministers and lesser leaders who have bought large farms
along the line of rail; but they are not formally representative of
organised farmer interests. Similarly, although some UNIP Members held directorships, organised business interests were not represented among the new UNIP candidates or established politicians.
Indeed, a few businessmen who had won UNIP seats in earlier by-
elections were not renominated in 1968. This was only partially
compensated for by the fact that ANC had a number of small
businessmen among its elected candidates. Trade union leaders,
whom one might expect to be the main articulators of workers'
interests in a country as heavily urbanised (some 28 per cent) as
Zambia, are also surprisingly under-represented in the Assembly.
It is true that many established UNIP leaders had been associated
with the unions before independence, but they either were, or had
become, first and foremost party men. Only one current trade
union official was selected by UNIP to stand in 1968. Women, too,
are remarkably under-represented in the Assembly, partly because
all UNIP regional secretaries are men, as were political assistants
and Assistants to the Ministers of State. At the start of the second
Assembly only two UNIP Members, one of whom was nominated
rather than elected, were women, and neither of them was elevated
to ministerial rank. Zambia has never had a female Cabinet Minister
or District Governor, although one woman MP in the first Assembly
was for a time a Minister of State. As for the opposition, no ANC
Member is a woman. Given this pattern of recruitment and the consequent under-representation of important segments of society,
interest groups continue to by-pass the Assembly in favour of direct

relations with the executive. The absence of constituency and interest-group pressures on MPs also makes it easier for them to accept without modification or opposition all legislative and budgetary requests of the executive; it inclines them, too, to refrain from any initiatives of their own.

The last important dimension of the process of candidate selection was its effect on the quality of the opposition. ANC's final list of candidates was very similar, in terms of occupational and educational background, to that of the previous election. Its elected members, with the important exception of the bloc of eight Lozi (ex-UP) MPs, did not, therefore, offer much promise of significantly more effective opposition to the government. The *de facto* merger with UP in mid-1968, which brought a greater militancy to the party in the field, provided ANC with a number of more articulate members, in particular Mr Mundia and two or three of his lieutenants, who proved to be vocal defenders of their province's interests and were also often outspoken on national issues. For the rest, the party failed to attract well educated opponents of UNIP and had few, if any, candidates from the higher civil service and trade unions.

*The campaign*

The disparity in resources available to UNIP and ANC for their respective campaigns was enormous. UNIP had massive organisational and material advantages. Its local structures were well organised and enthusiastic; it had access to considerable sums of money, and it received maximum publicity from the government-controlled mass media. By contrast, the scale of the ANC campaign was minuscule. It was badly organised, almost without funds, lacked adequate transport[42] and received no favourable publicity from the mass media. Operating under these restrictions and harassed by local UNIP officials, especially in Eastern and North-western Provinces, the party never really succeeded in contacting large numbers of the electorate outside its areas of strength.

In all but the Southern and Western Provinces the basis of the UNIP campaign was its strong, hierarchically organised local party. UNIP's director of elections tried to improve on this structure for the specific purpose of the election. A lengthy and remarkably unrealistic handbook entitled *General Elections Victory* was issued in

42. ANC's transport rarely exceeded three privately owned Land-Rovers in Western Province and one in Eastern Province, and the cars of its nine MPs. Most candidates had to cycle or walk on their rounds.

large numbers to party workers.[43] Written only in English and distributed a mere few weeks before election day, it required the grafting of additional electoral committees on to UNIP's structure at various levels and contained complicated bureaucratic procedures to regulate canvassing. The handbook was more a testimony to the director's organisational aspirations than a practical guide to UNIP party workers in their campaigning. Nevertheless, the intention, more or less met in different parts of the country, was for each parliamentary constituency to establish an election committee. Subcommittees were to be set up in every chief's area and in every UNIP branch, village and section. Detailed instructions were issued to these committees and to canvassers. They were to observe, *inter alia*, the requirements of the electoral law; they were informed of the best ways to display party propaganda and instructed in methods of canvassing. In the Southern Province, for example, UNIP tried to compensate for its lack of popular support by ordering its organisers to make a special effort to approach chiefs and headmen. Since chiefs are appointed and paid by the government and since the government had in a few cases dismissed chiefs who were pro-ANC, it was hoped that they would back UNIP and influence their village followers to do likewise.

The formal campaign lasted only three weeks and there was too little time for UNIP's new election committees to become operational. Moreover, it was unpractical to expect the performance of tasks by village committees where, as in the Southern and Western Provinces, the party organisation itself did not stretch to that level or had ceased to function. Thus in many areas the committees were not set up, and, even where they were established, reliance was placed primarily on the existing organisation. Nevertheless, the very strength of this organisation gave UNIP an inestimable advantage over its more poorly organised competitor.

UNIP's superior organisational capacity produced clear electoral dividends. In the first place, the party benefited from its considerable efforts to supplement the campaign of the PEO to teach voters the necessary skills involved in the new balloting procedure. As table 5.8 indicates, the percentage of spoilt papers in the strongly UNIP provinces was significantly and consistently much lower than in the three provinces with ANC strength. ANC's lesser ability to reach voters and teach them how to cast their ballots did reduce somewhat the number of valid votes cast for its presidential candidate, Mr Nkumbula. Secondly, UNIP's presidential candidate, Dr Kaunda, was also helped by his party's superior capacity to

43. 'General elections victory' (Lusaka, 1968).

achieve a high turn-out on election day (see table 5.8). In strongly UNIP provinces the percentage poll was appreciably higher than in Southern and (especially) Western Provinces, which largely supported ANC.

But the most important benefit to UNIP of its superior organisation was the impact on ANC's campaign. Harassment of ANC officials and of Nkumbula himself effectively restricted the party's sphere of operations to the Southern, Western and parts of Central Provinces, the Mufulira District on the Copperbelt and the Mwinilunga District in North-western Province. In Eastern Province, for example, ANC candidates arrived from Lusaka just before nomination day with high hopes of waging an effective and successful campaign on foot and by bicycle. But within a few days it became clear that they could not travel freely through their constituencies and, as a result, most of them spent the campaign living fearfully in two tiny township houses in Chipata and Katete. This kind of pattern resulted in ANC reaching almost no voters in areas where the party was weak and accounts for the significant drop in ANC support in (for example) Eastern and North-western Provinces, where the swing to UNIP was 11 and 16 per cent respectively.

Violence was a persistent feature throughout the election campaign. Physical intimidation of opponents has long been a feature of Zambia's political history. It dates back particularly to the late 1950s, when a vicious struggle developed between ANC and the newly formed UNIP. It reached a climax in the early 1960s and was continued in the card-checking campaigns which UNIP conducted on frequent occasions in the early years after independence. In the 1968 election violence again came to the fore. It started sporadically during the registration of voters when UNIP in some areas threatened 'to discipline on the spot' anyone who did not register.[44] As we have seen, it became more widespread on nomination day and continued during the subsequent campaign.[45] Indicative of its scale was the jump in the number of reported cases of riot, sedition and unlawful assembly from twenty-five in 1965 (a non-election year) to 100 in 1968. Several people were injured and a few died. The most serious violence, not UNIP-initiated, erupted in

44. ZIS press release No. 1091/68, 19 June 1968.
45. Symptomatic of the attitude of some UNIP officials to the use of politically directed violence was a cartoon issued by the Lusaka regional office depicting a man mutilating a lion (the ANC symbol) with a hoe (the UNIP symbol) and the lion bleeding profusely. For evidence of the frequent eruption of inter-party clashes and UNIP-inspired intimidation, see (*inter alia*) *Times of Zambia*, 12 September and 11 November 1968, and *Zambia Mail*, 3 and 10 December 1968.

Mwinilunga District in North-western Province when an armed group invaded from Angola and set fire to a number of villages. Although UNIP sought to capitalise on this by blaming ANC, the incident had deep historical roots and these, together with Portuguese instigation, rather than ANC, must be held responsible.[46] Finally, a wave of violence swept parts of the country after the results were announced. Particularly in Eastern Province, UNIP took punitive measures against ANC candidates and officials; these measures included assault, the destruction of homes, and the forcible removal of the candidates and officials by lorry to their home villages.

Poor communications existed throughout the campaign between Lusaka and the local ANC organisation. The latter had to manage as best it could in the absence of detailed instructions from the party leader, and finance and campaign material from party headquarters. Former UP officials tried to inject enthusiasm and a degree of local initiative into the ANC campaign, but, outside Western Province, they were usually faced with an apathetic or non-existent ANC organisation. The weakness of that organisation was dramatically reflected in the utterly unrealistic forecasts of support which it made in many constituencies.

ANC suffered from yet other difficulties. Not only was Mr Nkumbula ejected from the house which he occupied officially as Leader of the Opposition but the government also launched a series of prosecutions against him and other opposition leaders in 1968. Although a conviction was obtained in only one of these cases, the prosecutions took their toll in terms of time, anxiety and finance.

As compared with ANC, the financial position of UNIP was healthy. The UNIP treasurer, Mr Mudenda, budgeted for election expenses of K250,000. Apart from the party's normal sources of finance, election funds were raised by the party regions, by elitist fund-raising dinners at which President Kaunda was the guest of honour,[47] as well as by more plebeian party dances, and more or less forced requisitions from Asian businessmen. The latter source alone raised some K15,000 in the Southern Province and K60,000 on the Copperbelt.[48] The money was spent mainly on transport and publicity. Each of the forty-seven party regions was provided with at least one new Land-Rover and ten bicycles; the lake and swamp parts of the country were even supplied with six motorboats.

46. No criminal charges were laid against ANC members, and it is difficult to see what benefits the rampage could have brought ANC.

47. A double ticket cost K25.

48. *Times of Zambia*, 12 December 1968.

Yellow 'UNIP Election Worker' shirts were distributed to thousands of supporters and 300,000 election posters (in six standard formats)[49] were displayed throughout the country. Vast quantities of additional material were printed and distributed, including two lavish government publications, *Zambia's National Development Plan at Work*[50] and *Zambia: a Picture Progress Report on the First Four Years of Zambia's Independence*,[51] which outlined the government's achievements since October 1964. State funds to assist UNIP in its campaign were used in other ways. The State paid the salaries of over forty political assistants and Assistants to the Provincial Ministers of State, and UNIP used government vehicles for its campaign in certain constituencies. Moreover, while the PEO remained neutral between the two parties, the same did not always apply to other government agencies. The police issued far fewer permits for public meetings to ANC than to UNIP, and in any case, government Ministers did not require police permission to hold meetings. The Credit Organisation of Zambia employed many former party workers. Some of these employees, at least in Southern and Eastern Provinces, virtually turned their offices into supplementary UNIP campaign centres. As one COZ official stated, 'The COZ office is the UNIP office in Gwembe.' The mass media were also clearly biased against ANC. Radio and television gave almost no exposure to the views of the opposition; Mr Nkumbula made only one TV appearance and he was seldom mentioned on radio broadcasts except in derogatory references by UNIP leaders. In a survey of Radio Zambia, in which newscasts between 14 and 29 November were monitored, there were twenty-one references to UNIP and only two to the opposition. The two daily newspapers, one of which was government-owned and the other also favourably disposed towards the ruling party, gave more coverage than the radio to statements by the ANC leader but they too concentrated heavily on UNIP campaign material. In adition, UNIP bought vast quantities of advertising space which it filled with slogans such as 'Vote national, vote UNIP' and 'Polling day is UNIP day'.

ANC could not afford to match UNIP's expenditure, let alone compensate for the advantages to the ruling party of its use of the State machinery. After the election Mr Nkumbula noted that when the date for the election was set the party 'had not even a penny'.[52] He found it impossible to persuade businessmen to make contributions to the party on any scale. Candidates were required to find

49. *Ibid.*, 5 November 1968.
50. Lusaka, 1968.        51. Lusaka, 1968.
52. Minutes of the ANC post-election conference, *op. cit.*, p. 6.

most of the money for their own campaigns; indeed, the party could not always even raise the deposits for its candidates. One ANC candidate, for example, tried to claim from the party his 'candidature fees and the money he spent on transport (K986)' but the claim was disallowed on the grounds that the party had asked candidates to raise money themselves for election purposes.[53] Another consequence of ANC's desperate shortage of funds was that it was unable to reply to UNIP's extensive newspaper advertisements. It was only able to publish a few posters on the Copperbelt (which were rarely displayed for any length of time) and a certain number of duplicated hand-outs in Barotse. Even the quality of these was variable. One ANC leaflet proclaimed rather cryptically, 'African National Congress is our SALVATION. LION is a proverb of LIFE.'

Both parties held mass rallies and indoor meetings, although ANC's were very modest. UNIP, in addition, conducted a door-to-door campaign in the towns. Its rallies were attended by large crowds, and the candidate was almost always accompanied by government Ministers and leading party officials. They were lively affairs with over-long speeches prefaced by music and songs, and punctuated with the shouting of slogans: 'One Zambia, one nation; one leader, Kaunda'; 'UNIP—power, power, power'; and 'Kaunda, Kaunda'.

With thirty unopposed constituencies, UNIP could divert many of its leaders and local-level organisers to help in contested areas, though the inundation of the sensitive Southern and Western Provinces with mainly Bemba-speaking UNIP MPs may well have been counter-productive. UNIP certainly experienced great difficulty in penetrating the rural areas of the Southern Province, where (in the words of one perceptive District Secretary) 'ANC is a family thing.' President Kaunda played little part in the actual campaign, although shortly before polling day he spoke in Mwinilunga and Mankoya constituencies, which the party viewed as marginal. ANC meetings were generally poorly attended even in its Southern Province stronghold. Both parties supplemented the intensive attempts made by the PEO through Zambia Information Services to explain the new voting system to the electorate. In Chingola, on the Copperbelt, UNIP even held a mock election to ensure that the procedure had been understood.

Both parties made their appeal to the electorate on two distinct levels. The first and more dignified level concerned their actual policies. UNIP stood proudly on its considerable accomplishments

53. *Ibid.*

as a government. 'Nothing we promised the people has failed to materialise. We have developed the country,' said one Cabinet Minister.[54] 'Peace, progress and stability,' said the advertisements. Under the party's rule Zambia had experienced 'unprecedented expansion in all fields' and there had been a transformation 'not only [of] Zambia's landscape but even more important of the outlook of its citizens'.[55] In a wide-ranging speech to the UNIP national council in November the President outlined the four major achievements of the party.[56] These were the attainment of independence in 1964, the acceptance of the co-operative approach to economic development, the philosophy of Humanism, and the economic reforms of April 1968, all of which were seen as stages in the revolution achieved by UNIP. The party claimed that it had realised the goals contained in its 1964 election manifesto. Two documents distributed by the party—*A Promise Fulfilled* and *Economic Revolution in Zambia*[57]—described the advances made in the provision of social services, the development of the economy, and government participation in industry. Neither document made very specific commitments for the future, although it was stated that 'whatever benefits we reap from the action we are taking today should be used to develop our rural areas'.[58] This theme was developed by the President at the November national council meeting and became the leading commitment in theory of the second National Development Plan (1972–76). In the next decade the major emphasis was to be placed on rural development. Attempts would be made to raise average income in the rural areas to that of the line of rail, service centres were to be established to encourage people to stay in the countryside, and rural electrification was to be introduced.[59] To achieve these goals the civil service was to be decentralised. Cabinet Ministers were to be appointed to supervise development in each of Zambia's eight provinces. In each district a Governor would control the operations of both the party and the civil service and would co-ordinate their efforts. These reforms were introduced in January 1969 and have been subsequently continued and extended.

The party's industrial policy was unchanged. A new UNIP government would continue its efforts to diversify the economy in order to reduce reliance on the copper mines and to save foreign

54. ZIS press release No. 2132/68.
55. 'A promise fulfilled', *op. cit.*, p. 33.
56. Kaunda, *Zambia's Guidelines for the next Decade*, *op. cit.*
57. 'A promise fulfilled', *op. cit.*, and *Economic Revolution in Zambia* (Lusaka, 1968).
58. 'A promise fulfilled', *op. cit.*, p. 13.
59. *Zambia's Guidelines for the next Decade*, *op. cit.*, pp. 31–3.

exchange. The party's role in Zambianising major sectors of the economy and in raising the standard of living was stressed. Most of the references to foreign policy came in attacks on ANC's more compliant attitude towards relations with the white minority regimes to the south. UNIP would continue its opposition to those regimes; it would reduce further its trade reliance on them and give increased support for the liberation movements.

Overall, UNIP made no radical departures from the tenets on which it had fought the 1964 election. It did, however, indulge in a number of short-term, pork-barrel tactics, of which the most important was the temporary suspension of the collection of personal levy throughout the country before the election; this benefited several hundred thousand voters. Some UNIP Ministers and the President himself were sensitive to certain grievances in the country and promises were made that the cost of living would be lowered, that there would be more jobs, and that the slum areas would be helped. But no concrete proposals for the solution of these problems were offered. UNIP's policies, apart from the administrative reforms, were to be implemented only gradually in the course of the next decade.

The President's address to the national council provided a convenient platform for UNIP candidates to present a national appeal. This was especially useful since they did not feel free to make narrow electoral appeals on the basis of what they could do for the voter in their particular constituencies. The President's address enabled candidates to give a future-oriented message to the electorate without making local promises which might contradict the wider aims of the party. UNIP's national character was stressed both by the candidates and in the party's publicity; one UNIP poster, for example, read 'Vote national, vote UNIP'. This was contrasted with the ANC, which was portrayed by UNIP as sectional, moribund and without effective leadership. The implication of much of UNIP's campaign was that there simply was no credible alternative to a UNIP government under President Kaunda. This stress on the necessity of retaining Kaunda as the supreme leader of the country was embodied in the slogan 'Keep going with K.K.'

On the formal level, ANC's campaign did not convey effective policy alternatives to the voters; nor was there evidence that ANC supporters either understood clearly or were influenced much by the party's policy disagreements with UNIP. The candidates' speeches and the handful of policy pronouncements by Mr Nkumbula presented the party as a more moderate alternative to UNIP. Mr Nkumbula wanted closer trading links with the white minority-ruled south. He severely criticised the government's methods of development, particularly the economic reforms of April 1968. UNIP was slated for its wastage of public money, the Auditor General's report serving as a major source of ammunition. UNIP's use of intimidation, its advocacy of the one-party State, and alleged discrimination in the allocation of government jobs and loans, were all condemned by ANC. However, it is difficult to assess the effectiveness of the party's message Its manifesto was never produced and, although some ANC candidates did try to put out their own election manifestoes, these were supposed to require the approval of the party leader. In some cases they had been neither approved nor duplicated the week before the election. As with UNIP, local issues did not feature prominently in ANC candidates' speeches, although these tended to contain more conventional vote-catching promises than did UNIP speeches.

The two white independents who stood with ANC support produced identical manifestoes which accorded with the ANC message and were endorsed by Mr Nkumbula. They called for more schools, roads, hospitals, agricultural services and fertilisers. They also wanted legislation against UNIP-inspired youth movements, which ANC argued were a terror to law-abiding persons. The two manifestoes also urged respect for traditional authorities and the encouragement of 'rich people from Europe and America to come to Zambia to start new industries'.[60] The only other independent ran on a socialist platform. His manifesto, aptly produced on pink paper as a deliberate propaganda device, claimed that he would take 'a consistent stand for the Zambia proletariat, the general toiling masses and all oppressed members of our society'; he would protest against the squandering of public money and would support 'genuine' African liberation movements.[61]

Perhaps more important, the two parties also conducted their campaigns on a second, more slanderous level. UNIP accused ANC of being a tribal party, hostile to the national slogan 'One Zambia, one nation'. ANC was portrayed as potentially subversive, its alleged links with the south, its support of the two white independents and the Mwinilunga incident being adduced as evidence. In relation to the latter incident, the President himself stated that he believed beyond a doubt that it was ANC-trained men who had raided the villages.[62] And in a speech later in the campaign Vice-president Kapwepwe told the people of Mazabuka that Mr Nkumbula's

60. H. R. E. Mitchley, election manifesto.
61. J. W. Musole, election manifesto, p. 11.
62. ZIS press release No. 2073/68, 28 November 1968.

sponsorship of the two white independents showed his intention to
restore white minority rule![63] UNIP also charged ANC with falsi-
fying the government's record and thus deceiving the people, and
with using its extra-territorial links to engage in subversive activities.
It also sought to discredit Nkumbula personally: he was 'a twentieth century Uncle Tom', 'a stooge of the racists in the south',
and 'a sell-out of his own people'. For its part, ANC engaged in
an equally malicious 'whisper' campaign. In Western Province the
former UP organisers pointed to the fact that the Minister in
charge of the province was Bemba-speaking, as were several of the
civil servants there. They alleged that, if UNIP won, the Bemba
would dominate the government and would discriminate against
the Lozi, taking away their land and cattle. They also accused
UNIP of not taking adequate medical measures to prevent the aged
Litunga's death, which had taken place a short time previously.
The ANC leader, Mr Nkumbula, publicly hinted that President
Kaunda was a foreigner from Malawi and that at least two Cabinet
Ministers were Tanzanians. Again, it is difficult to assess the impact
of these scurrilous allegations. Certainly, however, they neither
reduced the tension of the campaign nor contributed to the poli-
tical education of the electorate.

In sum, the campaign embodied several remarkable features.
Until nomination day ANC genuinely thought that it had some
chance of a slim overall victory. For its part UNIP, until the
election results were announced, expected to crush ANC completely
even in the Southern Province. A great disparity in resources and
level of activity between the two parties existed from the start and
increased as election day approached. An undercurrent of violence
also persisted. And a low level of policy debate developed. UNIP
did not indicate important new lines of policy, and ANC proved
largely incapable either of effective detailed criticism or of presenting concrete alternative proposals.

Shortly after the polls closed, Zambia Broadcasting Services
began a non-stop radio and TV series of round-ups and analyses
of the election. Despite the transport problems of getting ballot
boxes to the counting centres (including washed-out roads, swollen
rivers and hostile elephants), the first results were received in the
early hours of 20 December. But it was only the next morning that
the sole dramatic result of the election—UNIP's defeat in Western
Province—became apparent.

63. Speech, Mazabuka District, 13 December 1968.

## The results[64]

Neither party was satisfied with the results of the election. UNIP had expected to realise its goal of a one-party State through the election of a National Assembly almost entirely dominated by the party. Its director of elections had forecast that the party would take all but six seats. Instead, despite the loss of its Mwinilunga seat in North-western Province, ANC increased its number of seats from nine to twenty-three. In addition, it secured the election of one of the two white independents it was backing. The party retained its seats in the Central Province and Southern Province, where it recaptured the Mazabuka constituency which UNIP had unexpectedly won in a 1967 by-election. It also took eight seats from UNIP in Western Province. The loss of eight of the eleven Barotse seats and the defeat in that province of three Cabinet Ministers, three Junior Ministers and the administrative secretary of the party considerably tempered the otherwise sweeping nature of UNIP's victory. It also resulted in a new Cabinet with much less Lozi representation than ever before.

The national swing to UNIP was 4 per cent and took place in both urban and rural seats. And the eighty-one seats it captured (compared to the fifty-six it held in the smaller first National Assembly) represented an overwhelming victory for the party (see table 5.8). In the simultaneous presidential race UNIP's candidate, Dr Kaunda, also won by an enormous margin. His 1,080,000 votes (including 421,000 votes, from the thirty uncontested UNIP seats, to which he was constitutionally entitled) constituted 68 per cent of the total registered electorate; Mr Nkumbula won only 15 per cent.[65]

It was not surprising, therefore, that ANC, despite its gains, was disgruntled by election results which did not even give it the one-third of Assembly seats necessary to block constitutional amendments. It had expected to capitalise on the popular grievances it assumed to exist against UNIP and to capture some of the ruling party's seats in Central, Eastern and Copperbelt Provinces. But apart from the upset in Western Province, which was entirely the work of the former United Party, ANC made no new inroads into UNIP's support. In four of the country's eight provinces there were significant swings away from ANC.[66] In Eastern Province the party

64. Some of the statistical analysis presented here is drawn from R. Young, 'The 1968 general elections', in Davies (ed.), *Zambia in Maps, op. cit.*

65. The remaining 17 per cent comprised spoilt papers and uncast ballots in the contested constituencies.

66. I.e. in Central, Eastern, North-western and Southern Provinces. In Copperbelt Province the swing away from ANC was only 0·8 per cent.

*Table 5.8*
Election results by province

| Province | No. of seats | | | Valid votes cast | | | Seats won | | | Spoilt papers | | Gross poll (%) | Swing to UNIP over 1964 (%) |
| | Total | Contested by ANC | Contested by independents | UNIP | ANC | Independents | UNIP | ANC | Independents | No. | As % of total votes cast | | |
|---|---|---|---|---|---|---|---|---|---|---|---|---|---|
| Western | 11 | 10 | – | 32,196 | 51,620 | – | 3 | 8 | – | 9,365 | 10·1 | 62·1 | –46·6 |
| Central | 16 | 15 | 1[a] | 141,772 | 48,439 | 4,962 | 13 | 3 | – | 17,660 | 8·3 | 82·0 | +12·3 |
| Eastern | 14 | 7 | – | 93,499 | 4,951 | – | 14 | – | – | 6,061 | 5·8 | 85·3 | +10·9 |
| Luapula | 10 | 2 | – | 22,511 | 278 | – | 10 | – | – | 835 | 3·5 | 91·0 | – 0·5 |
| Northern | 16 | – | – | 59,139 | 341 | – | 16 | – | – | 1,937 | 3·2 | 85·9 | – 0·3 |
| North-western | 6 | 2 | – | 27,195 | 3,161 | – | 6 | – | – | 2,023 | 6·3 | 79·7 | +16·1 |
| Southern | 14 | 13 | 1 | 34,427 | 98,737 | 7,657 | 1 | 12 | 1 | 13,783 | 8·9 | 81·0 | + 8·2 |
| Copperbelt | 18 | 18 | – | 247,025 | 20,750 | – | 18 | – | – | 11,826 | 4·2 | 91·3 | + 0·8 |
| *Total* | 105 | 73 | 3 | 657,764 | 228,277 | 12,619 | 105 | 23 | 1 | 63,490 | 6·6 | 82·4 | + 4·0 |

*Note*

a Contested by two independent candidates.

*Source.* Figures supplied by the Parliamentary Elections Office. Uncontested seats are not included.

was virtually annihilated, its share of votes cast falling from 16 per
cent in 1964 to 5 per cent. In two further provinces, Northern and
Luapula, UNIP retained its monopoly. The results in ANC's stronghold of Southern Province came as a particular shock to the ANC,
for it won only 56 per cent of the registered votes, compared with
79 per cent in 1964. Over 85 per cent of ANC's support was concentrated in three provinces and, although 25 per cent of the total
votes cast went to the party, this figure gave an exaggerated impression of its support, since all the uncontested seats were overwhelmingly UNIP.

The election results presented ANC with two problems. First,
having depicted party strength as much greater than it actually
was, morale among supporters fell sharply and special measures
to restore it had to be debated by the party at a post-mortem conference held early in January 1969.[67] Secondly, the acquisition of
UP support proved a mixed blessing. The former UP officials, with
their more militant ideas on organisation, had won most of
Western Province from UNIP and provided ANC with its only
real success. But they retained their identity within the party, and
their former leader, Mr Mundia, had to be rewarded with the
deputy leadership of the ANC. Some of his supporters were also
appointed to executive positions, but ex-UP members continued
to question ANC's lack of structure and the quality of its leadership.

The election results underlined several important characteristics
of voter behaviour in Zambia. First, political participation (measured
here in terms of votes cast) has declined somewhat since independence. As already pointed out, the proportion of the eligible population who registered as voters fell. The turn-out of the registered
electorate, at 82·4 per cent, was also significantly lower than in 1964
when 94 per cent of the voters cast valid ballots. Lower turn-out
particularly affected ANC areas and can perhaps be explained in
terms of ANC's reduced organisational effectiveness and the cross-
pressures which voters in those areas have been increasingly
under since UNIP came to power in 1964. But the lower voter
turn-out in the country as a whole is all the more remarkable in
view of the increase in the number of polling districts (by 369 to
1,622) and stations; this increase obviously made it easier for voters
to cast their ballots even in the very large constituencies (average
size 7,168 square kilometres) which exist in Zambia.

The election also disproved the fears of some observers that the
electorate would not be able to handle the new system of balloting,
which required each voter to mark his ballot paper. Despite the

67. Minutes of the ANC post-election conference, *op. cit.*

fact that some 72 per cent of electors were illiterate, the percentage of spoilt papers was extremely low—only 6·6 per cent. Although this represented a substantial rise from 0·5 per cent in 1964, when voters did not have to mark their ballots, the low overall figure showed that a largely illiterate electorate was capable of using a more sophisticated voting system which had been fully explained to them by the government and the political parties.

A third feature of Zambia's political culture is that voter orientations seem to adhere more strongly to parties than to individuals. This is not to deny, of course, that a party's image is heavily influenced by the composition of its leadership in terms of personalities and sectional origins, and that support for it could be reduced if local party organisers ran against the party's official candidates. But the fact remains that where UNIP candidates stood in constituencies which lay outside their provinces of origin there was no evidence of lower voter turn-out for the party. Similarly, ANC supporters in Gwembe North were equally prepared to heed party instructions and vote for Mr Mitchley, despite the fact that he was a European by birth and a former member of the defunct UFP, which, when it formed the Federal government in the pre-independence period, had built the Kariba dam and thus caused considerable hardship through the flooding of the Gwembe Valley. Even more interesting was the result in Libonda, where Mr Mundia, although the main architect of the UP which swept Western Province, won only 59 per cent of the votes, the second lowest score in the eight seats won by the opposition in that province. Furthermore, ANC's deliberate policy of selecting candidates with local roots in the constituencies where they were standing did not pay off. Clearly, the individual candidates are a relatively minor factor influencing voter behaviour in Zambia.[68]

Another interesting feature of the results was the stability of voter loyalties. Less than 10 per cent of seats changed hands—one each in North-western and Southern Provinces, and eight in Western. Moreover, the possibility of a significant shift in the relative strengths of the parties was limited by the very small number of marginal seats. In only twelve of the 105 constituencies did the losing party secure 30 per cent or more of the votes cast.

This stability of voter loyalties gives rise to another and most important question: what was the impact of the general election

68. This had already been indicated by the four by-elections held in Southern Province in March 1968. ANC won these easily in spite of the fact that UNIP put up as candidates the former ANC MPs who had crossed the floor.

on national integration? On the one hand, it can be argued that national unity was not undermined by the election. The campaign was fought out between only two parties, both of which sought to project a national image in their more dignified public propaganda. Of the three independent candidates (compared to ten in 1964), none stood on a sectional platform—one was an African socialist and two were white conservatives. UNIP had a very wide national spread. It contested all 105 seats, averaged 2,128 votes in the seats which it lost, and penetrated ANC areas of strength.[69] Even ANC could not be described as a sectionally based party, since it had considerable support among Ila–Tonga-, Lozi- and Lunda-speakers, as well as amongst people from Northern and Luapula Provinces in the three urban seats of Mufulira District, where it polled almost 30 per cent of the votes. It also retained some support in Eastern Province.

On the other hand, although it would be incorrect to argue that the results posed a real threat to national security, the election was not without its deleterious effects on national integration. ANC conducted much of its propaganda campaign in many areas on a sectional anti-Bemba platform. It also proved far less capable of penetrating UNIP areas than UNIP proved capable of penetrating ANC areas. Thus ANC failed to contest thirty seats—though, as we have seen, in some cases the party could not be blamed because its candidates were physically prevented by UNIP activists from lodging their nomination papers with the returning officers. Of the forty-one candidates who lost their deposits (by obtaining less than 10 per cent of the valid votes cast), thirty-seven were ANC. And in the eight Northern and Luapula seats which it contested, the party averaged only seventy-seven votes in each seat, or less than 1 per cent of the votes cast. Sectional tensions also persisted subterraneously within UNIP during the election period.

There was resentment among UNIP supporters in the Northwestern Province at the lack of any increase in their province's representation. UNIP was also unable to carry through its intention of placing most of its candidates outside their provinces of origin, and sectional conflicts resurrected themselves in the party almost immediately after the election. These were so serious that Dr Kaunda

69. UNIP's lowest poll was in Monze West and Mumbwa East: its candidate obtained only 481 votes in each case. Monze West was not only Mr Nkumbula's own seat but was also headed by a UNIP regional secretary whose discriminatory actions against ANC villages had excited the most bitter hostility. In Mumbwa East, the Sala community of Chief Shakumbila gave the UNIP candidate short shrift. (Information: Mr R. A. Young.)

felt obliged to dissolve the party's central committee in August 1969 and to assume absolute powers over the party. Finally, UNIP was prepared on occasion to resort to sectional appeals itself. In the closely contested constituencies of Mankoya and Luampa it used long-standing resentments against the 'true Lozi' on the plain to prevent defections to ANC.

The election weakened national integration most seriously because of the way in which some Zambians interpreted the results. In particular, many UNIP supporters perceived ANC's breakthrough into Western Province as a tribal defection of the Lozi from UNIP. The consequent wave of anti-Lozi sentiment in the party and the short-lived talk of secession by a few ANC leaders exacerbated the situation.

This raises a last question about voter motivation. The evidence casts the gravest doubts on the adequacy of relying too heavily on sectional variables to explain Zambian electoral behaviour. To take the case of Barotse, the swing away from UNIP cannot be explained simply in terms of the anti-Bemba appeal which the opposition undoubtedly made. For ANC made a similar, but unsuccessful, appeal in Eastern and North-western Provinces. The reason for the difference in voter response was perhaps that in the latter two areas the UNIP structure itself was effective in articulating anti-Bemba sentiments, while in Barotse the local UNIP organisation was so inactive as to lose the confidence of many people. Moreover, the swing away from UNIP in Western Province was a rural phenomenon in which special factors, other than the sectional appeal of the UP, were important. There were real grievances in the province. The operation of WENELA, whereby Lozi were recruited to work as migrants on the South African mines, had been terminated by the government in 1967; this had resulted in considerable economic hardship in the province. Secondly, there was a perceived lack of development in the province compared with the advances made in other provinces. Thirdly, there was resentment at the defeat of Lozi leaders in the UNIP central committee elections of 1967 and at the anti-Lozi witch-hunt which had followed the UNIP–UP clashes on the Copperbelt in August 1968. Lastly, although the UP made an overtly sectional appeal, it did articulate these felt grievances in a way that UNIP, with its crippled organisation, was unable to do. All these factors, which did not operate in any of the other provinces, clearly help to explain the swing away from UNIP in Western Province.

In addition, UNIP had been established in Western Province for a shorter time than elsewhere and voters were less stable in their identification with the party. There is further evidence that the swing to ANC was not a collective sectional defection by all Lozi. UNIP won the urban constituency of Livingstone (Southern Province) in a close fight and could have done so only with considerable support from those Livingstone voters coming from Western Province. Urban Lozi who were not affected by the economic factors operating in rural Barotseland do not seem to have abandoned UNIP. Moreover, even in Western Province itself UNIP still won 39 per cent of the votes cast, while nearly 40 per cent of the registered electorate abstained. These divisions within a particular area (and they were repeated in the Southern Province, where UNIP won 26 per cent of the valid votes cast) cannot be explained by the single sectional variable.

The relative weights to be attached to other variables must be taken into account. These variables include the party loyalties into which voters have been socialised over the years (and which explain the high degree of stability in party loyalty in most parts of the country); the degree of urbanisation (ANC did worse in urban than rural areas); the existence of cross-pressures (in particular, the government's ability to grant or withhold resources such as agricultural loans and trading licences, and the party's ability to escalate through violence the costs of opposition); and the attitudes adopted by local opinion leaders, including traditional chiefs and headmen.

The conclusions as to the role of sectionalism in the 1968 election are not simple. Sectionalism is clearly one factor influencing political behaviour. It affects the lines of division between and within the parties, and both preceded and postdated the election. The election did in practice result in a heightened perception of the political relevance of sectional loyalties; but the extent of their impact on electoral behaviour must remain doubtful.

## Conclusion

The 1968 election brought into sharp relief several problems facing the Zambian political system. First, both parties continued to recruit from amongst their organisation men who had led the independence struggle. But these men did not necessarily possess the skills needed to run a modern State, and they did not make it easy for the new post-independence generation of educated Zambians to assume an influential role in the political process. Secondly, the problem remained unsolved of attempting to legitimate a borrowed and foreign electoral system, with its assumptions of an impartial civil service and a multi-party competitive political system. This was demonstrated in 1972 when the UNIP government used the serious threat of the new opposition party, the UPP, to set up a one-party State with limited intra-party competition for seats in the National Assembly. Thirdly, the general election did not remove the basic Zambian problem of a declining sense of national unity. Indeed, the widespread interpretation of the results in sectional terms by Zambians accelerated this decline, as did the decision of the President to reward Eastern and North-western Provinces for eliminating ANC by giving them an increased proportion of Cabinet seats at the expense of the previously dominant Northern Province. These persistent problems, particularly of sectionalism, which faced the political system were not solved by the election and have continued to plague UNIP since. The temporary resignation of Vice-president Kapwepwe in August 1969, the struggle over the Chuula Commission's proposals for a new party constitution in 1970, and the break-away of several UNIP MPs to join the UPP in 1971—all reflected the growing discontent of Bemba-speaking elements after the 1968 general election. On the other hand, there was a positive, albeit limited, side to the election: neither the campaign nor the results led to the appearance of disruptive forces sufficiently strong to destroy the political system. In relative terms, the election was fairly conducted. The opposition was able to strengthen significantly its position in the Assembly, while the ruling party demonstrated the continuing and remarkably high level of structural vigour and popular consent which it has succeeded in maintaining since independence. The 1968 general election did not change the major contours of the political system or provide the occasion for major shifts in power between the parties or in the policies of the government. But it did reflect the maintenance of popular and, to some extent, democratic government.

# 6

# Parliament

## William Tordoff and Robert Molteno

Zambia's new National Assembly building occupies a dominant position some four miles from the commercial centre of Lusaka. Costing over one million kwacha, with the external walls of its four-sided chamber sheathed in copper, it reflects the scale and source of the country's opulence. Yet the building is in use for only a small part of the year. Its visitors' galleries are seldom full. No throngs of constituents toil up the hill to see their representatives. The very newness and quietness of the building, and the polished sophistication of its interior, symbolise the limited part which the National Assembly plays in the Zambian political scene. This chapter investigates the nature and limits of its contribution to the political life of the country during the First Zambian Republic (1964–72) through an analysis of its roles—its formal functions, its emergency powers, its representative nature, and its critical function.

### Formal roles of Parliament[1]

The Zambian Parliament[2] comprises the President and the single-chamber National Assembly,[3] to which all Ministers must belong. There must be a parliamentary session at least once a year, and since independence the Assembly has divided each of its sessions

---

1. For an analysis of Northern Rhodesia's pre-independence legislature, see Davidson, *The Northern Rhodesian Legislative Council, op. cit.*, and J. Helgerson, 'The Northern Rhodesian Legislative Council, 1959–63' (MA dissertation, Duke University, 1968). For a brief study of the Zambian Parliament just after independence, see A. Gupta, 'The Zambian National Assembly: study of an African legislature', *Parliamentary Affairs* (winter 1965–6), vol. XIX, No. 1.

2. Constitution of Zambia, s. 57.

3. The constitution provides for a unicameral legislature. But there is also an advisory House of Chiefs without any legislative powers. *Ibid.*, s. 86.

into three or four meetings. The life of Parliament is normally five years from its first sitting after a dissolution, unless the President dissolves it earlier;[4] dissolution simultaneously puts an end to the President's own term of office. The first Zambian Parliament was dissolved in November 1968; the second Parliament was elected in December of that year, met in January 1969 and was dissolved in October 1973.

In its formal powers and procedures, the Zambian Parliament is a variant of the Westminster system. The power of legislation is vested in it—including the right to confer on any person or authority the power to make statutory instruments. After a Bill has passed through the usual stages (first and second readings, committee and report stages, and third reading), it is presented to the President for his assent. This has never been withheld. In both the first and second Parliaments the President has belonged to, and has been leader of, UNIP and the latter has had a majority in the Assembly. More-over, UNIP discipline over its MPs has been tight, and all Bills presented to the President for his assent have been government-sponsored Bills which have been approved by the Cabinet[5] before they were introduced into the Assembly. Though the President does have a limited power of veto over legislation,[6] this power is likely to become important only when the President cannot command a majority in the National Assembly.

Parliament has sole power to amend the constitution—subject (since June 1969) only to the requirement that a constitutional amendment be supported at its second and third readings by at least two-thirds of the Assembly's total membership[7]—and to impose taxation.[8] It also authorises public expenditure. The Minister responsible for Finance has to lay before the Assembly each year the estimates of revenue and expenditure[9] for its approval and enact-ment in the annual Appropriation Bill. Through the Public Accounts Committee, whose ten members are appointed at the start of each session, the Assembly keeps itself informed of how the executive has spent the funds it has authorised.[10] The committee is assisted in its task by the annual financial report submitted by the

4. Constitution of Zambia, ss. 82 and 83.

5. Appendix D of Cabinet Office circular No. 74 of 1968, 9 September 1968, details the administrative stages involved in drafting public bills.

6. Constitution of Zambia, s. 71.

7. *Ibid.*, s. 72(2). In the referendum of June 1969 voters agreed to abolish their power to participate in amending certain parts of the constitution.

8. *Ibid.*, s. 106(1).

9. *Ibid.*, s. 109(1).

10. *National Assembly Standing Orders, 1967* (Lusaka), No. 140.

Minister responsible for Finance, and by the reports of the Auditor
General. Finally, the approval of the National Assembly is required
for a presidential declaration of a state of public emergency[11] to
remain in force, and the Assembly may end the state of emergency
at any time by revoking the President's declaration.

All these powers are formalistic—inevitably so in a parliamentary
system where strict party discipline has prevailed and which is
clearly modelled on Westminster. Despite the incorporation of
Zambian traditional culture in the internal architecture of the
chamber—its murals, its woodwork, and the presidential chair
framed by two huge elephant tusks—much of Westminster's formal
ceremony and custom is also reproduced. A costumed serjeant-at-
arms, bearing a splendid copper mace, precedes Mr Speaker, himself gowned and bewigged, into the chamber. The formal rules of
procedure follow those of the British Parliament closely and, in
cases of doubt, the Standing Orders (1967) of the National Assembly
are to be interpreted in the light of the relevant practice of the
House of Commons.[12] Indeed, it was well into the second National
Assembly before the Standing Orders Committee initiated a limited
Zambianisation of the Assembly's ceremonial. Traditional drum-
ming now welcomes the President on his rare visits to the legislature; 
the Speaker's gown now incorporates the national colours; it is even
permissible for MPs to wear national dress and safari suits; and the
national anthem is played at the start of proceedings each day.[13]

Until the establishment of a one-party State in December 1972
Zambia was a multi-party democracy on British lines. In the two
Parliaments since independence there has always been at least one
opposition party, a fact which has had an important impact on the
nature and proceedings of the National Assembly. Government and
opposition MPs faced one another from opposite sides of the House,
although their benches were ranged in a semi-circle in front of the
Speaker's chair. Even the British tradition of having a member of
the opposition as chairman of the Public Accounts Committee was
followed until the start of the second National Assembly. The new
Speaker then refused to recognise the ANC as the official opposition
on the grounds that it had three members too few with which to
constitute a quorum and execute the business of the House on its
own![14]

11. Under s. 29 of the constitution.
12. Standing Order No. 158(1).
13. *Nat. Ass. Deb.*, Hansard No. 24, 10 December 1970, cols 159 ff.
14. *Nat. Ass. Deb.*, Hansard No. 17, 22 January 1969, cols 27–9. This
(peculiar) ruling had an important effect when two ANC Members crossed the

There are, of course, significant departures from the parliamentary system in its British form. One stems from the fact that the Zambian President is chief executive as well as head of state, and shares the legislative role with the National Assembly. Unlike the British Prime Minister and the President of Kenya, he is not himself a member of this body, though he may at any time attend and address it. President Kaunda has regularly opened each parliamentary session, and his addresses have resulted in lengthy debates. Neither the President nor his Ministers are required to resign in the face of an adverse vote in the National Assembly. Under the First Republic, when inter-party competition was allowed, it was even possible for the President to belong to a party which did not command a majority in the Assembly. The person elected President was that presidential candidate who received more votes than any other candidate—a provision which still applies. In a general election if, as a result of party fragmentation, several fairly evenly matched parties had put up parliamentary candidates, the party of the person elected President might well not have had an overall Assembly majority. In such a situation the President would have found it much more difficult to carry on the government, and conflict between the executive and legislature might have ensued. The formalistic exercise of the Assembly's powers would then have assumed a real political importance.[15]

A second major difference between the Zambian and British Parliaments is the committee system. The Zambian Assembly has the usual sessional committees to regulate its affairs. There is the Standing Orders Committee, the Library Committee, and the House Committee, which looks after the comfort of Members. But in the field of committees which watch the activities of the executive, the Zambian Assembly has almost none. No select committee has ever been appointed to investigate some particular problem which is worrying Members or the general public. There is no select com-

floor in September 1970. Instead of being compelled to lose their seats in terms of Act No. 47 of 1966, the Speaker ruled that, since the notice informing him of this transfer came from Mr Nkumbula, whom he had not recognised as leader of a political party in the House, he was not obliged to pass the notice on to the Chief Justice. The MPs were therefore allowed to retain their seats. *Ibid.*, Hansard No. 23, 30 September 1970, cols 319–20. This ruling was later reversed by the courts, whose judgement was reluctantly accepted by the Speaker. *Ibid.*, Hansard No. 25, 19 January 1971, cols 29–34, and No. 29, 29 February 1972, cols 1381 ff.

15. In circumstances which forced both the President and the Vice-president (who succeeded him) to resign, the Assembly itself would have chosen the new President. Constitution of Zambia, s. 37(2)(b).

mittee on the estimates. While the economic reforms of April 1968 and subsequent years have vastly expanded the public sector, the Zambian National Assembly lacks a select committee on nationalised industries, or any other machinery to superintend the activities of the firms in which the State now has a major shareholding. The executive also enjoys wide powers of delegated legislation—more particularly since the National Assembly has prolonged the state of emergency which has existed continuously since before independence.[16] Yet no select committee on statutory instruments exists. The only select committee which does scrutinise the actions of the executive is the Public Accounts Committee. Even this committee during the first and second National Assemblies usually produced only one report a year. By its own admission, the committee has failed to have a corrective effect on the civil service's lax adherence to prescribed financial procedures[17] and to the detailed authorisations of public spending which the Assembly itself passes. At the very least, this absence of an effective committee system clearly reduces the weight which the Assembly carries in the eyes of the civil service.[18] Indeed, in December 1970 the Assembly itself became convinced of the need for more select and sessional committees 'on important subjects' but, despite the recommendations of its own Standing Orders Committee, no action was taken during the life of the second National Assembly.[19]

Under the First Republic and before the one-party State was established, the Zambian parliamentary system also differed from the British because of certain features of its party system. Following the 1964 general election, the state of the parties was: UNIP, fifty-five seats (plus five MPs nominated by the President in October 1964);[20] ANC, ten; NPP, ten.[21] Towards the end of 1968, when

16. Constitution of Zambia, s. 29.

17. See *Second Report of the Public Accounts Committee for the Fourth Session*, Hansard No. 16, October–November 1968, appendix A, col. 748, paras 11 and 12.

18. 'Your committee reports with regret that once again their work was seriously hampered by the failure of some controlling officers to appear in person.' *Ibid.*, para. 3.

19. *Nat. Ass. Deb.*, Hansard No. 24, 10 December 1970, cols 159 ff.

20. In 1964 and 1969 President Kaunda used the nominating powers conferred on him by s. 60 of the constitution both to increase the representation of communities which had few MPs in the Assembly and to bring in highly educated Zambians (usually former top civil servants).

21. The National Progress Party (NPP) was the name chosen for the former United Federal Party (UFP) when the Central African Federation was dissolved. Its MPs were all white. The party made a clean sweep of the ten reserved seats in the general election of January 1964. According to the

Parliament was dissolved, UNIP on aggregate had gained one seat from ANC and two seats formerly held by the NPP. Four seats were vacant. Thus ANC emerged with a net total of nine seats, while six independents (former NPP Members) remained at the end of the first Parliament. In the second Parliament (with 105 constituency Members, instead of seventy-five) elected in December 1968, the strength of the parties was: UNIP, eighty-one (plus five nominated Members); ANC, twenty-three; independent, one.[22] The combined opposition in 1969 formed less than a quarter of the Assembly, just as it had for so much of the life of the first Parliament. This remained the position throughout the second Parliament, despite the formation by Mr Simon Kapwepwe (former vice-president of UNIP and of the country) of his break-away United Progressive Party in August 1971 and the UPP's dramatic success in capturing the Copperbelt seat of Mufulira West from the ruling party in December of that year. This imbalance between the parties meant that the opposition ANC never seriously considered itself an alternative government. It never, for instance, formed a Shadow Cabinet. As for the ruling party, election results since 1962 enabled most of its leaders to discount the possibility of becoming the opposition. On several occasions Cabinet Ministers publicly advocated the creation of a one-party State,[23] though it was not until February 1972 after the rise of the UPP that President Kaunda yielded to their demands and appointed a commission to recommend what form the country's institutions should take under a 'one-party participatory democracy'. Not only before that date had the outcome of parliamentary contests between the parties seldom been in doubt, but inter-party competition had generally been of secondary importance and often less intense than competition within the ruling party.

In any parliamentary system the combination of party inequality and strict party discipline over MPs tends to make the legislature's major constitutional roles formalistic. Zambia has been no exception. The absence of an executive whose tenure of office was directly dependent on parliamentary votes of confidence, the lack of an

agreement reached at the Independence Conference, these seats were to be abolished within five years. The second Zambian Parliament therefore no longer contains this element.

22. The independent, Mr H. R. E. Mitchley, was a former UFP and later NPP Member of Parliament who entered an agreement with ANC whereby the latter gave him one of its safe seats. He backed the ANC leader, Mr H. Nkumbula, for the presidency.

23. For example, Mr H. D. Banda in January 1969. *Times of Zambia*, 6 January 1969.

effective committee system and the imbalance between parties increased the formalistic nature of these aspects of the Assembly's business.

### Emergency roles of the National Assembly

The National Assembly has certain constitutional powers (hitherto unexercised) which might, in an emergency, render it a greater force in the political system. These powers relate to the election and removal of the President. Under section 33 of the constitution, if the President-elect dies between polling day and his assumption of office,[24] the new Assembly (which has been elected simultaneously with him) chooses a new President. The same happens if the presidency becomes vacant and there is no Vice-president to succeed automatically.[25] Both these eventualities are very unlikely.

The second emergency power arises under section 36. If one-third or more of all MPs sign a motion alleging that the President has committed 'any violation of the constitution or any gross misconduct', and if the Assembly subsequently passes the motion by a two-thirds majority of its total membership, the Chief Justice is obliged to set up a tribunal to investigate the charges. Only if the tribunal finds the allegations substantiated may the National Assembly, by a three-quarters majority of all its members, remove the President from office. The constitution does not state that 'gross misconduct' is confined to serious criminal offences. If some time in the future strains within the ruling single party became so severe that party discipline disintegrated, the presidency might conceivably become a pawn in the power game played between rival party factions, and the legislature would have at its disposal a crucial mechanism for imposing its will on the political executive.

### The representative roles of the National Assembly

The formal roles and the emergency powers of the Assembly have been outlined. In addition, MPs are supposed to play an important part in the political system because of their representative roles. They can articulate particular ideological points of view and policies, they can represent the views of their constituents and defend their interests, and they can act as spokesmen on behalf of pressure groups. How far in Zambia does the National Assembly

24. In the 1968 general election Dr Kaunda was sworn in as President within hours of the results being declared.
25. Constitution of Zambia, s. 37(1).

act as a forum within which MPs represent the views and interests of the electorate in these three ways?

First, we consider how far an MP represents a certain policy or ideological point of view. To some extent he did so under the First Republic. As a member of a party, he acted as a spokesman for its policy in the Assembly. As between the two major parties, UNIP and ANC, there were differences of emphasis in several spheres. UNIP tended to be to the 'left' of ANC. It placed more stress on non-alignment. It did not wish to reduce confrontation with the white minority-ruled States which are Zambia's southern neighbours. In this respect Mr Nkumbula, the ANC leader, believed that the UNIP government was going too far:

*Mr Nkumbula.* Time and again the hon. Minister has made references to U.D.I. It is U.D.I. that has brought about inflationary pressures. Our imports from the south have dropped from 39 per cent to 25 per cent. With all due respect to Government's attempts to end the rebellion in Rhodesia, we should begin to think in terms of the remarks made by His Excellency the President yesterday when he was addressing the Committee of Five that 'first things first'. Our principal objective is to meet the requirements of Zambians. Indeed, we are all agreed that we must give our brethren in the south our moral support so that they also can achieve international personality in the same way as we have done. But we must be careful not to commit suicide ourselves.

Sir, the Republic of Zambia is the only country in the world that has thrown its strength in the liberation movement of the Rhodesian Africans. £31 million that we have so far spent on U.D.I. is not a joke. Other member States of the O.A.U. have treated U.D.I. as a subject for anyone to talk about when he has nothing to say at all. In other quarters U.D.I. is being used as a political gain for individuals who seek personal international reputation at the sufferance of the people of Zambia. Apart from our Republic other member States of O.A.U. have done nothing practical to end the illegal Smith regime.[26]

In economic development, UNIP placed more emphasis on State participation than on private foreign capital; ANC in turn reacted immediately to the first stage of UNIP's economic reforms by introducing a motion in the National Assembly condemning them and stating succinctly (if inaccurately): 'That is the philosophy of Humanism. It is nothing but communism.'[27] Finally, even before the 1972 decision to create a one-party State, UNIP had been less unanimously committed to a multi-party democracy than ANC

26. *Nat. Ass. Deb.*, Hansard No. 7, 11 August 1966, cols 599–600.

27. *Ibid.*, No. 14, 24 April 1968, cols 17 ff. (The speaker was Mr Nkumbula.)

claimed to be.[28] Since party discipline on both sides of the House was strong, MPs usually followed their respective party lines closely.

Party discipline was reinforced by the Constitution Amendment (No. 2) Act of 1966, which paralleled an arrangement made earlier in Kenya. It stipulated that an MP who left the party on whose ticket he was elected automatically forfeited his seat in the Assembly. Experience showed that it was unwise for an MP who wished to retain his seat to change parties in midstream. For, in the seven instances where this happened during the first Assembly, in not one were the electorate persuaded to follow their MP into his new party allegiance (and so policy stance). Three MPs (M. Mumbuna of ANC, D. M. Chikulo and N. Mundia of UNIP) defected in 1966–67 from the parties on whose tickets they were elected in order to join the United Party, a new party—largely Lozi in top leadership and local support—which was banned in August 1968 following the murder of two UNIP officials in a clash on the Copperbelt. Two of them did not feel strong enough to contest the by-elections, and the third, Mr Chikulo, was rejected by the voters. Indeed, between January 1964 and December 1968 UNIP never lost a by-election in any seat originally held by it and rendered vacant by the death or resignation of the incumbent. The other four cases took place early in 1968, when four ANC Members crossed the floor to join UNIP. In the by-elections which followed they stood on a UNIP ticket and lost to the new ANC candidates. For its part, ANC lost only one of its original ten seats—in the 1967 Mazabuka by-election, which UNIP won. A similar pattern manifested itself during the second Parliament: up to December 1972 ANC lost six of its original twenty-three MPs; they crossed the floor to join UNIP, but ANC won five of the ensuing by-elections. UNIP won all except one of the by-elections that resulted when one of its MPs joined ANC and another six left the party to found the UPP. The Constitution Amendment (No. 2) Act clearly went beyond the electoral procedures of most parliamentary systems in ensuring that voters were always represented by an MP who belonged to the party with majority electoral support in the constituency.

MPs of the third party in the first Assembly—the NPP—showed the least degree of policy cohesion. They dissolved their party in 1966 and sat thereafter as independents. Increasingly since independence the white community has withdrawn from political

28. For ANC's policies, see chapter 4. Interview with H. M. Nkumbula, MP, national president of ANC on 16 July 1968; ANC (Zambia) manifesto (n.d.), pp. 2 and 5; and referendum leaflet, issued by H. M. Nkumbula, MP, and dated 17 April 1969, which stated: 'Vote No to prevent one party state.'

activity, probably out of a conviction that it can no longer make any significant electoral impact on the future course of Zambian politics. Thus there was no public protest over President Kaunda's announcement in September 1965 that the reserved seats were to be abolished. In the three by-elections in these seats the white community put up and elected a candidate of its own only in the first (held in 1965). Although UNIP candidates won the two following by-elections, it was therefore by default—their only opponents were ANC candidates. Moreover the percentage polls were very low— much lower than in 1964. It cannot be said that UNIP has ever succeeded in capturing the loyalty of the white community.[29] Very few whites have applied for Zambian citizenship, which would have qualified them both to vote and to stand as parliamentary candidates after their reserved seats were abolished.

In so far as policy coincided with party, MPs fairly consistently represented the different policy stands of the parties to which they belonged. But this does not extend to the more significant level of policy divisions within UNIP. There are no definite 'left'- or 'right'-wing groups among MPs of the ruling party. The conservative end of the spectrum was pre-empted by ANC, and a UNIP Member who openly advocated ANC-type policies might be regarded as disloyal to his own party. Nor is there a strong group on the 'left': the pretensions to radicalism of Kapwepwe and the Bemba-speaking group which left UNIP in August 1971 to form the UPP must be viewed with the gravest caution.[30] Neither before nor after August 1971 have MPs of the ruling party divided along ideological lines. Party discipline and the fact that the social background of MPs has not by and large exposed them to radical ideological alternatives have meant that there has been no serious and public challenge inside the party to President Kaunda's personal monopoly of major ideological initiatives. Moreover the President's philosophy of Humanism, which has been espoused by UNIP and which includes a prospective code of leadership, has not yet demanded the personal sacrifices from government and party leaders required of their counterparts in Tanzania under President Nyerere's Arusha declaration. Again, South Africa, Rhodesia and Portugal have not put sufficient pressure on Zambia to force on her a choice between a change of policy on the one hand and a huge increase in defence spending (with a corresponding cut in development spending) on the other. Indeed, the large government revenues derived from high

29. In the 1964 general election UNIP polled (on aggregate) 6,177 votes in the ten reserved seats, or 26 per cent of the registered electorate.
30. Molteno, 'Zambia and the one-party State', op. cit., p. 8.

copper prices until 1970 enabled Zambia to be free of major policy choices as to priorities in government spending—whether, for example, investment in manufacturing and agricultural production should be stepped up at the expense of expanding the social services.[31] It is also because—at least in the first six years of independence—hard choices did not have to be made that strains or cleavages within UNIP on these policy issues have not emerged. On the other hand, changed circumstances since 1970, including a

*Table 6.1*
Parliamentary representation: extent to which MPs stood in their province of origin as at March 1964[a]

| Province (rural only) | Total No. of seats | 'Local' men | 'Outsiders' |
|---|---|---|---|
| Western (formerly Barotse) | 7 | 7 | – |
| Eastern | 10 | 9 | 1 |
| Luapula | 6 | 5 | 1 |
| Northern | 9 | 8 | 1 |
| North-western | 5[b] | 5 | – |
| Southern | 8 | 7 | 1 |
| *Total* | 45 | 41 | 4 |

*Notes*

a  For the reasons why the date March 1964 was chosen, see p. 219, n. 59.

b  In addition to these five seats, Solwezi constituency was partly in North-western Province and partly in Copperbelt Province; it has therefore been omitted from the table.

*Source*. MPs' own returns to Mr Speaker.

sharp fall in government revenue[32] and an increase in foreign pressures, presage growing conflict over the right policy decisions. Though the sharp criticism of certain government policies by Northern Province MPs early in 1971 was more a pointer to the intensity of the sectional competition within UNIP than to any fundamental disagreement over policy issues, such disagreement may

31. President Kaunda is well aware of the strains and policy changes which a large drop in the price of copper would cause. See Hall, *The High Price of Principles, op. cit.*, p. 6.

32. Fortunately the unexpected rise in the price of copper early in 1973 was sustained throughout that year.

well occur over the next few years. This will particularly be the case
if the more conservative of the former ANC MPs choose eventually
to integrate themselves into the ruling party now that the one-party
State has been established. In this event, ideological wings in the
single ruling party may emerge. In the meantime, however, there
are certain issues on which opinion within UNIP is divided, but no
major ideological cleavages whose varying views, MPs can express.

The second way in which parliamentary theory expects an MP to
be a representative stems from his being elected by a specific territorial area in order to voice the interests of all its residents in the
legislature. At first glance, Zambian MPs seem likely to be able to
do this effectively, since there is a strong tendency for them to be
'local men', standing for election in their own province of origin.
Table 6.1 (which is confined to the first National Assembly[33])
examines the provincial origins of MPs in relation to Zambia's
six predominantly rural provinces;[34] the Copperbelt[35] and Central
Provinces are examined separately.

A number of conclusions can be drawn from this table. Out of
forty-five seats in these six provinces, 'local men' stood, and were
elected, in forty-one. This strong local element in representation
may have had some bearing on the efficiency with which the MP
performed his representative functions. The 'local' MP could
speak the language of his people, he shared their culture and
traditions, and he might even have been born and grown up within
his own constituency. This was true of at least nine MPs. The hold
which they had on their seats by virtue of their provincial affiliation
was thus reinforced. It was not cast-iron, however, as was shown
in the general election of December 1968, when Arthur Wina was
defeated in his home area, Mongu, in the Western Province, and
L. B. Cheelo at Chikankata in the Southern Province.

We turn next to examine representation in the two provinces
which have sizeable urban populations—Copperbelt and Central.

33. Similar information for the second National Assembly is given in
chapter 5, table 5.4.

34. The province rather than language is taken here as the unit of assessment. Language and province do not coincide, since most of Zambia's
eight provinces are polyethnic. Nevertheless, within each province one
language group (and sometimes two) is politically dominant, as for example
the Nyanja-speaking peoples in the Eastern Province, the Lozi in Western
(formerly Barotse) Province, the Ila–Tonga in Southern, the Bemba in
Northern and Luapula, and the Lunda and Lovale in North-western Province.

35. In 1969 the names of two provinces were changed. Western Province
became Copperbelt Province, and Barotse became Western Province. The
new usage will be followed in this chapter.

While the pattern is more complex, it is somewhat similar to that in the predominantly rural provinces. Thus in these two provinces the parliamentary representation of the various language groups reflected fairly accurately the relative sizes of the latter.

The local people in the rural areas of Copperbelt Province are largely Lamba. They are the most vocal in asserting their rights against the immigrants who, from the 1920s onwards, have entered the province in large numbers to take up employment with the copper mining companies. The great mass of the Copperbelt's population today is an urban mixture of language groups, with Bemba predominating. The Central Province includes important urban areas—notably Lusaka, the capital, which has attracted many people from the Eastern and Southern Provinces, and Kabwe, the provincial headquarters. But it has also a substantial rural population. Alone of all the provinces, it is the meeting point of several linguistic groups: the Ila–Tonga inhabit the western part and mostly supported ANC; Bemba-speaking peoples dominate the north-eastern area and were pro-UNIP; while the Lenje and Soli peoples live in the middle belt and were divided in political allegiance, though a majority supported the ruling party. In tabular form, the pattern of representation in these two provinces in March 1964 was as shown in table 6.2.

This table shows that while three non-Africans (all UNIP) were elected in the urban areas of the two provinces, none was returned in the rural areas. In Central Province a high proportion of MPs were drawn from groups represented in the province's rural population. But no representative was an Easterner, despite the widespread use of Nyanja in Lusaka.[36] In Copperbelt Province, on the other hand, as many MPs were drawn from the Eastern Province as from Bemba-speaking areas. Indications were that Bemba UNIP leaders on the Copperbelt were successfully pushing themselves at the expense of other groups—during the 1964–68 Parliament they secured one extra seat on the main roll and provided two extra MPs on the reserved roll.

Bemba-speakers constituted, in fact, the biggest single bloc within the UNIP parliamentary party. They accounted for eighteen MPs in March 1964 and twenty-one in December 1967, as against fifteen drawn from the Eastern Province on both dates. Clearly, the Bemba- and Nyanja-speaking areas could have dominated the party if they had pulled together. In fact, they tended to constitute two rival blocs within UNIP, though the Eastern bloc was not monolithic

36. This changed in December 1968, when Mr H. D. Banda won the Lusaka City Central constituency for UNIP.

*Table 6.2*
Parliamentary representation in the two largely urban provinces as at
March 1964

| Members of Parliament | Copperbelt Province | | Central Province | |
|---|---|---|---|---|
| | Urban seats | Rural seats | Urban seats | Rural seats |
| *African MPs*[a] | | | | |
| Bemba[b] | 3 | – | – | 2 |
| Lamba | – | 1[c] | – | – |
| Lenje, Soli | – | – | – | 2 |
| Lozi | 1 | – | 1 | – |
| Nyanja | 3 | – | – | – |
| Tonga | 1 | – | 1 | 2 |
| *Other MPs* | | | | |
| Coloured | 1 | – | – | – |
| Indian | 1 | – | – | – |
| White | – | – | 1 | – |
| *Total number of seats*[d] | 10 | 1 | 3 | 6 |

*Notes*

a  Language group has been given for African MPs (instead of provincial origin as in table 6.1), since these two provinces are linguistically heterogeneous in both their urban and their rural areas. But to
list an MP as Bemba-speaking, for example, does not necessarily
imply that he was born in the Northern or Luapula Province. Mr
John Chisata, then MP for Mufulira, was born in the Copperbelt
town of Luanshya. At least four other MPs were born in the urban
areas.
b  Includes allied linguistic groups.
c  Mr Misheck Banda, MP for Ndola Rural (which embraced most
of the rural areas of Copperbelt Province), was only part Lamba.
d  This includes only main roll seats.

—for example, the sympathies of Dingiswayo Banda, a Cabinet
Minister from the Nyanja-speaking Eastern Province, were thought
to lie with the Bemba-speaking group at this time.[37] During the
1964–68 period the party's share of seats grew from fifty-five to
sixty-three (including five nominated MPs). Four of the extra seats

37. Rotberg, 'Tribalism and politics in Zambia', *op. cit.*, p. 30.

went to the Bemba–Tonga alliance that existed at the time within UNIP. None went to Easterners, although Lozis and North-westerners together gained three seats. One went to a nominated white, Mrs M. V. Robertson.

We have established the high degree to which MPs—both UNIP and ANC—spoke the home language of their constituents. Yet this seems to have had little beneficial effect on the MPs' representative role. Most Members, particularly in the first Assembly, seldom voiced the views, or pressed the interests, of their constituents in the National Assembly. This failure might of course have reflected a high level of political sophistication, MPs devoting most of their time to raising in debate matters of national rather than of particular concern. Yet this is hardly the case in Zambia, where UNIP back-benchers in the first Assembly rarely participated in proceedings.

There were, of course, a small number of MPs who did press their constituents' interests both through debates and through parlia-mentary questions. One UNIP back-bencher who had a clear-cut view of his responsibilities as a representative was Mr B. E. A. Mwelumuka, MP for Kasempa, 1964–68:

Moving in cars with flags and so on is good, but remember the common man in the village. We must speak for that man in the village who has sent us to this House ... I want them to be answered because I am the 100 per cent representative of the Government and of the common man in the village. I do not want to go home and tell people at home how good Lusaka is ... I cannot go there and tell them that we are having many cars and so on when the common man is suffering.[38]

Ironically, it was not coincidental that he was not re-nominated in the 1968 general election by the party. An example from ANC was Mr R. J. Japau, ANC Member for Mwinilunga until 1968, who asked many questions designed to ensure for his Lunda constituents a fair share of government posts.[39] The second National Assembly saw a considerably increased assertion of constituency interests by MPs. Both parties asked, on average, far more parliamentary questions each year than in the first Assembly (UNIP back-benchers averaged seventy a year compared to nil in the first Assembly, and even ANC raised its average from twenty to thirty-two) and, at least as far as UNIP was concerned, the percentage of questions which had a constituency referrent rose significantly from 44 per cent in 1969 to over 80 per cent in 1972.

38. *Nat. Ass. Deb.*, Hansard No. 14, 24 April 1968, cols 117–18.
39. For example, *Nat. Ass. Deb.*, Hansard No. 13, 21 March 1968, col. 1290.

Nevertheless, it remains true that most MPs were bound to their constituents by only the most tenuous links. In the 1968 election UNIP Members did not even choose the seats in which they stood;[40] President Kaunda chose for them. This led to occasional paradoxical situations: thus Mr Justin Chimba, an ardent Bemba protagonist from Northern Province, stood in the important Eastern Province district of Petauke. During the first Parliament many MPs rarely visited their constituents and received very little mail from them. They were not, therefore, sufficiently informed about local needs to voice those needs in the Assembly. The result has been, as President Kaunda stated, that rural people 'feel rather unconnected with the law-maker in Parliament in Lusaka'.[41] From 1969 onwards UNIP arranged for all its MPs to visit their constituencies on 'meet the people tours' which lasted up to ten days,[42] but it was not until the end of 1972 that the idea was accepted that all MPs should have permanent offices in their constituencies.

There were several reasons for the weakness of the links between MPs and constituents. Perhaps the most important was the fact that many MPs in the first Assembly held government posts or had other official duties to perform, making it difficult for them either to visit their constituencies regularly or to devote much time to constituency matters. This remained true of the second Assembly. As early as April 1969, out of eighty-one elected UNIP Members, seventeen (including the Vice-president) were Cabinet Ministers and sixteen were Ministers of State serving either in Lusaka or at provincial headquarters; seventeen were District Governors, and one was ambassador to Ethiopia. By August 1972 the number of Cabinet Ministers had risen to twenty-five, while a further twenty-nine MPs were Ministers of State and seven were senior diplomats; this left a mere twenty or so UNIP back-benchers. In general, it was more difficult for provincial Ministers and District Governors to undertake constituency duties than their colleagues at the centre. Whereas central Ministers could occasionally visit their constituencies during the course of an up-country tour to inspect Ministry projects, provincial Ministers were tied to the province in which they served, while their parliamentary seat was always in a different province. As for District Governors, it was presidential policy to station them outside their own constituencies; the latter might be close at hand but they might equally well be at the other end of the country.

40. See chapter 5.
41. Address by President Kaunda to the UNIP national council, 21 March 1969 (Lusaka, mimeo.), p. 8.
42. *Zambia Mail*, 2 April 1970.

Fortunately, the practice of appointing some MPs as District Governors as well was gradually discontinued and by late 1971 no MP was also a District Governor.

Other minor factors which also tended to reduce the links between the MP and his constituents included the occasional restrictions which President Kaunda placed on the movement of his Ministers, as in 1968 and July 1969.[43] Again, communications were poor between Lusaka and most of the rural areas. The fact, too, that only a tiny proportion of seats were marginal[44] meant that the great majority of MPs had no feeling that their chances of re-election would be substantially improved if they served their constituents well. This, of course, will change when some degree of intra-party electoral competition for Assembly seats is introduced under the one-party State constitution.

A special factor preventing certain opposition MPs from attending to their constituents' welfare was made clear by the 1968 general election. Mr N. Mundia, former UNIP Cabinet Minister and subsequently president of the United Party, had been in restriction in the Northern Province since the banning of his party in August 1968. Despite his restriction, he was able to stand as an ANC candidate in his home district of Kalabo in Western Province. He was elected—although unable to visit the constituency or to campaign. He remained in restriction until November 1969, so that nearly a year elapsed after the general election before he was able to take his seat in the Assembly. In June 1969 a further ANC Member, Mr E. Shooba, was placed under restriction following anti-UNIP disturbances in his constituency during the referendum campaign. In October 1969 two amendments to the constitution were passed which provided that any MP who is restricted or detained forfeits his seat after six months, and may not stand for re-election.[45] This goes well beyond the executive's existing power to restrict or detain an MP—thereby preventing him from attending the Assembly and carrying out his parliamentary duties. The executive can now, by administrative fiat and with no criminal charge having been laid, prevent the electorate from having the opportunity to choose again the man whom they had previously elected to represent them.[46] These provisions prevented those

43. *Times of Zambia*, 9 July 1969.

44. Marginal seats in 1972 included Livingstone, Mumbwa West and Kabwe South, Mufulira West, and one or two Western Province constituencies.

45. Constitution Amendment (No. 5) Act of 1969, ss. 10 and 11.

46. Cf. the operation of India's Preventive Detention Act, first enacted in 1950 and renewed subsequently. See N. D. Palmer, *The Indian Political System* (London, 1961), p. 129.

former UNIP MPs who were detained after they had joined UPP in 1971 from standing again.

The last important factor which reduces the role of the National Assembly as a forum for the articulation of constituency interests is the existence of alternative sources of redress for the voting public. President Kaunda has commented on the consequences of this fact. While 'Parliament must more and more effectively play its role as the custodian of this nation's interests,' he said, '...MPs cannot do this alone...MPs cannot continue to guess what people want. People must, through proper channels, put forward their suggestions in constructive form.'[47] Yet instead of approaching their MP it was easier, quicker and probably more effective for people at district level to go personally to the office of the District Secretary (a civil servant) or the UNIP regional secretary, or (from January 1969 onwards) the District Governor. All these officials tend to spend a good deal of time dealing with local anxieties and individual complaints. Moreover, if citizens want to raise matters at the Lusaka level they have two other avenues which they can use, apart from contacting their own MP. First, they can approach the MP or Minister who, though he represents a constituency other than the one in which they live, belongs to their own ethnic-linguistic group.[48] In other words, ethnic-linguistic ties might cut across the constitutionally orthodox links between the MP and his constituents. Secondly, people may choose to voice their needs through the chiefs.[49] The ability of the latter to fill a representational role should not be under-estimated. They have definite advantages over the MP: they are resident among their people for most of the year and are closer to them in terms of life-style; it is, moreover, traditional for them to safeguard the interests of their people. There is some evidence that chiefs perform this role, perhaps by means of a speech in the House of Chiefs,[50] and often by making a direct appeal to the President. Thus when President Kaunda spoke near

47. Address by President Kaunda to the UNIP national council, 21 March 1969, *op. cit.*, p. 8.

48. For example, Mr Peter Matoka, former Cabinet Minister, was regarded by many Lunda as 'their man' in Lusaka.

49. It should be noted that a small number of UNIP Members, including several Ministers, belonged to chiefly families—for example, Mainza Chona and Elijah Mudenda from the Southern Province, and Arthur and Sikota Wina from the Western Province. One UNIP Member in the first Assembly was a chief in her own right: Princess Nakatindi was Mulena Mukwae of Sesheke.

50. In June 1969, for example, Solwezi chiefs expressed their dissatisfaction in the House of Chiefs with the lack of development in their area.

Magoye in the Southern Province in April 1968 the chief, in his speech of welcome, laid before him a list of development demands for his area. Again, early in 1969 a deputation of chiefs, comprising one each from the Western, North-western and Eastern Provinces, complained to the President about the closure of foreign-owned shops and the lawless activities of the UNIP youth in their provinces.

We must conclude that these various factors prevent most MPs, even though they are local men, from serving as effective constituency spokesmen. They also disincline most constituents from looking to their MP as their first and most effective avenue of redress.

The third way in which MPs fulfil their representative function is by acting on behalf of interest groups in society. It is a common and accepted role for the MP in Britain and America to act as spokesmen for all sorts of voluntary associations, regardless of the fact that they cut across specific constituency boundaries. In Zambia, however, the MP does not play an equivalent role. Some voluntary associations—like the Council for the Blind and Handicapped, the National Road Safety Council, and the Red Cross Society—receive government subsidies and are therefore reluctant to mobilise political pressures in the normal way. Other associations—like Round Table, Rotary, and the Lions' Club—remain largely expatriate in composition in spite of calls by Ministers to Zambians to join them.[51] They either tend to steer clear of politics (like the Round Table) or prefer to work through the administration, as do the Commercial Farmers' Bureau and the Chambers of Commerce.[52] Moreover, these particular interest groups are often at variance with UNIP policy, so that it would in any case be difficult for them to find a spokesman among MPs of the ruling party. To a very limited extent they found representatives among the European NPP and independent Members up to the end of 1968.

One looks in vain for a wide range of specifically Zambian (in practice African) interest groups which are independent of government. There are, for example, virtually no consumer or peasant farmer organisations. Moreover, those that do exist tend to be weakly organised and have not recruited parliamentary spokesmen. Thus the Zambia Traders' Association (previously the Zambia African Traders' Association) is a vocal organisation which makes frequent demands through the press. But it knows where power lies:

51. *Zambia News*, 23 February 1969.
52. This is, of course, also true of established British interest groups such as the British Medical Association.

while it has (unsuccessfully) requested seats in UNIP's national
council, it has not contacted MPs and used them to raise matters
in the National Assembly.

There is one interest group in Zambia which is large, organised
and powerful—the trade union movement. In 1972 there were just
over a third of a million people in paid employment, of whom
about a half were trade union members.[53] As for the 72 per cent of
the population still living on the land, they are as yet a totally
unorganised and inarticulate interest group. Even the small proportion who have joined agricultural co-operatives since 1964
have not formed a federation of co-operative societies which can
make their collective voice heard. Yet these two economic interest
groups—the urban worker and the mainly subsistence farmer—constitute the overwhelming bulk of the electorate. The UNIP government has pursued vigorous policies to help both groups. Rapid
wage increases, accelerated Zambianisation of jobs, and housing
projects have combined to improve the lot of the urban worker.
Millions of kwacha in agricultural loans, a vastly expanded network of marketing and other services to encourage cash crop production, and education and health services have sought to do likewise for many rural Zambians.

But it cannot be said that the National Assembly has been a key
institution in communicating the views of these groups to the
government. The party structure of UNIP—with its often vigorous
local organisation—and the personal commitment of President
Kaunda to the 'common man'[54] are more important in keeping
government Ministers responsive to the demands of the poor. One
must not carry this argument too far. In their speeches and parliamentary questions many UNIP Members have pressed for better
rural communications; they have condemned the inefficiency of
marketing organisations, and raised other matters of concern to
their constituents. It is the things which they have not raised that
are so startling. They have seldom pressed for price increases for
crops. They have not argued in favour of including agricultural
training in primary school curricula so that children who are forced
to stay in the rural areas can learn how to farm profitably. In the

53. *Department of Labour, Annual Report for 1971* (Lusaka, 1972), tables
1(a) and 5(a).

54. This shines through all his pronouncements. See particularly the following speeches: 'Humanism in Zambia', 1967; 'Zambia moves towards
economic independence', 19 April 1968; 'Zambia's guidelines for the next
decade', 9 November 1968; and 'Towards complete independence', 11
August 1969.

huge strike by the Zambia Mineworkers' Union in 1966 no MPs
spoke up in the Assembly on behalf of the workers. When in 1968
the Ministry of Agriculture tried to boost beef production by an
enormous 22 per cent price rise, only one MP—and that a nominated one—raised the question of the implication of the price rise for
the cost of living and the level of nutrition of the man in the street.[55]

It is not surprising, therefore, that the country's largest organised
interest group—the trade unions—have not regarded UNIP or
ANC Members as political champions of the working class. There
are long-standing historical reasons why the trade union movement
in Zambia was suspicious of all political parties.[56] There are also
contemporary conflicts of interest between the trade union's role
of raising the standard of living of its worker members and government's concern since independence with closing the income gap
between rural and urban Zambians and accumulating capital for
development (both of which require that urban standards of living
be held down).[57] The role, as trade union spokesmen, of even those
MPs who represent urban constituencies (all UNIP) was reduced
still further by the complete absence in the 1964–68 Parliament of
any Members who were simultaneously trade union officials. Only
in 1969, for the first time, was an MP also a trade union office-
bearer. Mr Wilson Chakulya, MP for the Copperbelt seat of
Kantanshi, was also general secretary of the Zambia Congress of
Trade Unions. Until he was appointed a Cabinet Minister in 1971
he did put a number of parliamentary questions on trade union
matters, and was the only MP to do so.[58] But this doubling up of
roles caused some unrest in the trade union movement, where it was
felt that, as a UNIP Member, Mr Chakulya's first loyalty might
not be to the trade unions. This contrasts starkly with (for example)
Britain, where trade unions regard it as vital to their interests that
they should sponsor a large number of MPs.

The apparent lack of sensitivity on the part of UNIP and ANC
Members to the problems of ordinary people was due to the weakness of their links with their constituents. This has already been discussed. Another major factor has been the absence of a close
identity of economic interest between MPs and the bulk of the

55. *Nat. Ass. Deb.*, Hansard No. 13, 24 January 1968, col. 33.
56. See Mulford, *Zambia: the Politics of Independence, op. cit.*, pp. 170–4
and 341; E. J. Berg and J. Butler, 'Trade unions', in Coleman and Rosberg
(eds), *Political Parties and National Integration, op. cit.*, pp. 353–6.
57. Bates, *Unions, Parties and Development, op. cit.*, chapters 1 and 3. See
also chapter 8, below.
58. *Nat. Ass. Deb.*, Hansard No. 19, 1969, *passim*.

*Table 6.3*
Occupational background[a] of MPs at March 1964[b]

| Occupation | Cabinet Ministers and Mr Speaker | Parliamentary Secretaries | UNIP back-benchers | Total UNIP MPs | ANC | NPP[c] | Total of National Assembly |
|---|---|---|---|---|---|---|---|
| Professional in private sector | 2 | 1 | 5 | 8 | – | 7 | 15 |
| Teachers[a] | 5 | 5 | 1 | 11 | 3 | – | 14 |
| Civil servants[a] | 2 | 3 | 6 | 11 | 2 | 1 | 13 |
| Businessman/trader | 1 | 2 | 4 | 7 | 1 | 1 | 9 |
| Trade unionist[e] | 1 | 2 | 3 | 6 | – | – | 6 |
| Clerical[f] | 2 | 2 | 1 | 5 | – | – | 5 |
| Farmer–commercial | – | – | – | – | 1 | 2 | 3 |
| Manager of co-operative | 1 | – | – | 1 | – | – | 1 |
| Urban manual worker | – | – | 1 | 1 | – | – | 1 |
| No. for whom no data available | 1 | 1 | 3 | 5 | 3 | – | 8 |
| Total | 15 | 16 | 24 | 55 | 10 | 10 | 75 |

*Notes*

a  The occupation given is the last occupation the person had before becoming an MP or a full-time politician. Many, of course, come into this last category.

b  The data relate to those who were MPs in the first session of the first Legislative Assembly, elected by universal franchise. Most of these continued as MPs when the Legislative Assembly was transformed at independence (24 October 1964) into the first National Assembly of Zambia.

c  The NPP was the successor of the UFP. All its ten MPs were whites, elected on the reserved roll.

d  The civil servant total is in fact larger, since some of the teachers were also civil servants.

e  These former trade union officials were not simultaneously officials and MPs.

f  It is possible that some of these held clerical jobs in the civil service.

*Source.* MPs' returns to the Speaker's Office.

people—workers as well as peasants—by whom they are elected. This can be seen by examining the social background of MPs.[59]

Table 6.3 shows a sharp discontinuity, in terms of occupational background, between MPs of the first National Assembly and the people they represented, a discontinuity which persisted into the second Assembly, elected in December 1968.[60] Two-thirds of UNIP Members in 1964 were full-time political leaders before being elected to Parliament.[61] Forty-one (out of the fifty UNIP Members for whom details are available) were in white-collar jobs before turning to politics full-time, many as junior civil servants in the racially defined African civil service. Eight held professional posts outside the civil service and seven were in business, though few on their own account and then only in a modest way. Only one was an artisan (perhaps reflecting the very limited access of Africans to skilled wage-earning employment under colonial rule) and none came from the poorest wage-earning classes—domestic servants and unskilled workers. Six were trade union leaders, a few of whom may have worked in the mines; but, at the time of his election, no UNIP Member was a miner or trade union official. Even stranger in a predominantly rural country, not one UNIP Member was a farmer. Only one Member was associated with a marketing co-operative, while no MP came from the ranks of farm labourers, although they were one of the largest groups of employees in 1964. On the other hand, most UNIP (and ANC) Members had experienced village life. In the case of UNIP, nearly 90 per cent of its MPs were born and grew up in the rural areas. The reason for this is obvious.

59. There was a substantial turnover in the first Parliament's membership. By the end of 1968 twenty-one out of the seventy-five elected seats had changed hands. The reasons included death and resignation, the assumption of important public office, and loss of seats on the constitutional ground that their holders had left the party on whose ticket they were originally elected. It follows, therefore, that in assessing the social background of MPs the position will vary according to whether the beginning or end of the first Parliament is taken. March 1964 rather than December 1968 is chosen because more complete information is available for the former than for the latter date—mainly from biographical information supplied by MPs themselves at the request of the Speaker's Office. Information on a number of the seventy-five MPs is not available, while the five persons who were nominated as MPs at independence in October 1964 have been omitted from this analysis. There was a somewhat reduced turnover in the second Parliament: by December 1972 UNIP had lost twelve of its original eighty-six MPs (eighty-one elected, five nominated), as against eight out of twenty-three for ANC.

60. See chapter 5, tables 5.3 and 5.5.

61. For full details of the levels of the party from which these UNIP Members were drawn, see Mulford, 'Northern Rhodesia—some observations on the 1964 elections', *op. cit.*, p. 14.

Table 6.4
Educational background of MPs at March 1964

| Education | Cabinet Ministers and Mr Speaker | Parliamentary Secretaries | UNIP back-benchers | Total UNIP MPs | ANC | NPP | Total of National Assembly |
|---|---|---|---|---|---|---|---|
| Primary schooling only | 1 | 2 | 6 | 9 | – | – | 9 |
| Post-primary: teacher training only | 3 | 3 | 1 | 7 | 1 | – | 8 |
| Post-primary: other further education only | – | 2 | 4 | 6 | 1 | 1 | 8 |
| Secondary schooling only (usually not completed) | 3 | 5 | 6 | 14 | 1 | 2 | 17 |
| Post-secondary (non-university) | – | – | – | – | – | 2 | 2 |
| Study abroad:[a] university or equivalent | 8 | 3 | 2 | 13 | 2 | 5 | 20 |
| MPs for whom no data available | – | 1 | 5 | 6 | 5 | – | 11 |
| Total | 15 | 16 | 24 | 55 | 10 | 10 | 75 |

Note

a Some ten other MPs educated in Northern Rhodesia had studied abroad at post-primary level or above.

*Table 6.5*
Distribution of MPs by age at March 1964

| Age in years | Cabinet Ministers and Mr Speaker | Parliamentary Secretaries | UNIP back-benchers | Total UNIP MPs | ANC | NPP | Total of National Assembly |
|---|---|---|---|---|---|---|---|
| 20–29 | — | 1 | 2 | 3 | — | — | 3 |
| 30–39 | 9 | 8 | 13 | 30 | 2 | 2 | 34 |
| 40–49 | 6 | 5 | 4 | 15 | 1 | 6 | 22 |
| 50–59 | — | 1 | 1 | 2 | — | 1 | 3 |
| 60–69 | — | — | — | — | — | 1 | 1 |
| No. for whom no data available | — | 1 | 4 | 5 | 7 | — | 12 |
| *Total* | 15 | 16 | 24 | 55 | 10 | 10 | 75 |

The mining towns only began to mushroom in the 1930s and, as table 6.5 shows, not many UNIP Members were young enough to have been born in the Copperbelt towns.

The same discontinuity between MPs and constituents was true of the opposition ANC. Three of its Members were teachers, two were civil servants in the top two divisions of the civil service, and one was a farmer–businessman. Their Southern Province constituents were for the most part small farmers and farm labourers.

In contrast to UNIP and ANC, the white NPP Members shared the social backgrounds of their white constituents to a large extent. They were drawn from the commercial farming community, business, and the professions. Only the large number of white artisans on the mines were left without any representative who resembled them in background (see table 6.3).

Occupational discontinuity was further entrenched by educational factors, as can be seen from tables 6.4 and 6.5 About a quarter of the UNIP Members for whom data are available had attended university, though not all of them had studied for a degree. In only a few cases did an MP's education not extend beyond the primary level; it was generally supplemented either by vocational training (for example, as a teacher) or by study abroad, or both. Munali Secondary School, opened in Lusaka in 1941, served as the *alma mater* for many of Zambia's leading politicians. The Speaker of the first National Assembly and eleven out of the fourteen members of the March 1964 Cabinet attended the school, often at the same time. The fact that Munali was then the only secondary school for Africans, and the small age range of the Cabinet, must have resulted in a high degree of social contact among the future members of the Cabinet and so probably served as a cohesive factor bringing them together in the struggle for independence.

This study of the social background of MPs reveals several common elements in their experience which tended to make them a homogeneous group, but cut off from the rest of the population. Apart from their occupational and educational backgrounds, many of them had travelled abroad—this widened their experience far beyond that of their constituents. A majority of the MPs who went overseas for university education or other forms of training studied in Western countries (mainly Britain and the United States). A large number—including future UNIP Cabinet Ministers—went to South Africa. Other MPs again studied in India, the United Arab Republic, Uganda and Ghana. But none was educated in a communist State.

These common experiences linked Northern Rhodesian MPs in

many ways to their counterparts who were also struggling for independence elsewhere in Africa; at the same time, they marked them off from the great majority of Africans in Northern Rhodesia. Indeed, if it were not for the fact that the rural origins of MPs compensated in part for their overwhelmingly urban and non-manual occupational experience, it might otherwise have been very difficult to bridge the wide gap which separated the MP (in both the main parties) from the interests of his constituents. The point is so important that it is worth underlining. The MP had received a good deal of formal schooling—of necessity, in order to cope with the tasks of modern government—and Western education had opened up to him new job opportunities in the urban areas. He tended therefore to be both a town dweller and, before his election to the National Assembly, a white-collar worker. He was well paid, earning (in 1965–68) an annual salary of between K3,700 and K4,000, and could therefore afford to live in a low-density, often pre-dominantly European, housing area. In 1971 the MP's salary was raised to between K5,600 and K5,900 (a 51 per cent increase);[62] from March 1972 this salary was supplemented by a 12½ per cent gratuity so that, as Vice-president Mainza Chona explained, 'Hon. Members of this House . . . should not become paupers and beggars on ceasing to be hon. Members of this House.'[63] Most of the MP's constituents, on the other hand, were illiterate farmers with a small or no cash income; they lived in a traditional village which usually lacked such basic amenities as electricity and pipe-borne water. Other con-stituents were unskilled workers, living in one of the Copperbelt's mining towns or crowded together in the illegal and insanitary slums of Zambia's peri-urban areas. These points are as valid for the second National Assembly as they were for the first, and it is therefore not to be wondered at that the National Assembly is not the primary forum in Zambia for the articulation of the demands of economic interest groups.

However, this is not to assert that MPs play no representative role as spokesmen for interest groups. We have seen that MPs can be classified by language or province of origin. These are not just categoric groups; rather, they are units with which people identify.[64] To a certain extent, therefore, interest articulation follows the lines of these sectional groups, which are rooted in community

62. Ministerial and Parliamentary Offices (Emoluments) Act, No. 64 of 1965, as amended in 1971 and 1972.
63. *Nat. Ass. Deb.*, Hansard No. 29, 8 March 1972, cols 1760–1.
64. For a detailed analysis of sectional cleavages in Zambian politics, see chapter 3.

and language, and many MPs regard themselves as spokesmen for these groups. The most pronounced and persistent case was Western Province back-benchers of both parties, who, during the first four years of the second National Assembly, asked 38 per cent of all parliamentary questions and, more often than not, directed them at the interests of their Lozi constituents. But other MPs acted similarly. Mr R. J. Japau, ANC Member, was undisguised on occasion in his articulation of specifically Lunda interests, while Mr M. J. Banda, UNIP Member, defended Lamba interests,[65] as did Mr B. F. Kapulu in the second Assembly. Eastern Province MPs regarded themselves as the special custodians of the interests of the people in that province, as was shown in the debate on the provincial allocation of seats in 1968.[66]

From 1969 onwards, members of the Bemba-speaking Northern Province section of UNIP began to voice their discontent as they saw the political pendulum swinging away from them towards the Nyanja-speaking (Eastern) group. The discontent took the form of a rising number of constituency-oriented parliamentary questions by Bemba-speaking back-benchers, and of a general attack on the government's policies. This came to a peak early in 1971 just before the open formation of the UPP. In the debate following the President's address to the National Assembly, one Northern Province MP after another attacked the President's policy on citizenship and the economic reforms. Even Junior Ministers joined in, as is shown by the following extract from the speech made by Mr J. C. Sinyangwe, Minister of State for the Eastern Province and Member for the Kasama North constituency:

Sir, we have already started reverting the Economic Reforms in a different form. I have failed to understand why after a Zambian has taken over a shop, after one or two days one realises that a son or a daughter or a wife whoever may be as a Zambian should have taken over, this licence is transferred to this one. The next day you find that that one who bought that shop is asked to move out of that building so that the shop is taken over by a son or a wife of the expatriate.

Our Economic Reforms are failing, Sir. I wonder whether by doing this a Zambian would be able to own a shop according to His Excellency's reforms. After this shop has been taken over by a son, then the father or mother is made to be an employee in the same shop. I am questioning you, Sir, is it good for a father to be an employee . . .[67]

65. *Nat. Ass. Deb.*, Hansard No. 13, 13 February 1968, col. 207, and 16 February 1968, col. 403.
66. *Ibid.*, Hansard No. 14, 25 April 1968, cols 124, 138 and 152.
67. See *Ibid.*, Hansard No. 25, 22 January 1971, col. 229.

Such criticism was a product not so much of policy disagreements as of UNIP's basic problem: the growth of sectional conflict within itself. Sectional groups, of course, have used policy failures as sticks with which to beat their opponents. For example, early in 1971 UNIP back-benchers and Junior Ministers from the Northern Province criticised in speech after speech the three main Ministries run by Eastern Province Ministers—Rural Development, Education, and Power, Transport and Works.[68] In mid-February the President had to address a special meeting of the UNIP parliamentary caucus in an attempt to crush the growing attacks on his administration by MPs of his own party. Ministers, Ministers of State and District Governors were forbidden to attack government policy in public or to ask critical parliamentary questions, although UNIP back-benchers were to retain their parliamentary privilege of querying government on any aspect of policy.[69]

We can conclude that, to the extent that linguistic or provincial groups are self-conscious and regard themselves as distinct interest groups, the MPs' main representative role as the spokesmen of interests is on their behalf, and not on behalf of occupational and other voluntary associations.

*The critical role of the National Assembly*

The final role (already touched on above) which a Parliament can play in the political system is one of criticism of the executive. It can act as a forum of debate on government policy and behaviour. There are two sides to such debates. On the one hand, government Ministers, in principle supported by their back-benchers, seek to defend their actions. On the other hand, opposition MPs seek to expose the government's weak points and thereby, over a period of time, swing public opinion to their side. This is the practical political meaning of parliament's constitutional role of exercising control over the executive. How far did the Zambian National Assembly fulfil this role under the First Republic?

We start by examining the business of the National Assembly.[70] It has spent most of its time passing legislation, debating the budget, and debating the motion of thanks to the President for his address

---

68. See *ibid.*, January and February 1971.
69. ZIS background paper No. 17/71, 17 February 1971.
70. Most of the information which follows has been obtained from the records of the National Assembly and from Hansard.

Table 6.6
Parliamentary business, 1964–72

| | First Assembly | | | | | Second Assembly | | | |
|---|---|---|---|---|---|---|---|---|---|
| | 1964 | 1965 | 1966 | 1967 | 1968 | 1969 | 1970 | 1971 | 1972 |
| LEVEL OF ACTIVITY | | | | | | | | | |
| No. of sitting days | 47 | 60 | 59 | 33 | 66 | 65 | 47 | 49 | 42 |
| No. of columns spoken | 2,730 | 3,650 | 4,104 | 2,102 | 3,660 | 3,778 | 3,059 | 2,888 | 2,372 |
| BILLS | | | | | | | | | |
| No. of Bills passed | 66 | 69 | 73 | 56 | 49 | 57 | 57 | 44 | 40 |
| No. of Bills amended in committee[a] | 32 | 30 | 25 | 28 | 23 | 11 | 9 | n.a.[f] | n.a. |
| MOTIONS | | | | | | | | | |
| Total No. of notices of motions[b] | 63 | 46 | 44 | 38 | 36 | 43 | 34 | n.a. | n.a. |
| Government notices of motions | 45 | 40 | 32 | 29 | 27 | 35 | 28 | n.a. | n.a. |
| Private Members' notices of motions | | | | | | | | | |
| Wednesday adjournment debate | 5 | 2 | 3 | 1 | – | 2 | 3 | 5 | 3 |
| Other | 13 | 4 | 9 | 8 | 9 | 6 | 3 | – | – |
| Distribution of private Members' notices of motion | | | | | | | | | |
| UNIP[c] | 5 | 1 | 2 | 3 | 1 | 7 | 3 | – | – |
| ANC | – | 3 | 4 | 1 | 3 | – | 3 | 4 | 3 |
| NPP Independent | 3 | 2 | 6 | 5 | 5 | 1 | – | 1 | – |
| QUESTIONS | | | | | | | | | |
| Total No. of questions answered[d] | 127 | 35 | 11 | 36 | 21 | 147 | 77 | 117 | 72 |
| Oral | 79 | 28 | 11 | 29 | 16 | 129 | 66 | 91 | 66 |
| Written[e] | 48 | 7 | – | 7 | 5 | 18 | 11 | 26 | 6 |
| Distribution of questions | | | | | | | | | |
| UNIP | 1 | – | – | – | – | 116 | 50 | 53 | 61 |
| ANC | 62 | 25 | 6 | – | 7 | 29 | 25 | 64 | 11 |
| NPP Independent | 59 | 10 | 5 | 36 | 14 | 2 | 2 | – | – |

at the opening of each session.[71] Table 6.6 shows that between January 1964 and December 1968 the first Assembly sat for a total of 265 days, an average of fifty-three days each year; the second Assembly averaged slightly less—fifty-one days a year during its first four years. The length of time that the legislature is in session provides, however, an uncertain guide to the volume of business conducted. A more accurate index to the quantity of debate is given by extracting from Hansard the number of columns spoken. By this criterion the Assembly has (apart from 1967) been considerably more active since independence than was its predecessor, the Legislative Council, in the colonial period. Nevertheless, by the yardstick of established parliaments, and even some of the new ones like those of Ghana and Kenya, the Zambian Assembly's quantity and quality of debate are not impressive. With a formal membership of eighty (and often, in practice, rather less) until the first Assembly was dissolved in December 1968, each MP's annual average contribution to debate ranged from a minimum of twenty-six columns spoken throughout 1967 to a maximum of fifty-one columns in 1966. The volume of debate in the second Assembly was slightly less, with a maximum of thirty-four columns per MP in 1969, falling steadily to a minimum of twenty-one columns in 1972. As we shall see, these annual totals were distributed very unevenly between the different categories of MP.

71. The President's addresses to the National Assembly are lengthy speeches from the presidential Chair which review the past achievements of his government, and refer to future intentions.

---

*Notes to table 6.6*

a The great majority were government amendments. Private Members almost never moved amendments and, if they did, they were rarely accepted.

b This includes notices of motions by private Members for the Wednesday adjournment debate as well as all other notices of motions in the National Assembly's 'Notice of motions book'—excluding notices of motions in other adjournment debates.

c Motions moved by UNIP back-benchers were almost always formal. Thus in the years 1967 to 1970 only two out of twelve motions dealt with substantive issues.

d The number of questions asked usually exceeded the number answered, since several questions were withdrawn or lapsed, or in a few cases were not answered. For example, 1969: 191 questions asked, 147 answered.

e MPs very rarely requested a written reply, but a question was treated in this way if a Member was absent when his question was to be answered.

f Not available.

*Source.* Compiled from Hansard and from records of the Assembly, made available by the Clerk of the House.

Moreover, few speeches by back-benchers on either side of the House showed much evidence of careful preparation, with detailed research into the relevant government publications and other sources of information. The Assembly's library is not much used by Members, nor are the services of the research officer who was appointed by the second Assembly to assist MPs. One searches Hansard in vain for frequent penetrating analyses—defensive or critical—of the major problem areas facing Zambian government and society. Very few significant policy innovations are suggested from the floor of the House.

There were other indications that the first Assembly in particular was not a vigorous body. Limited use was made of the parliamentary question, and adjournment on a definite matter of urgent public importance (in terms of Standing Order No. 30) was never requested. Few substantive motions were tabled as a means of initiating debate on matters of national importance. The rare attempts made in this direction by UNIP back-benchers tended to be frustrated by the government. Thus Mr N. Mundia (Kabwe) was not able to secure a debate on the first National Development Plan in December 1966, but had to wait until October 1967 to discuss a plan which, said Mr Nkumbula, was 'introduced in a very bad manner'—it had been launched by President Kaunda at a UNIP rally in Lusaka instead of being laid before the National Assembly.[72] Government motions, which easily formed a majority of the whole, tended to be formal. So too did those tabled by UNIP back-benchers. Since independence, not only has no private Bill been passed by the Assembly, but no back-bencher has even introduced a private Member's Bill. The total number of Bills enacted remained at a high, albeit somewhat declining, level—the first Assembly passed an average of sixty-three Bills a year, while the second Assembly in its first four years passed on average forty-nine Bills per annum. But the great majority of Bills passed quite quickly (though usually less quickly than in Tanzania) and smoothly through the various stages of the legislative process. The lack of prolonged critical or constructive debate on government Bills was reflected in several ways. First, the average number of days it took for a Bill to pass through all its stages in the National Assembly was low, while a few Bills were rushed through the Assembly in one or two days only. In the second place, more than half of all government Bills were passed without amendment; back-benchers

72. *Nat. Ass. Deb.*, Hansard No. 8, 20 December 1966, cols 202–4, 300–1, and Hansard No. 11, 18 October 1967, col. 106.

almost never moved amendments to such Bills and, on the rare occasions when opposition MPs did so, their amendments were rejected.[73] Finally, it became customary for no debate at all to be held at the committee stage and third reading of a Bill. Thus the second-reading debate covered both the principle of the Bill and detailed criticism—if any—of its clauses. This is still the current practice.[74]

In assessing the contribution of Members to all these different kinds of parliamentary activity, four categories of MP can be clearly distinguished: UNIP Ministers, UNIP back-benchers, opposition ANC Members, and opposition NPP Members.[75] The great majority of those in the first three categories were Africans, while all those in the last category were whites.

Cabinet Ministers talked more than any other group. They introduced Bills, tabled government motions, answered questions and defended government policy. The second most active group during the first National Assembly was the NPP Members, and at times Assembly business appeared to be mainly a dialogue between them and Cabinet Ministers.[76] They made many speeches—including some not highly relevant to the problems of the country. They have not been prolific questioners since independence, though they tended to press Ministers more closely than ANC Members by asking more supplementaries on the replies given to their original questions. In tabling substantive motions NPP Members were more active than either ANC or UNIP back-benchers. But in their case too there was a decline in activity, as evidenced (for example) by the number of motions tabled for the Wednesday adjournment debate in the latter years of the 1964–68 Parliament—from having tabled five in 1964, they tabled only one in 1967 and none in 1968. Some of their motions dealt with wider issues, such as that in 1967 relating to the sale of maize to China on terms which Mr C. D.

73. This was the experience of Mr N. Mundia (ANC) in 1969, when he tried—unsuccessfully—to amend the Local Government Elections Bill and the Land Acquisition Bill.

74. On one noteworthy day, 17 October 1969, the Assembly gave second readings to ten Bills, went through the committee stage of thirteen Bills, the report stage of sixteen, and gave third readings to thirteen. *Nat. Ass. Deb.*, Hansard No. 19, 17 October 1969, cols 433 ff.

75. The NPP was formally dissolved in 1966, but its Members continued as independents. Of the latter, Mr H. R. E. Mitchley was returned in Gwembe North as an independent with ANC support in the December 1968 general election, while his former colleague, Mr R. E. Farmer, was elected ANC Member for Pemba in a by-election in 1971.

76. This situation changed completely with the second Parliament in 1969. Only one independent (ex-NPP) Member—Mr Mitchley—was returned at the 1968 general election.

Burney (Ndola) was rightly convinced would not be profitable to Zambia:

Thus the cost to us of this maize will be £31·4 per ton f.o.b. and we are being paid £20 10s per ton. That strikes me as involving this Government and this country in a stone-cold loss of £10·5 per ton, and if that is now multiplied by the quantity of maize involved we get a figure of £1,000,000 loss on the transaction . . .

*Mr Chona.* You are opposed to our trading with a communist country.[77]

A majority of NPP motions had a communal import and related to the interests of the large commercial farmers (who were mainly white), or to the well-being of the white community generally in Zambia. On a few occasions an NPP Member introduced politically embarrassing motions, such as Mr S. R. Malcolmson's motion of February 1968 on non-attendance and non-participation in the National Assembly,[78] and Mr J. J. Burnside's subsequent motion to reduce Members' salaries.[79]

NPP Members were better equipped than other back-benchers in terms of both parliamentary experience and formal education to take part in the work of the National Assembly.[80] Following the general election of January 1964, only sixteen out of seventy UNIP and ANC Members had ever been in Parliament before, and then (with two exceptions) only during the previous year.[81] All UNIP Members with parliamentary experience became office-holders. Not one of the UNIP back-benchers had therefore formerly served in Parliament, while only two out of ten ANC Members had done so. These facts are a pointer to the rushed and essentially unplanned nature of the decolonisation process in Northern Rhodesia;[82] they also illustrate the exclusion of the African nationalist parties from the protectorate's settler-dominated government and legislature. Such continuity as there was between the Legislative Council of September 1962 and the National Assembly of October 1964 was provided by the white NPP Members. These facts are not in dispute, though it would be rash to suggest that it was the lack of parliamentary experience which was the vital factor in explaining the relative

77. *Nat. Ass. Deb.*, Hansard No. 10, 12 July 1967, cols 951–2.
78. *Ibid.*, Hansard No. 13, 14 February 1968, cols 263 ff. See p. 237.
79. *Ibid.*, 6 March 1968, col. 659.
80. See table 6.4 above.
81. Mr H. Nkumbula (ANC) and Mr W. Nkanza (UNIP) had both been members of the 1959 Legislative Council for a time.
82. Kirkman, *Unscrambling an Empire, op. cit.*, chapters 7 and 8.

poor showing of non-NPP back-benchers in the first Assembly. Only one of the CPP Members returned to the Gold Coast Legislative Assembly in 1951 had served on the former Legislative Council, but unfamiliarity with parliamentary procedure did not detract from the effectiveness of their contribution to the work of the Assembly.

If we turn to the main opposition party, the ANC, it took almost as much part in debate as the NPP. ANC Members were fairly active questioners in 1964, when the party first went into opposition, but they almost gave up asking parliamentary questions from September 1965 onwards. They introduced no private Members' Bills, realising perhaps that such a Bill would not be passed if the government whips were put on against it. They also made very little use of the private Member's motion. They tabled only one motion for the Wednesday adjournment debate in each of the years 1965 and 1966. These dealt with alleged discontent in the civil and local government services, and with Rhodesia's UDI respectively. Subsequently, in 1967 and 1968, ANC Members failed to table any motion for this debate. With only one independent MP remaining in the House as a result of the December 1968 election, it seemed initially that the Wednesday adjournment debate would cease to be part of the Zambian parliamentary tradition. In fact, however, in the second National Assembly in 1969 the UNIP back-bencher Mr K. Jonasi, and the independent, Mr H. R. E. Mitchley, each introduced a motion for the Wednesday adjournment debate. In subsequent years ANC—and in particular, its able deputy leader, Nalumino Mundia—resorted increasingly to this device in order to initiate a series of debates on issues of major national importance such as education policy, various rural development topics, and the heavy-handed methods used by UNIP activists to check whether people possessed UNIP membership cards.[83]

We must conclude, however, that during the first Zambian Parliament, in contrast to the second, the ANC was not a very effective opposition. By and large it failed to take advantage of the opportunities which parliamentary procedure provided for criticism of the government. Even in debate it neither proved very tenacious in its opposition nor were the speeches of its Members replete with constructive policy alternatives. They tended towards angry invective, as did Mr Nkumbula when speaking to his adjournment motion on political youth organisations in August 1968:

83. For an example, see *Nat. Ass. Deb.*, Hansard No. 25, 27 January 1971, cols 351–79.

The youth organisation has been used to terrorise women and children in their own houses. The youth organisations have been interfering with the private lives of many people in this country. They have gone to the bus stops, to the railway stations stopping people intending to go to certain places from catching the bus or the train. They have gone to the same places forcing people to buy this wonderful UNIP card. And if one refuses to buy this UNIP card he is beaten up by the youths. In most cases you find that the police are looking on when this kind of thing is happening.
*Mr Mutemba.* Rubbish!
*Mr Nkumbula.* It could be as rubbish, Mr Speaker, as rubbish as the hon. Member is.[84]

Indications since 1969, however, showed that the ANC had the capacity to bear alone the full brunt of opposition in the second Parliament. The party's morale had been boosted by its 1968 electoral successes, when it not only retained its existing seats but broke into the hitherto UNIP area of Western Province. The party was confident that it was now too strong to suffer the UP's fate of being banned.[85] Over half its MPs were new men, including H. Noyoo, a former Ngambela to the Litunga,[86] and the experienced and highly educated M. Mumbuna, former MP and founding president of the UP. Though the Speaker denied the title of official opposition to the ANC, the party assumed an active role in the Assembly. It started to put parliamentary questions again and was much more pugnacious in its use of supplementary questions than UNIP back-benchers. In addition to the seventy-one oral questions which ANC Members asked in 1970–72, they put fifty-five supplementaries, as against only thirty-two supplementaries in support of the 52 oral questions asked by UNIP Members. In August 1969 ANC for the first time used a constitutional provision which allows seven MPs to request a report on the constitutional validity of a Bill or statutory instrument, in order to challenge a government ruling that all chiefs and headmen must attend meetings called by District Governors.[87] Various Bills were fought hard and even bitterly, including the Constitution Amendment (No. 5) Bill of 1969, which threatened, *inter alia*, to deprive at least one ANC Member

84. *Ibid.*, Hansard No. 15, 20 August 1968, col. 232.
85. ANC's new attitude of defiance was reflected, *inter alia*, in Mr Nkumbula's threat to allow his supporters to retaliate against intimidation by UNIP activists. *Zambia Mail*, 18 July 1969.
86. The Ngambela is a traditional office-holder; the nearest approximation is Chief Minister. The Litunga is Paramount Chief of the Lozi.
87. Constitution of Zambia, s. 27. The tribunal, comprising two High Court judges appointed by the Chief Justice, ruled that the statutory instrument in question was legal.

of his seat and to reduce the prerogatives of the Litunga. N. Mundia, ANC deputy leader (and the Member whose seat had been in jeopardy)[88] even tried unsuccessfully in the first session to persuade the government to accept amendments to two Bills—the Local Government Elections Bill (No. 44/69) and the Land Acquisition Bill (No. 45/69). On four occasions in the same session ANC Members used the motion to adjourn at the end of the day to raise matters they regarded as important. But the new Speaker ruled them out of order on three of those occasions and from 1970 ANC largely gave up its attempts to use the adjournment motion as a means of initiating debate. On the other hand, as we have seen, the party increased its use of the Wednesday adjournment debate. Clearly, the National Assembly provided the ANC with a vehicle of publicity. To a limited extent parliamentary immunity enabled its MPs to speak more freely than they could do outside the House. During 1969, however, three ANC Members were disciplined for over-stepping the bounds of parliamentary propriety. When some ANC Members threatened that the Constitution Amendment (No. 5) Bill would cause bloodshed in the country, President Kaunda himself responded and stated that such talk under the cover of parliamentary privilege must stop at once; if necessary, legislation would be introduced to curb speeches by MPs which would 'confuse the humble folk' of Zambia.[89] The most drastic penalty imposed on an opposition Member was in October 1970, when the secretary general of the ANC, Mr Mungoni Liso, was expelled for the rest of the second National Assembly for failing to substantiate his un-dignified allegation that the government had paid young women K4 a day to entertain delegates to the third Summit Conference of Non-aligned Nations, held in Lusaka.[90] The following year the deputy leader of ANC, Mr Mundia, was also suspended, though for only three months.[91] Another factor relevant to the effectiveness of ANC's parliamentary performance was the party's charge that the new Speaker of the second National Assembly had turned down its private Members' motions for debate without giving reasons, had refused to allow ANC Members to move adjournment debates, and that his rulings on interjections and points of order were

88. In the event, Mr Mundia (MP for Libonda) was released from restriction before the relevant clause in this Constitution Amendment Bill became operative. See p. 213 above.

89. President Kaunda was speaking at a Lusaka rally to celebrate the tenth anniversary of the founding of UNIP. See *Zambia Mail*, 27 October 1969.

90. *Nat. Ass. Deb.*, Hansard No. 23, 24 September 1970, col. 132, and 2 October 1970, col. 461.

91. *Ibid.*, Hansard No. 25, 24 February 1971, col. 1457.

usually weighted against the opposition.[92] The party felt so strongly
that it was being hampered by the Speaker that in July 1969 its
Members staged a two-day boycott of the House and called for
his resignation.[93]

Lastly, the closing months of the second Assembly saw the advent
of a new factor which adversely affected the parliamentary activity
of MPs from both parties. This was the new willingness of the
executive, following the formation of UPP in August 1971, to
detain not only ordinary opposition party activists but MPs as well.
The UPP party leader (Mr Simon Kapwepwe) was detained, as
were six UNIP Members who supported the UPP and one ANC
Member, Mufaya Mumbuna, one of the party's most able parliamentarians. One indication of the effect of these detentions was the
abrupt way in which Bemba-speaking UNIP Members from the
Northern and Luapula Provinces felt constrained to stop asking
parliamentary questions; the number (twenty-nine) which they asked
in 1971 fell sharply in 1972.

The extent to which ANC's parliamentary performance affected
public opinion must be doubted. The preconditions for Assembly
debate to serve as a factor influencing public opinion are largely
absent in Zambia. First, the mass media of newspapers, radio and
television are too under-developed to reach a wide audience. Even
the *Times of Zambia* averaged in 1968 a daily circulation of only
39,563[94] (about 1 per cent of the population) and the circulation of
all government publications was only about twice as large. Secondly,
most voters have not the money (to buy a radio, for example), the
literacy or the technical political knowledge to follow parliamentary
debates. In the circumstances the National Assembly must have
even less impact on public opinion than a legislature in a more
technologically developed Western country. What influence it may
have must be largely confined to the small, educated and mainly
urban strata of the population. Finally, there is no evidence that
swings of opinion away from UNIP (for example, in Western
Province, as reflected in the 1968 general election[95]) were the result
of a popular reaction to the course of parliamentary debate.[96]

92. *Times of Zambia*, 14 July 1969.          93. *Ibid.*, 11 July 1969.
94. *Ibid.*, 13 August 1969. By June 1969 it had risen to a daily circulation
of 50,954.
95. See chapter 5.
96. This is not to say that injudicious comment, whether made inside or
outside the National Assembly, may not have had important electoral consequences. An example is the anti-Lozi statement alleged to have been made
by Mr Peter Chanda, Minister of State for the Copperbelt Province, in
August 1968. See p. 115, n. 27.

The fourth category of MPs to be examined are UNIP back-benchers. Their role in the first Parliament was almost non-existent. They had a strong tendency not to attend, and an even stronger tendency not to participate. They were reluctant to make speeches in debate. With only one exception (June 1964), no UNIP back-bencher ever put a question between January 1964 and December 1968. One reason was that in 1963, when an ANC–UNIP coalition government was in office, ANC Members adopted a convention that they should not question their own government, and this convention was followed by UNIP back-benchers after the formation of an all-UNIP government in January 1964. Observance of this convention was made easier by the fact that UNIP Members already had alternative access to such information as they required— for example, they could approach a Minister direct. Moreover, they were not encouraged officially to question Ministers.

UNIP back-benchers tabled few motions and, with the exception of Mr Mundia's motion on the first National Development Plan,[97] these were all formal. Nor did UNIP Members bring any private Member's Bill before the Assembly. If they had legislation to propose they preferred to persuade the party to adopt it rather than run the risk of incurring official displeasure by introducing it into the National Assembly.[98] Lastly, UNIP Members in the 1964–68 Parliament tended not to speak their minds freely. There were, of course, a few exceptions. In 1966–67 Mr Mundia questioned the party's new philosophy of Humanism and criticised the budget and other government policies. Another instance took place on the eve of the general election in 1968, when a heated debate took place in the National Assembly on the allocation of seats between provinces.[99] UNIP Members from the North-western and Eastern Provinces regarded the constituency allocation as unfair and demanded that a population census should be held before the election. They attacked the impartiality of the Electoral Commission and predicted violent sectional conflict if their demands were not met. In the words of Mr J. C. P. Ngoma, Minister of State:

There are red skies overcasting Zambia ... We ought to put our house in order, Sir. Time and again we have pointed our fingers at our brothers in Nigeria at our political platforms ... Sir, as a Christian, I do not want this to happen here in Zambia.[100]

97. See p. 228 above.
98. There is no evidence, however, that any significant number of Bills originated in this way on the initiative of UNIP back-benchers.
99. *Nat. Ass. Deb.*, Hansard No. 14, 25 April 1968, cols 112 ff.
100. *Ibid.*, col. 151.

On this occasion MPs were secure in the knowledge that they were expressing the views of a section of the party leadership. Individual criticism was more risky and might have serious repercussions outside the House, even for a Cabinet Minister. Thus there was an angry reaction among UNIP officials on the Copperbelt to the speech made in the National Assembly on 5 March 1968 by Mr M. Sipalo, then Minister of Agriculture. In a reference to UNIP's card-checking campaign, Mr Sipalo said that it was senseless for the party 'to resort to primitive, archaic and fascist tactics'.[101] This speech, as well as Sipalo's earlier resignation in 1967 (subsequently retracted) from UNIP and the government, prompted a demonstration against him by party activists when he visited Kasama, capital of the Northern Province, in April 1968.

The failure of a majority of UNIP back-benchers either to participate or to attend the Assembly regularly became so marked in the first Parliament that Rodney Malcolmson (independent) suggested that the President should dissolve the Assembly because of the lack of interest shown by Ministers and MPs.[102] Several hypotheses can be advanced to explain the non-participation of UNIP back-benchers. A cultural hypothesis, stressing the African lack of attachment to 'Western' parliamentary traditions, can be rejected outright because it cannot explain why ANC Members (who are also Africans) participated more than UNIP back-benchers, the vigour of other African legislatures (that of Kenya, for example[103]), and the increased participation of back-benchers in the second Assembly. A second hypothesis is that key decisions were taken elsewhere and that UNIP was a sufficiently open party for MPs to find avenues for expressing their grievances within the party itself—at regional as well as national level. The locus of policy-making lay outside the Assembly, as it still does today. The President, sometimes in consultation with the Cabinet and the central committee of UNIP, took major policy decisions, while the civil service dealt with technical matters. At most, UNIP Members could trim the edges of government policy. But they could do this not in the National Assembly but in the national council of UNIP, to which they all belonged and which confirmed decisions taken by the central committee.[104] Moreover, impending government legislation was (and is) presented to a meeting of the UNIP parliamentary caucus, normally held immediately before each parliamentary

101. *Ibid.*, Hansard No. 13, 5 March 1968, col. 604.

102. *Ibid.*, 14 February 1968, cols 263 ff.

103. See C. Gertzel, *The Politics of Independent Kenya* (London, 1970), chapter 5.

104. See chapter 4.

session. Following discussion in caucus, MPs were expected to toe the party line. This, substantially, was the explanation for non-participation of backbenchers given by the caucus chairman, Mr Sikota Wina (who is also government Chief Whip), when replying to Mr Malcolmson's motion, referred to above. But this hypothesis cannot be pressed too far. It was only after the hotly contested elections to the central committee in August 1967 that the national council became temporarily the scene of lively debate, while the parliamentary caucus seems at most times to have been a quiescent body, meeting only a few times a year and then only for a couple of hours. Finally, an objection to this hypothesis is that it does not explain why ANC Members contributed a good deal when they also knew that government decisions were made off the floor of the House, that their own rhetoric and pressure would not alter those decisions, and that their criticisms would often be met with ridicule and abuse.

The non-participation of UNIP back-benchers in the first Parliament must be explained also in terms of other factors. First, there was the fact that the opposition was small—at its maximum strength, before December 1968, it could muster no more than twenty out of eighty MPs. Relatively few UNIP Members needed to attend in order to ensure the passage of government measures. Secondly, though the opposition was small numerically, individual opposition MPs—particularly those belonging to the NPP—criticised government policies and in this way did the work which would otherwise have fallen to UNIP back-benchers. Thirdly, in the 1964–68 Parliament standing orders did not provide any sanction which could be invoked against MPs who were lax in attendance. Fourthly, UNIP back-benchers operated within a framework of rules which discouraged participation. The fact that UNIP sought to present a united front in the National Assembly clearly circumscribed what a back-bencher could say, and there was little point in merely underlining what a Cabinet Minister (for example) had already said. Another discouraging factor (which, however, applied also to ANC Members) was that UNIP back-benchers tended to have had less formal schooling than Ministers; they were often uncertain of their ability to express their thoughts clearly in English. Since they were broadly in agreement with government policy, they might reasonably have concluded that unquestioning loyalty rather than participation would pave the way to public office. Finally, as we have seen, a UNIP Member lacked any strong inducement to impress his constituents with the extent and quality of his participation in the Assembly. The selection of candidates was the prerogative of President Kaunda rather than of the constituency organisations. Few people in the Member's constituency were likely to know about his parliamentary performance. The MP had, therefore, little feeling that he must play to a critical local gallery. This was reinforced by the virtual absence of marginal seats, so that MPs did not feel obliged to press vote-catching issues in the Assembly and to try and get into the public eye.

Leaders of UNIP were aware that the first National Assembly was not a lively institution. President Kaunda voiced his concern when he opened the new National Assembly building in mid-1967. He stated that he wanted to see three things happen: there should be 'more debates on matters of general policy'; increasing use should be made of questions and adjournment debates as a 'means of stimulating parliamentary life'; and in these and other ways back-benchers of all parties should become more active in the House.[105] The corollary of this statement, although not explicitly stated, was that the government would welcome constructive criticism. In 1968 other UNIP leaders expressed privately their fears that the position would deteriorate further with the disappearance of the indepen-dent MPs following the 1968 general election.

These fears appeared to be realised with the fiasco on the third day (28 January 1969) of the new Parliament. No MP rose to speak after hearing an opening address by President Kaunda, and the Assembly had to adjourn prematurely. This incident made it clear to the party leadership that, with only one independent remaining in the House, it lay squarely with UNIP Members, in-cluding back-benchers, to maintain the vigour of debate. Their response was swift. The next day the government Chief Whip, Mr Sikota Wina, announced that in future UNIP Members would be fined by the party for failure to attend the Assembly without adequate and prior explanation.[106] Subsequently, not only has the attendance of UNIP Members risen but there have also been signs of their greater participation in Assembly proceedings—several members have begun asking parliamentary questions and more speeches are being made by back-benchers. Indeed, just over half the UNIP back-benchers have at one time or another asked parlia-mentary questions since 1969. In April 1969 President Kaunda went so far as to say that:

since our opposition party has demonstrated its incapacity to provide any meaningful and constructive opposition in Parliament, the result is that

105. Press release No. 745/67, 2 May 1967.
106. *Times of Zambia*, 30 January 1969.

the representatives of the people in UNIP—the back-benchers—have taken over what is basically the role of the opposition. There is today constructive and meaningful debate in the Zambian Parliament on issues that matter. The Ministers ... are facing constructive criticism and piercing question from UNIP MPs who know their objectives and who know what the people really want. I must record my appreciation for this *new* feature in Parliament.[107]

Several factors account for the greater activity of UNIP Members in 1969. Nearly half these Members were new to Parliament;[108] several were highly educated and had previous experience in non-political occupations—for example, Mr Amock Phiri was a former lecturer in Sociology at the University of Zambia. UNIP Members were faced also with a large number of controversial issues on which the ANC attacked the government fiercely—the Bill to change the procedure for amending the constitution by abolishing the requirement that a referendum must be held in relation to certain entrenched clauses, the Matero economic reforms of August 1969, and a further spate of constitutional amendments in October. In the heightened activity which resulted, several MPs voiced their views fearlessly. Thus, following the presentation of the 1969 budget by the then Vice-president, Mr Simon Kapwepwe, Mrs Robertson (a nominated UNIP Member) criticised certain new taxes on necessities such as tinned fish, pointing out that the effect would be to raise the cost of living of the ordinary people. The government dropped the tax on some of these items.[109] Then, early in 1971, came the spate of criticism (noted above) directed at the President's policy on citizenship and the economic reforms. That such criticism came from Northern Province UNIP Members underlined the fact that by this time the balance of political power within the ruling party had tilted heavily towards the Nyanja-speaking group. Mindful of the major contribution which the people of their province had made to the freedom struggle, Northern MPs struck out angrily at Eastern Province Ministers; they were less prepared than their Eastern and Barotse counterparts had been after the central committee elections in August 1967 to wait for a further turn of the wheel of political fortune. Following Kapwepwe's defection from UNIP in August 1971, a few Northern MPs followed him into the UPP, while many others, though remaining

107. UNIP national council minutes, April 1969 (Lusaka, mimeo.), p. 23 (emphasis added).
108. For details of the composition of the new Parliament, see chapter 5, above.
109. *Nat. Ass. Deb.*, Hansard No. 17, 13 February 1969, cols 715–17.

within UNIP, were suspected of sympathising with the new party.

The increased size of the opposition in the second Assembly enhanced the need for strict discipline within UNIP. The parliamentary caucus was not abolished, and President Kaunda warned that he did not regard all contributions by UNIP back-benchers as constructive.[110] Several incidents showed how quickly the limits of party tolerance were reached. When, early in 1969, Mr Valentine Musakanya—nominated MP, Minister of State, and former head of the Zambian civil service—spoke in favour of mini-skirts, he was physically assaulted by UNIP youths at a State House reception held soon afterwards,[111] and was dropped as a nominated MP in the following year. Again, there was the 'Mutti affair' in April 1969. Mr J. M. Mutti, former Zambian ambassador to Ethiopia and newly elected MP for Livingstone, stated (incorrectly) in a maiden speech that Zambian Ministers were the highest paid in Africa and ought to give up their Mercedes-Benz cars. He was heavily barracked by UNIP Members during the course of his speech.[112] A few days later he announced that he was resigning as MP and Minister of State. The President then intervened, reprimanded Mr Mutti, but requested him to continue as a Minister.

*Conclusion*

We have examined the four roles of the National Assembly in relation to the Zambian political system. We have found that in most respects the Assembly is a comparatively unimportant institution. This is because it is poorly integrated into the main processes of the political system. Like most parliaments, it is certainly not the main locus of government decision-making. It is weakly linked to the executive because of the paucity of its committees whereby scrutiny of, and contact with, the civil service can be institutionalised. It is not even the main platform for major government pronouncements—it tends to take second place to the UNIP national council, and even to mass rallies. The parliamentary caucus of UNIP Members is a most insignificant body in the constellation of central organs of the party—the central committee, the national council and the general conference. The Assembly is not even the primary forum for the articulation of interests. The exercise of its constitutional powers was rendered largely formalistic by

110. UNIP national council minutes, April 1969, *op. cit.*, p. 23.
111. *Times of Zambia*, 21 February 1969.
112. *Nat. Ass. Deb.*, Hansard No. 17, 18 April 1969, cols 2349 ff.

the discipline and disparity in strength of the two main parties and, though its emergency powers could be vitally important, they are not likely to be called into play. While making due allowance for the indications since 1969 of the second Parliament's increasing vigour, we must still conclude that neither the National Assembly as an institution nor MPs in their individual capacities have played a crucial role in the Zambian political system.

# 7

# Government and administration

*William Tordoff and Robert Molteno*

In many African countries the legacy of Whitehall has been more important than that of Westminster. Thus at independence Ghana inherited a strong civil service, with 60 per cent of its senior posts filled by Ghanaians,[1] but a legislature which, though frequently lively, often seemed irrelevant to the real political life of the country. In contrast, Zambia in October 1964, because of its history of settler-dominated politics, was left with both a legislature whose African members were lacking in experience *and* an indifferent administration. In the critical pre-independence period between 1951 and 1957 Kwame Nkrumah's government took steps to localise the civil service. Northern Rhodesia, on the other hand, was throughout the 1950s part of the settler-ruled Central African Federation: little progress was therefore made in this direction until 1962, when it was decided to introduce a constitution which would make majority rule possible.[2] Only in 1963 was a staff training college set up. As late as February 1964 only thirty-eight of 848 administrative and professional posts were filled by Africans, and only 26 per cent of Division I and II posts.[3] The settler legacy complicated localisation in other ways. The task was made more urgent by the exodus of many white Rhodesian and South African civil servants after 1963—especially from the police force and the technical classes. The scale of the task was greater than in West Africa, since whites had monopolised posts down to very junior levels such as typists, road and building foremen, and mechanics. The

1. Austin, *Politics in Ghana, op. cit.*, p. 8.
2. See Kirkman, *Unscrambling an Empire, op. cit.*, chapter 7.
3. K. H. Nkwabilo (chairman of the Zambianisation and Training Committee for the Public Service), 'Remarks on manpower and Zambianisation' (Lusaka, mimeo., 26 June 1969), p. 3.

pool of educated Zambians from which to draw was also relatively smaller.[4]

There were further factors which weakened Zambia's administrative legacy. Almost to the eve of independence, the Northern Rhodesian administration was preoccupied with law-and-order functions. Again, while Ministries had been created in the 1950s out of a loose amalgam of departments, the latter were not fully integrated into the Ministries. Their organisation was often not based on rational principles, and inter-ministerial co-ordination was weak. Further structural disruption was caused in January 1964, when the formerly federal government departments were handed over to the Northern Rhodesian government. This necessitated extensive reorganisation, including the amalgamation of hitherto racially segregated Ministries such as African Education and European Education. These problems of administrative legacy were compounded because Zambia was in the ironical and unusual position of having more wealth and less local administrative and technical capability to utilise it than the countries to her north.[5] Moreover, the rapid growth of central government spending (from K91 million in 1963–1964 to K553 million in 1971)[6] and the consequently enormous expansion of activities and staff have forced the civil service to concentrate largely on keeping the inherited machinery going. No overall investigation into the suitability of that machinery for economic development has yet been held.

In this chapter we examine the machinery of government in order to assess its effectiveness for implementing the first and second National Development Plans. We start by looking at the Cabinet as the policy-formulating body of government, and then examine the ministerial (including the provincial and district) organisation, and certain aspects of the civil service. Against this background, we consider more specifically the implementation of the Development Plans.

*The Cabinet*

The independence constitution of Zambia confers wide powers on the President. The executive power of the republic vests in him, and

4. *Civil Service staff list* (Lusaka), September 1962; *First National Development Plan, op. cit.*, p. 2.

5. Cf President Kaunda: '. . . we entered Independence without a single African technician in one of the most highly industrialised societies on the continent.' Speech to UNIP national council at Mulungushi, 9 November 1968, ZIS background paper No. 84/68, 8 November 1968.

6. *Statistical Yearbook 1968* (Lusaka, 1969), tables 12-3, 12-4; *Monthly Digest of Statistics* (Lusaka, 1972), vol. VIII, No. 10, tables 30 and 31.

he is 'not obliged to follow the advice tendered by any other person or authority'.[7] From early 1968 onwards President Kaunda has taken, and announced publicly, certain decisions on vitally important matters—such as the economic reforms of 1968 and the take-over by the State of a 51 per cent capital share of the mines in 1969—without the prior concurrence of his Cabinet. One reason was probably that, following the bitterly contested elections to the UNIP central committee in August 1967, the Cabinet lacked unity and security was relaxed. But at least one Minister resented the assertion by the President of his constitutional powers.[8]

This is not to argue that the Cabinet was no longer important from 1968 onwards. It is still the meeting place of some of the country's leading politicians, behind whom are ranged strong sectional interests. Kaunda regularly consults it on a wide range of issues, including budget proposals, draft legislation, and any matter on which Ministries disagree and which has not been resolved at official or ministerial level. He may also seek the collective advice of his Cabinet Ministers on big questions of general policy. In examining the role of the Cabinet, we begin by looking at its composition.

*The composition of the Cabinet.* The size of the Cabinet has grown steadily since independence. Including both the President and the Vice-president, it numbered sixteen both at that date and in December 1966, seventeen in December 1968, and—following the first general election after independence—nineteen in January 1969. Since then it has risen to twenty-six—consisting in December 1972 of the President, Vice-president, Secretary General to the Government, one Minister heading each of the eight provinces, and fifteen in charge of central Ministries.[9] Moreover, while most Ministers have been reshuffled quite frequently, the turnover in Cabinet membership was low until the December 1968 election.[10] Following that election a complete reconstruction of the Cabinet took place, partly because of the electoral defeat of four former Ministers and partly because the major reorganisation of government which was then

7. Constitution of Zambia, *op. cit.*, s. 48(2).

8. In a forthright speech to the National Assembly, Munukayumbwa Sipalo, then Minister of Agriculture, warned against the 'Divine Right of Presidents'. *Nat. Ass. Deb.*, Hansard No. 13, 5 March 1968, col. 603. Sipalo's sentiments were shared, but not publicly expressed, by certain other Ministers.

9. Based on the Republic of Zambia *Government Directory*, issued by the Cabinet Office, and the *Government Gazette*.

10. Two Ministers were dismissed in 1966 for alleged financial impropriety and a third was named as ambassador to China in 1968.

undertaken entailed a drastic (although, as it turned out, not permanent) reduction in the number of central Ministries. Of six new
Ministers, only one was retained in Lusaka; the others became provincial Ministers, serving in each case outside their province of
political origin and strength in order to maintain the discipline of
the ruling party. While all Ministers belonged to the Cabinet,[11]
two tiers of Ministers now seemed to have been established. The
first tier comprised those administratively competent and often politically powerful Ministers who were in charge of (what were in
many cases) omnibus Ministries at the centre, while the second tier
was composed of (mostly new) Ministers in charge of provinces.[12]
This pattern continued throughout the second National Assembly
(1969–73).[13]

The major reconstruction of the Cabinet in early 1969 was
followed by frequent further changes in its composition, with new
men being brought in and certain existing Ministers removed. Thus
by late 1972 less than one-third of the Cabinet had been Ministers
since 1964 and this obviously reduced continuity in policy-making.
Also, the President's frequent reshuffling of Ministers between portfolios disrupted policy-making within Ministries. In the period from
1964 to 1968 most Ministers only kept their portfolios between one
and two years. Moreover, since the general election of December
1968 there has been no abatement of this tendency to move Ministers between provinces and between central Ministry portfolios.
Private and political misbehaviour (such as alleged corruption or
disloyalty to the party) were the causes of a Minister's downfall. In
no case was a Minister publicly criticised, reshuffled or removed
from the Cabinet because of incompetence in running his Ministry.

Another factor adversely affecting the Cabinet's policy-making
role has been the growth in its size since January 1969. Largely
because of the splitting up of five of the six huge omnibus Ministries
which were then created, the number of Lusaka-based Ministers
has steadily increased, resulting in a Cabinet of twenty-six at the
end of 1972. Moreover, the highly educated men who were given
office in 1964 despite their meagre record as UNIP activists were
by 1972 a tiny minority in the Cabinet. Though several men with

11. 'Government organisation. Working instruction for the new administration', Cabinet Office circular No. 13 of 1969, 1 February 1969, pp. 2 and 4.

12. An exception was Mr H. D. Banda, who was made Minister of the
important Copperbelt Province; he had been a member of the Cabinet since
January 1964.

13. While not one of the eight provincial Ministers in office at the end of
1972 had been in the Cabinet during the first National Assembly, nine of the
seventeen Lusaka-based Ministers had held Cabinet positions before 1969.

*Table 7.1*
Composition of the Cabinet

| Linguistic origins | *October 1964 (independence)* | *December 1968 (pre-general election)* | *January 1969 (post-general election)* | *August 1970* | *December 1972* |
|---|---|---|---|---|---|
| *Bemba* | | | | | |
| President | 1 | 1 | 1 | 1 | 1 |
| Vice-president | – | 1 | 1 | 1 | – |
| Secretary General | – | – | 1 | 1 | – |
| Other | 3 | 3 | 4 [a] | 5 [b] | 7 [c] |
| *Total* | 4 | 5 | 7 | 8 | 8 |
| *Nyanja (Eastern)* | | | | | |
| Vice-president | 1 | – | – | – | – |
| Other | 2 | 3 | 5 | 5 | 4 |
| *Total* | 3 | 3 | 5 | 5 | 4 |
| *Lozi (Western)* | 4 | 4 | 2 | 2 | 4 |
| *Lunda–Luvale–Kaonde (North-western)* | 1 | 1 | 2 | 4 | 4 |
| *Soli (Central)* | 1 | 1 | 1 | 2 [d] | 2 [d] |
| *Ila–Tonga (Southern)* | | | | | |
| Vice-president) | – | – | – | – | 1 |
| Other | 2 | 2 | 2 | 2 | 2 |
| *Total* | 2 | 2 | 2 | 2 | 3 |
| *Coloured* | | | | | |
| Secretary General | – | – | – | – | 1 |
| Other | – | – | – | 1 | – |
| *Total* | – | – | – | 1 | 1 |
| *White* | 1 | 1 | – | – | – |
| *Total size* | 16 | 17 [e] | 19 | 24 [f] | 26 |

*Notes*

a Including, for the first time, one Minister from Luapula Province.
b Including two Ministers from Luapula Province.
c Including only one Minister from Luapula Province.
d Including one Central Province Minister who is not Soli.
e Prior to Mr D. C. Mwiinga's removal from the Cabinet as Minister of Health in 1968 there had been eighteen members of the Cabinet.
f Including two ambassadors of Cabinet rank.

university education were made Cabinet Ministers during the second Parliament, more and more members seemed not to be greatly interested in many of the policy issues coming before them, and left discussion to a handful of their colleagues. When they did intervene they often did so only in matters affecting an area or group to which they felt politically beholden.

The linguistic composition of the Cabinet has also altered significantly since independence (see table 7.1). Up to the 1968 election the Cabinet reflected a careful balance between the country's various linguistic groups, and the image of a national government was projected. This balance had been retained despite individual changes in Cabinet membership. The UNIP elections of August 1967, which vitally affected the composition of the party's central committee, led at Cabinet level to important changes in the assignment of portfolios rather than to the actual displacement of Ministers.[14]

The basis of this balance was complex. In part, it indicated the numerical, political or bargaining strength of a particular group within the ruling party. Thus the dominant position of the large Bemba-speaking group within UNIP guaranteed that group substantial Cabinet representation. Again, in 1964 the Lozi-speaking group had threatened to withdraw from the party altogether unless it was granted adequate representation in the new Cabinet,[15] and Kaunda could not afford to ignore a threat which, if carried out, might have precipitated the secession of Barotseland. In securing four Cabinet posts the latter had received a more generous allocation than either its population or political record warranted. That the Lozi-speaking group's bargaining position was still strong two years later had been shown when the President dropped two Barotse Ministers from his Cabinet for alleged corrupt practices;[16] they were replaced by two others from the same province—M. Sipalo and Dr K. D. Konoso. Within the limitations imposed by the strength of the linguistic groups, Kaunda used his discretion to create a Cabinet which had both a national image and included competent administrators. Among the latter were Arthur Wina, Elijah Mudenda, John Mwanakatwe and Peter Matoka, all of whom had either no record or very short records as UNIP activists.[17]

The linguistic distribution of the Cabinet changed noticeably in

14. ZIS press release No. 1812/67, n.d. [September 1967]; *Gazette* notice No. 1465 of 1967.

15. Mulford, *Zambia: the Politics of Independence*, op. cit., pp. 329–30.

16. The Ministers were Nalumino Mundia and Mubiana Nalilungwe.

17. See Mulford, *Zambia: the Politics of Independence*, op. cit., p. 300.

January 1969,[18] following the general election the previous month, and has continued to change since then. In the election UNIP confirmed its monopoly control of the Northern and Luapula Provinces and swept the Copperbelt; Bemba-speaking representation in the slightly enlarged Cabinet was therefore increased, and an MP from Luapula was made a Cabinet Minister for the first time. The Eastern and North-Western Provinces voted more heavily UNIP than ever before, and this despite the disaffection openly shown by some leading politicians from these provinces immediately following the central committee elections in 1967. They were therefore rewarded with a collective jump in Cabinet representation from four to seven. Conversely, the Western Province electorate turned against UNIP, and three Lozi Cabinet Ministers lost their seats. Lozi leaders in the ruling party were weak electorally even in their alleged area of strength, and this fact, coupled with their discomfiture at Mulungushi in 1967, meant that their bargaining position collapsed. The President did not nominate any of the defeated Lozi Ministers (of whom the most important were Arthur Wina and Sipalo) to the National Assembly, although such nomination would have enabled him to re-appoint them to his Cabinet.

The 1969 Cabinet was more obviously a product of inter-group power relations than its predecessor. This was further demonstrated later in the year when Luapulan MPs almost unanimously became dissatisfied with their hitherto automatic membership of a Bemba-speaking bloc (within UNIP) dominated by Northern Province leaders. They approached the President with a request for increased Cabinet representation—to which he acceded with the appointment of S. M. Chisembele in October. Although sectional pressures such as these were important in shaping the composition of the Cabinet, President Kaunda remained anxious to project a government and party with a national image. He increased the Cabinet representation of numerically weaker groups in North-western and Central Provinces, and used his nominating powers to mitigate the effects of the 1968 election results. Among the (five) persons whom he nominated to the National Assembly were Mr F. M. Mulikita, a senior Lozi-speaking civil servant who was at once made a Cabinet Minister; Mr F. Chuula, a Tonga-speaking lawyer who was promoted Attorney General (outside the Cabinet); and Mrs M. V. Robertson, a white housewife.

The ministerial changes of 1969 reflected an intensified articula-

18. 'Government organisation—establishment of new Ministries: allocation of subjects to portfolios', Cabinet Office circular No. 4 of 1969, 4 January 1969.

tion of sectional interests within UNIP, and projected those interests into the arena of the Cabinet. Further dramatic illustration of this point came in 1971. By this time the balance of power inside the ruling party had swung so heavily away from the Northern Province Bemba-speaking faction that its disgruntled leaders indulged in bitter attacks on President Kaunda's government. In August Kaunda dismissed Chimba (who was already suspended) and three Junior Ministers, thereby precipitating the 'exit' from both UNIP and the Cabinet of his erstwhile deputy, Simon Kapwepwe.[19] It should be noted, too, that the existence of strong opposition areas has on occasion influenced the composition of the Cabinet in their favour. After 1969 President Kaunda did not give up hope of winning greater support in the ANC-dominated Southern and Western Provinces. When, therefore, his Bemba support showed signs of waning in late 1970, he increased the Cabinet representation of the two opposition provinces from four to seven Ministers.

There is also the fact that in recent years the Cabinet has become increasingly sensitive not merely to the demands of the rural areas but also to the competition among rural areas over the distribution of government resources. Thus of the eleven new Ministers appointed between January 1969 and August 1970, eight represented rural seats and at least six represented constituencies in their areas of political strength. To the extent that this political trend has affected the expenditure priorities of the government, it has influenced the growth of social services rather than the quantity of resources devoted to stimulating agriculture. Thus, while education and health spending rose from K60 million in 1968 to K99 million in 1971, the Ministry of Rural Development's spending rose only marginally. Indeed, the Cabinet's commitment to rural development in 1969 may have been weakened following the formation in 1971 of the UPP, with its appeal oriented to the Copperbelt and the Bemba-speaking people. Of the eight new appointments to the Cabinet between late 1970 and the end of 1972, not only were five Bemba-speaking but four represented urban seats and the two who were nominated MPs had urban affiliations.

*The working of the Cabinet.* The procedure of the Zambian Cabinet follows the Downing Street model and may be summarised briefly. The Secretary General to the Government, who replaced the former Secretary to the Cabinet in February 1969,[20] is in charge of the Cabinet Office. He arranges the Cabinet's business and

19. See pp. 118–19 above.
20. Constitution of Zambia, *op. cit.*, s. 47(2).

compiles an agenda which, together with memoranda and other supporting papers, is issued to Ministers in advance of a Cabinet meeting. Discussion in Cabinet is normally based on a memorandum
prepared by a particular Minister after consultation with other interested Ministries. The decisions reached by the Cabinet, as distinct
from the detailed discussion, are recorded; they are conveyed to the
appropriate person or authority by means of an extract from the
minutes.[21]

Until 1969 Cabinet meetings were held on Tuesday of each week.
Strictly, Cabinet business should have been limited to questions of
general policy requiring the collective advice of Ministers, and
questions on which there was a difference of view between Ministers which had not been resolved at official or ministerial level.
Draft legislation was also required to be submitted to Cabinet,
though not normally subordinate legislation made by a Minister.[22]
In fact, however, the Cabinet tended to discuss minor matters as
well as major policy issues. This is implied in the President's statement of 9 November 1968, when he announced that the Cabinet
would in future meet once or twice a month instead of weekly and
consider only major policy matters.[23] There was a fairly high
reference of material to the Cabinet in the first four years after
independence. While memoranda might be excluded from the
agenda because they did not comply with the rules laid down by the
Cabinet Office as to the time and method of submission, they were
rarely rejected on the grounds of substance.

There were several reasons why minor matters came within the
purview of the Cabinet. Some Ministers, particularly those new to
high office, liked to get the backing of their colleagues for matters
which clearly lay within their own discretion, while other Ministers—and their permanent secretaries—were sometimes genuinely
uncertain whether or not to refer a particular issue to the Cabinet.
Matters were also referred to the Cabinet which could have been
resolved at official or ministerial level if the rules relating to inter-
ministerial consultation laid down by the Cabinet Office had been
followed.[24]

*Cabinet committees.* The arrangement whereby any matter could be

21. In 1969 a revised system of follow-up action on Cabinet and Cabinet
committee conclusions was introduced, and took effect from 1 April. Cabinet
Office circulars No. 8 of 1969, 15 January 1969, and No. 15 of 1969, 1 April
1969.

22. Cabinet Office circular No. 74 of 1968, 9 September 1968, annexure c.

23. ZIS background paper No. 84/68, 8 November 1968.

24. Cabinet Office circular No. 74 of 1968, *op. cit.*, annexure c.

discussed if presented in the correct form placed a heavy burden on the Cabinet. Some of the load was therefore transferred to Cabinet committees. Whereas only two Cabinet committees existed before independence—the Capital Sentence Review Committee and the Capital Expenditure Planning Committee—sixteen committees operated during 1966. Some of these were standing committees, while others were *ad hoc* and official committees.[25] Among the nine main standing committees in existence following the ministerial reorganisation of January 1967 were an Economic Committee, a Foreign Affairs Committee, a Manpower Committee and a Legislation Committee.[26] Only Ministers could be full members of these committees, though civil servants—such as the Parliamentary Draftsman—could serve as advisers.

In addition, from mid-1965 onwards the President occasionally approved the establishment of committees of officials to service Cabinet standing committees, and thereby lighten the load on them.[27] Thus the Economic Intelligence Official Committee fed the Cabinet Economic Committee, as well as the Foreign Affairs Committee, with information on the economic affairs of the country. However, to the extent that official committees are composed of already overworked top civil servants, their effectiveness may be reduced. Moreover, Zambia has tended to establish more committees than she really needs, and this has tempted the Cabinet to shelve issues by referring them to the appropriate committee. This fact, as well as the unimportant nature of many of the matters so referred, has sometimes retarded the process of decision-making.

*The effectiveness of the Cabinet.* Several factors have helped to reduce the effectiveness of the Cabinet's role in policy-making and execution. In 1964 all its members lacked ministerial experience. By 1968 this problem had been largely overcome, but as a result of the general election at the end of that year the Cabinet lost several of its ablest and most educated members; over the next year and a half (1969–70) eleven new Ministers were appointed. Moreover, university graduates constituted only half the Cabinet in 1964, and from January 1969 an even smaller proportion. Inexperience, inadequate formal education and unfamiliarity with economic and

25. Cabinet Office circular No. 18 of 1968, 8 February 1968, lists the committees.
26. More information is available on this than on any other committee. See Cabinet Office circulars Nos 28 of 1967, 15 February 1967, and No. 11 of 1969, 19 January 1969.
27. Cabinet Office circular No. 65 of 1965, 16 June 1965.

legal matters (which inevitably consume a large part of the Cabinet's time) have made it difficult for many Ministers to play an active and constructive policy-making role in Cabinet. This problem has been exacerbated by the poor servicing the Cabinet has sometimes received from officials since 1964—in particular, the failures in the Cabinet memorandum system. These failures reached such serious proportions in 1968 that the Cabinet Office had to take special measures to improve the quality of Cabinet papers.[28]

The position of the President has also affected the Cabinet. Some Ministers have felt inhibited from criticising policy proposals contained in Cabinet memoranda submitted by Ministries in the office of the President and bearing the President's signature; criticism of these proposals might appear to be criticism of the President himself. This problem, however, disappeared from mid-1969 as the President gradually transferred all Ministries in his office (except Security) to Cabinet Ministers outside it. A more long-term factor which has reduced the importance of the Cabinet has been the President's creation of a corps of personal assistants and advisers. His most important assistant has been Mr Mark Chona, a former permanent secretary of the Ministry of Foreign Affairs who deals with both foreign policy and domestic political matters. Since 1968 the President has also had a development research team, which operates mainly in the fields of social, labour and agricultural policies. In addition he has had a variety of other assistants and advisers, both Zambian and expatriate. The result has been that, particularly since August 1967, the President has on occasion by-passed the Cabinet altogether in policy-making, signifying an increasing trend towards presidentialism in government.

Finally, the effectiveness of the Cabinet depends not merely on the range and quality of its decision-making but also on the machinery for executing its decisions. In 1964 the functions of the Cabinet Office were confined to servicing the Cabinet 'along secretarial lines'. Towards the end of 1967, however, the Secretary to the Cabinet took the initiative in reorganising the office in order to make it 'a much more effective central management agency of the government' so that it could serve the Cabinet 'fully in every sphere'.[29] The functions of an expanded Cabinet Office were to include responsibility for supervising and co-ordinating all other units on behalf of the Cabinet; to this end, a special Policy Co-

28. Cabinet Office circular No. 75 of 1968, 10 September 1968.
29. 'The future role and functions of the Cabinet Office', Cabinet Office circular No. 115 of 1967, 19 December 1967.

ordination and Cabinet Secretariat Section in the Cabinet Operations Division was to be created. The Cabinet was also to have a
Management Services Division, which would constantly look ahead
'to see what demands were likely to be made on the civil service',
advise how the latter should be expanded to meet the additional
load, and be responsible for efficiency. These were bold proposals,
which in principle could have tackled the growing problems of lack
of co-ordination, slowness of implementation, and inefficiency in the
civil service. They were not, however, fully carried through—Mr
Valentine Musakanya, their initiator, and Secretary to the Cabinet,
lost his post within a year. In spite of the changes that were made
(including the introduction of a Management Services Division),
the problems referred to continued to hamper the government's performance.

## The organisation of Ministries

In March 1964, seven months prior to independence, the organisation of government was based on the Offices of the Prime Minister
and Cabinet and thirteen supporting Ministries, each under a
Cabinet Minister. The Governor still had final control over defence
and internal security, as well as external affairs. Upon Northern
Rhodesia's attainment of independence as the Republic of Zambia
on 24 October 1964, the external affairs section of the former Prime
Minister's Office became the (only new) Ministry of Foreign Affairs.
In other respects, however, the organisation of the Office of the
President followed closely the previous organisation of the Office of
the Prime Minister.[30] Within his office the President was assisted by
the Vice-president, who was assigned special responsibility for certain
subjects which formed part of the portfolio of the President. Changes
in the allocation of subjects between Ministries were kept to a minimum.

Two years after independence (in October 1966) the picture had
not changed dramatically.[31] There were now separate Offices of
President and Vice-President, and more Junior Ministers: of these,
five were Ministers of State, eight were Resident Ministers (previously called Provincial Under-Ministers), and twelve were Parliamentary Secretaries. The really significant change by this date was
that the topmost civil service posts had been Africanised. Whereas

30. Cabinet Office circular No. 131 of 1964, 4 November 1964.
31. ZIS background paper No. 15/66, 27 June 1966, and amended 14 July
1966.

in October 1964 there had been no African permanent secretary in charge of a Ministry, by July 1966 every post at this level was held by an African. The way to this change-over had been paved with the appointment of thirty-eight top-level supernumerary officers in June 1964; these officers understudied for a period of six months the expatriates then holding key civil service posts.[32] Most of the expatriate permanent secretaries also stayed on as advisers to their new Zambian successors during 1965.

Not only were there no important changes in ministerial organisa-tion during the first two years of independence but most Ministries also retained the same Minister throughout this period—a period that coincided with the drawing up of the first National Development Plan. This continuity contrasts sharply with the ministerial game of musical chairs subsequently conducted. It began early in 1967, when, in a major reshuffle, the number of Cabinet Ministers was raised to sixteen and several had their portfolios changed. Con-siderable structural reorganisation also took place—a new and short-lived Ministry of Presidential Affairs was created, and several departments were moved from their existing Ministries to other Ministries. President Kaunda subsequently explained that the purpose of his reorganisation was to streamline the machinery of government, principally for the purposes of implementing the Development Plan.[33] In fact, however, the rationale behind much of this reorganisation was by no means clear, and it was probably also undertaken to satisfy political requirements and claims. Civil servants knew nothing about it until the changes had been an-nounced, and were then expected to justify them on administrative grounds. The process of adjusting the civil service's manpower to the reorganised structure was hardly complete when in September 1967 the President introduced further extensive changes in the assignment of portfolios. These were made necessary by the shift in the balance of power within UNIP, resulting from the central committee elections the previous month. Structurally, the main changes centred round the increasingly vast Office of the President, which was divided into seven separate divisions, each under the administrative control of a permanent secretary. The Vice-president carried out certain presidential functions on behalf of the President and had particular responsibilities of his own, including the Office

32. Of these 'trainee' officers, ten had degrees, four were under 30, seven-teen were under 40, while the two oldest were aged 53. ZIS press release No. 966/64, 22 June 1964.

33. Address by President Kaunda, 3 May 1967; ZIS press release, 3 May 1967.

of National Development and Planning (ONDP) and the Judicial
Department.[34]

It could have been hoped that once these further changes had
been made, individual Ministers would bring a new sense of purpose
to the Ministries for which they were now responsible, and that they
would work together as a team. The results, however, were disappointing. Though some Ministers did well—Munukayumbwa
Sipalo, for example, at the Ministry of Agriculture—others adopted
a half-hearted attitude towards their work. Morale among most
Ministers was low, and the Cabinet, as well as the UNIP central
committee, was disunited. Several of the non-Bemba-speaking
Ministers were reluctant to accept Simon Kapwepwe as national
Vice-president.[35]

*The administrative reforms of January 1969.* Moreover, from mid-
1968 the normal working of most Ministries was disrupted because
their political heads were engrossed in planning for, and campaigning in, the general election to be held at the end of that year. Before the election Dr Kaunda announced sweeping changes in the
organisation of government, with the aim of accelerating development
of the rural areas. He subsequently described the existing administrative machinery as 'cumbersome and inefficient', and as providing
insufficient contact between the Cabinet, the central policy-making
body of the government, and the people in the provinces and
districts.[36] Before describing the 1969 reforms we examine briefly the
background against which the President's criticisms were made.

In 1964 the UNIP government had changed the inherited system
of provincial administration on lines similar to those already mapped
out in Tanzania. Many of the duties formerly performed by officers
of the provincial administration were devolved on the police and
Ministries; thus field officers of the Ministry of Local Government
became responsible for supervising the rural local authorities which
(from 1965) operated under the provisions of the Local Government
Act.[37] The administration was politicised in that each of the

34. 'Ministerial reorganisation: division of the Office of the President',
Cabinet Office circular No. 91 of 1967, 18 September 1967.

35. This was subsequently admitted by Kapwepwe himself in his resignation statement. *Times of Zambia*, 26 August 1969.

36. President Kaunda's speeches to UNIP delegates at Mulungushi, 9
November 1968, ZIS background paper No. 84/68, 8 November 1968, and
to Ministers, Permanent Secretaries and District Governors at Lusaka, 30
December 1968, ZIS press release No. 2223/68, 30 December 1968.

37. This Act (No. 69 of 1965) was a consolidating measure which established a basically uniform pattern of local authorities throughout Zambia.

eight provinces into which Zambia was divided was headed by a politician called successively Under-Minister, Resident Minister, and Minister of State. The Minister was supported politically by at least one Public Relations Assistant (informally called Assistant Minister)[38] and between one and four political assistants, and administratively by a Resident Secretary and a development officer (both civil servants). He presided over a provincial development committee, which met, on average, every three months to consider ministerial progress reports and to identify and resolve bottlenecks in implementing a centrally formulated National Development Plan which was broken down into regional programmes.

For administrative purposes each province was divided into districts, of which there were forty-four in 1968; in addition, there were eight sub-districts (formed or in formation). The district was in the charge of a District Secretary, who was a civil servant rather than a politician. Like the Resident Secretary above him, he was the President's personal civil service representative in the area for which he was responsible and the chief government co-ordinating officer in his district 'with particular reference to the work of economic development'.[39] His co-ordinating role, however, was seriously undermined when, in mid-1967, the government replaced him as chairman of the district development committee (the counterpart at district level of the provincial development committee) by the UNIP regional secretary; he became secretary of the committee. For rural development to take place, a premium was placed upon a good working relationship being established between these two officials; this was made more difficult by the frequent presence in the district of the political assistant, who supervised a group of party regions and, therefore, administrative districts on behalf of the Minister of State.

Many complaints were voiced in the provinces and districts against the practices adopted by the Ministries in Lusaka, while individual Ministers of State constantly pressed for greater decentralisation. 'The bottleneck in the four-year plan is Lusaka,' said

Under the Act, there were until 1970 three city councils, five municipal councils, twenty-four township councils and thirty-four rural councils. On 1 July 1970 twelve township councils ceased to exist and the areas for which they had been responsible were absorbed into the municipal areas of Lusaka, Ndola, Kitwe, Mufulira, Chingola and Luanshya; Lusaka City also took over several square miles of the Rufunsa Rural Council area.

38. The full title of this officer was 'Special Presidential Public Relations Assistant to the Minister of State'.

39. President's directive of 19 June 1966, in *Annual Report of the Provincial and District Government, 1966* (Lusaka, 1966), p. 1.

one of them early in 1967.[40] Not only did Ministers of State have virtually no control over provincial heads of department, who were responsible direct to their parent Ministry, but the provincial heads themselves suffered from a sense of neglect. They complained that they were not brought in from the outset when projects for their provinces were being prepared and defined by ministerial head-quarters in Lusaka. They were not always consulted about the siting of projects within their province, and implementation was held up because of the failure of the Ministries to produce detailed plans and designs of projects. Another complaint from the provinces concerned the delay in the issue of funds for projects which had been approved in the plan and for which provision had been made in the estimates. The Ministry of Finance was blamed—often un-fairly, since the real cause of delay was the failure of Ministries to complete the preparation of individual projects preliminary to pre-senting capital expenditure requisitions to Finance.[41]

In announcing the administrative reforms which he intended to make, President Kaunda assumed (not unreasonably) that UNIP would be returned to power at the forthcoming election. He pro-posed a major decentralisation of both the party and the govern-ment, without, however, sacrificing central control in any way: '. . . we will decentralise most of our Party and Government activities while retaining effective control of the Party and Government machinery in the interests of unity.'[42] 'Centralism' was in fact the essential corollary of decentralisation, and was to be achieved by placing in every province a Cabinet Minister, who would be sup-ported politically by a Minister of State and District Governors[43] and administratively by a permanent secretary and other senior civil servants. Though neither the provincial Cabinet Minister nor the District Governor was made an *ex officio* UNIP office-holder, it was clearly Kaunda's intention in appointing District Governors

40. Statement by Minister of State for the Eastern Province, quoted by C. Hesse in 'Some political aspects of development planning and implementa-tion in Zambia with particular reference to the Eastern and Luapula Provinces', paper presented to the University of East Africa Social Science Conference, Dar es Salaam, January 1968 (mimeo.).

41. Office of National Development and Planning, *First National Develop-ment Plan, 1966–70: Progress Report, 1 July 1966 to 1 March 1967* (Lusaka, n.d.).

42. ZIS background paper No. 84/68, *op. cit.*, p. 19.

43. The President appointed a District Governor to head each one of the fifty-three districts and sub-districts into which the country was now divided for administrative purposes. Most Governors had held middle-level posts in the government (e.g. as Parliamentary Secretaries and political assistants) or party (notably as regional secretaries) a few had been civil servants.

to extend the use which had already been made[44] of the machinery of government both to buttress and to control the party organisation at the regional and sub-regional levels. UNIP was to fulfil a mobilising role and the rural economy was to become 'a dynamic force in the development of the country'.[45] The President envisaged that provincial Cabinet Ministers would be able to take more decisions locally than their predecessors, the Ministers of State, and that they would be better placed to overcome delays for which ministerial headquarters in Lusaka were responsible. It was, however, the District Governors who were to be the lynchpins of the reorganised system of administration. They were required to unite the people behind the government, and to foster the spirit of co-operation and self-reliance by establishing development committees at the sub-district level and by encouraging village regrouping, the growth of small-scale industries, private Zambian business enterprise, and increased agricultural production.[46]

The new organisation took effect after the general election of December 1968. Under it, Lusaka-based Ministers have overall responsibility for the formulation of policies and the planning of departmental programmes on a national scale after consultation with the Ministers in the provinces. Both sets of Ministers sit in the Cabinet, and provincial Ministers help to shape government policy on all subjects, including those which are not related to their respective provinces.[47] While the latter seemed likely to benefit from the new organisation, the load on many of the Ministers and their permanent secretaries remaining at the centre was considerably increased as a result of the drastic (but, as it turned out, temporary) reduction in the number of Ministries—apart from the Offices of President and Vice-president, only eight Ministries were retained at the centre in January 1969.[48] Each Minister, as well as the President and Vice-president, was assisted by one or more Ministers of State; the former post of Parliamentary Secretary was abolished, being open to most of the objections which had arisen in Tanzania.[49]

44. Mainly through provincial Ministers of State, 'Assistant Ministers' and political assistants; the two last categories were now abolished.

45. ZIS press release No. 2223/68, op. cit., p. 4.

46. Ibid., passim, and background paper No. 84/68, op. cit., passim. For a fuller discussion of the impact of the 1969 reforms at provincial and district levels, see Tordoff, 'Provincial and local government in Zambia', op. cit., pp. 23–35.

47. Cabinet Office circular No. 13 of 1969, op. cit., p. 4.

48. ZIS press release No. 2214/68, 23 December 1968, and Government Directory, April 1969.

49. See Tordoff, Government and Politics in Tanzania, op. cit., pp. 86–7.

By April 1969, when the main reorganisation was complete, the Office of the President had become enormous.[50] It included the Office of the newly created Secretary General to the Government (a Cabinet Minister controlling the Cabinet Office and Establishment Division); the Legal Affairs Division under the Attorney General; the Commission for Technical Education and Vocational Training, with its own Minister of State; a new agency called the Provincial and Local Government Division (an amalgamation of the former Provincial and District Government Division and the Ministry of Local Government), also under a Minister of State; Security; and three other Ministries—Defence; Trade, Industry and Mines (under a Minister of State); and National Guidance, a tiny new Ministry created in March to implement the national philosophy of Humanism.[51]

The creation of the post of Secretary General to the Government was particularly important and meant that President Kaunda intended to implement his new policy of making some senior political and administrative posts interchangeable at the very highest level. The Secretary General was both head of the civil service (replacing the former Secretary to the Cabinet on 1 February 1969) and a Minister of Cabinet rank. He was responsible to the President for securing the general efficiency of the public services, the smooth running of the Cabinet Office, and 'the co-ordination of the policy formulating and executing functions of both the central and the provincial Ministries'.[52] The first person appointed to this post, Mr John Mwanakatwe, had been a senior civil servant before his appointment as Parliamentary Secretary in 1962; he had been a Cabinet Minister between 1964 and 1968. The immediate (and private) reaction of many civil servants to this arrangement was unfavourable. They rightly saw it as formalising the already declining insulation of the civil service from politics. This was in fact intended by Dr Kaunda, who had invited permanent secretaries to attend a meeting of the UNIP national council in November 1968 and took the initiative in making them formal council members in March 1969.[53] Under Mwanakatwe the Cabinet Office was quickly given

50. *Government Directory*, April 1969, *op. cit.*, pp. 2–9.
51. It had only seventeen civil servants in October 1969. *Times of Zambia*, supplement, 23 October 1969.
52. Cabinet Office circular No. 13 of 1969, *op. cit.*, p. 2, para. 5.
53. 'Conditions of service—Participation in politics by civil servants', Cabinet Office circular No. 26 of 1969, 2 April 1969. This circular amended Establishment circular No. B363 of 28 September 1968, which had stated that any civil servant who intended to take an active part in politics would have to resign from his office or retire if eligible to do so.

a 'new look'. Its personnel was Zambianised, and it was arranged that, as from April 1969, officers of permanent secretary rank should be seconded in turn to the Cabinet Office for a period of twelve to fifteen months.[54]

The Secretary General was also ultimately responsible for the Establishment Division. This division, renamed the Personnel Division in 1972, formed part of his office but had its own permanent secretary. Unfortunately, the division continued to concern itself with personnel case work and to duplicate the functions of the Public Service Commission. The result was that inadequate personnel management practices still impaired the efficiency of government organisation.

Another important change at the centre was the linking of the Ministry of Finance with the Office of National Development and Planning (which housed the Central Planning Unit under the Director of Planning) to form the Finance and Development Divisions of the Office of the Vice-president.[55] In view of the lack of co-ordination between finance and development in the past, it seemed good sense to bring them together within the same Ministry. But the practical disadvantages of this move were considerable. Whereas formerly disagreement between the conservatively inclined Ministry of Finance and the progressive-minded ONDP had usually been resolved by compromise, development considerations now tended to be subordinated to financial ones. In August 1970 the Development Division lost its own separate permanent secretary and became merely one of three divisions in an integrated Ministry of Finance and Development, with the Director of Planning reporting to an Under-Secretary, who was not himself an economist. Only in 1972 did the division regain its status as a separate Ministry, although now linked with the very different function of National Guidance to form the Ministry of Development Planning and National Guidance.

Like the preceding, and by contrast minor, reorganisation of January 1967, the 1969 reforms were undertaken on the initiative of Dr Kaunda himself. They were the result of a political decision, tempered by advice from a number of quarters. First, a working party—composed of civil servants and appointed in January 1968 to consider the reorganisation of provincial and district government—had underlined the need for reform in an interim report submitted

54. Cabinet Office circular No. 28 of 1969, 3 April 1969.
55. Cultural Services and the Judicial Department were also part of the Vice-president's Office, *Government Directory*, April 1969, *op. cit.*, pp. 10–16.

to the Secretary to the Cabinet in March 1968.[56] While the reforms subsequently introduced by the President incorporated one of the working party's key proposals—the merger of the Provincial and District Government Division and the Ministry of Local Government at all levels into a single Ministry or Division of Provincial and Local Government—the President rejected its other major proposal. The working party had been anxious to free district administration of political entanglements, but the President deliberately politicised it by appointing District Governors. Moreover, his reforms related to central, as well as provincial and district, government and therefore dealt with matters well outside the terms of reference of the working party.

Dr Kaunda probably consulted Mr L. M. Lishomwa, former permanent secretary in ONDP who was assigned special duties in the President's Office late in 1968. His office had urged the need for government decentralisation in a progress report prepared in April 1967.[57]

The President may also have been influenced by the thinking of the small development research team in his own office. This team was headed by Dr G. A. Krapf, who was a former Director of Studies and Research at the Mindolo Ecumenical Centre on the Copperbelt. By 1968 (when it was formally constituted)[58] it comprised four West Germans (including Krapf), who were employed on contract terms and combined the complementary skills of a sociologist, an agronomist, an economist and a physical planner; a white Zambian (J. C. Oglethorpe) was added in 1969 and later tended to concentrate on foreign policy issues, particularly in relation to southern Africa. The team has undertaken a wide range of assignments—some at the request of the President (such as investigating worker participation in industry and the Ombudsman institution), and others on its own initiative.

Considerable doubt therefore remains as to who advised Dr Kaunda on this occasion—he has built up a substantial, although changing, corps of personal advisers who operate outside normal civil service channels. What is certain is that the extent and nature of the reforms surprised the great majority of Ministers and top civil

56. This report was not published.
57. *Progress Report: 1 July 1966 to 1 March 1967, op. cit.* This report (published for official circulation only) pointed to the tendency over the past two years to drain the provinces of economic resources—manpower, housing and office accommodation—at the very time when more of this capacity should have been channelled there.
58. Cabinet Office circular No. 20 of 1968, 9 February 1968.

servants. A few of the latter, particularly in the Cabinet Office, were concerned with examining the proposals as originally conceived and made some, though probably limited, changes to them.

*The significance of the 1969 reforms.* The January 1969 administrative reforms were not the product of a thorough and comprehensive investigation of the civil service's problems and weaknesses. No such enquiry was conducted during the life of the First Republic (1964–1972). Moreover, no unit exists with overall responsibility for promoting efficiency and reform in the civil service. The Personnel Division is preoccupied with personnel case work, and its specialised agencies—the Organisation and Methods Section and the Staff Inspection Unit—can investigate only at the invitation of the Ministry concerned; even then they examine limited aspects of the machinery of government and have no power to enforce their recommendations. As a result, the 1969 reforms dealt only with certain difficulties and provided no remedies for the growing problems of indiscipline, theft by public servants, delay, and inefficiency.[59] It is true that certain of these problems arise in part from factors—such as poor communications and lack of office accommodation—for which the civil servants involved cannot be held responsible. It was also understandable that in the first years of independence the civil service had to concentrate on keeping in operation a rapidly growing machine whose personnel was being speedily localised. But localisation outside the professional and technical classes is now largely accomplished;[60] and the rate of growth of the civil service establishment is falling off.

The 1969 reforms tackled three crucial problems with varying success: the relationship between the civil service and UNIP; over-centralisation; and the lack of co-ordination within the civil service. The nub of the first problem was to harmonise the two organisations so that they could work together for national development. However, a certain ambiguity in the civil service's relationship with UNIP was inevitable so long as Zambia remained a multi-party State and civil servants were required (under General Order No. 69) to be politically neutral. This factor was only removed with the establishment of a one-party State in December 1972.

59. For criticisms of the civil service, see the speech by the Minister of Information, Broadcasting and Tourism, March 1969, ZIS press release No. 132/69; and *National Convention on the Four-year Development Plan, op. cit.*, Committee B, pp. 25–6.

60. By 1968 there were 19,000 Zambians in Divisions I and II, being 76 per cent of all filled posts. *Zambian Manpower* (Lusaka, 1969), p. 6.

As to the second problem, the extent to which decentralisation has taken place must not be exaggerated. The basic structure of Ministries (other than the Ministry of Provincial and Local Government)—and the rules governing their operations—were not altered. Each department's provincial officer-in-charge remained administratively and financially responsible to his parent department in Lusaka. Government was very reluctant to devolve significant powers to provincial permanent secretaries, even in relation to their own staff. Permanent secretaries still do not control the structure of their provincial Ministries or the movement of their staff above the rank of assistant district secretary; and recurrent expenditure for each provincial Ministry is not sub-warranted to each provincial permanent secretary.[61] At the district level, a legal basis has now been provided for the new village and ward committee system,[62] but few District Governors have yet made any significant impact on rural development. The Governor's role remains ill-defined in relation to both the government and the party structures, and this helps to explain why there have been many cases both of unwarranted interference with the administration and of friction with regional level officials of UNIP.

Finally, the attempt to improve co-ordination through the amalgamation of related departments into 'umbrella' Ministries has largely failed. The huge new Ministry of Rural Development proved unable to adjust its structure to its enlarged responsibilities and had to be split into two as early as August 1969. In the case of the new Ministry of Finance and Development, not only did planning tend to be subordinated to finance but the already poor relations between the Central Planning Unit and other parts of government deteriorated further. By the end of 1972 only two of the original seven umbrella Ministries remained in existence.

Thus a somewhat depressing picture emerges, with new difficulties arising out of the January 1969 reforms, the continued emergence of fresh political considerations prompting reorganisation, and the persistence of problems not tackled by the reforms. There has been no abatement in the President's frequent reorganisation of government. The responsibilities of his own office proved so manifold and time-consuming that he progressively gave certain of his portfolios to Ministers outside his office—Provincial and Local Government went to Mr Mainza Chona in August 1969 and Defence to Mr Grey Zulu in January 1970. The President's decision in August 1969 to acquire for the State a controlling interest in the

61. Cabinet Office circular No. 24 of 1970, 1 May 1970.
62. By the Registration and Development of Villages Act, 1971.

copper mines led to the splitting up of another umbrella Ministry—Trade, Industry and Mines—into a Ministry of Trade and Industry and a short-lived Ministry of State Participation. The latter remained in the Office of the President. Its very small staff handled the take-over negotiations with the Anglo-American Corporation and Roan Selection Trust in late 1969. The Ministry became responsible for the newly formed parastatal body, the Zambia Industrial and Mining Corporation (Zimco)—which in turn controls the Industrial and Mining Development Corporations (Indeco and Mindeco)—as well as for certain other statutory boards. The political crisis of August 1969, when an alleged attempt in the UNIP national council to unseat Vice-president Kapwepwe was avoided only by closing the council prematurely, sparked off another Cabinet reconstruction.

Soon afterwards, in October, the President publicly admitted that

it is important that people get settled in their ministries so that they will learn the intricacies, the problems that are involved in their respective ministries. And so I want to say that I will really minimise the movement of Ministers and officials from now on.[63]

Unfortunately, this commitment has not been fully adhered to. Thus in January 1971 President Kaunda abolished the Ministry of State Participation, which had by that time become a huge affair, responsible for the majority of the government's vast undertakings in industry, commerce, mining and transport; he divided its responsibilities among five Ministries.[64] The practice by which Dr Kaunda undertakes major Cabinet reconstructions at least once or twice a year represents part of his continuing search for a solution to the seemingly intractable problems which face his government in the economic and social spheres. It is sometimes, too, the inevitable sequel to political events: for example, the President's dismissal of four Cabinet Ministers at various times during the second Parliament and the resignation of Kapwepwe from UNIP in August 1971 entailed consequential Cabinet changes.

## The civil service

The disruptive effects of such reconstructions on the administration cannot be overstated. The frequent movement of Ministers and civil

63. ZIS background paper No. 77/69, 1 November 1969.
64. S. W. Johns, 'Parastatal bodies in Zambia: a survey' (forthcoming).

servants[65] has made it difficult for them to build up experience in a particular field, and the quality and speed of their decision-making have been adversely affected. Provincial Ministers have not been exempt, and they, as well as District Governors, have often not had time to understand the problems of one area before being moved to another. The frequent transfer of departments among Ministries and the general reallocation of subject responsibilities have also imposed a heavy burden on the civil service. Chains of command at senior levels have been disrupted, resulting in delays which, for this and other reasons, have become a very serious problem. The work of the Ministry of Finance has been greatly complicated. Votes have had to be changed; the process of accounting has been made more difficult; mistakes in the coding of expenditure have soared; and the huge exercise of transferring balances of funds in votes during the financial year has had to be undertaken. Registries, which are the communications nerve centres of departments, have frequently had to be physically moved along with the rest of a department's staff and equipment. Files have had to be renumbered and relocated, not merely in the department being moved but in all departments which have files dealing with that department.

Only a strong civil service can carry such burdens without endangering the smooth working of government. But the Zambian civil service suffers from a number of internal weaknesses. As early as January 1967 the Kitwe National Convention on the Four-year Development Plan pointed to 'the deficiencies in the civil service structure', including:

the lack of sufficient co-ordination and communication between ministries and their field staff ... over-centralisation ... duplication of work ... and a cumbersome and involved administrative machinery which includes slowness by ministries to release funds to their provincial heads for approved projects.[66]

It also stated that the process of decision-making tended to involve more people than was really necessary and that there was an excess of paper work. Moreover, civil service regulations were outdated, and 'tribalism plays a part in appointments'. These criticisms related primarily to bureaucratic structure and procedures. Some years

65. In the August 1969 changes alone the President altered nine of the twenty-seven permanent secretaries in government. The Development Division (of the Vice-president's Office) had a succession of four permanent secretaries in little more than a year in 1969–70.

66. *National Convention on the Four-year Development Plan*, *op. cit.*, pp. 23, 25, 26, 30, 31.

later, in 1971, the Secretary General to the Government criticised
civil servants from a different angle. He attacked certain attitudes
which were prevalent among them: disobedience, drunkenness,
laziness, lack of commitment to the public service, and irrespon-
sibility.[67]

Other important flaws in the machinery of government exist.
There is a lack of cost-consciousness in the public sector which has
led to considerable waste of resources. Effective financial control
inside Ministries has often broken down owing to shortage of
accounting staff. Each year almost every Ministry comes to the
National Assembly with supplementary estimates of expenditure;
in 1970 these amounted to K43 million, or 18 per cent more than the
originally approved recurrent expenditure.[68] The lax attitude to
public funds on the part of many government officers is also shown
in the sharp rise in the number of reported cases of official corruption and accidents involving government vehicles.[69] In 1969 the
Finance (Control and Management) Act was passed, to empower
the Permanent Secretary (Finance) to recover losses from officers.
But the key provisions of the Act were not enforced, and it has not,
therefore, resulted in any significant improvement in civil servants'
handling of public funds and property. The parastatal sector has
also been criticised for 'financial indiscipline' and inefficiency which
have led to its growing dependence on central government subsidies
and grants.[70]

Another characteristic of the Zambian civil service is that it tends
to be over-formalised in its working, simple issues often being
referred in the form of a memorandum to committee instead of
being resolved informally by personal contact. One reason for this is
the lack of security felt by very senior civil servants, particularly permanent secretaries. They are under-educated—a survey of African
civil servants (senior executive officer and above) in 1969 revealed
that, at the time of joining the civil service, only 6 per cent had
university degrees, 22 per cent a secondary school-leaving certificate
at 'O' level, while 67 per cent had less education (fully a quarter
having completed only primary school). Even in early 1973 nearly
half the twenty-seven permanent secretaries in post had had no
university education. Civil servants tend also to be under-trained.

67. *Times of Zambia*, 3 April 1971.

68. *Estimates of Revenue and Expenditure for 1971* (Lusaka, 1971), p. 4.

69. *Zambia Police Annual Reports for 1964 and 1969* (Lusaka); *Sunday
Times of Zambia*, 21 March 1971.

70. ZIS press release No. 30/70, 30 January 1970, and *Daily Parl. Deb.*,
No. 25, 29 January 1971, col. 511.

Twenty-seven per cent of the officers surveyed in 1969 had not attended any in-service training course since joining the civil service.[71] The situation is even more serious at lower levels, owing to the fact that numbers have increased more quickly than places at the National Institute of Public Administration (the former Staff Training College) and other training institutions have become available.[72]

Most senior civil servants are also fairly young men, just over 40 years old,[73] with limited experience of high office. This is not surprising, since the colonial government only seriously began to localise the Northern Rhodesian civil service in 1962, when it became clear that the collapse of the Central African Federation was imminent and the country would in future be ruled by a black African government. Thus in December 1967 only some 5 per cent of the top civil servants had held their posts for four years or more, and all of them were whites. This situation has not improved greatly. Because of the departure from the civil service of almost all the original African permanent secretaries appointed in 1965, the average permanent secretary in 1972 had held post(s) at that level for only 2.8 years. There is also a high rate of turnover in the holding of senior posts, one reason being the large number of vacancies in government.[74] Over three years after independence, less than half these posts were held by Zambians, who tended to monopolise only key administrative posts, such as that of permanent secretary. Expatriate officers often served immediately below them and also filled nearly all the senior professional posts. Zambianisation has, of course, proceeded further since 1967, but the service remains a relatively young, under-educated, under-trained and inexperienced body of men, especially at the middle and senior levels. If La Palombara is right to argue that 'we are witnessing in many places the emergence of overpowering bureaucracies',[75] it can be said emphatically that Zambia is not yet one of those places.

Senior civil servants are often unsure of themselves and jealous

71. V. Subramaniam, 'The social background of Zambia's higher civil servants and undergraduates', paper presented to the University of East Africa Social Science Conference, Nairobi, December 1969, table 4.

72. I. Mackinson, 'The National Institute of Public Administration', *Service* (Lusaka, December 1967).

73. In December 1967 the average age of seventy-two Africans in senior posts (permanent secretary, director, etc.) was 37.9 years: the average age of 102 whites in equivalent posts was 46.5 years. Abridged staff list, December 1967 (Lusaka, 1968).

74. See 'Manpower: progress report and statistics, 1967' (Lusaka, mimeo.), pp. 17–18, paras 54–7.

75. J. La Palombara (ed.), *Bureaucracy and Political Development* (Princeton, 1963), p. 25.

of each other. They are sometimes afraid to take decisions lest a politically wrong decision should prejudice their career. In 1967, for example, they frequently referred papers to the Secretary to the Cabinet for his advice instead of recommending to him the course of action to be taken. This tendency continued, and in 1969 the Secretary General to the Government told senior officers that the service could not afford 'to employ civil servants at any level who flinch from decisions, hide behind files, and take refuge in delay and obstruction'.[76] At the same time, many permanent secretaries are reluctant to delegate authority to those below them. While they agree in principle that policy-making should reach down to the executive class, this rarely happens in practice—often because they doubt the competence of middle-level civil servants, perhaps promoted too rapidly from the junior grade. Over-centralisation is an extensive phenomenon. It pervades the system of financial control, personnel administration and policy-making. It manifests itself in the concentration of decision-making authority within Ministry headquarters in Lusaka (and away from the field) and at very senior levels within these headquarters. Some attempts have been made to remedy the situation. The Public Service Commission regulations were revised in 1968 to delegate specific powers to responsible officers so that indiscipline could be dealt with more promptly.[77] The 1969 reforms decentralised financial control by making provincial permanent secretaries controlling officers in respect of designated provincial development projects in any Ministry, although these projects constitute only a small proportion of the government's capital spending.[78] And 1969 also saw the re-establishment of provincial accounting units. But these changes have had only a limited effect. There remains an urgent need to overhaul the present ministerial structure and procedures with a view to institutionalising decentralisation. A comprehensive and fairly radical review along these lines was held early in 1972, but its recommendations have not yet been implemented. In the meantime the consequences of over-centralisation—over-burdening of the top levels, delay and frustration in the field—have as serious an effect on the civil service's

76. ZIS press release No. 117/69, 3 March 1969.
77. Statutory Instrument No. 200 of 1968, and *Public Service Commission Report for 1967* (Lusaka, 1968), p. 6.
78. In 1970 in North-western Province, for example, designated provincial projects were worth $K1·3$ million, or 25 per cent of government's capital spending in the province. The corresponding figures for Southern Province were $K1·7$ million, or 10 per cent. ZIS background paper Nos 27/70 and 28/70.

ability to implement the second National Development Plan as they had on the first.

Again, while the civil service has enormously increased its number of superscale posts (from 184 in 1964 to nearly 800 in 1969) and has greatly expanded the number of junior posts, it tends to be both understaffed and indifferently staffed at the middle level.[79] The reason is clear: as the Staff Inspection Unit pointed out in 1967, 'measures of expediency in staffing have been the rule rather than the exception'.[80] In particular, in the years immediately after independence the extreme shortage of educated citizen manpower, coupled with the huge expansion in the civil service's establishment (from 22,561 in 1963–64 to 51,497 in 1969)[81] and the desire for rapid localisation, led to a grave weakening in recruitment standards and procedures. Ministries tended to by-pass the Public Service Commission and to make appointments without the latter's consent, and the minimum educational levels required for direct entry were reduced.[82] Moreover, the consequences of the low-calibre staff recruited have been made worse by a sharp rise in the incidence of indiscipline of all kinds in the civil service, and the reluctance of both expatriate and Zambian supervisors to enforce discipline.[83]

Furthermore, the distribution of staff between Ministries is not always related to the government's stated priorities. In 1968, for example, only 9 per cent of all civil servants were in departments relating to rural development, despite the government's commitment to develop the economically backward parts of the country.[84] Weakness in staffing affects all Ministries and has particularly serious consequences for those which contain important departments—such as the Works Department in the Ministry of Power, Transport and Works. Some departments are not fully integrated into Ministries and, where this happens, departmental heads are often

79. ZIS background paper No. 84/68, *op. cit.*; 'Manpower: progress report and statistics, 1967', *op. cit.*, pp. 17–18, para. 55; *Report to the Government of Zambia on Incomes, Wages and Prices in Zambia: Policy and Machinery* (Turner report) (Lusaka, 1969), p. 27; and *Public Service Commission Report for 1965* (Lusaka, 1966), p. 7.

80.'Review of establishments and personnel work' (Lusaka, mimeo., 1967), p. 8.

81. *Annual Estimates of Revenue and Expenditure, 1963–69* (Lusaka).

82. *Second Report of the Public Accounts Committee*, Hansard No. 9, March 1967, appendix A, cols 327–45; *Public Service Commission Report for 1965*, *op. cit.*, pp. 8 and 9.

83. C. C. Greenfield, 'Manpower planning in Zambia', *Journal of Administration Overseas*, vol. VII, No. 4 (October 1968), p. 508.

84. Staff list, 1968; *First National Development Plan, op. cit.*, p. 81.

denied access at the level of permanent secretary and under-secretary. Technical departments still tend to be headed by expatriate officers recruited overseas, and until late 1968 the lack of a clearly formulated Zambianisation programme meant that there was general uncertainty how long the services of these (and most other) expatriates would be required. For almost four years after independence there was no co-ordinating body to plan and assess the staffing needs of individual Ministries and government as a whole.[85] In July 1968 an executive committee was established under the chairmanship of the Minister of State for the Cabinet and the Public Service and charged with the task of directing and co-ordinating all Zambianisation and training programmes in the public service.[86] Its work, however, was adversely affected by two factors. The first was the frequent change in the person of the Minister of State who chaired the committee, thus impairing continuity. Secondly, appointment and promotion procedures in the civil service were unsatisfactory, and for this individual Ministries, as well as the Personnel Division and the Public Service Commission, must share responsibility.

In the first two years after independence no attempt was made to examine critically establishments and personnel work in the civil service.[87] But in late 1966 the newly created Staff Inspection Unit of the Personnel (then called Establishment) Division was requested to make a service-wide review as a matter of urgency. The unit's report revealed a most unsatisfactory state of affairs. There was overlap and even duplication between the functions of the Personnel Division and the Public Service Commission. The Personnel Division concerned itself with case work arising from individual appointments and promotions, and its processing of cases was broadly the same as that carried out subsequently by the Public Service Commission. The Ministries had only very limited delegated authority in establishment and personnel matters, giving rise to the need for a constant stream of references from them to the Personnel Division and the Public Service Commission. The simplest cases passed through the hands of many individuals and registries,

85. Since 1966 a Staff Inspection Unit has existed and has performed this function for individual Ministries at their request.

86. Cabinet Office circular No. 61 of 1968, 9 July 1968. A new Zambianisation and Training Committee was established in 1969; *ibid.*, No. 30 of 1969, 10 April 1969.

87. The Staff Inspection Unit took establishment work to mean that group of functions which treats the staffing pattern of the organisation as a unitary whole, and personnel work as that group of functions which deals with individual officers as separate entities.

giving rise to serious delay. Moreover, the level of reference was far too high. Permanent secretaries and other senior officers often dealt with minor personnel cases, to the neglect of policy formulation and administration.[88]

The Staff Inspection Unit also found that the existing arrangements for the career advancement of officers in the junior and middle grades (especially clerical and executive) were most unsatisfactory, both from the viewpoint of the officers themselves and for the well-being of the service as a whole. Thus selection procedures and safeguards were totally inadequate. The unit concluded that the overall effect of rapid promotions over the last two or three years had been to lead to a lowering of standards of performance at executive level, and to some extent at clerical level also.[89]

The Staff Inspection Unit recommended that the Personnel Division should play no direct part in appointment and promotion procedures. Instead, its role should be advisory and interpretative; it should concentrate on a true central establishments function—the overall control of civil service complements and gradings. Certain large departments, such as Public Works, Mechanical Services and Roads, should be awarded semi-autonomous status in establishments and personnel work. Again, submissions made by a Ministry to the Public Service Commission should not pass any higher up the chain of command within the Ministry than was absolutely necessary; except in the very smallest Ministries, establishment sections should be organised as self-contained units. Changes were also recommended in promotion and disciplinary procedures, and the early introduction of formal training in establishments and personnel work was advocated.[90]

After submission in January 1967, the Staff Inspection Unit's report was referred by the Permanent Secretary, Personnel Division, to the Secretary to the Cabinet and, presumably, by the latter to the Cabinet. But then nothing happened. One reason was disagreement between the principal officials concerned as to the relationship of, and division of responsibilities between, the Public Service Commission and the Personnel Division. There was also a strong resistance to change on the part of some of the civil servants (both expatriate and Zambian) occupying key posts.

In the intervening five-year period some changes have been made along the lines recommended by the staff inspectorate. For example, the recommendation that schemes of service—on the basis of one

88. 'Review of establishments and personnel work', *op. cit.*, *passim*.
89. *Ibid.*, p. 28 and *passim*.
90. Summary of recommendations, *op. cit.*, pp. 42–4.

scheme for each stream—should be prepared has been implemented.[91]
But many of the main faults to which the unit's report drew attention remain uncorrected. Thus the Personnel Division continues to
play a direct part in appointments and promotions, and cannot
therefore devote adequate attention to the overall problems involved
in the efficient manning of the civil service. The duplication involved
has persisted, and in 1971 the O'Riordan Salaries Commission went
so far as to recommend the abolition of the Public Service Commission.[92] Again, semi-autonomous powers in establishments and
personnel matters are still denied to the large departments, with the
single exception of the Ministry of Education, which in 1971 became 'self-administrative' in the field of personnel management. An
executive Teaching Service Commission was created and relieved
the Public Service Commission of its functions in respect of all the
Ministry's staff, who constitute some 30 per cent of the total civil
service.[93] For the rest, submissions from Ministries still tend to be
referred automatically to the highest level of authority in the
Ministry concerned.

Finally, the morale of the civil service has been adversely affected
not only by the poor quality of personnel management but also by
the erosion of the principle of political neutrality. Top civil servants
can no longer be certain that they can count on a career in the
civil service, while those below them wonder whether proved political loyalty will be a more important criterion for promotion than
administrative or technical efficiency. In the circumstances it is
not surprising that many civil servants have either resigned from the
service to join private companies or have transferred to the parastatal sector.

The latter has grown rapidly since independence, particularly
in the aftermath of the Rhodesian UDI and the economic reforms
of 1968–70. Today there are some seventy State-owned companies
and statutory bodies in Zambia, operating to a varying extent
independently of civil service controls and extending the long arm

91. The appointment of a Working Party on Schemes of Service was
announced in Cabinet Office circular No. 38 of 1967, 15 March 1967. By
mid-1970 some fifteen schemes, embracing a large proportion of the service,
had been published.

92. *Report of the Commission appointed to Review the Salaries, Salary
Structure and Conditions of Service of the Zambia Public Service (including
the Zambia Police) and the Defence Force*: Government Paper No. 1 of 1971
(Lusaka, 1971).

93. See *Education in Transition—Report of the Administrative Working
Party Appointed to Examine Certain Aspects of the Teaching Service*
(Lusaka, 1969), p. 4.

of the State into the most vital areas of Zambian economic and political life.[94] As we saw in the case of the Ministry of State Participation, the growth of this sector has had profound effects on the organisation of government as a whole.[95] It has also had repercussions on the civil service because of the higher salaries prevailing in the parastatal sector. The consequent problems arising from such differences were examined in 1970 by the 'Report of the committee appointed to review the emoluments and conditions of service of statutory boards and corporations and State-owned enterprises'.[96] The committee found that the drain of high-level manpower from the public to the parastatal sector had not been great, but had probably been considerable at middle and junior management levels. There were also marked discrepancies in the terms offered by different bodies within the parastatal sector itself.

On broader issues the committee felt that the parastatal sector had done a reasonably good job (the Credit Organisation of Zambia, of course, always excepted) and that the government should not be deterred from creating new parastatal bodies where circumstances justified it. At the same time, the parastatal sector had grown too rapidly and the number of parastatal organisations in Zambia was now too large. A few organisations, such as the politically charged Zambia Youth Service, should become normal departments of government, while the criterion for the establishment of a parastatal body in the future should be whether that body would perform necessary functions which could not be so well performed by existing agencies or by the government itself.

Some of the recommendations of this useful report have now been implemented. But the committee was inhibited, both in its terms of reference and in its membership, from subjecting the huge parastatal sector to the really critical review which is still required. The relations between this sector on the one hand and the public sector and UNIP on the other continue to be uncertain. There is insufficient co-ordination between these agencies, all of which—in one way or another—have been, and are still, vitally concerned with the implementation of Zambia's National Development Plans.

94. The State-owned company is created by executive action and incorporated under the Companies Ordinance like any private company; the statutory body is established by an Act of Parliament as a separate body to carry out certain specific functions. Johns, 'Parastatal bodies in Zambia', op. cit.

95. See p. 264 above.

96. Lusaka, mimeo., March 1970 (restricted).

*The National Development Plans*

We turn finally to examine specifically the question: how adequate is the administrative machinery to fulfil the developmental role of the government, and particularly to implement its National Development Plans? We give most attention to the first plan, which covered the period from 1 July 1966 to 31 December 1970, but was then extended for a further year. It envisaged a minimum capital investment for the 1966–70 period of K858 million, of which K564 million was to be provided by the public sector (almost entirely from domestic resources), and K294 million was estimated to be available from the private sector, particularly for investment in the mining industry.[97]

The plan was the work of specialists in the ONDP, and was prepared in consultation with the Ministries and, as far as targets for agricultural production were concerned, with the provincial and district development committees. Because it was drawn up extremely hurriedly staff in the Ministries had not the time to make accurate cost estimates of projects even if (which is doubtful) they had the expertise to do so; consequently, costs were frequently found to have been underestimated.[98] The plan was a compromise between the different public interests involved. Under pressure from the conservative-minded Ministry of Finance, the ONDP had to accept a rather lower level of capital investment than it had envisaged, though the level was still higher than the Ministry of Finance considered prudent. In turn the ONDP slashed ministerial programmes.[99] The planners did not work to any ideological guidelines laid down by UNIP, but the plan was accepted by the Cabinet and can therefore be said to have embodied the main aspirations of the ruling party.[100] However, the plan was not published in a form readily comprehensible to either the non-economist civil servants or the political leaders who had to implement it. Further, not all

97. *First National Development Plan, op. cit.*, p. 12 (figures rounded).

98. S. H. Goodman, 'Investment policy in Zambia', in Fortman (ed.), *After Mulungushi, op. cit.*, chapter 9.

99. Estimates submitted by Ministries for the plan amounted to K1,250 million; they were reduced to K600 million by ONDP. The latter successfully resisted attempts by the Ministry of Finance to impose further cuts (to K300 million). Minutes of the fifth meeting of the Provincial Development Committee, Southern Province, 28 June 1966; Dev. 2/6, vol. 1, Office of the Minister, Southern Province.

100. Cf. the Seers mission in 1964, which took steps to ensure that the politicians' goals were embodied, but in an economically feasible form. See R. Jolly, 'The Seers report in retrospect', *African Social Research*, No. 11 (June 1971), p. 3.

sections of the community had been asked to contribute to its compilation. The private sector, for instance, was consulted only in the late stages on the ground that the public programme could not be revealed until it had been approved by the Cabinet. Nor was the opposition ANC involved: the party was not consulted before the plan was launched by President Kaunda at a UNIP rally in Lusaka, and therefore did not feel committed to a document which Mr Nkumbula, the ANC leader, described as 'purely academic and professional'.[101]

*The planning machinery.* The beginnings of a planning office were set up within the Ministry of Finance following the recommendation of the Seers mission report in 1964. It was moved to the Office of the President in 1965, and its first director arrived in September of that year, some nine months before the first National Development Plan was due to be launched. The Vice-president, assisted by a Minister of State, assumed direct responsibility for the office—an arrangement that has continued ever since, with only a short, politically motivated interruption in 1969–70.[102] The authority of the ONDP was reinforced by the President, the Cabinet, the Economic Committee of the Cabinet, and the National Development Committee. Understandably, the Cabinet was more skilled in political than in economic calculus, while the main concern of the Economic Committee was to assess the political implications of development projects. The National Development Committee kept the plan under critical review and discussed problems of implementation. A Contingency Planning Committee was also established to deal with the situation created by Rhodesia's UDI, and in particular to plan alternative supply routes and transport. The permanent secretary, ONDP, was a member of this committee, his main brief being to ensure that the National Plan was not thrown out of gear by contingency plans. UDI was a problem which persistently hampered the implementation of both the first and the second National Development Plans, as evidenced by Rhodesia's closure of the Zambian border (including Zambia's main rail link with the sea) from January 1973.

No attempt was made to effect a wholesale ministerial reorganisation when the first plan began in 1966, and the hierarchical system of administration, inherited from the British, was allowed to

101. *Nat. Ass. Deb.*, Hansard No. 11, 18 October 1967, col. 108.
102. Vice-president Kapwepwe was relieved of his main portfolio, Development and Planning, when he announced his resignation (albeit almost immediately withdrawn) in August 1969.

continue. Individual Ministries had to adjust as best they could to the change from law-and-order to development functions. Each of a number of officials in ONDP was made responsible for co-ordinating the work of a group of Ministries, and the office had the right to attend inter-ministerial meetings. In fact, however, inter-ministerial co-ordination remained weak, with adverse effects on vitally important sectors such as transport. The position was made worse because of conflicts within government on matters of economic policy and the lack of clearly defined lines of responsibility between development agencies.

Lack of co-ordination between Ministries in Lusaka added to the difficulties of the provincial and district development committees, which were established by administrative direction in 1966 and absorbed the economic committees established by UNIP in each district.[103] These committees were charged with implementing the regional programmes of a centrally formulated plan. Not only had they virtually no control over ministerial projects, but they had to try and resolve locally inter-ministerial conflicts which stemmed from the failure to reach agreement at the centre. In the circumstances their task of co-ordinating individual ministerial projects in the provinces and districts continued to be difficult even after the appointment of a development officer to each province in mid-1967.

*Implementation.* Our concern is with the difficulties which arose in implementation rather than with the achievements of the plan. The latter were considerable, but uneven—impressive in economic and social infrastructure (roads and schools, for example), and in the manufacturing sector, but much less successful in increasing jobs, raising agricultural production and reaching other physical output goals. The degree to which the plan was implemented also varied from province to province. Taking as the criterion actual (compared to planned) capital expenditure from 1966 to 1970, the Southern Province (for example) achieved an 85 per cent success, while the Northern Province achieved only 66 per cent.[104] In fact, slowness of implementation forced a postponement by one year of the second National Development Plan (which had to be rescheduled to start in January 1972) 'in order to ensure that all the carry-overs arising from the current Four-year Development Plan are either completed

103. Statement by Resident Minister. Minutes of the fifth meeting of the Provincial Development Committee, Southern Province, 28 June 1966, *op. cit.*
104. Minister of Finance and Development: ZIS background papers Nos 28 and 35 of 1970.

or significantly reduced'.[105] The difficulties of implementation can be grouped under three heads—non-administrative, administrative, and political.

Non-administrative difficulties occurred particularly in the period 1966–68. Physical resources (for example, fuel, replacements for machinery, and building materials) were in short supply because of Rhodesia's UDI, increased demand and the cumbersome procedures of government's own machinery for distributing supplies. Some Ministries were worse hit than others; in particular, fuel shortages adversely affected projects in agriculture, co-operatives and natural resources. Agricultural and construction projects away from the line of rail were hampered by additional factors. In 1964 the country's only tarred road ran from the Copperbelt to Livingstone. Roads to the other provincial capitals (let alone lesser roads) were almost impassable for several months of each year. The rainy season also held up construction, and many projects could be undertaken only during the dry season. Building in the rural areas was also affected by the absence of local artisans and small contractors.[106] Lack of rural repair facilities—of mechanics, tools and spare parts— not only led to the breakdown of the government's ambitious tractor mechanisation scheme but also prevented the speedy repair of other government vehicles. The absence of telephone links, coupled with slow postal services and over-centralisation, prevented speedy communication between Ministry headquarters and the field, thereby again slowing down implementation. There was also a sharp rise in costs in the economy. Higher prices had to be paid for materials and labour, and transport costs increased.[107]

Administrative difficulties were considerable. In the view of ONDP, the main problem was faulty administrative procedures, practices and attitudes in Lusaka. Whereas the rate of capital investment for economic development had increased enormously since independence, the ministerial structure in essentials remained unchanged. Ministries were not geared to large-scale economic and social change, and initially many ministerial officials and some Ministers lacked a sense of urgency in implementing development projects. Officials were often preoccupied with day-to-day routine matters and indulged in excessive minuting before taking a decision. Departmental and divisional heads were over-dependent on their

105. Minister of Finance and Development: ZIS press release No. 309/69, 11 December 1969.
106. See speech by the Minister of Finance and Development: ZIS background paper No. 27/70.
107. *Progress Report: 1 July 1966 to 1 March 1967, op. cit.*

permanent secretaries and lacked initiative. There was often no one person in a Ministry who regarded himself as personally responsible for the success or failure of a project. Civil servants tended to 'pass the buck'—from headquarters to field level and vice versa; from one Ministry to another; and from the civil service to the politicians. Departmentalism and over-centralisation, and the consequent lack of co-ordination and co-operation at lower levels, were further major constraints on implementation.

Not only did the provinces complain about the delays caused by the central Ministries in Lusaka and press for greater decentralisation,[108] the ONDP itself suffered from various difficulties. On the staff side it had a succession of seven permanent secretaries in the period 1964–70, only the first two of whom were economists. Its junior staff included some rather inexperienced economists, drawn from a number of different countries. For over a year and a half the office was without a Director of Planning and, until the appointment of provincial development officers, no permanent field representatives.[109] The results were a lack of internal co-ordination, an unevenly distributed work load, and low morale.

Relations between ONDP and the Ministries were far from harmonious. Initially, senior staff in the Ministries were not used to the concept of planning or ready to accept the controls which the office wished to impose. Some Ministries felt that they had not been consulted adequately by ONDP when the plan was being drawn up and did not therefore feel totally committed to it. In others, personal relations between senior civil servants and the Director of Planning were poor, thus making co-operation between them difficult. Attempts to institutionalise co-operation were made. Certain economists in ONDP were each given responsibility for working with a particular Ministry. But their job was made more difficult by the failure to set up programming units (called planning sections), which were supposed to be established within each Ministry directly concerned with economic development. Only the Ministries of Agriculture and Education eventually set up such units. A progress report system, to enable ONDP to check on project implementation by Ministries, was started. Despite its modification on several occasions, the quantity and complexity of data that were requested meant that no Ministry was able to supply all the details required, and some made little effort to operate the system at all.

A frequent source of tension between ONDP and the Ministries

108. See pp. 256–7 above.

109. Provincial development officers were appointed to the staff of Provincial and District Government, but worked closely with ONDP.

was the former's control over the annual capital estimates of all
Ministries. Although in principle such control was desirable in
order to ensure adherence to the plan's objectives, in practice
the office's control over Ministries was not complete. Moreover,
the office could not itself decide the size of the capital budget. The
Ministry of Finance guided the Cabinet to decisions as to the
overall level of government spending. The growth of the recurrent
budget was difficult to limit because of unavoidable increases in
staff, the payment of increments as large numbers of young civil
servants began to proceed up their scales, the running costs of completed projects, and the decision to expand free social services at the
expense of more immediately productive investment. This situation
meant that the size of the capital budget tended to be outside the
hands of ONDP. In particular, the inflation caused by the massive
rise in capital spending in 1968 enabled the Ministry of Finance to
persuade the Cabinet to keep the subsequent years' total expenditure
almost constant.[110] Although ONDP (until absorbed temporarily
by Finance in mid-1970) was able to put its case direct to the
Cabinet, it was the capital budget that was cut successively after
1968.[111] This trend was accelerated by the fall in the copper price
from 1970 and resulted in the 1973 level of capital spending being
the lowest since 1965–66 and in a decision not to implement any
new projects in 1973.

Late 1969 saw the installation of a new Director of Planning
from Yugoslavia. But his relations with many senior civil servants
were almost as poor as those of his British predecessor. Information
essential for both assessing the completion rate of the first plan
and preparing the second was withheld by several agencies. Certain
parastatal bodies, notably the Industrial Development Corporation,

110. Government's determination to hold down prices was a major theme
in Vice-president Kapwepwe's budget speech of January 1969. ZIS press
release No. 54/69.

111. The pattern of government spending changed as follows:

| | Recurrent expenditure (K million) | Capital expenditure (K million) | Capital expenditure as a percentage of total government expenditure |
|---|---|---|---|
| 1968 (actual) | 196 | 191 | 49 |
| 1969 ,, | 222 | 156 | 41 |
| 1970 ,, | 288 | 165 | 36 |
| 1971 ,, | 330 | 153 | 32 |
| 1972 ,, | 353 | 133 | 27 |
| 1973 (authorised) | 357 | 114 | 24 |

Source. Annual Estimates of Revenue and Expenditure (Lusaka).

were a law unto themselves, and communication with the Ministry of Rural Development virtually broke down. The status of the Central Planning Unit continued to fall. These developments must in part be held responsible for the departure from both the time schedule and project list of the first plan. They underline the enormous importance of a clearly defined division of responsibility between the central planning office and the Ministries—a division which is acceptable to both sides and made workable by good personal relations between their staffs.

Another administrative difficulty arose from Zambia's manpower problem, as revealed by the *Manpower Report* of 1966.[112] The solution to this problem was, of course, long-term and lay in the vigorous pursuit of educational and training programmes. But in the interim, available manpower was often not used to the best advantage. One reason for this was the lack (to which we have already pointed)[113] of firm central control of both establishment and personnel work in the civil service. The latter had little unity and cohesion. Again, the effect of the frequent ministerial reorganisations and reshuffles undertaken by President Kaunda from January 1967 onwards made it difficult to maintain staff continuity, especially at senior levels.

Finally, the plan's implementation was adversely affected by the low morale of many civil servants stationed in the rural areas; yet it was here that the success or failure of the rural development aspects of the plan was inevitably decided. Reasons for low morale included a higher cost of living than along the line of rail; the belief that rural social life was less pleasant; the fear among certain civil servants that they would be forgotten in the promotion race compared to their colleagues in Lusaka; and the frustration caused by over-centralisation. The result was a reluctance, and in some instances a point-blank refusal, on the part of (particularly senior) civil servants to be posted to the rural areas; and a strong desire by rural civil servants to be transferred to the line of rail. The performance of personnel in remote areas was further reduced because effective supervision could not be provided for most members of the field staff, such as agricultural extension officers.

Political difficulties also arose. That the ANC, which controlled the Western Province as well as the Southern Province after the 1968 election, did not feel committed to the plan was probably not serious: the Southern Province had a good record of project imple-

112. At independence 'the scarcity of educated Africans in Zambia was extreme'. *Manpower Report, 1965–66, op. cit.*, p. 1.

113. See pp. 270–1 above.

mentation, while the formidable problems facing the Western Province (including those of communications and ecology) would not have disappeared had UNIP retained its hold over the province in 1968. More serious were the poor relations between the private sector and UNIP. Until the economic take-overs in April 1968 and August 1969 the private sector remained largely outside government's control. The plan faced the problems which beset any plan in a predominantly private enterprise economy. In large measure it depended for its fulfilment on the voluntary co-operation of the private sector; but such co-operation was not always forthcoming. No doubt some blame attached to both sides. The private sector was overwhelmingly European- and Asian-owned, and in the past had been committed politically to the settler United Federal Party which had preceded the UNIP–ANC coalition as the government of Northern Rhodesia. It was therefore slow to adjust to the fact of UNIP dominance. Few Europeans or Asians took out Zambian citizenship, and many seemed mainly concerned to make a quick profit on a small investment. For its part, the government was slow to establish effective links with the private sector, which was consulted only in the late stages of formulating the Development Plan. It refused to adjust the tax formula in the mining industry, and until March 1968 did not make clear its future policy towards the private sector. As a result private investment—and, in particular, the inflow of foreign capital—did not measure up to the hopes of the plan.

Political difficulties also arose within UNIP and, as we have suggested, political considerations were often paramount in the President's ministerial reshuffles. An obvious example is Simon Kapwepwe's appointment as national Vice-president, with responsibility for development planning, following his success in the central committee elections of August 1967. The fact that Kapwepwe was unable to secure country-wide acceptance as Vice-president reacted unfavourably on his development role, and he could not maintain the vigorous lead in plan implementation that he first showed on assuming his new office. Again, following the UNIP crisis of August 1969 and Kapwepwe's resignation (subsequently withdrawn), responsibility for development planning was transferred to another member of the Cabinet. Predictably, a succession of political crises within UNIP meant that the implementation of the Development Plan often became subordinate to the need to maintain party unity.[114]

114. Cf. R. Cranford Pratt, 'The administration of economic planning in a newly independent State: the Tanzanian experience, 1963–66', *Journal of Commonwealth Political Studies*, vol. v, No. 1 (March 1967), pp. 55–6.

The lack of unity within the ruling party and the Cabinet formed out of it meant that the latter was not strong enough to resist the pursuit of projects which were not in the Development Plan. This is not to say, of course, that periodic revision of any plan is not essential. As Andrew Shonfield has pointed out:

A plan is a living body of economic policy adapting itself constantly to changing circumstances, sometimes undergoing drastic alteration in its component parts in order to secure particular objectives which come in time to acquire a new order or priority.[115]

Thus in the difficult field of rural development the government was right to de-emphasise strategies which had obviously failed, such as producer co-operatives, the tractor mechanisation scheme, and the Credit Organisation of Zambia.[116] What ought to be avoided, however, are alterations to national plans which are not justifiable in economic terms. In Zambia, already heavily burdened Ministries dissipated a great deal of effort in considering and planning new projects, thus slowing down the execution of projects which had already been approved and incorporated in the plan.[117] This was also serious because, with the rapid rise in costs, more funds were needed merely to execute existing projects.

Political factors also adversely affected agricultural production. A major reason for failure was the diversion of machinery for dispensing agricultural credit from its formal economic purpose of injecting capital into the subsistence sector in order to make possible higher output and so incorporate the sector into the market economy. The Credit Organisation of Zambia was heavily staffed by UNIP activists, and in granting loans the yardstick of party record often became more important than farming ability. COZ loans came to be popularly regarded as grants in reward for services rendered in the independence struggle, to be used as the recipient decided.[118] The inability of UNIP national leaders to resist the pressure of their own supporters was one factor in the plan's failure to reach almost any of its agricultural targets.

115. Andrew Shonfield, *Modern Capitalism: the Changing Balance of Public and Private Power* (London, 1965), p. 230.

116. The current stress is on the family as the unit of production; the ox-drawn plough; and a new credit agency, the Agricultural Finance Company, which, it is intended, shall not give loans to farmers on the political criterion of loyalty to the ruling party.

117. For opposition criticism, see *Nat. Ass. Deb.*, Hansard No. 11, 18 October 1967, col. 94 (Mr N. Mundia).

118. *The Friso Report on Rural Agricultural Credit in Zambia* (Lusaka, October 1968), *passim*.

Another political obstacle has been the frequency of contested elections since the year in which the first National Development Plan was launched. These elections not only imposed a heavy burden on the civil service but also absorbed the attention of political activists from Cabinet Minister level downwards. They took Ministers away from their Ministries for long periods and diverted regional and lower-level UNIP officials from the tasks of plan implementation. In fact the continuing necessity of fighting elections may have been one reason for the caution shown by UNIP in transforming itself from a political into an economic mobilisation instrument.

*Remedies.* Several of the non-administrative blockages were removed by the implementation of the first National Development Plan and of government contingency plans. The communication network was improved, the fuel problem solved, and the Mechanical Services Department opened several workshops in the outlying areas.

In the administrative sphere, we have noted that provincial Ministers of State pressed for more decentralisation of power from the centre to the provinces. Some concessions were made before the end of 1968: for example, a system of provincial block votes was introduced, enabling limited funds to be largely controlled at provincial level for the purpose of overcoming unexpected hold-ups or increased costs in already authorised projects. Then, towards the end of 1968, President Kaunda announced the major reorganisation of government to be implemented in 1969, which we have discussed above.[119] However, the decentralisation was by no means as far-reaching as Kaunda had led his followers to believe. Subsequent amendments—such as the grant of additional personnel management and financial powers to provincial permanent secretaries early in 1970[120]—were an indication that the exercise in decentralisation was not complete. In the meantime, in their dealings with Lusaka provincial Ministers still experience some of the frustrations felt by their predecessors, the Ministers of State, as they now seek to implement the second National Development Plan.

*The second National Development Plan.* The Development Planning Division, which has been housed within the Ministry of Development Planning and National Guidance since late 1970, drew up the second plan under a number of serious handicaps. Its status in

119. See pp. 255–8 above.
120. Cabinet Office circular No. 24 of 1970, *op. cit.*

government had fallen during the period of the first plan. The
planners' freedom of action was greatly limited by the fact that the
government was already committed to the extent of K350 million
on projects initiated during the first plan, and only due for completion during the second.[121] Their difficulties were compounded
by the hostility and uncertainty prevalent in the private sector
(whose performance is still essential to the achievement of any
plan's goals)[122] and the rapid fall in the copper price from 1970. It
was therefore impossible to make any certain estimates as to what
revenue might be expected during the plan period. Moreover, the
second plan stresses rural development and the need to develop
simultaneously Zambia's industry and agriculture;[123] yet the
national agricultural census, which alone can provide an adequate
statistical basis for agricultural expansion, was started only in
October 1970—too late to be of any real use.[124]

The staffing position of the Planning Division made for further
problems. As we have seen, the Yugoslav Director failed (like his
British predecessor) to establish good relations with many of his own
staff and with other agencies of government, and civil servants in
any case were often sceptical of the utility of planning. Consequent
resignations created what the Director regarded as a serious shortage
of planning staff. The absence of economists at provincial level
made effective decentralisation of planning very difficult, as the
Minister of Finance and Development admitted in March 1970.[125]
The Planning Division is still largely dependent on expatriates,
although the key post of Director was Zambianised in 1972.

Another serious weakness in the process of compiling the second
plan was the lack of close consultation with the political level. The
fourteen committees set up early in 1971 to knock the plan into
final shape did not include any Ministers or politicians, and most
of the papers produced by these committees were not sent to UNIP
headquarters. No UNIP national council meeting was held to discuss what the priorities of the plan should be or to consider its
subsequent implementation. Even the National Development Committee of the Cabinet did not meet regularly to decide these matters.
Inevitably, the activists of the ruling party lack a deep sense of

121. President Kaunda's address to the National Assembly. *Daily Parl.
Deb.*, No. 25a, 8 January 1971, col. 14.
122. See *Second National Development Plan, op. cit.*, p. 43. The SNDP
envisages a total outlay of K2,161 million, divided as follows: public sector,
K1,476 million; private sector, K685 million.
123. *Ibid.*, p. 33.
124. ZIS press release No. 58/70, 9 July 1970.
125. *Ibid.*, No. 40/70, 9 March 1970.

commitment to the plan, and, as far as implementation is concerned, this may prove a more vital factor than the new planning machinery to be created at central and provincial levels.[126]

## Conclusions

Very favourable terms of trade helped Zambia to achieve a remarkably high rate of growth of the national economy between 1966 and 1970. The abnormally high prices paid for copper throughout this period[127] not only made it possible for most of the capital investment in the first plan to be met from domestic resources, but also helped to offset the contingency plan expenditure consequent upon the Rhodesian UDI. Since 1970, however, the price of copper has fallen sharply and Zambia's leaders cannot 'count on any improvements in the terms of trade between copper prices on the one hand and import prices on the other'.[128] This means that the implementation of the second plan will take place under much less favourable conditions than those which prevailed during most of the first plan period. Given also the current monetary crisis in the world and the self-protective measures taken by the developed countries, it seems likely that Zambia will increasingly have to realise her development objectives through domestic effort and greater self-reliance.[129]

Shortage of trained and skilled manpower proved a bigger constraint on development in the first plan period than lack of financial resources. The extra drain on manpower caused by the economic take-overs of 1968–70 was considerable. Nonetheless, it is questionable whether the lack of skilled Zambian personnel—administrative, professional and technical—seriously slowed down the implementation of the plan. Richard Jolly explains the paradox of rapid economic growth at a time of acute shortage of skilled and educated manpower in two ways:

First, that growth, though rapid, was not as rapid as it would have been if skilled manpower had been in optimal balance with other resources,

126. 'A two-tier, closely related regional planning system will . . . be worked out: at the national level, through the Regional Planning Unit of the Development Planning Division, and at the level of Provinces, through Provincial Planning Units.' *Second National Development Plan, op. cit.*, p. 193.

127. The price was K1,300 a ton (pre-metric) in August 1969, when the State proposed to take over 51 per cent of the mines' capital.

128. *Ibid.*, p. 191. The average price for copper of K740 per metric ton has been used for the whole of the second-plan period (1972–76).

129. *Ibid.* Fortunately the sharp and unexpected rise in the price of copper early in 1973 was sustained throughout the year.

instead of in shortage and relative scarcity. Second, that growth as measured by statistics of output and national income misses out a great deal of what is important for assessing change in the quality and standard of living as well as change in the economic, political, and social structure on which future development will depend. Thus both in respect of consumption and investment, Zambia's growth of national income over recent years probably overstates the changes that have taken place.[130]

Probably more important in its effect on the plan than the actual shortage of manpower was the inadequate use that was often made of such manpower as was available, coupled with the fragmented structure of the civil service. In 1967 ONDP said that increased initiative, development-consciousness and a sense of urgency were the 'crucial factors' which were needed throughout the operation of the administrative structure.[131] This remains a valid comment. The importance of manpower is fully recognised in the second plan, which states that 'The manpower constraint is . . . more severe than the resources constraint and is, in fact, the principal limiting factor on the rate of growth of the country's economy. There is a shortage of adequately trained manpower in all sectors of the economy.'[132]

It can be argued that the quality of the personnel available to implement a country's development plan is of prime importance, whereas the administrative structure, political climate and fiscal resources are secondary matters. There may come a time, however, when this is a doubtful proposition and—so far, at least, as rural development in Zambia was concerned—we believe that that time was reached in August 1967, when UNIP held elections to its central committee, with disastrous consequences for the unity of the party and the government. Sectionalism within UNIP increased and adversely affected the civil service,[133] while development was retarded because of 'the snail-like speed with which the wheels of the bureaucratic machinery of government turn in the formulation of policy and the transmission of policy decisions to the field operators for execution'.[134]

130. R. Jolly, 'The skilled manpower constraint', in Elliott (ed.), *Constraints on the Economic Development of Zambia, op. cit.*, pp. 45–6.
131. *Progress Report: 1 July 1966 to 1 March 1967, op. cit.*
132. *Second National Development Plan, op. cit.*, p. 42.
133. Data collected by the Zambia Localised Civil Servants' Association in 1968 suggested that a significant number of civil servants believed that the treatment of members of the civil service was often heavily influenced by tribal considerations. Dresang shows the weak base of many such beliefs. D. L. Dresang, 'The civil service in Zambia' (forthcoming).
134. Address by President Kaunda, 30 December 1968, ZIS press release No. 2223/68, *op. cit.*, p. 9.

At the end of 1968 President Kaunda therefore took steps to restructure the administration and to discipline the ruling party by asserting his personal dominance over it. Both actions were necessary: on the one hand, implementation of the first National Development Plan in the rural areas was being delayed because decision-making was over-centralised in Lusaka,[135] and on the other hand, the deep and bitter divisions within UNIP were reducing the effectiveness and undermining the morale of the government. President Kaunda had in part diagnosed accurately the illness afflicting the Zambian body politic, but his remedies proved inadequate. Sectionalism still pervaded UNIP and became more intense, while the series of radical but unco-ordinated administrative changes in 1968–69 created at least as many problems as they solved.

In 1972 the President sought to overcome his political predicament by converting Zambia into a 'democratic' one-party State, claiming that such a State would be conducive both to political stability and to economic development. In the administrative sphere, a working party on the decentralised administration was appointed by the Secretary General to the Government early in 1972. Its report, which was accepted towards the end of the year, recommended a very thoroughly worked out, comprehensive and radical decentralisation of personnel, powers and responsibilities to the provincial level. In 1972, also, planning began on a new strategy for rural development—intensive development zones. Further administrative and political changes are therefore impending and may tackle the problem of what sort of governmental and party machinery is required to transform a sluggish rural economy. However, at the end of what may (as in 1968–69) be a much publicised exercise, the villager may in effect say once again, 'Plus ça change, plus c'est la même chose.'

135. Cf. 'We are now faced with a position in which the efficient execution of the Plan will demand greatly increased decentralisation of responsibility for execution.' *Progress Report: 1 July 1966 to 1 March 1967, op. cit.*

# 8

# Trade unionism and politics on the Copperbelt

*Anirudha Gupta*

In an over-simplistic way, the history of trade unionism on the
Zambian Copperbelt can be described as the story of a conflict
resulting from the attempts of the government and UNIP to control
the mineworkers and the determination of the latter to resist such
attempts. Yet the story is not one of conflict alone; underneath, one
discerns continuous effort on the part of the contending parties
to come to an understanding of each other's role. On the one hand,
the unions have been anxious to define the *political* role of the
government and the party in relation to the labour movement; on
the other, the government and the party have shown their determination to define the *economic* role of the trade unions. In the
process there have been many shifts from positions of confrontation
to compromise, until a stage has been reached in which the government and UNIP leaders have admitted the workers' right to
separate existence as an actively organised group, while the mineworkers have accepted the supreme authority of the government
in such industrial affairs as bear directly on political and policy
matters. The present stage can be roughly described as that of an
'equilibrium', although the relationship between the government
and the unions remains far from finally settled.

If a certain amount of latitude is allowed to conceptualise the
historical process, it can be said that the stage of 'equilibrium' has
been arrived at broadly through two phases. The first began at the
time of independence, when UNIP, emboldened by its political
success, attempted to establish full control over the labour movement.
Its actions then were guided by three motives. First, there was the
need to establish political control over an industry which was vitally
important to the nation's economy. Secondly, since a large number
of mineworkers were party members, it was hoped that UNIP would
succeed in having its trusted men elected to key union posts. In the

third place, the assimilation of an organisation with a paid membership of over 30,000 was expected to boost the image of the party
and facilitate its task of establishing political unity in the country.
But as we shall see, UNIP's attempts gave rise to new tensions
and conflicts during 1965–66 which proved that, notwithstanding
its official backing, the party was unable to break the organised
resistance of the mineworkers.

From 1967 onwards there were indications of a new phase when,
instead of trying to control the mineworkers' union, the government
concentrated on educating the workers and regularising the trade
union structure through available constitutional and administrative
means. Political considerations gave way to economic ones as the
national leaders realised the importance of conciliating the workers
in order to attain the goal of national development. In this stage
the party itself came to play a subordinate role, while central and
provincial Ministers and their officials and the officially sponsored
Zambia Congress of Trade Unions (ZCTU) were given greater
initiative and responsibility to maintain industrial peace on the
Copperbelt. This approach succeeded in bringing about closer
association between government and trade union structures, but
failed to educate politically the ordinary workers in favour of
development-oriented policies. Cases of unofficial strikes and defiance of their own executive by the miners to obtain immediate
economic relief continued unabated. In other words, this phase
resulted in an uneasy coexistence between the political elite and
the industrial worker, thus highlighting an interesting aspect of
Zambia's evolving political system.

In the following pages we shall try to study these two phases with
a view to obtaining a clearer understanding of the pattern of
relationships between the mineworkers' union and the party and
administration, the motivations which guided government and party
policies, the means adopted to achieve industrial peace, and finally
the constraints and limitations of the trade union structure itself.
To put the discussion into proper perspective, however, we give a
short description of, first, the socio-economic setting in which the
mineworkers live and, secondly, the pattern of relationships of
politicians and mineworkers during the nationalist period and its
bearing on the behaviour and attitude of both groups in the post-
independence era. For the sake of clarity, we discuss these two
aspects under the sub-heading:

*Basic determinants*

*Socio-economic environment.* In the Zambian economy the copper industry—wholly owned until recently by two expatriate firms[1]—plays a key role. This is evident from the fact that copper contributes over 45 per cent of the country's gross domestic product and provides 96·5 per cent of its total exports. In terms of employment, although the industry employs only 19 per cent of the total labour force, it pays about 38 per cent of the country's total wage bill.[2] It is again the earnings from copper that provide a major share of the expenses involved in the execution of various developmental projects and the National Development Plans. The overwhelming dependence of the State-structure on the industry can be understood from the fact that any sustained fall in copper production or in the world price of copper would not only reduce government revenue but also affect development plans and result in widespread unemployment. This makes it obvious why—unless the economy becomes more viable and diversified—the government is very sensitive about the mining sector and regards it as essential both to maintain industrial peace and discipline and to raise production. Further, because of the persistence of a mono-type economy, the government must keep a strict watch on the wage structure in the mines so as to prevent inflation and a further widening of the substantial income gap between the miners and those engaged in other sectors, especially agriculture. As we shall see, the attempt to evolve an incomes and wages policy has occasionally brought the government into direct confrontation with the mineworkers' union.

The dominant place occupied by copper in the nation's economy also invests the labour force engaged in the industry with a sense of its own importance. In the first place, the sustained growth and continuing prosperity of the mining industry have helped to raise the wage level of the miners to such an extent that they are 'among the most highly paid mining labour in Africa'.[3] Secondly, working conditions on the mines have facilitated the growth of a stabilised

1. The Anglo-American Corporation group and the Roan Selection Trust group. The first own Bancroft, Nchanga, Broken Hill and Rhokana mines; the second, Chambishi, Chibuluma, Mufulira, Ndola and Luanshya mines. The Anglo-American group, which produced about 53 per cent of the copper output, is owned predominantly by South African and British interests, whereas the RST group is owned predominantly by American and British interests.

2. Deposition by Mr Mars-Jones on behalf of the mining companies to the Brown Commission on 20 May 1966. *Times of Zambia*, 21 May 1966.

3. *Report of the Commission Appointed to Enquire into the Mining Industry in Northern Rhodesia* (Morrison report) (Lusaka, 1962), p. 18.

labour force. By 1968 it was estimated that about one-third of the
local labour force had been working on the mines for more than
ten years (see table 8.1). Length of service also accounts for the
higher technical skill the Africans have obtained in certain surface
and underground jobs. Hence, even though the literacy rate among
the mineworkers is relatively low, the latter are considered to be

*Table 8.1*
Distribution of labour force on the mines according to length of
service, as at December 1968

| Length of service (years) | Expatriate employees (%) | Local employees (%) |
|---|---|---|
| 0–5 | 63·0 | 32·9 |
| 6–10 | 19·0 | 34·5 |
| 11–15 | 8·6 | 15·1 |
| 16–20 | 5·7 | 12·1 |
| Over 20 | 3·7 | 5·4 |

*Source. Copperbelt of Zambia Mining Industry Year Book, 1968* (Kitwe, n.d.),
p. 47.

more advanced, more urbanised and more adept in industrial techniques than workers in other sectors. Thirdly, employment in the
mines gives the workers the privilege of living in mine townships
with various facilities such as housing, hospitals, schools and ration
shops, all run and owned by the companies. The physical setting of
these towns instils in the worker a sense of communal exclusiveness:
his social relations are regulated by a strange amalgam of traditional
and tribal ties and new affiliations based on job performance in the
mines, as (for example) surface and underground workers, shift
bosses, and shop stewards. It is, as Epstein points out, 'the unitary
structure of mine society'[4] that determines the miners' world outlook. As an over-privileged elite who are greatly envied by others,
they are conscious of their own importance and also know that if
they so desire they can stop the mines and disrupt the country's
economy. Behind this knowledge lies a long tradition of militancy
and collective action which has made the mineworkers' union one
of the strongest in Africa.

However, though privileged, the mineworkers do not represent
a satiated group: in an industry in which a large number of expatriates—over 4,500 in December 1968—are employed on better

4. Epstein, *Politics in an Urban African Community, op. cit.,* pp. 123 ff.

conditions of service and higher pay, an amount of dissatisfaction among the local employees is bound to be endemic. Sometimes this dissatisfaction finds an outlet through incidents which have racial overtones and demands for the promotion of Africans to higher jobs and for parity in the pay-scales of both expatriates and Africans.[5] The racial element also induces among the mineworkers a pattern of behaviour which leads them, even on minor issues involving the European and African staff, to demand immediate redress from union and party leaders; if the latter fail to satisfy them, they resort to illegal stoppage of work. The result is that at the local level there is a regular competition between UNIP and union officials to win the sympathy of the miners by consciously supporting their demands, even when such action runs counter to the directives of the higher authorities. As we shall see, this over-enthusiasm on the part of the local UNIP leaders to back and encourage miners' militancy in racial matters has at times caused great embarrassment to the central leaders and has persuaded the latter to direct UNIP followers to keep out of industrial disputes altogether.[6]

To summarise, the Copperbelt miners play a key role, out of all proportion to their limited numbers. They represent the largest organised working force in Zambia; their collective bargaining capacity is derived from the central place which the mining sector occupies in the nation's economy; as the 'best paid, best housed, and best provided for',[7] they constitute a privileged group in society; while the racial factor complicates and sometimes aggravates industrial relations on the mines.

5. The dual wage structure—i.e. different scales of pay for expatriate and African workers for similar jobs—which was introduced by the mining companies in 1964, ran counter to a way of thinking about wages shared by Africans and Europeans. 'It did so at the very point of racial division, and for this reason became a focus for dissatisfaction amongst African workers at a time when their co-operation with the management was essential if the industry was to be successfully organized to meet the needs of an independent Zambia.' *Report of the Commission of Enquiry into the Mining Industry, 1966* (Brown report) (Lusaka, 1966), p. 16.

Although, in accordance with the recommendation of the Brown report, the dual structure has been abolished, the various incentives in the form of allowances, leave pay, etc., which the expatriates enjoy give them a standard of living which is far higher than that of the Zambian workers.

6. In the National Assembly Mr Chakulya thanked the President and the second National Convention 'for deciding that there should be no more interference in industrial relations matters by friends and brothers and people who are not directly connected'. *Nat. Ass. Deb.*, Hansard No. 21, 22 January 1970, col. 510.

7. *Africa Digest* (London), February 1967, p. 72.

*The mineworkers' union and the nationalists.* As has been noted earlier, the relationship between the mineworkers' union and the nationalist parties in the colonial era was complex: as the largest organisation of African workers, the union sometimes came into close contact with political movements and sometimes drew apart, but at all times it took care to maintain its own organisational independence. In the process the union developed what can be called a 'code of conduct' which governed its relationship with the nationalist politicians. For the present discussion it is not necessary to review this relationship in detail;[8] instead, we shall identify those features which persisted and influenced UNIP–union relations in the post-independence period.

It is a coincidence that the African Mineworkers' Union (AMU) came into being in the same year, 1949, as the first nationalist organisation, the African National Congress (ANC), was founded. The formation of the AMU was the culmination of a long struggle on the part of the African miners to have their own union as distinct from the European Mineworkers' Union. Their efforts succeeded partly because of the changed attitude of the colonial government and the mining companies in the post-war period, when they favoured the formation of African trade unions on the Copperbelt,[9] and partly because of the dynamic leadership of Lawrence Katilungu, who became the first president of the AMU. Under his guidance Africans in other industries also formed their own unions and, in 1950, the AMU and these other unions federated to form the Trades Union Congress (TUC), again with Katilungu as president.

Among the African mineworkers Katilungu enjoyed the status of a near-charismatic leader and for a decade from 1950 his personal leadership of the AMU and the TUC was unchallenged. For some time during 1951–52 the AMU leadership became closely associated with the ANC, led by Nkumbula, giving cause for anxiety to both the employers and the government.[10] While co-operating with the politicians, however, Katilungu followed a clear policy of

8. For a detailed study, see Mulford, *Zambia: the Politics of Independence, op. cit.*; Gray, *The Two Nations, op. cit.*; Mason, *Year of Decision, op. cit.*; and Hall, *Zambia, op. cit.*

9. In 1947 William Comrie, a British trade union expert, was appointed Labour Officer on the Copperbelt. He arrived in March and proceeded to implement government's policy on African trade unions.

10. Many of the earlier leaders of the mineworkers' union endorsed a conception of the labour movement which emphasised political action and this made them support the political views of Simon Zukas, an important European ally of the trade union and nationalist leaders. In response, the government deported Zukas in 1952.

keeping the trade union movement strictly under his own control
and of stressing the fact that, as an organisation interested in promoting the workers' economic welfare, the AMU had no political
role to play except when it benefited the mass of the workers. This
demarcation of the roles—the economic from the political—seems
to have been the most important contribution of Katilungu to
Zambia's labour movement. Thus both in 1953 and 1956, when
the ANC called upon the mineworkers to stop work in support of
its political demands, Katilungu refused to co-operate. On the
other hand, in 1952 AMU waged a successful struggle for wage
increases. In 1955, when a dispute arose over the promotion of
Africans to supervisory positions and the recognition by the companies of a new union of Africans in staff and supervisory posts
called the Mines African Staff Association (MASA), the mineworkers resorted to intermittent stoppages of work which came to be
known as the 'rolling strikes of 1956'.[11]

In 1959, although the formation of the Zambia African National
Congress (ZANC) received support from the ranks of militant
workers, it does not appear that the AMU was anxious to play any
role in the ZANC programme. Later, when the United National
Independence Party (UNIP) was formed, some important trade
union leaders on the Copperbelt joined it; but as an organisation
AMU kept aloof from UNIP.[12] In view of these events it was surprising that Katilungu, who had maintained the primacy of
workers' economic interests, himself became actively involved in
politics. In 1959 he accepted an invitation to serve on the Monckton
Commission, which was boycotted by both the nationalist parties,
and in 1960 he became acting president of the ANC. Katilungu's
political pronouncements aroused bitter controversy, and this led
to the first crack in his leadership. In 1960 the TUC was split on
Katilungu's controversial role and a new Reformed Trade Union
Congress (RTUC) was formed under the leadership of J. Chivunga,
A. Kalyati and M. Mwendapole.[13] The new organisation worked in
close alliance with UNIP, but it did not affect Katilungu's position
so long as he held the presidency of the AMU. However, Katilungu's
involvement in politics dissatisfied his own followers, and in December 1960 he was dismissed by the union's supreme council. He was
replaced by John Chisata, a former chairman of the Mufulira
branch of the AMU and a UNIP supporter.[14]

11. See Mason, *Year of Decision*, *op. cit.*, p. 116.
12. Berg and Butler, 'Trade unions', *op. cit.*, pp. 356 ff.
13. Mulford, *Zambia: the Politics of Independence*, *op. cit.*, pp. 172–3.
14. *Ibid.*, p. 174.

The dismissal of Katilungu marked a turning point in Northern Rhodesia's labour movement: first, it broke the personal link that existed at the leadership level between the AMU and the TUC and, secondly, it ended the era of charismatic leadership—no trade union leader subsequently enjoyed the same measure of popularity among the mineworkers. What is more interesting, however, is that by removing Katilungu from office the union reasserted its principle of non-involvement in politics. In other words, the non-political and essentially economic role of the AMU was institutionalised. This can be seen from the fact that, though the new leadership was sympathetic to UNIP's programme, it did not accept party supervision in industrial matters. Thus in July 1962, following a wage dispute, the union withdrew from the RTUC, which was renamed the United Trades Union Congress (UTUC), and threatened to go on indefinite strike. Fearing that the proposed strike would interfere with the general election of 1962, UNIP workers went round the mining towns and advised the workers to ignore the strike call. This infuriated the leaders of the AMU, and its president, John Chisata, warned Kaunda and his followers that they 'had no business interfering in an industrial dispute'.[15]

While this incident showed that the AMU was jealous in guarding its independence from outside political interference, another development made it abundantly clear that, as the largest labour organisation, it was equally determined to maintain its primacy in the mining industry. Thus in 1963, when the MASA changed its name to the United Mineworkers' Union (UMU) and claimed to be representative of all employees, its aims clashed with those of the AMU. For several months the two organisations competed with each other, but before the end of the year the UMU was in serious difficulties and had to be dissolved; it was reorganised as the Mines Local Staff Association (MLSA) to cover only supervisory and staff employees in the mines.[16]

The AMU's withdrawal from the UTUC, on the other hand, facilitated the disintegration of the latter. For some time the Congress leadership had been split into several factions, and the UNIP government eventually stepped in to dissolve the rival executives and appoint a caretaker committee pending proper elections. The finances of the Congress were so mismanaged that in 1965 the government had to extend a grant of £5,614 to wind up its business so that the Zambia Congress of Trade Unions (ZCTU), which

15. See *Central African Examiner*, 6 August 1962.
16. Report of the Registrar of Trade Unions for the year ended 31 December 1964 (Lusaka, mimeo., n.d.), p. 5.

was formed by an Act of Parliament, 'could begin [functioning] with a new slate'.[17] The purpose of the officially sponsored ZCTU was said to be to bring about, 'by wise leadership', the integration of various competing trade unions in a single industry.[18]

This brief historical survey helps us to indicate the main features of UNIP–union relations until 1964. In some respects UNIP had reason to be satisfied with the mineworkers' union, since it received overwhelming support from the Copperbelt in both the 1962 and 1964 elections.[19] A number of trade unionists also joined the UNIP administration, perhaps suggesting that the ordinary members of the AMU were in full support of the government. On the other hand, the unpredictable and generally apolitical role of the mineworkers gave UNIP cause for anxiety. The fact that the AMU had originally been formed under the active guidance of a British trade unionist and that it was for a long time dominated by 'unreliable' leaders, especially Katilungu, gave rise to the suspicion that the union was motivated by outside influences and that it was solely guided by its own narrow economic interests. Moreover, the fact that the mining industry was entirely owned by expatriate companies increased the fear that labour leaders could easily be used by 'imperialist' or foreign agents.[20] A general belief also grew up that most of the labour leaders were irresponsible and illiterate, especially after the co-option by the government of some of their best talents. At the local level, however, the job security of the miners became a source of continuous envy for the roving bands of unemployed youth who had been most active in UNIP. Thus immediately after independence both government and party leaders launched an attack on the AMU leadership and urged a wholesale change in the union structure.[21]

For its part, the union also inherited a set of legacies. First, resentment at political interference in union affairs became an article of faith in all grades of the organisation. In order to maintain its autonomy the union developed a kind of defence mechanism by which it could unite all sections of its ranks against outsiders, even when fissures and factional rivalries remained within the organisa-

17. *Nat. Ass. Deb.*, Hansard No. 5, 14 December 1965, col. 136.
18. J. M. Mwanakatwe, Minister of Education, *ibid.*, Hansard No. 6, 6 April 1966, col. 1175.
19. See Mulford, *Zambia: the Politics of Independence, op. cit.*, pp. 277–8.
20. See *Nat. Ass. Deb.*, Hansard No. 6, 31 March 1966, col. 897. A UNIP Member of Parliament, Mr E. Chirwa, accused the colonial government of giving lots of money to 'globe-trotting union leaders'. *Ibid.*
21. See pp. 297–302 below.

tion. Secondly, the tradition of intermittent struggles against racial discrimination on the mines gave the workers a kind of militancy which was not paralleled even by the extremist section of UNIP's youth brigade. Ideologically, therefore, it is hard to say whether the AMU was on the 'left' or the 'right' of UNIP; above all, it was intensely concerned with guarding its autonomy. Thirdly, as Katilungu's downfall demonstrated, it became a part of AMU's policy not to regard highly those who had left trade union activity and joined the administration. For all practical purposes, the role of such leaders in the labour movement became redundant.

## UNIP–union confrontation

It was against this background that the stage was set for a direct confrontation between UNIP and AMU, which was renamed the Zambia Mineworkers' Union (ZMU) in January 1965. In regard to the mining industry, the objective of the government was clear: it wanted full co-operation from both the management and the workers to maintain and expand production for the successful operation of its economic policies. While some sort of agreement could be negotiated with the management, it was less easy to decide how best to control and persuade the workers to play their role in the changed post-independence situation. The choices before the government were three: it could split the ZMU by forming a rival body; or it could dissolve the union; or it could encourage UNIP to take over the leadership of the existing organisation. That the first approach was not feasible had already been proved by the events of 1962–64. The UMU, which functioned as a wing of UNIP, had failed to convert the mineworkers; and the UTUC, led by UNIP faithfuls, had gone bankrupt. The second choice was ruled out, both because any step to dissolve the union would have met with the united opposition of the mineworkers and because, being nationalists themselves, the new leaders were unwilling to destroy the trade union movement in an industry which was wholly owned by foreign capital. Under the circumstances, only the third choice remained open. This choice was additionally favoured because disciplining the workers in their new role was felt to be essentially a political task and the extension of control over the ZMU was not considered incompatible with UNIP's goal of establishing a one-party system in the country. Further, there was a built-in tension between the union leaders and local supporters of UNIP in the mining towns, so that the government was under some pressure to give greater initiative to the party in industrial affairs.

*The Trade Unions and Trade Disputes Ordinance.* It was, therefore, with a view to facilitating this objective that the government
introduced a Bill to amend the Trades Union and Trades Dispute
Ordinance (see chapter 25 of the Laws). It was passed in December
1964 and came into effect early in 1965. Introducing the Bill in
Parliament, the Minister of Labour, Justin Chimba, stated that it
would create stable industrial relations between employers and employees, check the trade unions from receiving financial and other
forms of assistance from outside, and establish a new trades union
congress (ZCTU) to which 'it is hoped all trade unions should
affiliate'.[22]

Certain provisions of the amending Act seemed to be indeed
in favour of strengthening the trade union movement. For instance,
the minimum number of members required for a trade union to
be registered was raised from seven to 100 in order to stop the
mushrooming of smaller unions. Trade unions were required to
provide for taking decisions by secret ballot on a wide range of
matters such as the election of delegates to a general meeting,
election of officers, calling a strike or lock-out, dissolution, amalgamation, imposition of a levy and increasing subscriptions and
decreasing benefits. By this provision it was hoped that ordinary
members would have greater control over the affairs of their own
unions.

The keynote of the amending ordinance, however, was the considerable powers which it bestowed on the Registrar of Trade
Unions, the ZCTU and the Minister of Labour. Thus the Registrar
could refuse to give consent to the election of an officer of a trade
union; he could suspend from office any officer who failed in his
duties under the ordinance (and the Minister of Labour could
appoint a person to perform the duties of the suspended official);
and he could summon witnesses 'to give any information as to the
existence or as to the operation of any trade union, or federation of
trade unions'. Finally, every secret ballot required to be taken under
the provisions of the ordinance must be supervised by the Registrar
or a person appointed by him.

The powers of the proposed ZCTU were clearly defined: it was
proposed to be a federating body of trade unions to which, after
affiliation, trade unions were required to remit a part of their sub-

22. Chimba added, 'Membership of the Congress will confer considerable
benefits upon the affiliated unions and will have the effect of strengthening
their position and making it extremely difficult for any rival organisation to
set up in opposition.' *Nat. Ass. Deb.*, Hansard No. 1, 15 December 1964,
col. 72.

scriptions; its approval was also needed for certain 'prescribed decisions' such as a strike ballot, strikes, dissolution and amalgamation. The ordinance provided that the Minister of Labour should appoint the first officers of the Congress, to hold office until elections were held.

The Minister was given far-reaching powers: if he was satisfied that a trade union was sufficiently representative of the employees concerned he could make an order for the deduction of union dues by the employer for payment to the union (check-off facility); and, if the membership exceeded 60 per cent of the total employees, he might make an order to deduct subscriptions for all employees unless exempted in the order (dues shop facility). Such an order, however, could be made only if the union was affiliated to the Congress. Moreover, no trade union could accept aid from foreign agencies or affiliate with any organisation outside Zambia without the approval of the Minister. Finally, the Minister could, if he thought necessary, dissolve the ZCTU, and his decision could not be questioned in any proceedings whatsoever.

These provisions aimed at centralising the labour movement under the personal authority of the Minister of Labour. In performing his duties the Minister was to be assisted by the Registrar, who was from the beginning a political appointee, and the ZCTU, which—according to Chimba—was to have 'considerable control over the affairs of the labour movement as a whole'.[23] In one important matter, however, the jurisdiction of ZCTU was limited: it could not intervene directly in a dispute between employers and employees in any particular industry. This limitation, as we shall discuss, became a source of irritation for the ZCTU activists.[24]

*UNIP and ZMU.* From the beginning it was clear that while the smaller and financially insolvent unions were very willing to be affiliated to the ZCTU, especially for the check-off benefits, the ZMU was openly suspicious of the new move. The mineworkers' union did not think that it would benefit from affiliation; on the contrary, it would have to contribute a portion of its regular income from membership fees to the Congress. Further, the ZMU leaders were afraid that, after affiliation, they would be subject to Congress rules on strike action and, more important, would be

23. *Ibid.*, col. 76.
24. As the general secretary of ZCTU, Wilson Chakulya, subsequently complained, 'the present constitution keeps the union autonomous and the national centre is there mainly to provide advice and guidance without authority'. *Times of Zambia*, 4 January 1969.

required to hold elections for a new executive. It was, therefore, not until July 1966 that the union decided to affiliate. Before that date the first round of confrontation between UNIP and union leaders had begun in earnest.

It was not, however, on the question of affiliation that the confrontation took place: the immediate issue was one of converting the mineworkers to the development-oriented goals of the government. To achieve this conversion, the central leaders eagerly attempted to assert their authority over the mining industry. The trade unionists reacted by denying the right of the central leadership to have any say in matters which concerned themselves and their employers. This sharp divergence between the two stands was noted by the *Times of Zambia*:[25]

The trade unionists see their role in life as to fight for all they can get for their own members; the government thinks that instead of being 'selfish' the union should be an arm of the nation, assisting in the general progress.

The first clash took place when the ZMU, representing the local daily rated employees, declared a dispute concerning the rates of pay for senior operators and craftsmen not covered by any previous agreements. The government appointed a conciliation board, but after a few months, in September, the union decided to hold a strike ballot. The Registrar of Trade Unions insisted that ZMU should amend its constitution and hold new elections, under the 1965 ordinance, before taking a strike ballot. Controversy flared up when union leaders accused the government of trying to install hand-picked UNIP men to run the union. In reply, at a meeting held in Kitwe, Dr Kaunda accused the workers of living in the world of the 1940s.[26] In November ZMU agreed to change its constitution to allow the Registrar to supervise the strike ballot, and 22 December was fixed as the date for election to the ZMU executive. It soon became clear that the Registrar was acting on the advice of the government when he declared these elections void, and, in turn, ZMU blamed the UNIP workers for indulging in hooliganism. At the centre of the controversy what appeared to be crucial was UNIP's open bid to replace the trade union leadership at any cost. This attitude surprised the latter: the ZMU president, Cosmos Mwene, wondered why the party wanted a change in the leadership when most officials of the union were also UNIP mem-

25. 25 October 1965.
26. *Times of Zambia*, 25 October 1965.

bers.[27] Another date for election in all the seven branches of the ZMU was fixed in January 1966, and UNIP branches were put into full swing to present their slate of nominees for the various posts to be filled. In contrast to the curious silence maintained by union officials, UNIP held noisy meetings in the mine townships and openly denounced the labour leaders. Thus in Ndola a gathering was told that the party had put up its two candidates for the ZMU's special conference in Kitwe and that they were going to be elected whether the miners liked it or not.[28] Again, in Kalulushi township a leaflet, entitled 'Kasupato', was circulated which mentioned some union men and accused them of plotting against the President and of receiving money from the mining companies.

The results of the elections, however, came as a great shock to the party as well as to the government. Of some 8,000 votes cast, UNIP received only 1,000 votes, or only $12\frac{1}{2}$ per cent of the total; and of the fifty-three branch delegates elected to the annual conference of the Mineworkers' Union, only twelve were UNIP candidates. Even these candidates succeeded only because they had the support of the leading elements in the union's own hierarchy.

The election controversy and the results served to emphasise several important aspects of union–party relations. From the manner in which UNIP conducted the campaign, it was evident that it had overestimated its own strength. It believed—rather naively—that its views about the union leaders as 'irresponsible' would be largely shared by the mineworkers. Moreover, certain remarks—notably that the party would get its candidates elected 'whether the miners like them or not'—betrayed a supercilious attitude towards the mineworkers. Party workers often tried to give the impression that their actions had the backing of the government and, therefore, that those who opposed the party would have reasons to regret their stand at a later date. In this respect even top UNIP officials and government leaders indulged in threats and intimidation; and in an angry speech in Chingola, Kaunda declared that he would arrest labour leaders 'in broad daylight and imprison them to show them that they have no support'.[29]

Yet the results underlined an astounding degree of organisational solidarity among the miners. They showed that, despite their internal divisions, the ZMU members were united in their opposition to outsiders and 'loafers', as some UNIP men were called. Politically, the results demonstrated that an organised labour force of

27. *Ibid.*, 24 December 1965.
28. *Ibid.*, 13 January 1966.
29. *Ibid.* 10 January 1966.

over 35,000 could not be brought to submission by means of threats and intimidation. Further, the failure of the miners to respond even to Kaunda's appeal reflected their determination to differentiate the roles of active politicians (including the national leaders) from those of active trade unionists. This aspect became increasingly important in the later stages of union–government relations.

*Deterioration of industrial relations.* The immediate result of UNIP's ill-calculated bid to oust the ZMU leaders was a clear deterioration of industrial relations. In August 1966 the Minister of Labour and Social Services, M. Sipalo, reported to Parliament that during the first six months of the year there were 138 strikes in Zambia, involving 152,000 workers. Most of the strikes took place on the mines, particularly at the Nchanga open-cast mine, where there were sixteen stoppages. Giving reasons for this unprecedented spurt of labour unrest, the Minister regretted the 'get rich quick' attitude of the workers, blamed the management for failing to take adequate disciplinary action, and in general held the racial element responsible for the unrest on the Copperbelt.[30]

At this stage, however, two tendencies became more pronounced: first, the tendency among the miners and junior union officials to defy the authority of their own executive and, secondly, the tendency to suspect all moves on the part of government to rationalise the labour movement. The first was responsible for frequent stoppages of work; the miners did not even refer their grievances to the proper organs of the union. Sometimes they resorted to strike action simply because they did not like the manner in which their leaders conducted negotiations with the management. In fact the immediate cause of the appointment of the Brown Commission (May 1966) to report on all aspects of the mining industry was a three-week unofficial strike by the open-pit workers at Nchanga against a wage agreement signed by the union executive and the mining companies.[31]

30. *Nat. Ass. Deb.*, Hansard No. 7, 3 August 1966, cols 326 ff.
31. On 21 March there was a minor stoppage of work at Nchanga which subsequently proved to be the beginning of a mass withdrawal of labour by ZMU members throughout the Copperbelt. Describing the sequence of events, the Brown Commission observed, '. . . we are satisfied that the strikes were spontaneous and took by surprise both the unions and the companies. They affected all categories of employment in the ZMU field of representation and were supported by a number of workers in staff and supervisory jobs. From this we have drawn two conclusions:

(1) That the agreement signed by the union on 19th January, 1966, was unacceptable to the majority of workers covered by its terms.

The second tendency contributed to the famous crisis over the National Provident Fund (NPF) during August–September 1966, resulting in a complete breakdown of communication between the government and the union on the one hand and between the union leadership and ordinary members on the other. Briefly stated, the facts were as follows. Early in 1966 the government announced its intention of introducing the NPF, thereby causing concern among the ZMU leaders lest the amounts standing to the credit of the members in the companies' contributory pension fund (ZAMINLO) would be transferred to the NPF and the members would not be able to withdraw their credits when they retired, but would have to wait until they reached the age of fifty-five years. Opposition to the idea of having to contribute to two schemes began to grow and, when the NPF came into force, mining employees refused to produce their national registration cards. In August workers in the Mufulira mines stopped work on the advice of the ZMU branch officials. By 2 September the strike was 100 per cent effective throughout the Copperbelt, and the daily loss of production was estimated to be close to K2 million. On 3 September an emergency ordinance was issued on the Copperbelt and the government declared mining to be an essential service. Despite repeated threats and appeals and Kaunda's personal visits to the mining towns, the strikers refused to budge, until, on 14 September, the government retracted and promised to introduce new regulations to provide for the winding up of ZAMINLO and the paying out to the employees, over a period, of their credits under the old scheme.[32] Two days later thirty-three men were arrested, including ZMU and MLSA officials as well as UNIP workers, who were accused of spreading 'malicious' rumours on the Copperbelt.[33] Normality, however, returned on 23 September, when all strikers reported for duty.

The manner in which the government retreated from its original stand and accepted the miners' demand to release the ZAMINLO fund showed that in a trial of strength the government preferred to appease the workers rather than wreck the most vital sector of the economy. John Burnside, independent Member for the Zambezi constituency, summed up the situation: 'the workers had the government

(2) There is widespread dissatisfaction in the industry with the conditions of service laid down by the companies.'

Brown report, *op. cit.*, p. 30. For the text of the agreement between ZMU and the companies, see *ibid.*, appendix XII.

32. *Times of Zambia*, 15 September 1966 (broadcast by M. Sipalo).

33. *Ibid.*, 17 September 1966.

over a barrel, and were blackmailing them'.[34] The question
was not only one of retreat; what was more remarkable was that
when in the initial stages trade union leaders expressed doubts,
the government did little to clarify the implications and advantages
of the new scheme. Moreover, the UNIP workers on whom the
administration mainly relied to educate the miners were themselves
responsible for causing new misunderstandings. Reports alleged
that they discredited the ZAMINLO and in some cases even encouraged the strike.[35] Thus, at a meeting with President Kaunda
in Kitwe, union leaders complained about the lack of communication between the government and their members and the executive,
and pointed to the disruptive activities of some men close to the
ruling party.[36]

Finally, the strike underscored the trend towards what can be
described as a weakening of authority in the ZMU structure.
During the crisis some branch officials openly defied their leaders,
while in other cases the branch officials were themselves unable
to control their members. This lack of centralised authority which
marked the union structure, as distinct from that of UNIP, emerged
as one of the most pressing problems requiring solution at a later
stage when government–union relations were greatly normalised.

## Normalisation of relations

Towards the end of 1966 the government took fuller stock of the
labour situation than it had done hitherto. By then it had become
clear that party leaders had seriously underestimated the strength
of the mineworkers. Attempts to intimidate the workers by punitive
action had succeeded only in hardening their resistance, while
UNIP's failure to gain control over the union had shown that the
latter was unwilling to become a 'puppet' of the ruling party.
At the same time, it was not deemed possible to adopt a policy
of non-interference in industrial affairs: the mining industry was
much too important for the survival of the State structure, as well
as of the country as a whole, to be altogether ignored. Moreover,
economic considerations were now uppermost in shaping policies.
On the one hand, development programmes demanded a more
active intervention by the State in the private sector; and on the
other, runaway prices and highly inflationary conditions—caused
partly by the Rhodesian emergency and partly by the 20 per cent

34. Quoted in *ibid.*, 24 September 1966.
35. *Ibid.*, 31 August 1966.
36. *Ibid.*, 1 September 1966.

wage rise in the mining industry as a result of the recommendations of the Brown Commission—made it obligatory for the government to adopt a firmer prices and incomes policy. That the country was facing a serious situation was stressed by all: by the end of 1968 it was estimated that whereas wage and salary bills had risen by 26 per cent and labour costs per unit of output had grown by 38 per cent over the 1964 level, the employment rate showed an alarming tendency to fall. The failure of the mining industry to expand production also gave cause for general anxiety.

All these factors—rising prices, higher labour costs, unemployment and stagnation in the copper industry—called for a new line of thinking. It was felt that the State should have a greater say in the private sector, both in management and in policy matters, and that by expanding such participation it would be possible to convince the workers that they were serving the State and not a group of private capitalists and 'profiteers'. It was partly in order to inculcate a new spirit of dedication among the workers that the philosophy of Humanism was devised, while the economic reforms of 1968 were announced with a view to securing larger participation by the State in economic and entrepreneurial activities.

At the Mulungushi conference held in April 1968, President Kaunda called on certain foreign companies to sell 51 per cent of their enterprises to the government. He explained that, although their present managements would continue, the 'policy and control of the industries will be with the directors', a majority of whom would belong to the government.[37] Following this statement, twenty-six principal companies entered into agreement to have the government as a major shareholder. A year later, on 11 August, Kaunda announced that the copper industry was to be 'nationalised'. He said that he did not think that Zambia could achieve economic independence without national control of the mines. Hence he asked the owners of the mines to offer 51 per cent of their shares to the government.[38] On 1 January 1970 the new arrangement came into effect, making the State the largest employer in the country.[39]

While these policies had an immediate bearing on the labour movement, it is also necessary to note how the developing pattern of party politics, especially changes within UNIP, were affecting

37. In the same statement Kaunda expressed disappointment at the lack of mining development since independence. He thought profits were being sent abroad instead of reinvested. *Africa Digest*, June 1968, pp. 46–8.

38. *Ibid.*, October 1969, pp. 82–3.

39. Mines Acquisition (Special Provisions) Bill, 1970; *Nat. Ass. Deb.*, Hansard No. 21, 17 March 1970, cols 2076–93.

government–union relations. In direct contrast to the centralising tendency in administration, new fissures began to appear in the structure of UNIP. In August 1967, at the Mulungushi conference, its central leadership was divided into rival camps. Following defeat in the elections to the central committee, the Lozi leaders wavered in their allegiance to the ruling party, while the United Party, which merged with the ANC to contest the general election of 1968, began to draw support from the Lozi elements both in Barotseland and on the Copperbelt. A year later, inner party tensions caused further rifts when Simon Kapwepwe resigned from the vice-presidency of both UNIP and the government and, dissolving the central committee, Kaunda appointed an interim committee until a new party constitution was adopted.[40]

These events brought new complications to the Copperbelt. The support which the UP received from a section of the mining population angered the ruling party. Some UNIP local leaders began accusing the miners of harbouring anti-UNIP elements. Subsequently rival factions in the party attempted to draw the miners' support on tribal lines.[41] Though these efforts failed, it appeared as if mounting political tensions would finally suck in the mineworkers. On the other hand, the government revised its policy of using the party against the union, for a party which itself needed disciplining could not have been a reliable instrument to control the labour movement. In the second stage, therefore, greater emphasis was placed on regularising the trade union movement through normal channels and on establishing closer association with the labour leaders, without directly involving the party. In the following section we discuss the steps taken by the government in this direction and assess how far they have succeeded.

*Steps towards regularisation.* Already, before the major political events (noted above) took place, the government had inaugurated a seemingly endless series of seminars and labour conferences in which representatives of the government, the management and the unions took part. Aided by reports and experts and solemnised by the somewhat rarefied atmosphere of the seminar rooms, these round-table meetings provided opportunities for the exchange of ideas and the extension of the areas of agreement among the participants. Further, they aided the process of educating government and union leaders about their respective problems. Thus from these

40. See Tordoff, 'Political crisis in Zambia', *op. cit.*, pp. 225–36, and chapter 4 above.
41. See also p. 316, n. 59 below.

meetings there emerged a more objective understanding than had existed hitherto of the causes of labour unrest on the Copperbelt. The important causes were: lack of communication between the policy-making organs of the government and the unions; inefficient management and sometimes poor selection of supervisors; intimidation of supervisors and insubordination on the part of some workers; political interference in union affairs; ignorance on the part of workers about the machinery for settling disputes through negotiation; racial friction; and the slow pace of Zambianisation on the mines.

In the light of these findings the government proceeded to give effect to its new labour policy. Priority was given to the pace of Zambianising the industry. In order to provide Africans with rapid training so that they could hold more responsible jobs, a committee was set up under the chairmanship of Aaron Milner, Minister of State for the Cabinet and Public Service. Secondly, steps were taken to promote 'one union in one industry', since it was felt that mushroom organisations only encouraged indiscipline. Although the mining companies were somewhat sceptical about this particular policy, negotiations between the three African unions concerned— ZMU, MLSA and the Mines Police Association (MPA)—proceeded in earnest, and in April 1967 they merged to form the Mineworkers' Union of Zambia (MUZ). Similarly, the two expatriate organisations, the Mines Workers' Society (MWS) and the Mines Officials and Salaried Staff Association (MOSSA), amalgamated and formed the Zambia Expatriate Miners' Association (ZEMA). Considerable difficulty, however, was experienced in trying to combine the African and expatriate associations in a single organisation. Members of ZEMA were not willing to have Africans to represent their case, while the MUZ flatly refused to make any concession to the European association. Negotiations broke down repeatedly until, early in 1969, the Minister of Labour declared that he no longer recognised ZEMA. This move did not, however, vitally affect the expatriates, since they had only come to Zambia for a fixed period and on contractual terms of service.

Another innovation was a thoroughgoing restructuring of the administration to provide for direct communication links between government and union leaders. Labour inspectors and assistants, who worked directly under the supervision of the Minister of Labour, were encouraged to acquaint themselves with the day-to-day problems of the workers. In January 1969, under a new package of administrative reforms, Kaunda created two new posts: a Cabinet Minister in each province to be chairman of both a provincial

development committee and provincial UNIP committees, and a
District Governor in each administrative district to serve as a
'political technician' and to co-ordinate and supervise all development projects in his district.[42] In the Copperbelt Province development projects were so intimately connected with the mining industry that the primary task of both the provincial Minister and
the District Governors became one of establishing direct contacts with the mineworkers.

Finally, attempts were made to convert the ZCTU from a
'talking shop' into a dynamic organisation with increased control
over the functioning of the affiliated unions. Early in 1967 Wilson
Chakulya, who had served for some time in the Foreign Ministry
and was an old hand in the trade union movement, became secretary
general of the ZCTU. His energy and drive were soon felt in all
spheres of the labour movement. He declared that urban unrest
could not be controlled so long as Congress was weak and did not
participate in the negotiating process both before and after a dispute. At a conference attended by 150 delegates of all affiliated
unions, Chakulya secured the adoption of a new constitution for
Congress which obliged member unions to keep the ZCTU informed about their activities, and empowered Congress to discipline
workers by withholding union protection for strikers.[43] In a further
memorandum Chakulya asked for an assurance from the member
unions that they would not resort to strike action without the consent of Congress.[44] In order to strengthen Congress he decided to
establish a country-wide network of information centres as a means
of keeping contact with the government as well as the workers,
independently of the unions to which the latter belonged. Again,
in order to streamline labour relations he proposed the appointment of specialised agents who would assist the unions with their
accounts and negotiations. Chakulya was seeking, in other words,
to modernise the trade union structure by by-passing the existing
unions.

Predictably, Chakulya's activities gave rise to heated controversy.
The opposition regarded him as a 'stooge' of the government, and
an ANC Member of Parliament, Edward Liso, thought it was 'a
shame to call him general secretary of [the] trade union movement
in this country'.[45] The MUZ leaders also disliked Chakulya's inter-

42. President Kaunda's address, *Nat. Ass. Deb.*, Hansard No. 17, 22
January 1969, cols 35–6.
43. *Zambia Mail*, 5 December 1967.
44. *Southern Africa News Week*, 16 February 1968.
45. *Nat. Ass. Deb.*, Hansard No. 17, 4 March 1969, col. 1450.

ference in union affairs, and at one time tried hard to oust him from the Congress executive. However, Chakulya survived the storm, partly because he had the backing of the government and partly because of his superb skill as a tactician.

*Results.* How far have these efforts, taken together, succeeded in normalising labour relations? The question is hard to answer. In terms of administrative control the government has gained increased initiative in containing the workers' demands for wage rises. The unions have also improved their internal organisation in the sense that accounts and membership records are now kept more scientifically. The overall importance of the ZCTU can no longer be ignored and, despite its continuing suspicions of Congress, the MUZ has agreed to co-operate with it. Nonetheless, the communication gap at the union–government level and within the MUZ structure still continues. In particular, the credibility of the MUZ leadership in the eyes of branch officials and members seems to have declined considerably. This is exemplified by the spate of 'wild-cat strikes' on the mines. Thus during 1968 a total of 65,898 man-days was lost by unofficial stoppages, mainly in the mining industry.[46] What seems to have complicated the matter is that the overlapping jurisdictions of union leaders and various agents of the government have given rise to new types of tension. The union leaders complain that labour officers and District Governors interfere too often with their work and give misleading directions to the miners. They are aggrieved, too, because the government does not confide in them fully.

For example, when, in March 1969, MUZ declared a dispute over job gradings, salaries and leave pay, other factors intervened to turn the issue into a full-fledged crisis. The new budget proposals, which cut a slice out of the miner's pay packet, and a stray remark by the Minister of Labour, Mr Lewis Changufu, that Zambianisation had done more harm than good to the country, aroused great resentment among the mineworkers. The declaration of the dispute thus became an occasion for the miners to press for a strike call, starting from 1 April. The strike became overlaid with other issues; as the *Times of Zambia* noted,[47] 'some mention it [the strike call] is because of the wages negotiation deadlock; others think it is because of the Budget'. The attitude of the miners quickly

46. This compared unfavourably with the 1967 figure of 46,088 man-days lost. See the statement of the Minister of Labour and Social Services, *ibid.*, 14 February 1969, col. 813.
47. 28 March 1969.

crystallised, and even personal appeals by the Vice-president and top
government and union officials failed to convert them. The efforts
of UNIP to persuade the miners to reverse their stand were also unsuccessful. Except at Mufulira and Bancroft, the meetings organised
by UNIP were disrupted by the miners. In Kitwe more than 2,000
people walked out of a meeting as the national anthem was being
sung. At another gathering UNIP's acting regional secretary and
mayor of Kitwe, Councillor R. Mwale, was shouted down by the
audience. When he warned that the party would see that the workers
lost their jobs if they went on strike, many shouted back, 'It is all
right, we will go back to our villages.' In the end the government
appointed a four-man conciliation board, and the assurances of the
latter somehow succeeded in averting the strike. This episode once
more illustrated the weakness of the central leaders *vis-à-vis* the
miners, who were clearly capable of paralysing the nation's economy.
Moreover, notwithstanding the official measures which had been
taken, the communication gap between the union and administration remained unbridged.

In May 1969 in a major policy declaration, the government
outlined its approach to labour problems. It stated that the need
was to have negotiating machinery for the conduct of industrial
relations 'which will be between the two extremes of complete
centralisation of negotiations as found in communist countries, and
that based on voluntary negotiations as obtained in capitalist
countries'. The other points listed in the declaration were: (1) to
devise a means of setting limits to wage increases; (2) to endeavour
to intervene and make government's stand clearly known to the
negotiating parties; (3) to ask all trade unions to incorporate in
their constitution a declaration that 'the union will protect and
promote industry for the benefit of its members and the nation as
a whole, and that it will strive to promote increased efficiency and
higher productivity'; (4) to ensure more unionisation of the labour
force and increase the area of representation by employees at a
national level; and (5) not to tolerate any 'window dressing'
Zambianisation from any sector.[48]

### Limitations and constraints

In the preceding pages we have described the evolution and
direction of the trade union movement in Zambia since independence. Two stages in this evolution have been distinguished. First,
UNIP attempted to dominate and impose its hegemony on the

48. *Times of Zambia*, 2 May 1969.

mineworkers; secondly, when this attempt failed, the government adopted new methods to integrate the trade unions into the administrative structure. Although these methods helped to achieve a degree of normalisation, the basic issues underlying labour unrest remained unresolved. Short of complete centralisation on communist lines, it does not seem likely that the Zambian political leaders can achieve a more permanent solution of the problem. This is so not because the leaders lack the necessary means or resolution, but because several inherent limitations and constraints in the structure of the mineworkers' union and its relations with the party and government inhibit their capacities in this sphere. These limiting factors are discussed in a final section.

*The structure of MUZ.* The formal structure of MUZ resembles that of a pyramid: each mine has a branch elected by the members; the branches, in turn, send delegates to a conference which elects a seven-man executive and a supreme council. The latter is a policy-making body, which reviews and endorses the actions of the executive. Not all criteria that govern the choice of a trade union leader are clear, but some of the basic ones are apparent. In the first place, in order to gain the confidence of his colleagues he should have been working on the mines for some time.[49] Apart from a natural aptitude for organisation, he should show the ability to take quick decisions; possess a certain amount of militancy (particularly in relation to those who are in supervisory jobs), and invariably champion the African cause in matters affecting Africans and Europeans. At the local level it is the low-paid, daily rated workers whose voice is decisive in the making of a leader—the history of the mineworkers' union shows that in times of organised action it is the pressure from below that maintains the tempo of the movement. Hence, even though at the top level some former MLSA leaders have found a place, on the mines it is the old and experienced activists of the ZMU who still form the backbone of the union.

Personal commitment to fight for the cause of the workers is considered to be the highest quality in a leader. Sometimes, when a popular and militant branch official is removed or demoted by the executive, the members continue to give him their full support. By the same token, the growing tendency at the top level of leadership to be closely associated with the administration has come to be

49. According to the Trade Union Ordinance of 1965, no person is qualified for election as an officer of a trade union unless he has been engaged or employed for a period of at least three years in a trade, occupation or industry with which the trade union is directly concerned.

regarded with suspicion by the mineworkers. 'Very soon they will treat us as stooges of the government,' one leading unionist told the writer.[50] As a result, the leaders find themselves in a dilemma: on the one hand, if they participate too frequently in officially sponsored meetings and conferences they will lose the confidence of the miners; on the other hand, if they do not do so they will be accused of non-co-operation by the government. Recently there has been much talk about 'participatory democracy', by which is meant greater participation of workers' representatives in the management of industry. However, it does not appear that mineworkers are over-enthusiastic to participate in this way. Their attitude was summed up by one of their number, who said, 'What sort of a worker is he if he becomes a member of a board of directors?'[51]

These factors doubtless inhibit the initiative of top union leaders. If they decide to associate themselves fully with the government, they will have to resort increasingly to threats and disciplinary action to maintain their authority in the union. But by doing so they may forfeit the support of the members. They therefore adopt an ambivalent attitude which has at times greatly annoyed the government. Thus at a labour seminar organised by the ZCTU an Assistant Labour Commissioner bitterly attacked the trade unionists. 'It would appear,' he said, 'that these leaders are double-tongued in trying to please the workers but find themselves in difficulty when approached to explain the strikes.' He added, 'Union leaders must be frank with their members. If a claim has no merit or justification, tell them they are flogging a dead horse and throw the complaint into a wastepaper basket.'[52]

It is easy for the outsider to give this kind of advice, but the trade unionists know that if they ever follow it they will cease to have any voice in the labour movement. Unlike the politician, the trade unionist has no patronage which he can freely distribute to retain the loyalty of his followers. His continuing leadership depends on what concrete benefits he is able to achieve for the members, and he must therefore not only be active but also *appear* to be active in fighting for the cause of the workers. His militancy is inherent in the situation in which he works.

It would be interesting to speculate how party men would themselves behave if they were to occupy all the important places in the MUZ. Would they be political activists or trade unionists first?

50. Interview with Edwin Thawe, 24 July 1970.
51. Interview with an old mineworker in Kitwe, 24 July 1970.
52. *Times of Zambia*, 24 January 1969.

The conflict of roles would certainly cause them acute embarrassment: if they tried to push the workers too hard, the latter would desert them; if they did not do so, they would forfeit all chances of promotion to higher grades of the party or administration.

Finally, it should be noted that MUZ is not an organisation in which central authority is as directly effective at the base as in a dominant political party. It is true that central leaders can take disciplinary action against junior officials, but this cannot be done without regard to the sentiments of the ordinary members. Moreover, at the local level it is the category of job as well as the position he holds in the union hierarchy that ultimately determines the effectiveness of a trade unionist. In other words, mineworkers are more likely to accept the lead of a shop steward or veteran on the mines than of a man who holds a senior post in the union hierarchy but who lacks experience in mine jobs. It is this horizontal link that diffuses the exercise of union authority at the base level. This fact does not seem to be appreciated by either UNIP or the government.

*UNIP–union relations.* We have seen how the mineworkers' union refused to play a very active political role in the colonial era and how it has subsequently resisted the power drives of UNIP. The organisational resilience of the union poses a twofold problem for UNIP: first, so long as MUZ preserves its functional autonomy the party cannot hope to gain the undivided loyalty of the mineworkers; and secondly, since UNIP now has a legal monopoly of power, it cannot permit 19 per cent of the country's labour force to belong to an organisation which it cannot control. Hence attempts are continually being made by the ruling party to undermine the union's structure, often with the official backing of the central leadership. In the process, however, the party has become increasingly identified with the government, and the miners are more suspicious than ever before of its overtures.

At the local level the problem is compounded by what one observer described as the overlapping jurisdiction and membership of the union and the party.[53] Since the miners belong to both UNIP and MUZ, they approach officials of both organisations to present their complaints. The latter may arise on any number of issues, such as housing, water supply, sanitation and safety measures, or a dispute involving European supervisors and African employees. In matters which directly affect town life the local councils, which

53. See Bates, *Unions, Parties, and Political Development, op. cit.,* pp. 136–141.

are largely filled by UNIP members, claim jurisdiction, and this claim is not usually challenged by union officials. However, certain other issues, such as fixing the level of house rents or disciplinary action against a miner, do give rise to the problem of overlapping jurisdiction. On these occasions the union wants to negotiate a settlement with the management without interference from the party. But UNIP is not always willing to be excluded in this way. As a result, there is a competition between party and union officials to adopt such postures as will please the maximum number of workers. Again, instances occur when the mineworkers take their disputes to party officials simply because they are not satisfied with the arrangement reached by their own union. This causes further friction, and union officials blame the party for encouraging indiscipline. Yet so long as UNIP is regarded as the most reliable instrument of political control, national party leaders will hesitate to restrict its role in such matters. Instead they assert that as a mass party UNIP has every right to intervene in such disputes (even in marriage disputes), and that party interference is always positive because it is 'trying to achieve what is good'.[54]

Another factor which intensifies UNIP–union competition is the varying social structure of the mine towns. The mineworkers and their families are provided with accommodation by the companies and, relatively speaking, live in a better style than those who are outside the mining industry. The pressure of new arrivals, overcrowding and the acute shortage of housing have widened further the disparity between the stabilised and non-stabilised sections of the urban community. Moreover, in recent years the size of squatter families has grown so large that it sometimes outnumbers the settled population, leading to general conditions of squalor and unrest in the mine townships. As Fines Bulawayo, Minister of State for the Copperbelt Province, warned the National Assembly, 'If the squatters go on, we will find our people now are going to have two types of society in one Republic.'[55]

These squatters, and the unemployed youth who come to the towns in search of jobs, constitute the two most desperate elements of Copperbelt society. Mineworkers appear to them to be an overpaid and overprivileged elite rather than what is known in Marxist parlance as the exploited proletariat. It is they who provide the raw material for such political agitation as threatens the security of the mineworkers. Thus when UNIP started a campaign early

54. *Nat. Ass. Deb.*, Hansard No. 13, 2 March 1968, col. 1301 (Lazarus Cheelo).

55. *Ibid.*, Hansard No. 21, 14 January 1970, col. 142.

in 1969 to eliminate ANC elements in the mine townships, it soon turned out to be a campaign of indiscriminate eviction of workers, fanned and encouraged by these social outcasts.[56]

In short, UNIP's ideology, the overlapping jurisdiction and membership of the party and union, and the social setting of the Copperbelt have led to intermittent friction between the local activists of UNIP and MUZ officials.

*Government–union relations.* In contrast, the various packages of administrative reorganisation and reforms undertaken by the government since 1967 have brought about a greater degree of stability in industrial relations. Briefly stated, the present structure of the government–union relationship depends on the following: (1) labour inspectors and assistants, who, as agents of the Minister of Labour, are attached to the mines; (2) the Registrar of Trade Unions, who has overall charge of the trade unions and is directly supervised by the Minister of Labour; (3) the ZCTU, which, as an officially sponsored organisation, has considerable control over the affairs of the labour movement; (4) the Cabinet Minister for the Copperbelt Province, who, with his staff, is responsible for increasing the production capacity of the mining industry; and (5) District Governors, who are entrusted with supervising and co-ordinating development planning in their districts. (See also fig. 8.1.)

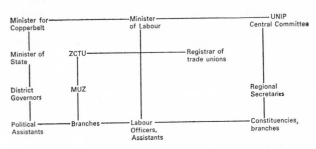

Fig. 8.1. The structure of government–union relations

This top-heavy and rather cumbersome structure has succeeded in facilitating closer association between government and union leaders. The participation of the latter in different policy-making organs has greatly helped in normalising labour relations on the

56. The campaign created such bitterness that the President's Office finally intervened and denounced categorically the policy of eviction.

Copperbelt. Further, although there is tension between ZCTU and MUZ, the two have maintained a close working relationship. Finally, prompt intervention by the provincial Minister or a District Governor has sometimes averted a labour crisis on the mines.

But the limitations of the system have also become apparent. In the first place, owing to the fact that all these officials and organs are engaged in the same activity—i.e., each is seeking to achieve industrial peace and to increase production—there is considerable confusion and overlapping of functions. Labour officials entrusted with specific jobs find their authority overshadowed, and sometimes even overruled, by top dignitaries in the province. The ZCTU secretary, Chakulya, complained in Parliament that District Governors exceeded their functions and meddled in labour matters.[57] Moreover, since the Minister and Governors are political appointees, they are also expected to look after and promote party interests. The eviction campaign mentioned earlier afforded a clear example of official position being used to favour the ruling party: H. D. Banda, the provincial Minister, declared that he would cleanse his province of all ANC elements. Another example concerned Ndola's District Governor, who checked a list of thirty people recommended by the Labour Office for jobs in a Dunlop factory. The Governor warned the applicants: 'If you are not UNIP and if you merely want to incite trouble in industries you will be imprisoned. We intend to employ only UNIP, not ANC members.'[58]

Again, tensions and divisions within the upper echelons of the government and party can adversely affect the labour movement. Thus, following Kapwepwe's resignation in August 1969, some elements close to him (including Cabinet Ministers) were reported to have visited the Copperbelt to organise the mineworkers on sectional lines.[59] There have also been (perhaps associated) attempts to arouse tribal feeling among the predominantly Bemba population of the Copperbelt by emphasising Bemba culture, dress and language. All these factors may neutralise the progress made in normalising government–union relations.

57. *Nat. Ass. Deb.*, Hansard No. 18, 22 January 1970, cols 458–9.
58. *Times of Zambia*, 21 January 1969.
59. During a visit to the Copperbelt in July 1970 the writer was told that Kapwepwe had been assured by some of his associates that the majority of mineworkers would give him solid support in a crisis. One does not know if this precipitated Kapwepwe's decision to resign; in any event, mineworkers remained supremely indifferent to the constitutional crisis of August 1969.

## Conclusions

Notwithstanding UNIP's dominant position and its goal (now realised) of establishing a one-party system, the mineworkers' union has been able to defend and largely preserve its organisational autonomy. This does not mean that the union has continuously defied the authority of the party and government; in fact the various reforms initiated by the latter have gone a long way to integrate the trade union movement into the various organs of the State. By agreeing to co-operate with the official agencies and by affiliating with the ZCTU the union has more or less accepted the overall authority of the government in industrial matters. In return, union leaders have been given expanded representation in various policy-making bodies of the government, and, with the increased emphasis on 'participatory democracy', it is intended that they shall have a greater say in industrial management.

However, it is when the question of the economic and material benefits of the workers arises that the union asserts its independence and comes at times into headlong conflict with government and party policies. In this way it underlines the fact that, as an organisation of a particular section of urban society, it cannot function in terms of the whole nation, even though (except when its own interests are endangered) it may not overtly try to oppose national goals. As an organised labour force engaged in the country's most vital industry, the mineworkers know that the skills and experience they have acquired cannot be easily dispensed with or replaced by alternative labour. Hence they ignore threats of dismissal and, as in the meeting at Kitwe, retort, 'It is all right, we shall go back to our villages.' This realisation of their own indispensability enables the mineworkers, in turn, to threaten both the management and government in times of crisis. In an industry in which the expatriate standard of living sets the norm, it is natural for the miners to shape their aspirations according to that norm rather than in accordance with the living conditions of the average Zambian. Moreover, the mining industry is the only sector of the economy in which higher wage demands can be met by the companies. The mineworkers therefore continually press for higher wages and refuse to accept a voluntary wage freeze as demanded by the central leadership.

It is curious that even after independence both the government and UNIP encouraged the economic demands of the mineworkers. One reason may have been that, so long as the mining industry was wholly owned by foreign companies, they thought that this was

one way of fighting 'neo-colonialism'. In its submission to the
Brown Commission UNIP went to the extent of asserting:

The companies' attempt to justify the local wage level on the basis of
wage levels throughout Zambia, without reference to productivity or
ability to pay, means that they are putting forward a low wage policy
cloaked in the garb of a privately sponsored wages and incomes policy
for the country at large.

If increased wages in the mining industry would result in upward pressures on wages in other sectors, this is a matter for the government of the
Republic of Zambia and not a point on which any private group can
legitimately seek to base its wages policy.[60]

Similarly, in view of their nationalist traditions, the new leaders
tended to exaggerate the racial factor in the mining industry.
Statements that the expatriates were 'white racists', 'saboteurs'
or 'anti-national' provided a section of the miners with the excuse
they wanted to create trouble as a means of furthering their own
interests. Local UNIP leaders often tried to patronise these elements
by acts of violence against Europeans. The result was a general
deterioration of discipline in the industry.

It was not so much UNIP's failure to capture the union leadership in 1966 as the alarming economic situation and rising prices
that forced the government to restrain the party and initiate administrative reforms. While this action helped to minimise the political factor and to normalise labour relations, it also gave rise to a
new set of problems. The closer association of union leaders with the
government served only to alienate the average miner. Moreover,
the MUZ failed to meet the challenge of playing a constructive
role in the development process because it was organised on principles that were incompatible with such a role. In trying at the same
time to be more receptive to official directions and to maintain the
primacy of the miners' interests, the union has weakened its own
authority structure.

Curiously enough, with increased State participation in the
private sector, and especially in the mining industry, the national
leaders of UNIP have tried to re-shape the party as an agency of
development rather than as an instrument of political control.
In other words, the task of disciplining the trade unions has now
become secondary to that of reorganising the party along new lines.
At a conference of UNIP leaders in Kitwe in March 1970 Kaunda
said:

60. Brown report, *op. cit.*, pp. 40–1.

The role of the United National Independence Party and its leaders must be to ensure that industries increase production so that the total welfare of the country will increase the capacity of the party and Government to discharge its responsibilities to the people, and so enable us to increase the economic and social benefits of the people in the Republic.[61]

Thus in terms of goal orientation and structure UNIP may have experienced in recent years more radical changes than the mineworkers' union.

61. ZIS background paper No. 22/69.

# 9
# Zambia's response to the Rhodesian unilateral declaration of independence[1]

*Richard L. Sklar*

It is notorious that over thirty million Africans are held in sub-jugation by racialist regimes in southern Africa. Of the various confrontations which have occurred between these regimes and the independent African States, that between Rhodesia and Zambia has been the most complex and has called for the most imaginative exercise of statecraft. Indeed, the purely logistical aspects of statecraft in this situation are remarkable in the annals of newly independent nations. This chapter presents a survey and appraisal of Zambia's employment of its diplomatic, economic and logistical resources in the aftermath of the Rhodesian rebellion.[2]

Zambia possesses a great economic asset: its giant copper mining industry, which has accounted for more than 12 per cent of world production in recent years, on a par with the output of Chile. Between 1964 and 1968 this one industry contributed about 93 per cent of the value of Zambian exports, some 60 per cent of central government revenues, and approximately 44 per cent of net domestic product.[3] Although this industry has provided the wherewithal for basic national development, its operations have also been central to the continuation of economic dependence upon Rhodesia, a con-dition that Zambia cannot tolerate.

On the Zambian Copperbelt, which lies adjacent to the Congo pedicle, the operating mines have been controlled by two groups

1. An earlier version of this chapter appeared as 'Zambia's response to UDI', *Mawazo*, vol. 1, No. 3 (June 1968), pp. 11–32.
2. See also the excellent accounts by F. T. Ostrander, 'Zambia in the aftermath of Rhodesian UDI: logistical and economic problems', *African Forum*, vol. 2, No. 3 (winter, 1967), pp. 50–65; and R. B. Sutcliffe, 'Zambia and the strains of UDI', *The World Today*, vol. 23, No. 12 (December 1967), pp. 506–11.
3. *Zambia Mining Industry Year Book, 1968, op. cit.*, p. 35.

of companies.[4] Recently mines of the Anglo-American Corporation group have produced roughly 53 per cent of Zambia's copper output. They form part of a vast international business network headed by the Anglo-American Corporation of South Africa Ltd. Despite its name, American participation in the latter company is relatively minor. It is owned mainly by South Africans, and nationals of South Africa predominate in the managerial staffs of the Anglo-American Corporation group companies in Zambia. Some 47 per cent of the output is produced by mines of the Roan Selection Trust group. While the management of this group is mainly British, the owners have been predominantly American, with the largest and controlling interest of 42 per cent held by American Metal–Climax Inc. In 1970 the Zambian government acquired a 51 per cent interest in the ownership of all of the operating mines. The two foreign groups, now minority shareholders, were given contracts to provide management and marketing services for a period of ten years.

Apart from the mining industry and its appurtenances, like the railways, Zambia inherited little of lasting economic value from her colonial past. The neglect of educational development during that era was also appalling. At the time of independence in 1964 there were only some 1,200 Africans in Zambia who had earned secondary school certificates. Only 109 Zambians had graduated from a university.[5] In 1966 there were only two Zambian graduates in agriculture, one in engineering, and four in medicine.[6] A deformed economy and crass disregard for the human aspects of development: this is a common yet fair judgement on the effects of the Central African Federation in Zambia. For ten years (1954–63) the wealth of Zambia (then Northern Rhodesia) was diverted to Southern Rhodesia, where it was used mainly to benefit the ruling white minority.[7]

4. For good brief accounts of the Zambia copper mining industry, see L. H. Gann, 'The Northern Rhodesian copper industry and the world of copper, 1923–52', *Rhodes-Livingstone Journal*, vol. XVIII (1955), pp. 1–18; Hall, *Zambia*, *op. cit.*, pp. 245–67; Baldwin, *Economic Development and Export Growth*, *op. cit.*, pp. 29–35.

5. *Manpower Report*, *op. cit.*, pp. 1–2.

6. K. D. Kaunda, 'Installation address by the Chancellor', *University of Zambia Inauguration Ceremony, July 1966* (Lusaka, n.d.), p. 20.

7. See W. J. Barber, 'Federation and the distribution of economic benefits', in Leys and Pratt (eds), *A New Deal in Central Africa*, *op. cit.*, pp. 81–97; A. Hazlewood and P. D. Henderson, *Nyasaland: the Economics of Federation* (Oxford, 1960); S. Williams, *Central Africa: the Economics of Inequality*, an African Bureau pamphlet (London, 1960). It is generally thought that as a

When the Federation was finally dissolved, and Zambian resources were no longer subject to simple appropriation by the
Rhodesians, the true interdependence of these two countries was
more clearly revealed. Zambia depended upon Rhodesia for essential
supplies, technical services, transport facilities and communications.[8]
In 1965 Rhodesia was the largest supplier of Zambian imports,
accounting for 34 per cent of the total, valued at K70 million.[9] This
represented 25 per cent of the value of Rhodesian exports. Inevitably, the wrenching apart of these two economies would give rise
to ambivalent feelings in Zambia. On the one hand, Zambians
had little desire to trade with Rhodesia in preference to other
partners. The old relationship had been exploitative at Zambia's
expense, and a general reduction or severance of economic ties with
Rhodesia would signal the end of a despised era. On the other
hand, most of what remained of the relationship was economically
rational for both countries; there would be no question of breaking
it if white supremacy did not prevail in Rhodesia. Furthermore, a
drastic reorientation away from Rhodesia might appear to mark
the acceptance of a great divide and *cordon sanitaire* along the
Zambezi river, and therefore to signal the end of an era of African
liberation.

*Rules of the game*

While the collapse of the Federation liberated Zambia, it also
strengthened the resolve of Rhodesian whites to secure their independence from Britain before the advent of majority rule. Zambia
asserted the common view of all independent African States that
it was Britain's responsibility to establish majority rule in Rhodesia
as quickly as possible, certainly before the concession of, or
acquiescence in, Rhodesian independence. Britain's failure on this
score would be regarded by Africans as a sell-out of the African
people to the British 'kith and kin' in Rhodesia. To assist Britain,
Zambia offered to provide a military base in her territory from
which an attack on Rhodesia could be mounted in the event of a
unilateral declaration of independence.[10]

result of the redistribution of wealth among governments following the creation of the Federation, Northern Rhodesia lost about K14 million per annum
to Southern Rhodesia—a total of K140 million during the ten-year span.

8. As late as 1966 telephone calls to Kitwe from Lusaka were sometimes
completed more quickly via Salisbury than by direct connection.

9. *Economic Report, 1966* (Lusaka, 1966), pp. 42–3.

10. See *Zambia Mail*, 29 September 1965; also C. Legum (ed.), *Zambia:
Independence and Beyond: the Speeches of Kenneth Kaunda* (London, 1966),
p. 237.

But the British government was unwilling to use force. Harold Wilson, then Prime Minister, made this clear in late October 1965, during his visit to Salisbury, where he met the leading African nationalists, in particular Joshua Nkomo (Zimbabwe African People's Union) and Ndabaningi Sithole (Zimbabwe African National Union), who were then in detention, as well as the leaders of the Rhodesian government. Upon his return he informed the House of Commons that he had told the African leaders that Britain would not exert military power in Rhodesia, either before or after UDI. Nor, he said, would Britain require the immediate introduction of majority rule, since time was needed to alleviate racial fears and suspicions. In discussions with the government of Rhodesia he made it clear that in the event of an illegal seizure of power there would be dire legal, constitutional and economic, *but not military*, consequences.[11]

When UDI was declared on 11 November, Britain immediately imposed a number of economic and financial sanctions. Rhodesia was expelled from the sterling area and excluded from the London capital market, while preferential tariff arrangements for Rhodesian exports were suspended. A ban was imposed on the purchase of Rhodesia's main export crops, namely tobacco and sugar. In December exchange and trade controls were tightened, while Rhodesian assets in London, valued at к18 million, were frozen. Finally, in compliance with a resolution of the United Nations Security Council, taken on 20 November, which called upon all States 'to break all economic relations with Southern Rhodesia, including an embargo on oil and petroleum products', Britain acted on 17 December to ban the sale of oil to Rhodesia by British firms.[12]

From the outset President Kaunda insisted that economic sanctions alone would not end the rebellion and that military action was required. The outcome of Britain's failure to quell the rebellion by force, he warned, would be 'a bloody racial or ideological war'.[13] Time and again thereafter Kaunda has returned to the theme of 'racial and ideological war' as the probable result of white minority rule in Rhodesia.[14] Short of military action to end the rebellion, Zambia made two minimum requests. First, she renewed her previous request for the posting of British troops at the Kariba

11. *H. of C. Deb.*, Hansard vol. 718, 1 November 1965, cols 633–4.
12. For an account of British sanctions and an early appraisal of their effectiveness, see R. B. Sutcliffe, *Sanctions against Rhodesia*, an Africa Bureau pamphlet (London, 21 January 1966).
13. *Zambia Mail*, 26 November 1965.
14. See, for example, his statement on Africa Freedom Day in Lusaka, 25 May 1967.

dam and hydro-electric station, which then supplied 68 per cent of all electricity used in Zambia, including some 90 per cent of the electric power requirements of the Copperbelt. Although the power station is located at the south bank of the Kariba dam, the entire facility is owned jointly by Rhodesia and Zambia.

Britain refused to comply with this request. However, the Prime Minister did inform the House of Commons that he had given President Kaunda an assurance that 'we shall not stand idly by if Rhodesia cuts off power supplies to the Copperbelt'.[15] Furthermore, an RAF squadron of jet fighters was dispatched to Zambia 'purely for defensive purposes'. Richard Hall has observed that Wilson had settled upon the threat of retaliation against Rhodesia's own supply of electricity from Kariba to deter possible Rhodesian sabotage of the Zambian supply.[16] One of the reasons given by the British government for its refusal to seize and occupy the south bank power station was its fear that the Rhodesians had mined that facility, and possibly even the dam itself, and would blow it up in the event of an attack from Zambia.[17] This information was never substantiated and appears to have been disbelieved in Zambia.[18] Nonetheless, it would not have been difficult for the Rhodesians to destroy the power station at short notice.[19]

Zambia's second minimum request was for compensatory aid to offset the costs to Zambia of Britain's policy of economic sanctions. The magnitude of these costs would depend upon the duration of the sanctions war and the extent of Zambia's involvement in it. In this regard, Zambia faced a deep dilemma in the formulation of her policy. Kaunda and his colleagues were convinced that economic sanctions would not succeed, owing to South Africa's non-compliance, if for no other reason. If Zambia endeavoured to support sanctions faithfully and to the best of her ability, she was bound to

15. *H. of C. Deb.*, Hansard, vol. 721, 1 December 1965, col. 1430.

16. *The High Price of Principles, op. cit.*, p. 128. Hall has also suggested that Wilson's primary concern at this time, shared by the Conservative Party opposition to his government, was to preclude the commitment of a planned OAU expeditionary force, which might have led to Soviet and Chinese military involvement. *Ibid.*, pp. 125–31. Cf. *H. of C. Deb.*, Hansard vol. 721, 1 December 1965, col. 1433. The RAF fighter squadron was withdrawn from Zambia by mutual agreement in August 1966, by which time the possibility of OAU military action had ceased to exist.

17. See *H. of C. Deb.*, Hansard vol. 722, 7 December 1965, col. 384; *ibid.*, written answers, 14 December 1965, col. 233.

18. A senior British official of the Central African Power Corporation, custodian of the Kariba project, was reported to have assured Kaunda that 'this talk was absolute nonsense'. *New York Times*, 9 December 1965.

19. See Hall, *The High Price of Principles, op. cit.*, p. 138.

incur economic reprisals and pay dearly in shortages of supply without securing her political objective. Yet Zambia had a moral obligation to support the United Nations' decision. If Zambia did not support sanctions, she could hardly escape a measure of blame for their failure. Moreover, Zambia's dereliction would make it that much easier for Britain to reconcile with the Rhodesian regime.

Once the die had been cast for economic sanctions, Zambia favoured extreme measures calculated to produce a quick kill. It has been suggested to the present writer that a total break with Rhodesia was seriously considered by the Zambian Cabinet in December 1965. This would have meant the rupture of railway services between the two countries, the suspension of coal shipments from Rhodesia, and possibly the loss of electrical power transmission from Kariba. The risks to Zambia would have been great, among them the following: an indeterminately great loss of revenue from copper exports that would set back the country's economic development; the possibility of disastrous floods in underground mines when the coal required to operate thermal power facilities had been exhausted, if sufficient electrical energy could not be imported from reserve sources in the Congo; unemployment and unrest on the Copperbelt, including the possibility of racial strife; severe shortages of consumer goods, resulting in widespread urban discontent and a precipitous exodus of skilled European labour. With encouragement from Britain in the form of massive material aid, Zambia might have taken these risks.[20] But Britain did not want Zambia to 'go to the mat' with Rhodesia, since the costs of unlimited economic warfare to Britain herself might have spiralled out of control. For one thing, Britain would have been deprived of 40 per cent of her normal copper imports for as long as the impasse continued. For another, Britain might have felt obliged to give Zambia far more aid than she would ever have to give so long as the Zambian economy remained viable. Finally, Britain might have been drawn by circumstance to the use of force, which British policy was designed to avoid. Wilson was too shrewd a statesman to aid Zambia in a course of action that could have undermined his own policy of 'no force'. It seems probable that Britain took care to exert a restraining influence on Zambia in December 1965.[21]

20. Answering a question at a press conference on 12 May 1966, President Kaunda said that Zambia did offer 'to make a total break with Rhodesia' at the time of UDI on condition of adequate British assistance. ZIS background paper No. 12/66.

21. A report to this effect was filed from Lusaka by the expert correspondent of the *New York Times*, Anthony Lewis, who wrote as follows:

Short of a total break, Zambia had few effective economic weapons at her disposal to use against Rhodesia. Theoretically, she could refuse to buy Rhodesian goods and prohibit transfers of money from Zambia to Rhodesia. In practice, restrictions on Rhodesian imports were applied gradually so as to minimise their disruptive effects upon Zambia's economy. Exchange control was implemented less cautiously and proved, as we shall see in our review of the railway crisis, to be a double-edged sword. For her part, Rhodesia had several potentially effective leverages against Zambia. She could (and did) cut off Zambia's supply of oil; she could disrupt the flow of essential supplies, including coal supplies vital to the copper industry; she could interfere with the export of Zambian copper. However, these weapons might also prove to be double-edged.

On 1 December Wilson had indicated that Britain would retaliate with force if the Rhodesians cut off Zambia's supply of electrical power from the Kariba station. On 9 December Kaunda declared that he would regard Rhodesian interference with the jointly owned common services, providing electrical power and transport, as an act of war and would respond in kind. Previously, in October, Smith had given an assurance that Rhodesia would not cut off Zambia's power or interfere with Zambia's transport rights unless Zambia became a 'launching pad' against Rhodesia.[22] In short, *de facto* ground rules for the contest, backed up by suggestions of ultimate threats, were established by the end of 1965. They were as follows: Zambia would take warlike action *if* Rhodesia interfered with her essential services; Rhodesia would cut off Zambia's electricity and cripple her transport/supply system *if* Zambia became a 'launching pad' for armed attacks; Britain would use troops *if* Rhodesia interfered with the transmission of electricity to Zambia.

'Zambian leaders . . . say resentfully that they were taken in by Mr Wilson last winter on the issue of the British sanctions program.

'The story told is that Zambia wanted to begin last December to cut off her Rhodesian trade, but Britain resisted the idea and said she would not help Zambia in the difficult economic transition.

'The reason assertedly given was that the Rhodesian rebels would fall under the weight of sanctions in a few weeks anyway, and that Britain did not want to upset the trade patterns for a Rhodesia about to be restored to grace.

' "If Britain had not bluffed us," a member of the Zambian Government said, "we'd be much farther along now to where we must go." ' *New York Times*, international edition, 17 August 1966.

22. *Financial Times* (London), 11 October 1965; and *Times of Zambia*, 28 October 1965.

## The common services

When the Federation of Rhodesia and Nyasaland was dissolved at the end of 1963, three existing inter-territorial services became international agencies, namely the Central African Airways Corporation, the Central African Power Corporation and the Rhodesia Railways. The assets and liabilities of the latter two were divided evenly between Rhodesia and Zambia. In the case of the Airways, 45 per cent was assigned to Rhodesia, an equal proportion to Zambia, and 10 per cent to Malawi.

UDI disrupted the legal basis of the operations of these agencies. In each case, the power of direction has been vested in a 'Higher Authority', comprising an equal number of Ministers from each of the governments concerned. It was provided that the decisions of any one of the Higher Authorities must be taken by unanimous vote. After UDI Britain decreed, in effect, that the rebel government of Rhodesia was illegal and that its acts were, therefore, null and void. This largely paralysed the inter-governmental agencies; although their routine operations might continue thereafter as a matter of convenience, policy decisions, involving their Higher Authorities, were clearly out of the question.

*The railway crisis.* In 1965 the Rhodesia Railways carried nearly all Zambia's exports and imports over routes of approximately 1,500 miles from the Copperbelt to the ports of Beira and Lourenço Marques in Moçambique. Ownership and control of the railway, excluding its Moçambique extensions, was vested jointly and equally in the governments of Rhodesia and Zambia.[23] Under the terms of an agreement between them, each country's trade was virtually tied to the Rhodesia Railways. If either country diverted traffic to an alternative route, the government of that country would have to pay the Rhodesia Railways compensation equal to the revenue it would otherwise have earned.[24]

23. Most of this railway system was constructed during the 1890s and early 1900s. Between 1929 and 1949 it was wholly owned by the British South Africa Company. In 1949 the system was nationalised by the British and Portuguese colonial governments. Four years later ownership of the Rhodesia Railways was transferred to the Federation of Rhodesia and Nyasaland, where it remained until the end of 1963. For an account of the Central African railway system, see E. T. Haefele and E. B. Steinberg, *Government Controls on Transport: an African Case* (Washington, 1965).

24. 'Agreement between the Government of Southern Rhodesia and the Government of Northern Rhodesia relating to the Rhodesia Railways', ss. 33–45, *Northern Rhodesia Gazette*, 13 December 1963.

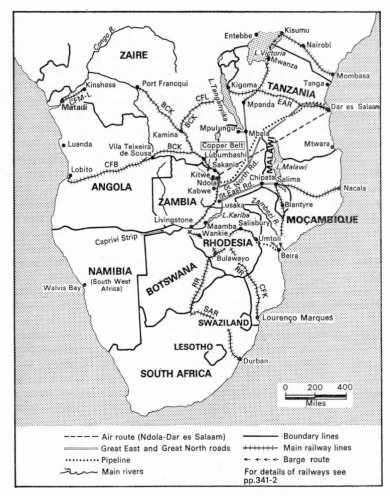

Fig. 9.1. Zambia: rail, road and other main supply routes

In rail transport, as in other respects, Zambia's mineral wealth
benefited Rhodesia. Specifically, after 1956 high railing rates imposed upon Zambian (and Congolese) copper exports have supported
the generally low rates charged for most other commodities.[25] Even

25. Before UDI, revenues earned by Rhodesia Railways from copper
shipments alone were nearly 30 per cent of total freight revenues, although
copper tonnage was only 8 per cent of the total freight tonnage. See
*Rhodesia Railways Reports and Accounts*, 30 June 1965.

with traditionally low rates for the transport of coal to the Copper-belt, Zambian traffic earned much higher revenues per ton–mile than Rhodesian traffic. Naturally, Rhodesia was inclined to favour a continued high railage on copper exports, although such rates might hinder the expansion of the copper mining industry in Zambia. For her part, Zambia would have preferred a lower railage as an incentive to expansion of the mining industry, since Zambia depends mainly upon revenues from mining taxation to finance her development. Lower railing rates would be especially desirable to Zambia in the event of a decline in copper prices from the abnormally high levels of recent years. However, the rating pattern of the Rhodesia Railways was virtually frozen by the inter-government agreement of December 1963, which, as noted above, imposed a penalty on the diversion of traffic to alternative routes.

The rupture of established railway relations occurred after UDI as a result of Zambia's attempt to implement financial sanctions against Rhodesia. Briefly, the Rhodesia Railways had two accounting centres, at Bulawayo in Rhodesia and at Broken Hill (now Kabwe) in Zambia. Bulawayo was also the principal administrative and technical centre from which most expenditures were made. But most of the revenue earned by the railway, including all freight charges on most Zambian imports, was collected at Broken Hill. The Zambian mining companies alone paid rates in excess of K2 million per month for the export of copper, and the Broken Hill account normally transferred some K2 million to the Bulawayo account every month. Interference with these payments would inevitably jeopardise the normal operations of the railway.

While Zambia agreed to support Britain's policy of sanctions against Rhodesia, she did not, as we have seen, expect that policy to succeed, and was duly cautious in her own approach. However, money transfers to Rhodesia were scrutinised and subject to increasingly restrictive controls by the Bank of Zambia. Between UDI and March 1966 payments from the Rhodesia Railways Broken Hill account to its Bulawayo account were reduced by more than 25 per cent by means of exchange control. Suddenly, in April, the Zambian government decided to block all further payments from the railway's account at Broken Hill to that at Bulawayo. This was a precipitous and daring step for Zambia to take, since the line carried over 90 per cent of Zambia's imports and exports. Unless Zambia was prepared to sacrifice her own planned development, there was no question of giving up the Rhodesia Railways for years to come. The timing of this gambit, shortly after the British Labour Party's decisive victory in the general election of March 1966, may not have been coincidental, since Zambian leaders now expected the British government to act more resolutely against the rebel regime.

A disruption of rail transport would immediately affect the copper companies; ultimately it would affect Britain herself, which obtains 40 per cent of her copper from Zambia. Perhaps Zambia hoped to induce the companies to 'lobby' for a more militant policy against Rhodesia. The British government too might have been spurred to take more decisive action. Seen in this perspective, Zambia's decision to block the transfer of railway funds to Rhodesia appears to have been a major initiative in foreign policy.

In her direct confrontation with Rhodesia, however, Zambia's position was weak. In May, following the Zambian government's refusal to reconsider its decision, the Rhodesia Railways, acting in consultation with the Moçambique Railways and the South African Railways, demanded payment in advance for all freight coming into Zambia via the Rhodesia Railways system. Until then the railway had, for some months past, been requiring payments of railage in advance on traffic originating in Rhodesia. Henceforth the Broken Hill centre would be deprived of the bulk of its accustomed receipts from imports. Furthermore, it was announced that railing charges on exports from Zambia earned outside Zambia would have to be pre-paid in Rhodesia; alternatively, the total railage could be paid on delivery at the point of destination in Rhodesia, South Africa or Moçambique. These decisions were taken by the Rhodesia Railways board, consisting of a chairman, three Rhodesian members and three Zambians, the latter voting against them. Theoretically the board was subordinate to a Higher Authority for Railways, comprising two Ministers from each government, but that body, as we have noted, had not been able to function since UDI.

On 24 May the retaliatory payments procedure was put into effect by the Rhodesia, Moçambique and South African railways. Copper exports were affected immediately, since the Zambian government would not permit the Zambian copper companies to make the required railing payments either directly or indirectly (through Moçambique or South Africa) to the Rhodesia Railways. On 25 May Zambia's copper companies declared *force majeure* on their contracts with buyers, thereby relieving themselves of liability for damages because of conditions beyond their control. On 28 May the Zambian High Court issued an injunction against implementation of the new payment procedure, on the grounds that it was harmful to Zambia and could not be adopted without the consent of the (now defunct) Higher Authority for Railways. Thereupon the railway management suspended the new procedure in Zambia, although it remained in force in Rhodesia, Moçambique and South Africa, where Zambian imports were held up pending advance payments for railage to be incurred south of the Zambezi. On 31 May the Zambian government instructed the Bank of Zambia to refuse applications for foreign exchange needed to pay the railage on goods coming over the Rhodesia Railways. (Exceptions were made for medical supplies and coal, although the copper companies had actually been making dollar payments in advance for coal shipments since December 1965.) At this time Zambia was importing over 100,000 tons of general goods, exclusive of coal, per month via the Rhodesia Railways. Clearly, Zambia had overreached her striking ability and would not be able to maintain a comprehensive ban on foreign exchange for railage.

On 3 June the Zambian government relented and authorised the payment of railage to the Rhodesia Railways for goods ordered under contracts made before 24 May. In addition the Import Licensing Department of the Ministry of Commerce and Industry was authorised to permit pre-payment of railing costs for an indeterminate range of 'essential supplies'. Thereafter, until the disruptive events of January 1973, Zambia relied upon the Rhodesia Railways for at least three-quarters of her imported general goods, exclusive of oil, for which the entire cost of railage south of the Zambezi was pre-paid in Moçambique and South Africa, rather than Bulawayo.

The copper export snarl was also resolved, after much difficulty, on Rhodesian terms. Between 29 May and 9 June the copper companies railed 16,000 tons of copper, worth K20 million, into Rhodesia, where it was held up until the Zambian government would allow the companies to pay charges required by the Rhodesia Railways. Further shipments were prohibited, and by mid-July there were 90,000 tons of copper awaiting export from the Copperbelt. Amidst rumours that the copper companies might restrict production and retrench workers, Zambia's Parliament enacted a law that empowered the President to prohibit the dismissal of employees during periods of public emergency.[26]

On 22 July the Zambian government ended the impasse by announcing that copper shipments via the Rhodesia Railways could be resumed. It was agreed that the copper companies would pay the railage incurred within Zambia to the Zambian section of the Rhodesia Railways. Arrangements were made whereby an agency

26. *Nat. Ass. Deb.*, Hansard No. 7, 21 July 1966, cols 17–82. Regulations under this Act were in effect from 3 to 25 August 1966.

company, or intermediary, associated with each of the two copper mining groups would take title to the copper at the Rhodesian border and pay the railage due from there to the seaports, at which points title to the copper would be transferred to sales companies associated with each group. While these sales companies are registered in Great Britain, the two intermediary companies are registered in Switzerland. By this device the rail payments issue was resolved and the crisis ended without a technical breach of sanctions by the Zambian producers, their British customers, or either the British or Zambian governments.

*Towards autonomy:* (a) *railways.* When Zambia refused to permit any further money transfers to the Bulawayo account of the Rhodesia Railways, the Broken Hill account was reported to total к8 million. This sum was retained by the Zambian section of the railway. However, Broken Hill no longer received any portion of the revenues earned outside Zambian territory. The income of the Zambian section was far from sufficient to meet its rising costs of operation. To make matters worse, in May 1966 the Rhodesians manipulated the railways to ensure that most of the rolling stock was on their side of the border. By mid-June the Zambian section was seriously deficient in railway cars. Belatedly, a 'one-for-one' vehicle exchange agreement was negotiated, thereby stabilising the unbalanced distribution of rolling stock. This was the best that the Zambian section could do under the circumstances. For months thereafter Zambia suffered from a critical shortage of the wagons needed to carry coal to the Copperbelt.

One area of agreement between Zambia and Rhodesia was their common resolve to divide the Rhodesia Railways. Rhodesia is known to have pressed for division since 1963,[27] while Zambia, fearing the possibility of dislocation and oppressive rates, was at first reluctant. But Rhodesia was insistent, and by November 1965 the Zambian government was prepared to accept division on principle. Beyond that, it would be necessary to undertake complicated negotiations for an equitable division of the railway's assets and liabilities.

Zambia's desire to split the unitary railway system was heightened during the payments crisis. But Zambia wanted to negotiate the terms of division with Britain, since Britain was still legally responsible for the government of Rhodesia, and it was politically un-

27. See R. Hall, 'Zambia and Rhodesia: links and fetters', *Africa Report*, vol. 11, No. 1 (January 1966), pp. 8–12, for informed speculation on Rhodesian motives.

palatable for Zambia to negotiate with the rebel regime. On 15 November 1966 President Kaunda gave the British government a seven-day ultimatum to open negotiations with Zambia for division of the railway. If Britain refused to do so, he declared, Zambia would negotiate directly with the Smith government, however distasteful to Zambia that might be. This was a foregone conclusion, since the British government did not propose to negotiate while it lacked effective control of the railway. On 23 November the Rhodesia Railways board, including Zambian members, met at Bulawayo to begin negotiations. After seven months of hard and secret bargaining the railway was formally divided at the end of June 1967, although agreement had still not been reached on division of the assets and liabilities.[28]

Meanwhile deficiencies of rail transport have continued to hamper Zambia's economic performance. In addition to equipment shortages and maintenance problems, it has been difficult to recruit skilled railwaymen to replace departing white Rhodesians. By 1968 Zambia Railways had augmented its rolling stock substantially with the acquisition of twenty-six diesel locomotives and 1,300 wagons. Furthermore, the opening of a new к6 million railway workshop at Kabwe in 1971 has removed the necessity to contract for services at the Bulawayo workshop of Rhodesia Railways. However, the financial outlook for the new Zambia Railways is far from favourable. Since Zambia intends to reorient her trade away from the Rhodesian route, the old lines stand to lose money, in particular their traditionally high revenues earned on copper exports. Inevitably, the new Rhodesia Railways announced a substantial increase (of about 25 per cent) in the rates for Zambian imports and metal exports shortly after the break-up of the unitary system. Both the Zambia Railways and the new Rhodesia Railways continue to operate at a loss; both require financial support from their governments;[29] both need large injections of capital investment. Neither is likely to regain economic health until amicable relations between their two countries have been restored.

28. Under the 1963 inter-governmental agreement, Rhodesia and Zambia were equally responsible for the assets and liabilities of the enterprise. These were reported to have been worth к200 million and к144 million respectively at the time of the split. Among the many technical problems of division was a disproportion of physical assets between the two countries, with some 70 per cent being located in Rhodesia. See 'Railway break-up: the key questions', *Business and Economy* (Ndola), June 1967, pp. 13–14.

29. In 1967 the Rhodesia Railways obtained a к10 million loan from the Rhodesia Reserve Bank, while the Zambian government guaranteed a к9 million commercial loan for the Zambian section.

*Towards autonomy:* (b) *airways and power.* At the end of 1967 the Central African Airways Corporation was dissolved and its assets were distributed among the owners—Rhodesia, Zambia and Malawi—in proportion to their interests. Direct air services between Zambia and Rhodesia were then discontinued on political grounds. A management contract to operate the new Zambia Airways was awarded to the Italian State airline, Alitalia.

Unlike the railways and the airline, nothing could be done about the remaining common service, namely the Central African Power Corporation, which owns the Kariba dam and the south bank power station. In 1967 the Kariba station supplied Zambian users with approximately 350 megawatts, which was nearly 80 per cent of the country's electricity requirement.[30] Since UDI steps have been taken to increase the capacity of the Victoria Falls power station from 8 to 100 megawatts. In addition, various small hydro and thermal stations are maintained on a stand-by basis. On the Copperbelt electricity is required to operate pumps that prevent flooding in all the underground mines. In an emergency, thermal power stations there could supply about one-third of the current power requirement. While this would suffice to maintain essential services and save the mines, there would be very little, if any, power left over from local sources for actual production. The mines could also import electricity from the Congo (now Zaïre), but not in sufficient quantity to offset a crippling stroke at Kariba.

It was known that by 1970 Zambia's growing need for electricity would strain the capacity of existing sources of supply. From the economic and technical viewpoint it was logical to proceed with the planned installation of a second 600-megawatt power station at Kariba—this one on the north or Zambian bank of the Zambezi river. Yet Zambia did not want to increase the degree of its reliance upon the jointly owned Central African Power Corporation. Furthermore, the corporation cannot undertake new capital expenditures while its Higher Authority remains legally disabled as a result of UDI. Consequently Zambia decided to construct a new, internal hydro-electric facility on the Kafue river. The first stage of this project, destined for completion in 1971 and designed to generate 500 megawatts, was originally estimated to cost K74 million. This figure, which proved to be unrealistically low, was about twice

30. J. E. Mitchell, General Manager of the Copperbelt Power Company Ltd, 'Electricity supply in Zambia', an address (mimeo., 1967). The Copperbelt Power Company distributes electricity on the Copperbelt from all sources, including Kariba, Zaïre, and local stations. It is jointly owned by the two copper-mining groups.

as high as the total estimated cost of completing the relatively simple
second stage at Kariba. What is more, the World Bank, a principal
financier of the original Kariba project, was prepared to finance
a major portion of the cost of expansion there, while the balance
would be derived from revenues accruing to operations of the
existing plant.

It was painful for Zambia to forego these immediate economic
opportunities, even though its preferred Kafue project is truly consistent with long-range development goals. By 1968 the main
financial obstacles to the Kafue scheme appeared to have been
overcome. An approach had been made to the World Bank; informed sources say that despite that institution's deep commitment
to completion of the Kariba project, it had been willing to finance a
250-megawatt scheme at the Kafue gorge. This offer is said to
have been deemed inadequate and turned down by the Zambian
government, which then made arrangements with a Yugoslav
engineering firm to provide most of the capital required. The Kafue
project became operational at less than full capacity in 1971.

Meanwhile, it has been determined that Zambia's ever-increasing
need for electricity would outstrip her planned generating capacity
by the end of the current decade. Deciding that it could not really
afford to snub the abundant source of inexpensive power at its door-
step, the government asked Britain and the World Bank to assist with
the financing of a power station at the north bank of Kariba.
Britain then agreed to be responsible for the unpaid balance of the
original World Bank loan, so that Zambia, free of her inherited debt,
could qualify for a new loan. Arrangements to by-pass the virtually
defunct Central African Power Corporation were also devised. This
project, which will be capable of expansion from an initial 600
megawatts to a potential 900, is due for completion in 1974. It
will supplant the south bank station as a source of supply, so that
Zambia will have become self-sufficient in electricity.

## Essential supplies

*Petroleum products.* At the time of UDI Zambia imported 90 per
cent of her supplies of petrol, oil and lubricants via Rhodesia. In
December 1965 Britain acted in pursuance of a resolution by the
UN Security Council to prohibit the shipment or delivery of
petroleum products to Rhodesia by British nationals. As expected,
Rhodesia retaliated by prohibiting the conveyance of petroleum
products through her territory to Zambia. Thereafter Zambia's
entire supply had to be imported via precarious land routes or by

air. The most dramatic and immediately effective relief was provided by an airlift of petroleum products mounted and financed by
the British, Canadian and United States governments from December 1965 until May 1966.

Despite immense transport problems and continuous rationing,
Zambia's consumption of petrol, oil and lubricants in 1967, estimated at 360,000 tons, was more than twice that of 1964.[31] The vast
bulk of this supply was imported by road from Tanzania. Periodi-
cally this route was disrupted by heavy rainfall. In the absence of
adequate storage facilities, Zambia experienced recurrent severe
shortages. Meanwhile Rhodesia has been able to obtain all the oil
she needs from South Africa and Moçambique. In Zambian eyes
the oil embargo on Rhodesia has been 'a gigantic miscalculation'.[32]

A lasting solution to this problem has been sought through the
construction of an eight-inch 1,060-mile underground pipeline
from the refinery at Dar es Salaam to the Copperbelt centre of
Ndola. Financed by an Italian banking group and constructed by
the Italian State Petroleum Company (ENI), the pipeline was
opened in September 1968, ending thirty-two months of petrol
rationing. It is two-thirds owned by the government of Zambia and
one-third by the government of Tanzania.

*Coal.* In 1965 Zambian coal consumption was of the order of
110,000 short tons per month, of which about 60 per cent was
used by the copper industry and about 30 per cent by the railway.
Nearly all of it was railed from the Wankie colliery in Rhodesia,
which property is controlled by the Anglo-American Corporation.
Coal shipments from Wankie, representing about one-third of that
colliery's output, then comprised some 45 per cent of the total net
tonnage of all goods railed into Zambia. In addition to normal uses,
the mining companies also rely upon coal to operate their stand-by
thermal generators in the event of a failure of the hydro-electric
power facilities. At UDI the stockpile of coal on the Copperbelt
was barely sufficient to keep the pumps in service for thirty days.
If the power supply from Kariba had been cut, and Wankie coal
had also become unavailable, the mines would have been pre-
cariously dependent upon power from the Congo to prevent irre-
parable losses from flooding.

In August 1965 Zambia's newly created National Coal Supply
Commission, comprising representatives of the government and

31. See J. de St Jorre, 'Zambia's economy: progress and perils', *Africa
Report*, vol. 12, No. 9 (December 1967), pp. 36–9.
32. Editorial comment in the *Times of Zambia*, 30 March 1967.

both mining groups, decided to open a low-grade coal mine at Nkandabwe in the Gwembe Valley, adjoining Lake Kariba. The venture was 50 per cent government-owned, while each mining group held 25 per cent of the shares. Initially the Commission aimed merely to mine and stockpile 300,000 tons as a safeguard against emergency. UDI increased the magnitude of the challenge.

In December 1965 the Rhodesians suddenly imposed export taxes on coal and coke of K10 and K16 respectively per short ton. Although these charges were retracted within two weeks' time, a fivefold increase in the cost of coal, however temporary, spurred the development of domestic supplies in Zambia. Soon the suitability of Nkandabwe coal was found to exceed previous expectations. For some uses it replaced Wankie, while increasing proportions of it were mixed with Wankie imports at the copper mines and elsewhere. In comparison with Wankie, however, Nkandabwe coal was markedly inferior in quality and relatively difficult to mine and transport to the railhead. Its comparatively low calorific value and high ash content made for inefficient smelting, among other technical drawbacks. The excessive use of this product resulted in production cuts caused by damaged equipment early in 1968. Its limited purpose had been served by 1969, when the deposits were exhausted and the mine was closed. Fortunately, a much better and larger coalfield was discovered at Maamba in the Gwembe Valley in 1966. This mine, wholly owned by the Zambian government, began to produce in 1968. Meanwhile the mining companies stockpiled reserves of Wankie coal for their own use at the southern town of Livingstone. In addition, small quantities of German coal reached the Copperbelt via the Angola–Congo rail route. With the installation of a washing plant at Maamba in 1970, the quality of this mine's product was enhanced to approximate that of Wankie. By 1972 production at Maamba was actually greater than Zambia's need, since dieselisation of the railway system had resulted in a substantial reduction of the domestic demand for coal.

Before completion of the Maamba colliery, Zambian consumers still used high-grade foreign coal, preponderantly from Wankie, for about 50 per cent of their needs. Their attempt to maximise the use of a domestic product, despite its lower energy value, meant that greater tonnages had to be shipped over more difficult routes, albeit for slightly shorter distances and entirely within Zambia. For a time copper production was plagued by coal shortages resulting mainly from chronic railway problems, and periodic cuts in production were attributed to this cause. Fortunately for Zambia, the market price of copper during most of this critical period was abnormally high, owing to the Vietnam war and a prolonged strike by copper industry workers in the United States during 1967–68, among other causes.

*General imports.* In 1965 the value of Zambian imports totalled K210 million. Rhodesia supplied 34 per cent of that total; Britain and South Africa each supplied 20 per cent. In 1966 the value of imports rose to K246 million. South Africa and Britain accounted for 23 per cent and 22 per cent respectively, while Rhodesian imports, accounting for 18 per cent of the total, were down to about two-thirds of their 1965 level.[33] In 1967 the value of imports was up to K306·3 million.[34] The South African and British portions remained relatively constant at 23·5 per cent and 21 per cent; the Rhodesian portion had declined to 10·5 per cent (K32·2 million), including electricity and coal. This was less than one-third of the expected level of imports from Rhodesia had there been no UDI.

As a matter of policy, attempts have been made to diversify the sources of Zambian imports at the expense of both Rhodesia and South Africa. Import (and export) licensing was adopted in December 1965 and applied restrictively against non-essential commodities from those countries. For example, in April 1967 permits were refused for the importation of South African clothing that was not shipped through Tanzanian ports. Since Tanzania has refused entry to all South African goods, a line of trade worth K2 million in 1966 was destroyed.[35] Despite governmental pressures of this kind, Zambian importers have generally been either unable or unwilling to switch rapidly to new sources of supply. Officials have alleged that many Zambian businesses are traditionally subsidiaries of Rhodesian firms and are therefore reluctant to dispense with their old suppliers.[36] But the greatest obstacle to change is the inadequacy of facilities for trade and transport between Zambia and countries to the north. In 1967 it was correct to say that 'the main effect of import licensing to date has been to increase South African exports to Zambia at the expense of Rhodesia'.[37]

*Transport routes*

The railway crisis of 1966 nullified those international and com-

33. *Economic Report, 1967* (Lusaka, 1968), p. 43.
34. *Economic Report, 1968* (Lusaka, 1969), p. 54.
35. *Times of Zambia*, 3 August 1967.
36. *Ibid.*, 29 July 1967.
37. *Business and Economy*, September 1967, p. 33.

mercial agreements which obliged both government and business organisations in Zambia to support the Rhodesia Railways at the expense of other routes. Steps then taken to divert copper exports in particular from the Rhodesia Railways met with moderate success, as we shall see. But it was impossible to break drastically with the traditional route for imports. Before UDI the net tonnage of imports per month via the Rhodesia Railways averaged approximately 215,000 short tons, including 100,000 tons of coal and coke, 15,000 tons of petroleum products, and 100,000 tons of general goods. By September 1966 the total net tonnage had fallen to 170,000 tons; coal was down to 67,000 tons, but general goods had actually increased to 103,000 tons. At this time a mere 15,000 tons of general goods entered Zambia via other routes. By 1968 the import capacity of the alternative routes had climbed to 40,000 tons. No major alteration of this picture will be possible until significant progress has been made in the development of alternative routes.[38]

In this brief account of problems and achievements relating to transport we shall consider, first, options that were within Zambia's reach immediately or soon after UDI; secondly, the efforts of the copper companies to use new routes; and thirdly, the search for durable solutions.

### Early options

*By air.* In addition to the American–British–Canadian emergency airlift of petroleum products noted previously, one of the mining groups, namely Roan Selection Trust, decided to experiment with a 'copper air bridge' between Ndola and Dar es Salaam. RST's wholly owned subsidiary, Zambian Air Cargoes Ltd, purchased two turboprop air-freighters from Lockheed Aircraft Corporation of the USA. Operations were initiated in April 1966; subsequently

38. In 1968 the Zambian government informed the Secretary General of the United Nations that 25 per cent of its transported foreign trade had been routed away from the Rhodesia Railways. Financial pressures appear to have reinforced Rhodesia's logistical hold over Zambian trade, thus: 'The remaining traffic still moved by the Rhodesia railways is the outcome of calculations by the Southern Rhodesians of the largest amount of money they consider they can safely extort from Zambia and the largest amount of traffic Zambia can route through Southern Rhodesia without paying more. Any further attempt to direct traffic from the Southern Rhodesian route would result in additional payments to Southern Rhodesia for less traffic, which Zambia could not afford.' UN Doc. S/8786/Add. 2, 10 October 1968, p. 5.

the Zambian government purchased three more air-freighters for operation by Zambian Air Cargoes under contract. By the end of 1967 the five-plane fleet was able to transport up to 4,000 tons of copper per month, importing (on return flights) fuels, mining materials and general goods.

*By road.* Since UDI Zambian commercial traffic has depended increasingly upon the condition of two motor roads. By far the most important is the Great North Road, which runs 1,200 miles from central Zambia to Tanzania's seaport capital of Dar es Salaam. The Great East Road covers more than 500 miles from Lusaka to Salima, in Malawi, which is connected by rail with the port of Beira in Moçambique. Both roads have been improved with the aid of loans from the World Bank. But the Great North Road, which is vastly preferred for external political reasons, has been over-burdened, and long stretches of it are very difficult to maintain during the heavy rains between November and April. This road's deplorable condition, great volume of traffic and high accident rate have earned it the apt nickname of 'hell run'.

At first, emergency motor transport services over the Great North and Great East Roads were provided by private companies, including many small operators who rented government-owned tankers and lorries. In 1966 the Zambian and Tanzanian governments joined with the Italian Fiat organisation to form Zambia–Tanzania Road Services Ltd. This enterprise has activated a fleet of lorries, including dual-purpose tankers, which have carried both petroleum imports and copper exports on the Great North Road. Private and mixed enterprises have supplemented this operation and have provided similar services on the Great East Road. Two subsidiary road (and road–rail–barge) routes branch from the Great North Road. One goes to the southern Tanzanian port of Mtwara, which some planners have visualised as the potential 'gateway to Zambia'. In fact improvements of the harbour facilities and airport at Mtwara have been financed by the Zambian government. A second road branches from the Great North Road in Zambia and goes due north via Mbala (formerly Abercorn) to the railhead at Mpanda in Tanzania. From there the railway links both to Dar es Salaam and the port of Mwanza on Lake Victoria, where ferry boats provide a link to the Kenya railways. Yet another road link, of twenty-six miles, branches from Mbala to Mpulungu on Lake Tanganyika, where barges connect with the Tanzania railways at Kigoma. While these experimental routes have been used sparingly, the costs of developing them have been defrayed by the Zambian government, and they have continued to attract interest in view of the present limitations of the congested port of Dar es Salaam.

*By rail.* Zambia Railways connects with the Congo–Katanga system (BCK, or Chemin de Fer du Bas-Congo au Katanga). One branch of the BCK connects with the Benguela Railway (CFB or Caminho de Ferro de Benguela) of Angola, terminating at the Atlantic port of Lobito. This route from the Zambian Copperbelt is almost exactly as long as the southern routes to Beira and Lourenço Marques. Moreover, the port of Lobito is some 2,000 miles nearer to destinations in Europe than are the seaports of Moçambique.

The Benguela Railway, opened in 1931, was constructed by a British firm, Tanganyika Concessions Ltd (Tanks), which also acquired about 15 per cent of the Union Minière du Haute-Katanga. Tanks owns 90 per cent of the Benguela Railway, while 10 per cent belongs to the Portuguese government of Angola. For many years the BCK–Benguela line was denied access to the lucrative trade of the Copperbelt. Thus in 1936 the Northern Rhodesian copper companies agreed to ship all their production via the Rhodesia Railways for the next twenty years. In exchange, the mining companies were given very low rates on both their copper exports and their imports of coal from the Wankie colliery in Southern Rhodesia. To assure the continuation of two-way (copper–coal) traffic, the mining companies also agreed not to develop hydro-electric power as a substitute for coal. When this agreement expired in 1956, rates on copper from Northern Rhodesia were raised from about κ6 per ton to κ29·70. By then the copper companies wanted a second route to relieve congestion on the Rhodesia Railways. In 1956 an inter-railway agreement between the Rhodesia, BCK and Benguela railways stipulated that a maximum of 20 per cent of total copper exports from Northern Rhodesia could be shipped via the Lobito route. It was also agreed that both routes would charge identical rates for Northern Rhodesian copper. After this agreement was renewed in 1960, the Rhodesia Railways acted unilaterally to offer the copper companies a substantial rebate on exports diverted to it from the BCK–Benguela system. As a result, the Lobito route was virtually abandoned by the Northern Rhodesian (later Zambian) producers for several years.[39] Interest in the Lobito route was renewed prior to UDI when the copper companies found it necessary to supplement the coal-carrying capacity of the Rhodesia

39. See Haefele and Steinberg, *Government Controls on Transport, op. cit.*, and Baldwin, *Economic Development and Export Growth, op. cit.*, pp. 171–174.

Railways. By the end of 1965 small quantities of South African coal
and Zambian copper were being transported via the Benguela–BCK
railway system. But it remained for the railway payments crisis of
1966 to stimulate a massive redirection to the Lobito route.

It will be recalled that in June and July 1966 an immense
stockpile of exportable copper, about 90,000 tons, accumulated at the
Copperbelt mines. From 12 to 15 July ministerial talks concerning
rail transport were held at Kinshasa, capital of the Democratic
Republic of the Congo, including representatives of the Congo,
Zambia and Tanzania, in addition to observers from the several
railway systems involved.[40] An agreement was reached to facilitate
the export of 40,000 metric tons of copper per month,[41] equal to
about two-thirds of Zambia's current copper exports, via Congolese
and related routes.[42] However, various technical and logistical im-
pediments foiled the implementation of most of this agreement.
Moreover, the crucial Benguela Railway insisted upon a five-year
guarantee, backed by the Congolese and Zambian governments,
for 20,000 metric tons per month at a fixed rate of railage that
would be 25 per cent higher than the rate then in effect. Since this
guarantee could not be obtained, the agreement as a whole never
came into force, and traffic via the Lobito route has never attained
the desired level.

Nonetheless, the Kinshasa agreement represents a real achievement of Zambian diplomacy towards inter-State co-operation.
Copper shipments via the Lobito route were sustained at more than
10,000 metric tons per month for nearly a year, until acts of
sabotage, attributed variously to Angolan freedom fighters, Tshomb-
ist saboteurs, and mercenaries, in both Angola and the Congo,
disrupted transport in 1967. Periodic incidents of this kind have
served to underscore the hazards of reliance upon exit routes
through countries like Angola and Moçambique, which are likely
to be military theatres for years to come. It was also seen that the
Portuguese might take reprisals against Zambian and Congolese

40. The railways represented were the Congo railway companies, namely
the BCK, Otraco (from Kinshasa to Matadi), and Chemin de Fer aux
Grands Lacs Africains (CFL, between BCK and Albertville), the Benguela
Railway, and East African Railways & Harbours. The Zambian delegation, led by the Minister of Transport and Works, also included the
administrator of the Zambian section of the Rhodesia Railways and an
official of the mining companies.

41. There are 2,205 lb in one metric ton, compared with 2,240 lb in one
long ton, and 2,000 lb in one short ton.

42. For the text of the final joint communique of the Kinshasa meeting of
12–15 July 1966, see ZIS background paper No. 16/66.

traffic for guerrilla activities thought to be supported by either country. Despite these risks, an agreement between Zambia and the Congo in December 1967, reaffirming the principle of complete co-operation between the two countries in the field of rail transport, called for the negotiation of a new agreement by the BCK, Zambia and Benguela railways to supplement the Kinshasa decisions and replace the inter-railway accords of 1956 and 1960. The Benguela Railway has since undertaken to make major improvements that are expected to double its capacity by 1974. Meanwhile, the Zambian government has contracted to use this route for at least 20 per cent of copper exports in return for favourable tariffs.

*Copper exports.* From June to September 1966, during the height of the railway crisis, the two mining groups agreed to share the available capacity for copper exports and the importation of mining supplies according to a ratio of 4 to 3 for the Anglo-American Corporation group and the Roan Selection Trust group respectively. From October 1966 until May 1967 the two groups fixed their rates of production in accordance with this formula. Since then there have been no such restrictions, but the groups have continued to co-operate closely, sharing transport costs, supply costs and coal stocks in proportion to their actual rates of production. With the fear of comparative losses thus eliminated, the mining companies have been encouraged to experiment with transport and production methods designed to ease the post-UDI crisis.

Despite strenuous efforts to develop reliable alternative routes, the companies have remained dependent upon the Rhodesia Railways to carry a large percentage of their exports. The Lobito route has never been able to carry anything near its Kinshasa agreement target of 34,000 short tons per month; it has often fallen short of the 15,000 tons that it was thought to be able to carry in mid-1966. Given the availability of more than 60,000 short tons of exportable copper per month, it was possible, in an average month during 1967–1968, to ship it via various routes approximately as follows:

| *Via:* | *Tons* |
|---|---|
| Rail to Lobito | 15,000–16,000 |
| Road to Dar es Salaam | 15,000–16,000 |
| Air to Dar es Salaam | 3,000–4,000 |
| Road to Malawi and rail to Beira | 4,000–5,000 |
| Miscellaneous routes | 2,000–3,000 |
| Rhodesia Railways to Beira and Lourenço Marques | 20,000–22,000 |
|  | Total 59,000–66,000 |

The actual decision on each month's export allocation to the various routes, including the Rhodesia Railways, has been made by officials of the Ministry responsible for foreign trade after consultation with officials of other Ministries and the mining companies. In practice, more often than not one or another alternative route has fallen short of its expected capacity. For example, in June and July 1967 the Lobito route was rendered largely inoperative as a result of sabotage to a bridge in Katanga. In September and October this route was endangered again by the actions of both nationalist guerrillas and mercenary troops moving between Angola and Katanga. At this time, also, a few of the air-freighters had to be withdrawn from service for repairs. It therefore became necessary to export about 40,000 short tons per month, or nearly two-thirds of copper exports, via the Rhodesia Railways. In both 1968 and 1969 nationalist guerrillas disrupted the rail route to Lobito. From time to time, stretches of the Great North Road have been washed away by torrential rains. Consequently, until 1973 Zambian copper exports via the Rhodesian rail route rarely dipped beneath 20,000 tons, or one-third of the total; they were often considerably higher. Indeed, the Rhodesian authorities eventually required Zambia to ship a minimum of 22,700 metric tons of copper per month via the Rhodesian Railways. Failure to comply with this requirement would be penalised by the imposition of a surcharge of 50 per cent on all Zambian imports using that railway.

*Long-term solutions.* The most obvious long-term solution to Zambia's transport problem envisages the overthrow of white minority rule in Rhodesia and a consequent resumption of normal trade relations between Zambia and her southern neighbour. But the Rhodesia–Moçambique route would still not be safe until minority rule had been abolished in the latter country too. This observation applies with equal cogency to other routes through Portuguese-held territory, notably the Lobito route, where major improvements have been projected, and the Beira route via Malawi. Similarly, a major shift to reliance upon the South African Railways—for example, the Durban route via Rhodesia and Botswana— is also ruled out on political grounds. Among the various northern routes, the all-Zaïre rail and river route to the Atlantic Ocean, and the rail routes via Zaïre and Lake Tanganyika to East African ports, have very limited capacities or potentials.[43] A more promising route

43. The all-Zaïre system would be reappraised if the proposal of a British company, Lonrho Ltd, to construct links for an unbroken rail route to the Atlantic, were to be implemented. *Financial Times* (London), 22 May 1969.

in the long run may be the road, rail and barge route to Lake Victoria and Kenya. Far and away the most promising northern prospects lie with the construction and improvement of direct rail and road links between Zambia and the Tanzanian ports of Dar es Salaam and Mtwara.

In 1966–67 studies commissioned by the United States Agency for International Development and the World Bank set the stage for major improvements in road transport between Tanzania and Zambia.[44] With financial assistance from Britain, Sweden and the United States as well as the World Bank, a vastly improved Tanzam highway has been constructed. The most significant development of all involves construction of a 1,000-mile Tanzam railway between the Zambian centre and Dar es Salaam. This project had been rejected by the World Bank, which favours highway development, in 1964, but its financial feasibility was demonstrated in a 1966 study sponsored by the British and Canadian governments. The total cost was estimated at about K280 million, including construction, rolling stock, and the improvement of port facilities at Dar es Salaam.[45] In 1967 a firm proposal to build the Tanzam railway was made by the People's Republic of China, which offered to extend a K200 million interest-free loan for the purpose. An agreement between China, Tanzania and Zambia was then signed, and a survey undertaken by Chinese engineers. Subsequently it was reported that the interest-free loan would amount to K286·6 million and be repayable over a thirty-year period. Zambia and Tanzania have also agreed to purchase consumer goods from China equal in value to the local construction costs that will be incurred by the Chinese. Actual construction was begun in 1970 and has proceeded ahead of schedule, so that completion is anticipated in 1974.

In January 1973 Zambia's ability to dispense with the Rhodesian rail route was tested by Rhodesia's sudden decision to close her border in reprisal for the actions of nationalist guerrillas who were alleged to operate from Zambia. Although copper shipments to Beira were specifically exempted from this embargo, Zambia herself resolved to grasp the nettle and discontinue all trading relations

44. A report on the economic and engineering feasibility of upgrading and relocating the road link between Zambia and Tanzania was submitted by the Stanford Research Institute in 1966. Engineering studies in Tanzania, where major problems arise, were undertaken the following year.

45. See articles in *The Economist* (London), 12 August 1967, pp. 565–6, and *Business and Economy*, August 1967, pp. 7–9. The study was performed by a British firm of economic consultants, Maxwell Stamp (Africa) Ltd.

with Rhodesia. Neither Portugal nor South Africa approved the disruption of trading relations with Zambia. Upon reflection, and facing the prospect of a substantial loss of revenue from railage, Rhodesia rescinded the blockade. But the Zambian government was now resolved to rely upon alternative routes, especially the reconstructed Great North Road and the partially usable Tanzam railway, which then reached to within 150 miles of the Zambian border. Shipments via the Angolan rail route would also be increased. While these facilities were adequate for copper exports, their import capabilities would depend upon the ability of Dar es Salaam and other East African ports, such as Mtwara and Tanga in Tanzania, Mombasa in Kenya, and possibly even Malawi's outlet at Nacala in Moçambique, to accommodate Zambia's needs.

Finally, the long-term perspective on Zambia's economy should not overlook the intriguing potential of modern air transport. During three years of operations, between 1966 and 1969, Zambian Air Cargoes carried about 150,000 tons of freight—over half being outbound copper wire bars—between Ndola and Dar es Salaam. Although the costs of this operation were much higher than originally anticipated, new vistas in transportation have been perceived. Visionaries anticipate the future development of giant air-freighters that could carry finished copper all the way to Europe and other destinations.

## Relations with Britain

Against this economic background, let us examine the record of public diplomatic relations between Zambia and Britain in the aftermath of UDI. This record is largely unrelieved in its progression of dismal events. Needless to say, Zambia was in no position to implement an ultimatum by the Council of Ministers of the OAU, on 5 December 1965, calling upon all member States to sever diplomatic relations with Britain if the Rhodesian rebellion had not been quelled by 15 December. Only ten member States, including two Commonwealth members, Ghana and Tanzania, complied. As President Nyerere remarked, 'no sane person' could ask Zambia to implement that resolution.[46]

In January 1966 Mr Wilson hopefully reassured the Commonwealth Prime Ministers and other heads of government meeting in Lagos, Nigeria, that the cumulative effects of economic sanctions might bring the Rhodesian rebellion to an end 'within a matter of weeks rather than months'. The meeting then set up a committee of

46. *Foreign Affairs Bulletin*, Tanzania, vol. II, No. 1 (January 1966), p. 15.

representatives of all Commonwealth countries to review regularly both the effects of sanctions and the needs of Zambia. The heads of government also agreed to reconvene in July if the rebellion had not been ended before then. A few of them, notably Lester Pearson, the Prime Minister of Canada, reserved the right to propose mandatory sanctions under chapter VII of the UN charter.

In March the Labour Party, which had survived with a precarious and dwindling majority in the House of Commons, was returned to power with a rousing majority of ninety-seven. Now President Kaunda expected Wilson to take firm measures against Rhodesia.[47] He was deeply disappointed when, in April, Britain resumed negotiations with representatives of the Rhodesian government in London. Amidst reports of a softening of Britain's attitude towards the Smith regime, Kaunda threatened to propose the expulsion of Britain herself from the Commonwealth. In a radio address he expressed his contempt for Britain's 'shifty and evasive' policy; he also alleged that by holding informal talks with Rhodesian officials Britain had given *de facto* recognition to the Smith government.[48] When Wilson managed to obtain a postponement of the expected Commonwealth conference from July to September, Kaunda was moved to warn that Zambia might withdraw from the Commonwealth.[49]

At the Commonwealth conference of September 1966 Britain was urged by most of the heads of government to 'make a categorical declaration that independence would not be granted before majority rule is established on the basis of universal adult franchise and that this declaration should not be conditional on whether the illegal regime agreed to surrender or not'.[50] However, Wilson refused to strengthen his previous undertaking that any basis for independence must be 'acceptable to the people of Rhodesia as a whole'. In other words, Britain refused to rule out the possibility of a settlement involving independence before majority rule. But the British Prime Minister did announce that if Rhodesia failed to comply with British terms for ending the rebellion, Britain would both withdraw her offer of a settlement that allowed for the grant of independence before majority rule, and ask the United Nations Security Council,

47. See Hall, *The High Price of Principles*, *op. cit.*, pp. 43, 133–4, for the basis of Kaunda's trust in Wilson at this time.
48. *Africa Research Bulletin*, Political, Social and Cultural Series (Exeter), vol. 3, No. 5, p. 540.
49. Kaunda, 'Installation address by the Chancellor', 1966, *op. cit.*, pp. 29–30.
50. 'Commonwealth Prime Ministers' meeting: Rhodesia communique' (mimeo.).

before the end of 1966, to vote for selective mandatory economic sanctions against Rhodesia.[51]

Pursuant to these aims but contrary to the expressed wish of most heads of government at the Commonwealth conference, Wilson met Smith aboard a British warship off Gibraltar. As the Africans feared, he offered to concede independence before majority rule, but his specific proposals for an interim government under gubernatorial rule were rejected by the Rhodesian Cabinet.[52] Thereupon Britain asked the United Nations Security Council to vote mandatory sanctions both on selected Rhodesian exports, including tobacco, sugar, asbestos, and chrome, and on the sale of armaments to Rhodesia. Presenting this proposal in the form of a draft resolution to the Security Council, Britain's Secretary of State for Foreign Affairs, George Brown, said that his delegation would not oppose the addition of oil to the sanctions list, 'on the basis of the full understanding ... of the importance of not allowing sanctions to escalate into economic confrontation with third countries'.[53] This meant, in effect, that sanctions on oil could not be enforced if South Africa chose to disregard the resolution. If the Security Council approved this resolution, the British Foreign Secretary confirmed that his government would 'not thereafter be prepared to submit to the British Parliament any settlement which involves independence before majority rule'.

Zambia's position was explained to the Security Council by her Foreign Minister, Simon Kapwepwe. His government continued to believe that military intervention was 'the only sure and speedy way to topple the illegal Smith regime'. The record thus far, he said,

51. The Security Council's resolution of 12 November 1965 had condemned Rhodesia's declaration of independence and called upon all States to refrain from recognition. On 20 November 1965 the Security Council called upon the United Kingdom 'to quell this rebellion of the racist minority', and upon all States to desist from providing the illegal regime with arms or military materials, and 'to do their utmost in order to break all economic relations with Southern Rhodesia, including an embargo on oil and petroleum products'. These injunctions, under chapter VI of the UN charter, were not mandatory. On 9 April 1966 the Security Council authorised Britain to use force to prevent the arrival at Beira of vessels believed to be carrying oil destined for Rhodesia. The adoption of mandatory sanctions, under chapter VII of the charter, imposes an obligation of compliance upon all member States of the UN.

52. See L. W. Bowman, 'Rhodesia since UDI', *Africa Report*, vol. 12, No. 2 (February 1967), pp. 5–13, where 'The working document prepared aboard HMS *Tiger*' is also reproduced.

53. *United Nations Security Council, Official Records*, s/PV. 1331, 8 December 1966, p. 9.

indicates 'that the Wilson Government is acting in collusion with Smith; that the Wilson Government is motivated by racialism in its policy towards Africa'. In Zambia's view, 'the collusion of Smith and Wilson is substantiated by Wilson's ruling out of the use of force before Smith's unilateral declaration of independence'. Furthermore, 'Wilson now seeks to rule out a total embargo on oil so as to make his long-advocated economic sanctions totally futile and unworkable'. Kapwepwe said that Zambia was 'willing to go all the way with mandatory comprehensive sanctions in which South Africa and Portuguese Moçambique would be forced to comply; but Zambia is not prepared to go half the way, thereby subjecting itself to greater economic sacrifices to no avail'. To satisfy Zambia, the British draft resolution would have to be amended 'to include a complete embargo on oil coming from all sources, that is, South Africa, Moçambique, and overseas. Britain must bring a halt to all financial operations with or for the Smith regime; its banks in Southern Rhodesia must be closed. We ask Britain to improve the draft to include all imports and exports, making it a mandatory comprehensive endeavour.'[54]

An amendment submitted by Mali, Nigeria and Uganda on behalf of the African group of States proposed the addition of coal and all manufactured goods originating in Rhodesia, as well as oil, to the sanctions list. The sponsors were not unmindful of the immense strain that this would impose upon Zambia's economy, but they noted that Zambia's agreement had been obtained. Indeed, Kapwepwe had advocated the adoption of comprehensive sanctions in his address to the Security Council. Here, as in the case of the railway crisis of mid-1966, Zambia appeared ready to run an open-ended risk in order to create a situation that might dispose Britain to regard the use of force in a more positive light. At length, the Security Council adopted the substance of the British draft resolution with the addition of sanctions on oil supplies for Rhodesia. In the course of debate Kapwepwe warned that Zambia 'would not participate in the British proposals because these, in short, mean only one thing, and that is to kill Zambia, bit by bit'.[55]

It should be acknowledged that in some ways the prolonged strain of UDI has stimulated economic development in Zambia, notably in coal mining and the field of transport. But the short-term financial costs have been high. In July 1966 the Minister of Finance revealed that as a result of UDI Zambia was committed to expenditures totalling K62 million by mid-1967. He also reported a current

54. *Ibid.*, s/pv. 1332, 9 December 1966, pp. 8–11.
55. *Ibid.*, s/pv. 1336, 13 December 1966, p. 10.

British offer to commit K7·2 million for the development of alternative transport routes.[56] Throughout 1966 there was sporadic wrang-
ling over the factual question of how much aid Britain would
actually contribute, over and above the K20 million already spent
on the emergency fuel airlift, an RAF fighter squadron, and sundry
projects. Ultimately, in February 1967, the two countries agreed on
a sum of K27,700,000, mainly to improve transport routes to the
East African coast and to develop the port and airfield at Mtwara,
Tanzania. Zambia's Foreign Minister described this contribution
derisorily as 'chicken-feed', adding that Britain was 'responsible
for the whole mess'.[57] A few days later Kaunda announced his
government's decision to participate after all in the imposition of
selective sanctions. His government would, however, continue to
press for the adoption of more stringent measures. Zambia, he said,
was still prepared for a period of 'belt-tightening', *provided* the
end in sight was 'a clear victory for freedom and independence of
Zimbabwe under a One Man One Vote constitution'.[58]

Since then the prospect of liberation of Zimbabwe by means of
collective action under United Nations auspices has become increasingly remote. In May 1968 the Security Council set aside an
Afro-Asian draft resolution censuring Portugal and South Africa
for their continued assistance to Rhodesia and urging the United
Kingdom to use force against the rebel regime. In its place, a
resolution based largely on a British proposal for comprehensive
non-military sanctions, under chapter VII of the charter, was
adopted.[59] This imposed a virtually complete ban on all trade
with Rhodesia, on the supply of funds to that country, and on
the provision of airline services for it. However, the position taken
by the British delegate during the course of a prolonged debate on
this matter, as well as the phrasing of paragraph 17 of the resolution
itself, appeared to foreshadow a retreat from Britain's pledge of
December 1966 not to renew the previous offer of independence
before majority rule.[60] Several months later, in October 1968,
Wilson and Smith met once again aboard a British warship at

56. *Nat. Ass. Deb.*, Hansard No. 7, 22 July 1966, col. 120.
57. *East African Standard* (Nairobi), 2 February 1967.
58. President's press conference, 6 February 1967; ZIS background paper
No. 6/67.
59. S/RES/253 of 29 May 1968.
60. See especially Lord Caradon's address of 19 March 1968. The interpretation suggested here was developed by the present writer in a paper
presented at the annual meeting of the (US) African Studies Association,
October 1968, entitled 'On returning to the road of legality in Rhodesia'.
(See *Pan-African Journal*, vol. 1, No. 4 (autumn, 1968), pp. 168–71.)

Gibraltar. Not only did the British Prime Minister renew his offer of independence before majority rule; he no longer proposed to exert an effective British presence in Rhodesia before the conclusion of a settlement.[61] These negotiations came to naught because the Rhodesians were unwilling to accept external judicial guarantees against unjust racial discrimination in the form of constitutional amendments.

In June 1969 Zambia, now a member of the Security Council, joined in sponsoring a draft resolution that would have required member States to sever all relations, including all means of communication, with the regime in Southern Rhodesia. In addition, this draft would have extended the application of sanctions against Rhodesia to Moçambique and South Africa, while it urged Britain to use force against the rebels. As seven delegations, including Britain, France and the United States, abstained from voting, the resolution was not adopted.[62]

Following the proclamation of a republic by the Rhodesian regime in March 1970, the Security Council debated another African–Asian draft resolution, with Zambia as a sponsor, which would have condemned Britain's 'persistent refusal' to end the rebellion through the use of force, and required member States to sever postal, telegraphic, wireless and other means of communication with Rhodesia. Nationalist China and Spain voted in favour of this resolution after paragraphs that would have condemned Portugal and South Africa, and extended the application of sanctions to them, had been rejected in separate votes. Despite nine affirmative votes, the minimum required to adopt a Security Council resolution, this draft failed in the face of negative votes by two permanent members—the United Kingdom and the United States. Another resolution, condemning the proclamation of republican status in Rhodesia, was then adopted. This resolution also enjoined member States to sever all diplomatic, including consular, relations with Rhodesia, and to 'immediately interrupt any existing means of transportation to and from Southern Rhodesia'.[63] Zambia, Botswana and Malawi would not be expected to implement the latter injunction.[64]

61. See 'Constitutional talks on HMS *Fearless*', in C. Legum and J. Drysdale (eds), *African Contemporary Record: Annual Survey and Documents, 1968–69* (London, 1969), pp. 698–705.

62. *UN Monthly Chronicle*, vol. VI, No. 7 (July 1969), pp. 10–34.

63. s/res/277 of 18 March 1970; *UN Monthly Chronicle*, vol. VII, No. 4 (April 1970), pp. 3–35.

64. Article 50 of the charter of the United Nations provides that any State which 'finds itself confronted with special economic problems' as a result of enforcement measures taken by the Security Council 'shall have the

Like the resolution of May 1968, that of March 1970 did *request* member States, specialised agencies and international organisations within the United Nations system to 'extend' (1968) and 'increase' their assistance to Zambia as a matter of priority with a view to helping her solve such special economic problems as she may be confronted with arising from the carrying out of the decisions of the Security Council in this question'. However, the Security Council has not imposed an obligation upon member States or organisations to provide such assistance, and Zambia does not feel that the international community has been truly responsive to this appeal.[65] A recent study concludes that the omission of a binding requirement to compensate Zambia has been a grave defect in the UN strategy of economic sanctions.[66] Indeed, the drain of Zambia's wealth into expenditures needed to sustain an ineffectual UN policy only rubs salt into the wound inflicted by racial oppression in Rhodesia.

On two occasions noted in this study Zambia went to the brink of all-out economic warfare against Rhodesia. At the time of UDI Britain appears to have cautioned Zambia against a total break with Rhodesia. Had Zambia sealed her border with Rhodesia, thereby preventing both the importation of coal and the export of copper, the crisis might have been brought to a head. The copper companies might then have become the 'most insistent and powerful lobbyists at Westminster for Britain to restore normal relations at all costs; they would have advocated the use of troops in Rhodesia to end the crisis'.[67]

Again in April 1966 Zambia seemed ready to risk everything in an attempt to provoke action by the British. By prohibiting the payment of funds, including copper railing charges to the

right to consult the Security Council with regard to a solution of those problems'. It may be noted that the United Kingdom had proposed to qualify explicitly the obligations of 'landlocked States of southern Africa' in its draft resolution of 22 April 1968. However, no clause to that effect was included in the resolution finally adopted on 29 May 1968. Any such clause may have been regarded by proponents of stronger measures as an undesirable provision that might undermine the UN's commitment to prosecute an effective sanctions programme.

65. In October 1968 the Zambian government reported 'with regret' to the Secretary General of the United Nations 'that no United Nations Member States or organisations have offered Zambia assistance as a result of this resolution [of 29 May 1968]'. 'Report by the Secretary General in pursuance of Resolution 235 (1968)', UN Doc. S/8786/Add. 2, 10 October 1968, p. 4.

66. R. Zacklin, 'Challenge of Rhodesia', *International Conciliation*, No. 575 (November 1969), pp. 62, 68.

67. Guy Arnold in the *Times of Zambia*, 9 December 1967.

Rhodesia Railways, Zambia put British interests and those of the copper companies directly in the line of fire. With what result? 'The British Government', said Simon Kapwepwe, Zambia's Foreign Minister in an address to the Security Council, 'flew immediately to say "Don't close it"—and yet they were responsible for the sanctions. They said they were prepared to pay money for transporting their copper; they were prepared to pay Smith the foreign currency.'[68] Eventually a face-saving procedure was devised to permit payment of the railage.[69] Zambia's moral posture was unimpaired, although her attempt to bring the sanctions war to a climax had misfired. Clearly, Britain, which imports 40 per cent of her copper from Zambia, did not want Zambia to endanger the flow of copper exports. Zambia was prepared to pay a great price for the sake of a decisive stroke against Rhodesia. Only Britain could deliver that stroke. Unwilling to do so, Britain was anxious to avert the costs of extreme measures to herself, Zambia and the copper companies. Britain's tactical position was described succinctly by *The Times* of London: 'The British case has been that Zambia should cut its trade with Rhodesia first, and only discontinue the use of the Rhodesia Railways when assured of alternative routes and alternative supplies of coking coal.'[70] At best, and with a much greater commitment of economic support than Britain was prepared to make, this strategy *may* have been sound from a parochial, Zambian *realpolitik* standpoint.[71] However, as Zambian leaders knew, its adoption would not have hastened the overthrow of the Smith regime.

To quell the rebellion itself, coercive action beyond the limits set by the British government would be required. Short of direct military action against the Rhodesian regime, it would be necessary at least to ensure that the effects of economic sanctions, particularly in the case of oil, would not be nullified by South Africa. But British spokesmen left no doubt that sanctions would not be enforced to the extent of a 'confrontation—economic or military' with

68. *United Nations Security Council, Official Records*, s/pv. 1336, 13 December 1966, p. 9.

69. See pp. 331–2 above.

70. *The Times*, 23 August 1966.

71. It should be noted that the Zambian government was realistically wary of this approach. Richard Hall has disclosed that in July 1966 the Zambian government rejected a British proposal for Zambia to cut off all Rhodesian imports by the end of that year on the ground that it would expose Zambia to immense economic dangers without adequate support or reason to expect a successful result. *The High Price of Principles, op. cit.*, pp. 163–4.

South Africa.[72] Britain's economic stake in South Africa, in trade
and investment, was too crucial to be jeopardised.[73] Therefore
sanctions were bound to fail.

It is widely believed, in Africa and elsewhere, that Britain's
refusal to quell the rebellion by force was, and is, the result of
racial and national solicitude for the white Rhodesians. Many, like
Kaunda and Nyerere, had hoped that the anti-colonial and humani-
tarian traditions of the Labour Party would finally prevail against
the 'kith and kin brigade'. We have remarked that Zambia acted
to precipitate the railway crisis immediately following the Labour
Party's great victory in the British general election of March 1966.
In April, however, the British government, in consultation with the
South African government, reopened negotiations with the Rhodesian
regime. From that moment nothing has occurred to change the
Zambian view that Britain would ultimately recognise Rhodesian
independence under white minority rule. This is why the domestic
strains and costs of the prolonged sanctions war—petrol rationing,
chronic shortages of both producers' and consumers' goods, emergency expenditures, including government subsidies, on a variety of
alternative import–export routes, and inflation, not to mention
racial and political tensions—have been so deeply resented in
Zambia.[74] In the eyes of Kaunda and his colleagues, Britain's policy
of 'No sell-out and no force' (this phrase was used by George
Thomson, the Commonwealth Secretary, during a visit to Lusaka
in November 1967) is, to all intents and purposes, a sell-out to the
white minority regime.

## National security

If Britain had been willing to back Zambia in a supreme effort
to defeat the Rhodesian regime, the Zambian leaders would have
been willing to pay a great economic price for that purpose. But
Britain was not prepared to prosecute a total sanctions war. In-

72. *United Nations Security Council, Official Records*, s/PV. 1331, 8
December 1966, p. 7.

73. Commenting in Lusaka on Britain's policy towards Rhodesia, David
Kerr, Parliamentary Private Secretary to the British Minister of State for
Commonwealth Affairs, said, 'It is the stocks and shares and blue chips—
not the white skins—which inhibit the British government's actions.' *Times
of Zambia*, 3 November 1968. On the nature and extent of British interests in
South Africa, see D. Austin, *Britain and South Africa* (London, 1966).

74. In October 1968 the Zambian government estimated its net contingency costs resulting from the Rhodesian crisis at the figure of K142·4
million. UN Doc. S/8786/Add. 2, 10 October 1968, pp. 6–7.

creasingly it became clear that the measures adopted would not compel the rebel regime to submit. In these circumstances Zambia refrained from sealing her Rhodesian frontier and sought instead to reduce her dependence upon her southern neighbour by degrees and without serious damage to her own economic well-being.

Had Zambia resolved to seal her border with Rhodesia, the strain upon her own economy and government might have become unbearable. At the same time, Britain and the copper companies would have suffered too, and more effective means might have been taken against Rhodesia as a result. In any case, the risk of violence and destruction of facilities, like the Kariba hydro-electric station, would have grown. Zambia's ability both to contain the racial and political tensions that would have been engendered and to counter threats to her security and survival might have been seriously tested. Undoubtedly, Zambia's response to UDI was restrained by exigent problems of internal and external security. These should be considered, despite the purely speculative judgements to which they give rise.

*Enemies within?* In 1966 the population of Zambia was 3·8 million, of whom nearly 70,000 were Europeans and 10,000 Asians. Over half the Europeans lived on the Copperbelt, 18 per cent in Lusaka, and some 95 per cent in all near the line of rail from the Copperbelt to the Victoria Falls. While there was little or no reason to suppose that Europeans generally were not reconciled to African rule in Zambia, most of them were widely and plausibly thought to favour the continuation of white rule in Rhodesia and South Africa. That judgement is unlikely to be questioned by anyone familiar with the European element in Zambia. Recently Zambia has ranked second to Britain as a source of white immigrants to South Africa—approximately 4,000, or 10 per cent of the total number of such immigrants in 1967. In Zambia's crucial mining industry, at the end of 1965, 40 per cent of the expatriate labour force of some 6,500 employees were South Africans. Many more, in all branches of industrial, professional and public employment, were South Africans at heart, intending to settle there at some future time.

In principle the Zambian leaders have been sincerely dedicated to a policy of strict non-racialism. Furthermore, they fully appreciate the immense contribution of expatriate skills to national development. But hard-core racialism among Europeans has provoked both official retaliation and ruffianism from time to time, most notably in the latter part of 1966. In accordance with Zambia's constitution, those permanent residents who were not automatically citizens of Zambia by birth were given two years from the date of independence to register as citizens. During the interim period most Europeans in the country were entitled to citizenship status. When the period of choice expired on 24 October 1966 President Kaunda made a scathing condemnation of persisting racialism on the Copperbelt. A few days later twenty-three Europeans were deported for promoting 'racial and industrial unrest'.[75] On top of this, a fire broke out at a Kitwe oil depot, destroying 400,000 gallons of fuel. Believing that saboteurs were responsible, Africans in Kitwe rioted and a European woman was killed. Tempers remained high for several weeks thereafter, while the rate of resignations by white mineworkers markedly increased.

Just before the Kitwe fire, a plot to destroy a railway bridge and other installations in Zambia, involving American, British and Israeli nationals, was detected by the Israeli secret service and disclosed to Zambia. Naturally the Kitwe fire, which appears to have been accidental, was linked in the minds of high government and party officials with the threat of sabotage, and army units were assigned to guard vital installations throughout the country.[76] Arrests were made in Israel and the United States, where three men were charged with violating the American Neutrality Act. Although the indictment alleged that the plotters, two of whom were officials of a small metal trading company, aimed to induce an increase in the price of copper by creating shortages of supply, President Kaunda asserted that their true motivations were political rather than economic.[77]

In April 1967 five Europeans were placed in detention by order of the President under regulations in force for the preservation of public security.[78] Two of them were employed by the mining com-

75. Twenty-five people in all, including two African women, were deported. President Kaunda stated that he had taken care to convince himself that these people endangered the State. Some months later the President admitted that one man had been wrongly deported. He publicly apologised to that individual and welcomed him back to Zambia.

76. See Martin Meredith in the *Zambia News*, 13 November 1966. There had been an instance of major sabotage near Kitwe shortly after the Rhodesian UDI, involving the wreckage of an electrical power pylon on the Kariba line. This crime was never solved. See Hall, *The High Price of Principles*, *op. cit.*, pp. 124–5.

77. Speech of 10 November 1966, ZIS background paper No. 36/66.

78. These regulations have been in effect in parts of northern and eastern Zambia since the Lumpa Church crisis of 1964. The President extended their application to cover the entire country at the time of UDI, and the declaration enabling their enforcement has been renewed by the National Assembly every six months thereafter as required by s. 29 of the constitution of Zambia.

panies and more than 100 expatriate miners took part in brief, unauthorised protest strikes. In June a special tribunal, chaired by a High Court judge, found that four of the detainees were engaged in supplying information to the Rhodesian intelligence service.[79] Feeling that the evidence that would be admissible in a court of law might not result in convictions, the tribunal recommended that the detainees be deported, and this was done. In an introduction to the published report President Kaunda observed that, as a result of UDI, Zambia had been threatened by many hostile acts 'ranging from psychological warfare to actual sabotage'. Shortly thereafter other persons, including a former civil servant, were detained and deported on security grounds. Although reports of attempted sabotage in Zambia have not been frequent, the occasional incidents have been most disquieting. For example, in October 1967 time-bombs were discovered and disarmed at a vital railhead near the Rhodesian border.

Zambia does appear to have acquired a reasonable capacity for counter-intelligence. Yet the reliability of police and military personnel has been a constant preoccupation. In June 1966 President Kaunda suddenly retired seventeen white police officers, including the Inspector General, his deputy and fifteen officers of the Special Branch, on grounds of security. Subsequently he disclosed that it had been necessary to continue to purge the police and army establishments for similar reasons.[80]

*External dangers.* Zambia borders on eight States—namely Malawi, Tanzania, Zaïre, Botswana, Angola, Moçambique, Rhodesia and South West Africa (Namibia), the latter four of which are subject to colonial or white minority rule. In view of her own vulnerability to reprisals, Zambia has prudently shied away from overt belligerency. Official spokesmen have often denied that Zambia is a source of arms and other forms of assistance to guerrillas. Angolan refugees, in particular, have been sternly warned not to stage guerrilla operations in Zambia. In 1967 the residence permit of an Angolan nationalist leader, whose organisation had interfered with rail transport in eastern Angola, was not renewed.[81] Nonetheless, Zambia is a key and devoted member of the OAU

79. *Report of the Tribunal on Detainees, op. cit.*

80. *Times of Zambia,* 1 May 1967.

81. Jonas Savimbi, president of UNITA (National Union for the Total Liberation of Angola). The Portuguese were reported to have delayed Zambian traffic on the Lobito route following guerrilla attacks in eastern Angola that were alleged to have originated in Zambia or the Congo.

Liberation Committee. A Liberation Centre, to which officials of revolutionary groups are posted, is maintained in Lusaka, and freedom fighters, trained and equipped in Tanzania, appear to be accorded transit facilities through Zambian territory. For all her caution, Zambia's geographical position, strong commitment to the cause of liberation, and acceptance of both refugees and active political exiles from neighbouring States make frontier incidents virtually inevitable. Reports indicate that more than 10,000 refugees entered Zambia from Angola and Moçambique between 1965 and 1967, with many more to follow. Incursions by Portuguese troops and military aircraft have also been confirmed. In July 1966 a Zambian village on the Angolan border, was bombarded by Portuguese forces; in March 1968 Portuguese aircraft bombed a few Zambian villages near the Angolan border causing seven reported civilian deaths. Several attacks on Zambian villages near the Moçambique border, and at least one skirmish between Portuguese and Zambian troops in that sector, were also reported in 1968.[82] Furthermore, the sabotage of a vital bridge over the Luangwa river on the Great East Road in June 1968 is suspected to have been an act of retaliation against the intensification of African guerrilla activities in that area.[83]

South African soldiers and policemen have occasionally entered Zambia from the Caprivi Strip, a strategic protrusion of South West African territory that separates Botswana from Angola and Zambia. In August 1967 South African forces were deployed in north-western Rhodesia to assist in operations against an African guerrilla force, mounted by the African National Congress of South Africa–Zimbabwe African People's Union alliance, which had crossed the Zambezi from Zambia. A spate of verbal recriminations followed. Rhodesia warned Zambia against continuing incursions. Zambia denied that she was involved in the provision of arms or material assistance to the freedom fighters. In turn, Zambia remonstrated with Britain against the unpunished invasion of a British 'colony' by South African forces. Britain's response was even-handed. A mild protest was lodged with the South African government, while Zambia was politely admonished to refrain from affording support to guerrillas. Meanwhile, Rhodesian aircraft on re-

82. Legum and Drysdale (eds), *Africa Contemporary Record, op. cit.,* p. 250.

83. Hall, *The High Price of Principles, op. cit.,* p. 249. Douglas Anglin estimates that between 1966 and 1969, there were no fewer than sixty-five 'armed intrusions across Zambia's borders' by Portuguese land or air forces; at least thirteen of these incidents involved loss of life. 'Confrontation in southern Africa', *op. cit.,* p. 513.

connaissance missions intruded into Zambian air space and dropped leaflets intended to discourage the guerrillas. Zambia then protested to Britain against the repeated violation of her territory and air space by the Rhodesians. (On one occasion, in November 1966, Rhodesian soldiers shot and killed a Zambian woman on Zambian territorial waters in the Zambezi river.) President Kaunda also intimated that Zambia would seek military assistance from unspecified 'friends' if it became necessary to do so.

These exchanges reached a climax in October 1967, when Balthazar Vorster, the Prime Minister of South Africa, warned Zambia bluntly: 'If you want to try violence, as you have advised other States in Africa, we will hit you so hard that you will never forget it.' Kaunda replied that Zambia could defend herself. Vorster then said that South Africa desired peaceful relations with Zambia, and the exchanges ceased. When all had been said, Zambians could not mistake the South African build-up in Rhodesia, for which Britain was blamed.

*Strains on security.* Apart from the hazards of UDI, Zambia was fated by her strategic location and mineral wealth to attract big power ideological competition. President Kaunda's doctrine of 'Humanism' is partly intended to blunt the impact of so-called 'foreign ideologies' in Zambia.[84] In the absence of restraints, foreign powers might easily exploit existing social and political tensions, including the grievances of sectarian religious groups[85] and

84. See Kaunda, *Humanism in Zambia and a Guide to its Implementation, op. cit.*

85. Two religious groups have been at odds with the Zambian government. The Lumpa Church, inspired by the prophetess Alice Lenshina, defied the ruling party and clashed violently with government forces in 1963 and 1964. See R. I. Rotberg, 'The Lenshina movement of Northern Rhodesia', *Rhodes-Livingstone Journal*, vol. xxix (1963), pp. 63–78; and Hall, *Zambia, op. cit.*, pp. 229–30. Lenshina was then placed in restriction, but many of her followers, thought to number 65,000 in all, fled to the Congo, where they settled in areas adjacent to Zambia. In 1967 Lenshina escaped from restriction and remained at large for a week. At that time the exiled Lumpa community was reported to number more than 10,000. Its existence was cited by leaders of the Zambian government as one of several security threats which justified the further extension of a declaration of public emergency. *Nat. Ass. Deb.*, Hansard No. 11, 17 October 1967, cols 3–52.

A second group, the Watch Tower Society (Jehovah's Witnesses), has also disturbed the Zambian government by its members' characteristic refusal to permit their children to participate in patriotic school ceremonies involving the national anthem and flag. Government officials have publicly threatened to proscribe the sect, as was done in Malawi in October 1967. In January 1968 the Zambian government deported some thirty non-Zambian leaders of

tribal separatist groups.[86] It would be difficult to imagine a greater threat to Zambia's stability than a major tribal cleavage intensified by rival ideologies.

Until mid-1967 racial tensions were markedly greater than tribal tensions in Zambia. Yet there have been very few serious racial incidents. The only notorious blemishes on Zambia's record in this regard are the Kitwe riot of October 1966, the sacking of a Lusaka butchery by UNIP youths in February 1967, and a riotous demonstration at the High Court in 1969, following a controversial decision involving two unarmed Portuguese soldiers who had been seized in Zambia. It might even be suggested that moderate racial tensions are functional to Zambian unity. To state this bluntly: while Bemba and Lozi compete vigorously with one another in Lusaka, they are both black *vis-à-vis* whites on the Copperbelt.[87] Crude balance-of-power notions, like this one, need not be pressed too far to remind us that cross-pressures do reduce tensions in an ethnically heterogeneous society.

Yet it cannot be denied that the protracted crisis over Rhodesia has threatened to aggravate racial tensions past the point of safety. For one thing, resurgent racialism in southern Africa has been thought to have encouraged the activities of white mercenaries in the Congo. In September 1967 fourteen whites were deported from Zambia on grounds of their alleged connections with mercenaries from the Congo. Secondly, prolonged economic hardships resulting from the Rhodesian impasse might strain the loyalties of certain relatively privileged people, both Zambians and expatriates, with harmful effects on the conduct of government. Thirdly, the prospect of a racial war across the Zambezi river poses special security problems for the Zambian armed services, which rely upon many white

the sect. The total number of Watch Tower adherents in Zambia is thought to exceed 100,000.

86. Lozi separatism was effectively counteracted by UNIP in the period before independence. See Hall, 'The integration of Barotseland', in *Zambia, op. cit.*, pp. 237–42; and Mulford, *Zambia: the Politics of Independence, op. cit., passim*. However, Lozi disaffection within UNIP was apparent during an intra-party struggle over offices in 1967. See Rotberg, 'Tribalism and politics in Zambia', *op. cit.*, pp. 29–35, and pp. 112–15 above. A separatist threat among the Lunda of north-western Zambia was also revealed in 1967 at a treason trial which ended with the acquittal of an opposition Member of Parliament. Lunda people live in adjacent areas of Zambia, Angola and Zaïre. In 1968 President Banda of Malawi attempted to stir separatist sentiment among Nyanja-speaking peoples of eastern Zambia. Legum and Drysdale (eds), *Africa Contemporary Record, op. cit.*, pp. 180, 250.

87. The reader should not, however, infer that intra-African tensions are insignificant on the Copperbelt or that racial tensions are absent from Lusaka. It is a question of degree.

officers and technicians. Fourthly, racial tensions engender a climate of suspicion that is detrimental to the attraction and retention of expatriate skills.[88] Finally, the sustained crisis imposes a great strain on the modest capacity of Zambia's security establishment.

Zambia's army is reported to comprise three battalions of 1,000 men each. There is also a paramilitary mobile police unit of 1,000 men. Until 1970 most of the officers, including the army commander, were seconded from the British army. In 1967 Zambia decided to recruit expatriate officers (mainly British and Irish) on contract, ostensibly to minimise the potential for conflicts of loyalty.[89] Subsequently Zambia terminated her training agreement with the British armed services. However, the air force, so far restricted to non-combatant missions, has continued to rely largely upon RAF personnel. To counter the construction of a South African air base in the Caprivi Strip, and repeated violations of her air space, Zambia has taken steps to acquire a modest missile-type air defence system from British suppliers.

By way of comparison, the Rhodesian army is thought to comprise some 4,000–5,000 regular troops and twice as many fully trained white reservists. It has modern communications equipment and is backed by a small but effective air force, comprising at least two squadrons of fighter planes and one of bombers. Since the guerrilla alert of 1967 South African forces have also been stationed in Rhodesia.

In the period under review, Zambia did not approach the military capacity of her enemies. Military training schemes for the National Youth Service were designed, but not implemented effectively.[90] However, UNIP leaders, including the President, have suggested the introduction of military training for all young Zambians in conjunction with a national service and Home Guard training system. Meanwhile military weakness, in addition to grave

88. Confidence among expatriates is hardly enhanced by this kind of public exhortation by a high government official to members of UNIP on the Copperbelt: 'Act as a watchman and report anybody who speaks ill of the government and its leaders.' In this speech the official also said that 'most of the country's enemies' were on the Copperbelt. He had been pleased when someone reported a white man who had spoken against the government. 'I dealt with this white man,' he said. *Times of Zambia*, 7 May 1966.

89. President Kaunda cited the possibility of armed conflicts between Zambia and Portugal, which, like Britain, is a member of the NATO alliance. *Times of Zambia*, 6 May 1967.

90. A youth training programme with military and land settlement aspects was inaugurated by Israeli instructors in 1966. But the programme faltered on administrative snags and the Israeli mission appears to have been withdrawn.

internal security defects, have been among the chief dictates of caution in the development of Zambia's response to UDI.

## Conclusion

In the world of nations *realpolitik*—the realistic pursuit of one's narrowly defined national interest—is an accepted norm of State behaviour. From the Zambian standpoint, *realpolitik* would imply a 'business as usual' policy towards Rhodesia. At the very most, Zambia might seek to diversify her trade and reduce her dependence upon Rhodesia as rapidly as her means and circumstances would permit. In no wise would Zambia deliberately place her cherished programme of national development in jeopardy.

To a degree, as this study shows, the norm of *realpolitik* has prevailed. Zambia has refrained from extreme measures that might have entailed disastrous results at home without producing the desired effect in Rhodesia. But revolutionary idealism has a powerful claim of its own upon the Zambian government. Nor could that claim be denied without shattering the Zambian government's valued image as an exemplar of fortitude in the African liberation struggle. Zambia has always been willing to accept the economic and military risks of participation in collective action against Rhodesia, if they are realistically designed to dislodge the white minority regime. On the eighth anniversary of the South African Sharpeville massacre, President Kaunda declared, 'Zambia has done what it can to fight for justice. The hardships which we have undergone ever since UDI will not deter us from making further sacrifices *if justice is assured*.'[91]

This mixture of liberationist principle and *realpolitik* displeases the doctrinaire proponent of either persuasion. The pure realist regrets an approach that is costly in terms of the rational allocation of scarce resources in a newly developing country, especially since the sacrifices made by Zambia do not result in corresponding injuries or dangers to the Rhodesian regime. To the ardent liberationist nothing is more painful than the steady entrenchment of white supremacy in Rhodesia. But all Zambians may derive satisfaction from the knowledge that the national effort to which their country is committed will yield a rich harvest of pride, confidence and material progress. One day African nations will negotiate from strength.

91. 'Broadcast speech by His Excellency on the eve of the International Day for the Elimination of Racial Discrimination', ZIS press release No. 520/68, p. 7 (italics added).

# 10

## Conclusion

# Independent Zambia: achievements and prospects

### Robert Molteno and William Tordoff

### Achievements since 1964

The United National Independence Party first participated in the government of Northern Rhodesia in December 1962 in an uneasy coalition with the African National Congress. When the first universal franchise elections were held a year later, UNIP swept to victory, winning fifty-five of the sixty-five main roll seats. At independence in October 1964 its leader, Kenneth Kaunda, became executive President of the new Republic of Zambia. This concluding chapter examines the ways in which President Kaunda and UNIP, who have been in power ever since, have influenced the early destiny of this new State. Relying on a not always happy triumvirate of the private sector, the public sector and the ruling party, President Kaunda's government has built up a remarkable record of achievement, particularly in the early years after independence.

There was rapid economic expansion. The very high price of copper resulted in the economy averaging a 13 per cent annual growth rate in real terms until 1970.[1] The most rapidly growing sector was manufacturing, which almost doubled its output in the same period. Total employment expanded fast, from 268,700 in 1964 to 372,130 by June 1970, although it grew very little in the three years thereafter. Employed workers also enjoyed a considerable rise in their real standard of living. Average annual earnings of Africans rose 97 per cent between 1964 and 1969, while the consumer price index rose only 37 per cent.[2] The economy's performance did deteriorate in the early 1970s, but this was largely due to factors beyond the government's control. Moreover, the position

---

1. *Zambia: Six Years After, op. cit.*
2. *Monthly Digest of Statistics, op. cit.*, tables 4, 5, 14, 49 and 53.

may improve if the unexpectedly high copper prices prevailing early in 1973 are sustained over a long period.[3]

Another major achievement has been the expansion of the country's economic infrastructure. This expansion has taken two directions. In the first place, Zambia responded to Rhodesia's UDI by accelerating measures to reduce the country's inherited dependence on the white-ruled territories to the south. An oil pipeline from Dar es Salaam was completed in 1968; extensive coal deposits within Zambia are now being mined; self-sufficiency in electric power will be achieved by 1974; the Great North and Great East Roads have been tarred; and the Tanzam railway will be completed at the end of 1974. These measures proved so effective that in early 1973 Zambia was not dismayed when the Rhodesian government closed its border with Zambia as an economic reprisal for the support allegedly given by the latter to terrorists operating against Rhodesia. Though copper shipments from Zambia over the Rhodesian railway to Beira were exempted from the ban, Zambia reacted by announcing the permanent diversion of all her external trade to alternative routes. The copper price was thereby given an upward boost (on the assumption that the volume of exports would decline) and imports were curtailed—an outcome not unwelcome in the short term to the Zambian government, which was facing a deteriorating balance-of-payments problem. Secondly, the government has expanded into the rural areas away from the line of rail. An ambitious road construction programme has been undertaken;[4] outlying urban centres have been provided with piped water and electricity, telecommunications links have been improved; mechanical workshops have been created or expanded in provincial and district headquarters; and new services, notably credit and marketing, have been extended to the rural areas.

Another important development in the economic sphere has been the localisation of manpower. Overall, the proportion of non-African (almost synonymous with non-citizen) workers fell from 12 per cent in 1964 to 7 per cent in 1970,[5] although thereafter the rate of decline became much slower. In the civil service Zambianisation is almost complete in the administrative cadres, but inevitably less progress has been made in localising secondary school teachers and the professional/technical levels of departments. In the key sector of the mines, the number of Zambians in the field of

3. The LME price of copper exceeded K1,050 per ton at the beginning of March 1973.

4. See *Times of Zambia*, 26 March 1971.

5. *Monthly Digest of Statistics, op. cit.*, table 4.

expatriate employment has risen from a total of 704 in December 1964 to a projected 4,661 in December 1970, thereby permitting a 50 per cent reduction in the size of the expatriate work force over the same period.[6] The overall progress is all the more remarkable given the lack of educated Zambians at independence and the subsequent growth of total employment.

In the long term the most significant economic changes have been in the field of ownership. Beginning with the Mulungushi economic reforms of 19 April 1968, and carried further by the Matero reforms of 11 August 1969 and the additional reforms of 10 November 1970, President Kaunda has laid the foundation for a basic restructuring of the Zambian economy. The overall goal has been to increase local control over an economy which at independence was completely dominated by foreigners at the ownership and managerial levels. Even as late as 1968 only 15 per cent of bank credit was channelled to the Zambian citizen sector.[7] A parallel aim was to ensure that a larger proportion of the gross national product remained in the country. Each stage of the reforms set about achieving its goals along two paths. First, the government invited large firms to accept State participation on a 51 per cent shareholding basis, usually with the original firm receiving a management contract and costly compensation. In 1968 twenty-six large firms in the construction sector, commerce, road transport and one or two other fields were taken over. In 1969 the reforms assumed a new magnitude with the take-over of the mining companies. In 1970 they were extended to the financial sector— the insurance companies and building societies, but excluding the banks, which successfully resisted being taken over.[8] These measures, together with the new manufacturing ventures of the Industrial Development Corporation (Indeco), have given government ultimate control over all major sectors of the economy, with the exception of large-scale commercial agriculture and the banks. Of course, the management contracts usually given to the companies being taken over, together with the continuing acute shortage of local managerial and professional manpower, may in the short run reduce the reality of public control.

The second leg of the economic reforms has been a series of

6. *The Progress of Zambianisation in the Mining Industry* (Lusaka, December 1968), p. 9.

7. Minister of Finance, ZIS press release No. 17/70, 30 January 1970.

8. Kaunda, *Zambia: towards Economic Independence, op. cit.*, pp. 35 ff; *Towards Complete Independence, op. cit.*, pp. 29 ff; *Take up the Challenge, op. cit.*, pp. 64 ff.

measures to increase participation of Zambians in the remaining private sector. In 1968 curbs were put on the right of resident expatriate enterprises to borrow money locally, in the hope that more credit would be made available to citizens. Foreigners were also excluded from the retail trade outside the centres of ten major urban areas, and they were not to be granted any additional trading licences even in those areas. Restrictions were also placed on them in the fields of transport, while building material permits, as well as Public Works Department contracts worth κ100,000 or less, were in the future to be given only to Zambians. These measures were taken further in 1969, when foreigners' participation in the wholesale trade was restricted to the ten major urban centres and the eight provincial headquarters. In 1970 came the announcement of the most dramatic extension of this policy. From 1 January 1972 no foreigner has been able to get a retail or wholesale licence anywhere in the country; and existing licences to retail prescribed goods as well as existing transport licences and building material permits have been cancelled.[9] While Zambia remains a predominantly capitalist economy, these reforms have greatly increased the participation of, and control by, the State, and have created massive new opportunities for citizen entrepreneurs. The problem remains that many of the latter are non-Africans, although the Financial Development Corporation (Findeco) has helped finance African businessmen to some extent.

In its social policy the government has made equally significant strides both by removing those elements of institutionalised and overt racism which remained from the settler past and by progressing towards a Welfare State. Not only has the range of State-provided social services been expanded, but the scale of social services has also grown enormously.[10] To give only the most dramatic example, education expenditure rose from κ13 million in 1963–64 to κ85 million in 1973. Primary school enrolment doubled in the eight years following independence, and secondary, technical and university education expanded even faster. Indeed, the only criticism of substance that can be made is that the government has pursued its priority of free and near-universal social services at the expense of investment in more directly productive, job-generating sectors.

9. *Zambia: towards Economic Independence, op. cit.*, pp. 25–31; *Towards Complete Independence, op. cit.*, p. 9; *Take up the Challenge, op. cit.*, pp. 59–60.

10. *Zambia: a Picture Progress Report on the First Four Years of Zambian Independence, 1964–68* (Lusaka, 1968), p. 31; and *Zambia: Six Years After, op. cit.*, p. 11.

On the political front there have also been successes. Until December 1972, when the constitution was amended to allow a phased transition to a one-party State, Zambia practised democracy on the multi-party model. New opposition parties were formed and, together with the ANC, contested with UNIP elections for local authorities, the National Assembly and the presidency. UNIP has accepted its rare defeats in elections, which since 1968 have been supervised by an independent and impartial commission presided over by a judge. In various voluntary associations, such as trade unions and UNIP itself, there have also been frequent electoral contests at all levels.

However, in the political sphere UNIP remained in principle committed to the virtues of a one-party State. For President Kaunda, the fact that any other party existed was 'a confession of failure and challenge. The work of evangelism has not been done well. There are still people who do not trust the party to understand its ideas.' Until 1972, however, Kaunda rejected a legalised one-party system in favour of trying to destroy rival parties only at the polls.[11] Certain UNIP activists at various levels did not fully accept this position and used violence to prevent ANC candidates being nominated and receiving electoral support. There was also considerable discrimination against ANC supporters in the granting of agricultural loans and trading licences.[12] Several opposition leaders were prosecuted, albeit usually unsuccessfully. Their freedom was further limited to some extent both inside and outside the National Assembly. Multi-party competition clearly did not attain legitimacy during the First Zambian Republic (1964–72), but it remains to be seen whether or not individual competition for office will suffer the same fate under the Second Republic's one-party constitution. That constitution was enacted in August 1973 and followed closely Government Paper No. 1 of 1972, in which the government gave its somewhat negative reaction to the far-reaching proposals of the National Commission on the Establishment of a One-party Participatory Democracy in Zambia. The commission's report laid the basis for widespread popular participation and electoral competition; a more powerful and active National Assembly; an executive reflecting the principles of collective leadership and limited government; an independent judiciary; and a wide-ranging Ombudsman to protect the individual against party and government. It also sought to reform the ruling party extensively

11. K. D. Kaunda, *Ten Thoughts on Humanism* (Kitwe, 1970), p. 5.
12. See chapter 5, and *Report of . . . the Affairs of the Lusaka City Council, op. cit.*, pp. 6 and 18.

and recommended subjecting both political and bureaucratic leaders to a stringent code of leadership. However, the Cabinet and central committee seriously modified or rejected most of the commission's main proposals,[13] and within a month introduced legislation ending the existence of the opposition ANC.[14] ANC Members were allowed to remain sitting in the Assembly until Parliament was dissolved in October 1973.

Turning to the judiciary, it has remained independent of the executive, thus fulfilling the pledge given by Dr Kaunda when still Prime Minister in March 1964.[15] Although for the first five and a half years of independence the Bench was composed only of whites, not all of whom were even Zambian citizens, there was significant tension between the judiciary and the executive on only two occasions. In 1967 the President freed a UNIP youth leader who had been gaoled for criminal contempt. The judges were resentful and were reassured only after a meeting with Dr Kaunda.[16] The second clash was less amicably settled. In July 1969 Mr Justice Evans, in releasing two Portuguese soldiers who had been arrested by Zambian immigration officials for illegal entry, set in motion a train of events which led to a public clash between the President and the newly appointed Chief Justice (Mr J. Skinner, formerly the only European UNIP member to be a Cabinet Minister) and the ransacking of the High Court by the Zambia Youth Service. Although the President reaffirmed the independence of the judiciary, the Chief Justice resigned[17] and the constitution was amended to enable relatively inexperienced (in effect, African) lawyers to be appointed as judges.[18] The gradual Africanisation of the Bench began early in 1970.

The continuing independence of the judiciary is most clearly demonstrated by the willingness, in almost every case, of the executive to allow the prosecution of UNIP office-holders both for offences arising out of political activities, usually at election time, and for ordinary criminal offences. The verdicts of the courts have been respected; the only partial qualification to this was President

13. *Report of the National Commission on . . . a One-party Participatory Democracy*, op. cit., *passim*, and Government Paper No. 1 of 1972, op. cit., *passim*.

14. The Constitution (Amendment) (No. 5) Act, 1972.

15. *Leg. Co. Deb.*, 20 March 1964, col. 420.

16. Rotberg, 'Tribalism and Politics in Zambia', op. cit., and Mubako, *The Presidential System*, op. cit., p. 401.

17. *Times of Zambia*, 15 July 1969; Mubako, *ibid.*, pp. 401 ff.; Roberts, 'White Judges Under Attack', op. cit.

18. The Constitution (Amendment) (No. 5) Act, 1969, s. 12.

Kaunda's use of his prerogative of mercy to declare, in celebration of the fifth anniversary of independence (24 October 1969), a general amnesty of all prisoners gaoled for offences arising out of political activities.

Individual liberties were by and large respected during the First Republic in spite of the tensions in society and within the ruling party, as well as the external threat posed by Zambia's white minority-ruled neighbours. However, a number of points need to be made. While the constitution of Zambia (sections 14 to 25) guarantees a range of civil rights,[19] the effectiveness of these guarantees is limited by the widely drawn qualifications to them written into the constitution itself. Moreover, in the few cases where acts of the executive have been challenged,[20] the courts have tended to be cautious about restricting the State's freedom of action.[21] The very extensive security powers of the executive are a further limitation, although they were used with restraint until the rise of significant opposition to UNIP in the form of UPP in 1971. While one political party (the UP, in August 1968) had been banned *in toto* before this, the UPP was banned in February 1972 and all opposition parties outlawed with the creation of a one-party State in December of that year. Similarly, while very few people were detained in prison without trial or restricted to a particular area before 1971, large numbers were detained, and some ill-treated while under detention, from late 1971 onwards. As to the press in Zambia, this has remained free, although even the privately owned *Times of Zambia* (one of the country's two dailies) has its editor appointed by the President, is pro-UNIP and is never directly critical of the President. Again, freedom of debate has prevailed in the National Assembly. Vigorous criticism of government came from NPP and ANC Members during the first Parliament, and increasingly during the second Parliament from UNIP back-benchers and the Western Province wing of ANC.[22] While some voluntary associations were closed down in 1972, others have remained independent of the ruling party. Trade union leaders, in particular, have publicly

19. Only one of these rights (section 18, relating to property rights) has been amended to restrict its ambit and thereby facilitate the carrying through of the Matero economic reforms.

20. The main cases are: *Chilufya* v. *City Council of Kitwe* (1967), 9 S.J.Z. bb; *Attorney General* v. *Thixton* (1967), 1 S.J.Z. 1; *Kachasu* v. *Attorney General* (1967), H.P./273; *Patel* v. *Attorney General* (No. 1) (1968), 33 S.J.Z. 111 (H.C.); and *Patel* v. *Attorney General* (No. 2) (1969), Court/Ref./ H.P./8.

21. Mubako, *The Presidential System, op. cit.*, pp. 442 and 488.

22. See chapter 6.

resisted UNIP interference in industrial disputes and have frequently exercised their right to call strikes.

In practice, the most serious limitations on liberty in the early years after independence were not the actions of the executive but the pressure (including violence) which UNIP party workers sometimes exerted against supporters of the ANC and the other opposition parties, as well as members of the Watch Tower sect who refused to vote UNIP in the general election of December 1968 and the referendum of June 1969. Violence also erupted very occasionally inside UNIP itself; four Ministers—Sipalo, Musakanya, Mwananshiku and Siyomunji—have been assaulted by UNIP members since 1964. Nonetheless, Zambia has remained a fairly free society. The reasons include the usually non-coercive style of President Kaunda's leadership, the composition of the Bench, which has ensured its commitment to liberty, and a strong trade union movement with a long tradition of autonomy.[23]

A different but major political achievement has been the success with which President Kaunda and certain of his lieutenants in UNIP have largely contained sectional tensions within the party and society. These have grown to very serious proportions since 1964 and are continuing to grow.[24] Nevertheless, despite the creation of UP in 1968 and UPP in 1971 (both with sectional bases of support) the State and the ruling party have (by and large) held together—a remarkable achievement in tension management for a State as new as Zambia, as lacking in national integration, and as subject to serious fragmentary forces.

But in the long term the most important political achievement may prove to be the process, initiated and sustained by President Kaunda, of redefining the dominant values of Zambian society and rebuilding its institutions to embody those values. The transfer of political power which took place at independence, while important in itself, also created a precondition for even more important possibilities: the achievement of greater economic independence, and of cultural and institutional change. Such change was particularly urgent, in view of Zambia's previous domination by white settlers. The focus of the President's philosophy of Humanism, which was first enunciated in 1967, is on the importance of each individual human being as an end in himself; his welfare must never be overridden in the pursuit of some collective goal. From the importance of the individual flows his right to participate in controlling not

23. Epstein, *Politics in an Urban African Community, op. cit.*, chapters 4 and 5.
24. See chapters 3 and 4, and pp. 382–3 below.

merely the State but all associations affecting his environment (hence party, trade union, company and village democracy). The State is obliged, as are political leaders and other institutions, to serve the interests of ordinary workers and villagers. The economic system must exist to benefit primarily the citizens of the country and, within the country, the State must limit exploitation. The humanist's assertion of the importance of every man leads on to a belief in non-racialism and non-violence, and a desire to avoid sectional and class conflict. This absence of conflict in turn enables stress to be placed on communal co-operation for economic development, social betterment and national security. Finally, Zambian Humanism argues the right of every nation to create autochthonous institutions at home and to pursue independent non-aligned policies abroad.

The institutionalisation of these basic values of Zambian Humanism has already been taken some way. Democratic forms have been preserved and local control over the economy increased, while some social inequalities have been removed. Steps have also been taken to bridge the rural–urban gap. But the importance of Humanism is not just that it has provided the guidelines within which improvements in the quality of life may take place. Humanism has also led Zambians to begin questioning themselves about the kind of society they want. Indeed, as we show below, the growing controversy which may well attend the further institutionalisation of Humanism is likely to become a key characteristic of Zambian politics.

These very considerable achievements have involved a rapid growth in the size and role of the public sector. The civil service has grown from 22,000 in 1963 to about 54,000 in 1971, and is responsible for greatly increased capital expenditure.[25] Many new parastatal bodies have also been set up. The government ultimately determines the capital programmes of the State-controlled firms which now dominate the economy. It also intervenes in the private sector in ever more numerous ways: helping to settle labour disputes, controlling prices and wages, determining import routes, pressing for Zambianisation, reshaping worker–management relations, and so on. It has assumed a growing burden of social services. These and other changes reflect a clear shift in emphasis in the basic philosophy of the role of government in society. Whereas the colonial government's approach was relatively *laissez-faire*, except

25. Establishment registers, 1963–64 and 1971 (Lusaka); *Monthly Digest of Statistics, op. cit.*, tables 29 and 30. Capital spending, however, has declined sharply since 1970.

where its action was required to entrench the racial privileges of whites, today government's approach is more generally interventionist and activist.

The reason for this change is obvious. UNIP came to power on the support of a very poor black population, subject not merely to foreign rule but to local white settler domination and exploitation. Africans had been excluded from most skilled occupations and from participation in the modern economy at capital-owning and managerial levels; and they had been grossly underpaid in relation to Europeans, who enjoyed far superior public services. From January 1964 UNIP used its newly captured power over the State to redress the economic situation in favour of the African majority. Its policies—for example, on taxation, manpower localisation, and licensing—benefited its own supporters but hit the wealthy European and Asian communities hard.[26] This process was made easier by the refusal of most Europeans and Asians in 1964 to take advantage of the offer of Zambian citizenship; many of those who did so have prospered greatly.

Since independence UNIP has retained considerable vigour compared with ruling parties elsewhere in Africa, such as KANU in Kenya, the former CPP in Ghana and UPC in Uganda.[27] It has been able to finance itself, even if sometimes with difficulty, through rent from building investments, participation in a large construction company, massive membership card sales, and periodic requisitions from businessmen (especially Asians). It has not milked the State in the way that the CPP did in Ghana, or, like TANU in Tanzania, sought refuge in a government subvention to maintain its full-time cadres of three officials in each of the fifty-three regions, a small headquarters staff in Lusaka, and drivers and office orderlies. Moreover, in many areas UNIP has maintained a well articulated structure extending from national to regional, constituency, branch and village levels. And, despite the disruption caused by the crises of August 1967, August 1969, and August 1971, its various organs have continued to meet at frequent intervals.

An important dimension of the vigour of UNIP has been the increasing domination by politicians of the rest of society. This is reflected in the growing importance of the public sector, and in the increasingly close control of government agencies exercised by UNIP politicians at all levels. They have not been content with

26. Europeans: 43,390 in 1969; 74,549 in 1961. Asians: 10,785 in 1969; 7,790 in 1961. *Zambia Six Years After, op. cit.*, p. 8.

27. KANU: Kenya African National Union; CPP: Convention People's Party; UPC: Uganda People's Congress.

laying down broad lines of policy for public officers to execute.
Despite the complaints of public officers, politicians have busied
themselves with a host of minutiae: the recruitment of personnel
and their political reliability, the location of projects, and the
granting of loans to Zambian farmers and businessmen.[28] UNIP
members have also been recruited on a large scale to certain civil
service posts, the police, and parastatal bodies like the Credit
Organisation of Zambia.[29]

UNIP activists have expanded their roles in society in a multitude
of directions. All sorts of matters now come within the competence
of District Governors and junior party officials. As one District
Governor put it, people 'will bring to us all kinds of problems—
including their domestic squabbles. We are supposed to settle everything.'[30] They often settle labour disputes; attempt to control prices;
and try to mobilise villagers for economic development. Clearly,
the boundaries between the traditional sphere of politics and other
sub-systems in society have both moved in favour of the former and
become blurred.

There are several reasons for the continuing vigour of UNIP.
One was the electoral challenge posed by the ANC; a second has
been the importance which President Kaunda has attached to the
party as 'the principal tool' for consolidating 'the revolution in the
interests of the common man'.[31] He has devoted considerable time
to party matters, and works from time to time at the party headquarters. The party has also served as an avenue for the upward
mobility of party activists. In the latter's view, it must continue to
do so, especially since, as Mr Kaushi (MP for Samfya) explained,
'... some of the freedom fighters in branch constituencies, regional
leaders, have not even enjoyed the fruits of this Independence. . . .
They should enjoy the fruits of this Government because they
suffered for it.'[32] The feeling in the party is widespread that loyal
service can, and should, be rewarded. There is, in fact, a clear ladder
of promotion from part-time constituency official to full-time
regional official, and thereafter to MP, District Governor, and even
ministerial office. Equally important, faithful service to the party,
even at the lowest level, has frequently been rewarded with jobs in
the civil service or certain parastatal bodies like the Zambia Youth
Service (now the Zambia National Service since 1971). Thus the

28. There have been complaints of both political discrimination and
political favouritism even in this field. *Zambia Daily Mail*, 6 April 1971.

29. *Daily Parl. Deb.*, No. 21bb, 17 March 1970, col. 2066.

30. *Times of Zambia*, 27 March 1971.

31. ZIS background paper No. 84/68, 9 November 1968, p. 11.

32. *Daily Parl. Deb.*, No. 25e, 22 January 1971, col. 248.

latter recruited many of its members from the UNIP Youth
Brigade. It is perhaps this factor of reward which accounts for the
readiness of so many people to continue working for the party,
and in part explains their reluctance in 1971–72 to transfer their
allegiance to the UPP.

An important consequence of the vigour which UNIP has maintained since independence is that government has remained responsive to popular demands and group interests. While the party has
assumed (not always very effectively) the new role of explaining
government policies to the people, it has continued to be the major
forum for the articulation of local level interests and their communication to government. The party's responsiveness explains the
fairly high level of consent which UNIP managed to maintain
during its first decade in power. This is reflected in table 10.1,
which portrays UNIP's political mobilisation capacity over time
and by area.

*Table 10.1*
UNIP's electoral performance since 1964

|  | General election, January 1964[a] | General election, December 1968[a] | Referendum, June 1969[b] |
|---|---|---|---|
| Population | 3,490,540 | 4,000,000 (approx.) | 4,056,995 |
| Registered electorate | 1,379,804 | 1,587,966 | 1,584,574 |
| Percentage of registered electorate voting UNIP: | | | |
| Nation-wide | 65·1 | 56·4 | 50·3 |
| Urban seats | 79·0 | 73·9 | 65·6 |
| Rural seats | 58·4 | 47·5 | 40·4 |

*Notes*

a  Uncontested seats are omitted and the extent of support for UNIP is
   therefore understated.

b  The 1969 figures relate only to constituencies contested in December
   1968; the figures for 1968 and 1969 are thus exactly comparable.

*Source.* From electoral statistics compiled by Mr R. A. Young.

UNIP's capacity to mobilise electoral support varies significantly
from area to area. Its greatest strength is in the towns, particularly
the Copperbelt; ANC won only seven out of 274 urban wards in
the 1970 local authority elections. The most interesting area of

weakness, apart from the former ANC's strongholds in Southern, most of Western, and parts of Central Province, has been North-western Province, where UNIP has been extremely weak, despite the failure of ANC to penetrate the area. The backbone of UNIP remains the Copperbelt and Northern, Luapula and Eastern Provinces.

## Problems of load and capacity

In spite of the achievements of the UNIP government since 1964 and the considerable support the party retains, it has been clear since at least early 1971 that the Zambian political and governmental system faces a basic difficulty: the load on it continues to rise at a time when its capacity to carry that load is weakening.

The attainment of independence itself imposed two new loads on government: the conduct of foreign affairs and defence. The burden created by these new loads has risen since 1964. For example, Zambia has expanded her diplomatic contacts within Africa, in the West, and with various communist States. And she has been diplomatically active, particularly on east and southern African issues. The defence load has also increased since the start of guerrilla warfare in Moçambique in 1964 and its escalation in eastern Angola from 1967. Zambia is unique in that she is the only African State to share borders with all the white minority-ruled States in southern Africa. They have subjected her to various forms of pressure: diplomatic, economic and military.[33] The early 1970s saw a significant escalation of these pressures on Zambia, including Rhodesia's attempt in January 1973 to deny Zambia access to the sea by closing the border. These trends forced a rapid and costly upgrading of the Zambia Defence Force after 1969.

Meeting aspirations aroused by the independence struggle has also increased the load on the system by raising the volume of demand inputs. UNIP activists wanted jobs as a reward for services rendered; villagers expected government to improve their lot; and everybody wanted more social services. The government's success in meeting these demands has not led to any slackening, nor is it likely to do so, since the population is growing at the rate of 2·5 per cent each year and 46 per cent of the people are 14 years and under.[34]

Another socio-demographic problem has been the unprecedented

33. Hall, *The High Price of Principles, op. cit.*, and R. V. Molteno, 'National security and institutional stability' (forthcoming).

34. ZIS press release No. 66/70, 7 September 1970.

movement of villagers to towns. Between 1963 and 1969 the population of Lusaka, Kabwe and Copperbelt urban districts rose by 60
per cent—from 740,000 to 1,183,000.[35] Urban growth has averaged
8 per cent a year, posing new problems for the government: huge
slums, rising crime rates, escalating demands for housing services
and jobs.

There have been other increasing loads. Government has tried
to accelerate economic development by stepping up its own capital
spending sevenfold between 1964 and 1970. Consequent problems
of inflation have had to be dealt with. The economic take-overs
since 1968 have also imposed new demands. They have increased
enormously the decision-making responsibility of the public sector
as a whole. And they have led to the setting up of two new parastatal bodies (Mindeco and Findeco) and a vast expansion of the
existing Indeco. These in turn have detached from the civil service
scarce top-level manpower.

At the same time, the capacity of the political and governmental
system to meet these ever-rising loads was already being reduced by
1971 and is likely to be reduced further. In the first place, in 1971
UNIP was operating in a very different historical context from 1964.
At independence it embodied the prestige of a successful freedom
struggle and could be judged only by the lack-lustre record of the
settler-dominated administrations which had preceded it. It had
clear policy objectives. Various features of the economy facilitated
the achievement of its goals, including the industrialisation opportunities created by the end of the Central African Federation in
December 1963, the rising copper price, the withdrawal of many
whites round about independence and the consequent opening up of
more jobs, and the opportunity for a much stiffer tax system. But
today the party's position is very different. It has been in power for
nine years. In that time there have been both serious policy failures
and actions by the party and government which have excited criticism. In foreign policy, for reasons beyond the government's control,
Mr Smith's regime is still in power in Rhodesia. The Portuguese
remain entrenched throughout most of their colonial territories.
South Africa has been increasingly successful in obtaining sophisticated arms supplies, and in penetrating both the white-ruled and
several of the black-ruled States of Africa economically and politically.[36] Zambia is more isolated than before in her courageous
stand against these white-minority-ruled regimes.

At home the government saw problems developing in the

35. *Monthly Digest, op. cit.*, table 1.
36. Molteno, 'South Africa's forward policy in Africa', *op. cit.*

economy after 1964, especially the spiralling of wages, the rising
cost of living, and the growing urban–rural income gap. But it
did not take adequate counter-measures, at least until 1969.[37] The
biggest domestic disappointment has been rural development,
especially in the five provinces off the line of rail. With the exception
only of cotton, sugar and poultry, most agricultural production has
stagnated or fallen. Between 1964 and 1969 food imports jumped
from K14·3 million to K30·4 million, which is nearly twice the value
of marketed domestic agricultural production.[38] Government's
attempts during the first National Development Plan to accelerate
rural development were partly frustrated by the inability of the
backward areas to absorb rapidly rising capital inputs.[39] Specific
strategies to raise output also failed. The producer co-operatives
launched without adequate preparation in 1965 did not reverse
this trend, and many are now defunct.[40] The tens of millions of
kwacha distributed annually to villagers in the form of Credit
Organisation loans have by and large not been repaid, nor have
they had any impact on agricultural output.[41] Village self-help
projects, which were launched with high hopes shortly after independence in order to build rural clinics and primary schools, have
mostly petered out. The ambitious and expensive tractor mechanisation scheme has also failed. The result is that the cash incomes of
Zambia's rural population today are probably no larger than they
were at independence, and the average farmer is probably only
half as well off in 1973 in relation to the urban worker as he was in
1964.[42] Another economic problem is that the restructuring of the
economy has not yet gone far enough to escape from its almost total
reliance on copper; or to place most of the economy effectively in
Zambian hands—whether public or private; or to give urban
workers a sense that they control their own destiny.

Another consequence of the years in power is that the UNIP
government has incurred popular criticism for certain of its actions.
It spent K7·8 million on a prestige hall and housing for the Non-

37. See President Kaunda's speech before the second Kitwe National
Convention: ZIS background paper No. 91/69, 12 December 1969.

38. *Monthly Digest, op. cit.*, table 19.

39. President Kaunda's address to the National Assembly, *Daily Parl. Deb.*,
No. 25a, 8 January 1971, col. 15.

40. The failure of the co-operatives' drive was tacitly admitted by the
introduction of new legislation, the Co-operative Societies Bill, in December
1970.

41. Elliott *et al., Some Determinants of Agricultural Labour Productivity,*
*op. cit.*

42. *Zambia: Six Years After, op. cit.*, p. 53.

aligned Summit Conference in 1970[43] at a time when the national housing shortage was acute. It made more of the lower income groups liable for income tax in the 1969 budget, and limited wage increases to 5 per cent in 1970. The economic reforms of April 1968 and subsequent years also ran into various difficulties: several hundred of the 850 foreign-owned shops were closed prematurely, and not enough government loans were available to finance new Zambian businessmen in taking over all foreign-owned enterprises.[44] The trade unions have also frequently resented interference by UNIP politicians in industrial disputes and intra-union affairs.

The result of many years in power is that more and more people now feel ready to criticise the party and government both secretly and in public. 1970 saw a large number of anonymous circulars attacking President Kaunda's government. Editorials in the only independent daily, the *Times of Zambia*, became so critical of government inefficiency and the behaviour of UNIP politicians[45] that President Kaunda removed its editor in 1972. Certain Church and trade union leaders also began to criticise UNIP's leadership.[46]

It seems clear also that there has been a fall in the popular standing of many major UNIP leaders. The reasons go deeper than the much publicised in-fighting within the ruling party. The years following the 1968 general election saw a succession of criminal prosecutions against certain Ministers, and the dismissal of four others for alleged corruption and of two more for sectional politicking.[47] These events tarnished the image of a party dedicated to the principles of Humanism. In addition, the rough handling of opposition parties, the creation of a one-party State by legislation, and the rejection of free electoral competition as proposed by the Chona Commission created the impression that the existing political elite was more preoccupied with its own survival in power than with the welfare of the mass of the population.

Indeed, as early as 1971 several UNIP politicians had themselves become aware of this. One Minister of State went so far as to call for the phasing out of certain old-guard leaders.[48] This was a view

43. See the criticism by Mrs Robertson (UNIP nominated MP) of this expenditure. *Daily Parl. Deb.*, No. 25b, 19 January 1971, col. 69.

44. *Times of Zambia*, 1 January 1968; *Daily Parl. Deb.*, No. 25e, 22 January 1971, col. 242.

45. See, for instance, the editorial in the *Times of Zambia* of 15 April 1971, criticising UNIP for its card-checking campaigns.

46. *Ibid.*, 5 April 1971.

47. ZIS press release No. 82/70, 9 November 1970; *Report . . . into the allegations made by Mr Justin Chimba and Mr John Chisata, op. cit.*

48. *Daily Parl. Deb.*, No. 25b, 19 January 1971, col. 55.

shared by one or two more senior Ministers, as well as by informal groups which sprang up in the party in 1969 and 1970. In Eastern Province they wanted to oust many of the existing MPs and Ministers, and in Luapula they alleged that UNIP Members were doing nothing for the people.[49] In recent years Lusaka-based UNIP leaders have also been accused of promoting sectionalism in the country.

But the inevitable dross which the government has accumulated during its years in power is not the major reason for its reduced capacity to meet rising loads. The economic resources available to it in the early 1970s were considerably less than in the late 1960s. Foreign exchange, government revenue, and the general level of economic activity in Zambia are peculiarly dependent on the output and price of copper. Between 1963 and 1970 the price rose more or less steadily, but then fell dramatically to a level which was only marginally higher than the price in 1964.[50] Since there has been no significant diversification away from copper (in 1965 42 per cent of the gross domestic product was generated by mining, as against 39 per cent in 1968) the government was faced from 1971 with a huge drop in revenue, exacerbated temporarily by the simultaneous fall in physical output due to the massive cave-in disaster at Mufulira mine in September 1970. The use of foreign exchange revenue, which reached an all-time high in 1970, forestalled an immediate cut-back in government spending. But a low copper price persisted, and government was forced to choose between cutting either its recurrent or its capital spending. It chose the latter course. Indeed, since 1968 it has preferred to avoid the immediate dissatisfaction which a curtailment of the current level of services would cause by allowing recurrent expenditure to rise while cutting capital spending. But this policy has slowed down the rate of economic growth and so reduced the government's long-term capacity to meet demands for more jobs and higher standards of living. There is a second factor which has reduced the economic resources available to meet the load on the political system. As President Kaunda has admitted, the private sector has experienced a hostile atmosphere since independence.[51] Government has by and

49. *Sunday Times of Zambia*, 3 January 1971; *Daily Parl. Deb.*, No. 25c, 20 January 1971, col. 140.

50. *Monthly Digest, op. cit.*, tables 18, 20, 29, 52, 55; and Mindeco, *Prospects for Zambia's Mining Industry* (Lusaka, 1970), p. 6. However, as we have noted, the price of copper rose sharply early in 1973.

51. President Kaunda's address to the first National Convention, *National Convention on the Four-year Development Plan, op. cit.*, pp. 8 and 9.

large neglected even to consult the private sector, for example in drawing up the first National Development Plan. This was particularly true of the large-scale and mostly expatriate farming and commercial communities. The annual budget has imposed increasingly heavy tax burdens on the private sector and failed at the same time to use fiscal measures to encourage new investment. The most blatant case was the tax formula for the mines, which positively discouraged expansion and which was not scrapped until April 1970.[52] Government has also been ham-handed in its handling of the private sector in other ways.[53] In particular, the expanding network of often inefficient and unsympathetic bureaucratic control has depressed morale and throttled initiative within a sector on which the government still relies heavily for the achievement of its growth targets.

But the most basic factor which has shaken the confidence of private investors has been the trend of government economic policy since the first economic reforms of April 1968. There has been no certainty on three fundamental points: what limits, if any, the philosophy of Humanism puts to the process of State take-overs of private firms; how fast and in what fields the policy of protecting citizen entrepreneurs against established foreign competition will be pursued; and whether foreigners who wish to take out Zambian citizenship will be allowed to do so, and if not, to what extent and for how long there is a role for them in the economy. Moreover, the government's promise in April 1968 of a Foreign Investments Protection Act has never been fulfilled,[54] putting Zambia at a disadvantage as compared with certain nearby States such as Kenya. The inevitable result of this uncertainty is that the still foreign-dominated private sector is reluctant to invest, particularly in long-term projects. To take one important example, the mining companies chose to distribute over 80 per cent of their net profits as dividends.[55] It is not surprising, therefore, that the response to the Mulungushi economic reforms was an immediate downturn in the private sector. The index of manufacturing production, which had risen fast between 1964 and 1968, fell in 1969.[56] There was an immediate drop in private sector employment, which had scarcely recovered two years later. Indeed, ever since 1968 private investment has remained at a

52. *Prospects for Zambia's Mining Industry, op. cit.*, pp. 3 and 16.
53. *Zambia Daily Mail*, 13 April 1971.
54. Kaunda, *Zambia: towards Economic Independence, op. cit.*, p. 45.
55. *Ibid.*
56. *Monthly Digest, op. cit.*, table 14.

depressed level, and the non-copper sectors of the economy have shown very little growth.[57]

By reducing employment, tax revenue and the rate of economic growth, this slow-down lowers the political system's capacity to meet demands. The results have been rising industrial unrest. The number of man days lost owing to strikes rose from 65,900 in 1968 to 125,317 in 1970.[58] Significantly, following its formation in August 1971, the weight of the UPP's appeal was directed to the Copperbelt.

Indeed, a further dimension of the political system's reduced capacity to carry its rising load is that the administrative and political structures which are essential to convert demand and resource inputs into outputs are proving increasingly feeble. By 1971 Zambia had both a public service and a ruling party which exhibited grave and growing weaknesses, and in 1973 it remained an open question whether the formal institutional changes to a one-party State would have any significant and progressive impact on the performance of either of them.

The level of efficiency of public agencies in Zambia clearly varies. The small rural councils are far less efficient than the large urban local authorities, while certain parastatal bodies are also less efficient than others. The Credit Organisation of Zambia, after several enquiries, had to be wound up in 1970. Zambia Railways, with only just over 650 miles of track, suffered an appalling accident rate after the break-up of Rhodesia Railways in 1967; some 80 per cent of these accidents were attributed to human error, in particular inexperience, carelessness and drunkenness.[59] Various civil service departments have also gained a reputation for exceptional inefficiency.[60]

The kinds and causes of inefficiency have been analysed in chapter 7. They pervade the processes of planning, financial control, personnel management and general implementation. Many individual civil servants are, of course, both conscientious and capable.

57. Minister of Finance, *Daily Parl. Deb.*, No. 25i, 29 January 1971, especially col. 493.

58. Owing to a presidential ban on strikes in August 1969, only 21,000 man-days were lost in that year. *Daily Parl. Deb.*, No. 25i, 29 January 1971, col. 506.

59. ZIS background paper No. 32/70; *Zambia Mail*, 28 April 1970.

60. See the Minister of Power, Transport and Works' criticism of rude telephone operators (ZIS press release No. 16/70, 11 February 1970), and UNIP MPs' criticism of inefficiency in the General Post Office (*Daily Parl. Deb.*, 25b, 19 January 1971, col. 65; 25c, 20 January 1971, col. 135; 25f, 26 January 1971, col. 305).

And various piecemeal reforms have been undertaken, notably the decentralisation reforms of 1969. It remains true, however, that individual officers who are efficient are severely hampered by the general bureaucratic environment; piecemeal reforms have had little impact; and no overall commission of enquiry into the machinery of government has been held since independence. Consequently, while it would be difficult to *prove* that the civil service as a whole has continued to decline in efficiency, the morale of civil servants has fallen to a very low level,[61] decentralisation has not reached down to district level, relations between UNIP politicians and civil servants are often still strained,[62] and the public service's implementation capacity cannot carry properly the rising load facing the government.

The second major structure on which government has relied to meet its rising load is the ruling party itself. But UNIP's capacity in this direction, while assisted by the high level of mass support it has retained and its structural strength, has been increasingly weakened by other factors. We have seen that it operates today in a more difficult situation than before and with a leadership whose prestige has fallen. Since early 1969 even President Kaunda has come under growing criticism, although usually private or indirect, especially from members of the Bemba-speaking Northern Province section in the party. This criticism reached a crescendo in early 1971 during the debate following the President's address to the National Assembly,[63] and erupted finally in the formation of the UPP in August of the same year. This criticism is a product not so much of policy disagreements as of the party's basic problem: the growth of sectional conflict within itself. The growth of conflict within UNIP has been uneven. Tensions rose to a peak over the central committee elections of August 1967, which were the first to be contested freely without the outgoing committee presenting a single slate of candidates for unanimous endorsement. Tension died down after the President's verbal resignation in February 1968, only to rise once more with the attempt to unseat Vice-president Kapwepwe at the national council meeting of August 1969. The President handled this crisis by suspending the party constitution and assuming supreme powers as secretary general. Conflict intensified again

61. This was admitted in the National Assembly by Mr A. Masiye, Minister of State and former permanent secretary. *Daily Parl. Deb.*, No. 25b, 19 January 1971, cols 82 ff.

62. See debate in the first sitting of the second National Assembly's third session. *Ibid.*, No. 25, January 1971, *passim*.

63. See *ibid*.

after November 1970, this time with the Northern Province section taking the initiative and accusing the President of bowing to Eastern Province pressure to cover up various alleged criminal offences, including corruption, by Ministers from that area.[64] This contributed to the formation of UPP, which was the catalyst for the formation of a one-party State in December 1972.

The basic issue in all these crises has been the same: which sectional group of leaders shall, under President Kaunda, hold preponderant power within the party and government. In August 1967 the pendulum swung in favour of the Bemba-speaking group, led by Kapwepwe, when he ousted Kamanga as Vice-president. By August 1969 it had swung away from them towards the Nyanja-speaking group. Today the divisions are less clear-cut, and differences have appeared within both camps.

UNIP has shown a remarkable capacity for tension management, compromise and survival. Nonetheless, as events before Mulungushi 1971 and after clearly show,[65] competition within UNIP has not decreased. It has taken new forms, but continues to dominate Zambian political life. A number of serious consequences have followed. Rivalries within the party have spilled over into society and divided other institutions, including the trade unions. Even public agencies have not remained unaffected.[66]

Ministers have been preoccupied with political in-fighting, to the neglect of their Ministries and of party organisation. In the process, as President Kaunda pointed out when dissolving the central committee in August 1969, 'development is necessarily retarded due to lack of time for effective planning and decision-making'.[67] Since 1967, too, the Cabinet has been bitterly divided, and its members have been increasingly prone to attack one another in public. Open clashes between Ministers broke out in 1970 and 1971. Understandably, therefore, the Cabinet has become a less important forum for decision-making than it was in the first few years after independence.

Collective decision-making has been further undermined by President Kaunda himself. Particularly since the end of 1967, he has responded to the in-fighting among leading members of his party and government by taking more and more decision-making into his own hands. After 1970 he did this not by adding to but by steadily

64. Speech by Mr J. Chisata, MP, in the National Assembly. *Daily Parl. Deb.*, No. 25d, 21 January 1971, cols 156 ff.
65. See chapter 4.
66. For example, Zambia Railways; *Times of Zambia*, 8 April 1971.
67. K. D. Kaunda, *I Wish to Inform the Nation* (Lusaka, 1969), p. 5.

divesting himself of all portfolio responsibilities and by building up a sizeable corps of personal advisers, mostly located in State House itself. He has used them increasingly to by-pass his official advisers, both Cabinet colleagues and senior civil servants, much to the chagrin of both groups.

This trend towards presidentialism in government decision-making has been paralleled by Dr Kaunda's centralisation of party power in his own hands. The members of the interim executive committee appointed by him in August 1969 were dependent on him for office. In the national council the President's approach has not been consultative; instead he has used the national council as a platform for major policy pronouncements like the Chifubu declaration on co-operatives in 1965 or the series of economic reforms. These are acclaimed, rather than seriously discussed, by the members.

There is an obvious contradiction between the President's style of increasingly personalised decision-making and his own stress on participatory democracy. It can be argued that the divisions among his party lieutenants left him no choice and that dramatically timed announcements of radical measures were a means of diverting attention from internal divisions. The President has sought to reduce the contradiction by maintaining a high degree of accessibility. He has very diverse advisers; it is fairly easy for people to see him; and he holds more or less regular meetings with party activists (like District Governors), Church and student leaders, and trade unionists. In these ways he keeps in touch with important interests in society.

The most serious consequence of UNIP's internal divisions has been to retard the party's transformation into an instrument of economic mobilisation. As the President stated in August 1969, 'there have been people among us who have been engaged in fostering purely sectional interests. The result has been to sap the energy from this nation necessary to make national unity and economic development a real success. The Party has almost missed direction.'[68] That the party is in principle committed to an economic mobilisation role is evident from the preamble to its 1967 constitution and innumerable presidential statements which declare, for example, that 'the Party [UNIP] is the only sufficiently widespread instrument we can use to reach the common man'.[69] To this end, as early as 1967 Dr Kaunda elaborated a structure of village- and ward-level committees which the party would organise to mobilise

68. *Ibid.*
69. Kaunda, *Humanism in Zambia, op. cit.*, p. 33.

villagers for development. And in the same year the Kitwe National Convention on the First Four-year Development Plan decided that at the lowest level the party should continue to initiate voluntary projects such as road links, small bridges and canal drainage.[70]

Yet these attempts have consistently met with failure. Increasingly the people have looked to government to do everything for them, and this at a time when the relevant agencies—the extension officers of the Department of Agriculture, and the credit and marketing organisations—are extremely weak.[71] President Kaunda has had to express repeatedly his disappointment at the party's failure to get village productivity committees going.[72] In spite of renewed efforts in 1970 and 1972 it is not certain, even in areas where the party is strongly organised politically, how far the committees which exist on paper are in fact operating and changing villagers' behaviour.

As was pointed out above,[73] the reasons for UNIP's failure to transform itself into an economic mobilisation agency go well beyond the growing preoccupation of its cadres with competition among themselves. They include the loss of party manpower to the civil service and elsewhere since 1964; lack of funds and insufficient full-time officials; the sapping of the people's confidence in political (and managerial) elites who are so obviously better off than themselves; and the heavy drain to the towns of villagers with initiative.

For reasons such as these, UNIP has not achieved the transition from being the vehicle of political liberation to becoming an agency of economic development. While UNIP may still play a vital role in mediating conflict, it cannot be relied on as a structure capable of enhancing significantly the capacity of the political and governmental system to meet its rising load.

## The institutionalisation of Humanism

The growing imbalance between load and capacity has been analysed, as have the tensions within the ruling United National

70. *National Convention on the Four-year Development Plan, op. cit.*, p. 30.

71. Minister of State Sefelino Mulenga, *Daily Parl. Deb.*, No. 25g, 27 January 1971, col. 410. See also the views of another UNIP MP, Mrs M. V. Robertson, *ibid.*, No. 25b, 19 January 1971, cols 75 and 76; and of the Minister of Finance, *ibid.*, No. 25i, 29 January 1971, col. 501.

72. See Kaunda, *Zambia: towards Economic Independence, op. cit.*, p. 2, and *Zambia's Guidelines for the next Decade, op. cit.*, p. 22.

73. See pp. 132–3.

Independence Party.[74] One way in which President Kaunda has tried to manage these tensions, which have sprung in part from this imbalance, has been to divert the attention of the party from its internal divisions by articulating his philosophy of Humanism. At the same time he has made dramatic attempts to institutionalise the values of Humanism and thereby to radicalise Zambian society. Most of the key steps in this process—August 1967, August 1969, November 1970 and December 1972—coincided with periods of crisis in the party which the President overcame by announcing further instalments in the long process of transforming colonial, capitalist Northern Rhodesian society into an independent, humanist Zambia. But this process is itself creating new tensions. Perhaps the most fundamental question the country now faces is: how much further can the institutionalisation of humanist values be taken? Or, to put it at a lower level, to what extent is the existing degree of institutionalisation an almost irreversible restructuring of the society's values? The answers to these questions will provide the key to the kind of society Zambia will become.

Zambian Humanism was first elaborated by the President in April 1967, two and a half years after independence. Its essence is the assertion of the 'high valuation of Man and respect for human dignity which is a legacy of our tradition' and a determination that 'we in Zambia intend to do everything in our power to keep our society man-centred'.[75] The implications of this general value and determination were first spelled out in Dr Kaunda's *Humanism in Zambia* (April 1967) and, a few months later, in *A Guide to the Implementation of Humanism in Zambia*. The President from the start began to institutionalise humanist values. At its general conference of August 1967 UNIP formally adopted the achievement of Humanism as the first of its objects.[76] And although the detailed timing of subsequent announcements has been largely dictated by the periodic eruption of tensions within the party, there is a clear logic in the steady unfolding of the President's design. Three stages can be detected.

The first drive, launched after August 1967, concentrated on the rural areas and stemmed from the President's concern at the widening gap between urban and rural standards of living. He argued that this gap was both immoral (anti-humanist) and socially dangerous, since it was creating two nations and could lead in the long

74. See chapters 3 and 4.
75. Kaunda, *Humanism in Zambia, op. cit.*, p. 7.
76. UNIP constitution (1967), *op. cit.*, clause IV(a).

run to a rural explosion.[77] Humanism in Zambia was therefore 'a decision in favour of rural areas'.[78] The strategy was to transform the rural areas by raising the range and volume of agricultural output, encouraging new social modes of production (in particular, co-operatives and village regrouping), and reorienting the party to play its part in these changes. These efforts, although largely unsuccessful so far, have not been abandoned. In December 1970 a new Co-operative Societies Bill was introduced into the National Assembly to put these bodies on a sounder legal and organisational footing. In January the following year the President reaffirmed that:

we shall expect the principle of self-reliance to be applied with renewed vigour in the rural areas... To this end Village Productivity Committees, Ward Councils, and Ward Development Committees are being established not only as instruments for administration and strengthening democracy but also for inculcating a sense of responsibility in the rural people for their own development... Self-reliance is our goal but we have to organise the people to be self-reliant.[79]

Three months later, on the President's initiative, a pocket manual was published to guide village productivity and ward development committees as to their functions.[80] In October legislation was passed to give a legal basis for development committees at the lower levels.

But the preconditions for the success of these efforts, which are directed towards the institutionalisation of Humanism and the entrenchment of the party in the fabric of society, have not yet been met. First, village and ward committees lack trained leaders. Village headmen, who are supposed to lead the village productivity committees, tend to be elderly and ill-educated; many of them lost the confidence of their people during the struggle for independence, and others have lost authority since. The party itself has taken no steps to train its own activists, while the field-level civil servants are both too thin on the ground and too lacking in basic skills to win the people's confidence.[81] Secondly, the villagers have not been trained on a large scale in the simple technical skills needed for undertaking successful self-help schemes; only in agriculture has

77. President Kaunda, speaking at the second National Convention at Kitwe, ZIS background paper No. 91/69, 12 December 1969.

78. Kaunda, *Zambia: towards Economic Independence, op. cit.*, p. 14.

79. *Address to Parliament on the Opening of the Third Session of the Second National Assembly*, 8 January 1971 (Lusaka, 1971), p. 8.

80. *Village Productivity and Ward Development Committees, op. cit.*

81. Elliott *et al.*, *Some Determinants of Agricultural Labour Productivity, op. cit.* There was an establishment of only 166 Community Development Assistants in 1971 and 788 senior and other Agricultural Assistants.

some training taken place. A third possible precondition, which has also not been met, is that in the early years these village committees should control small quantities of public money to spend on the tools and supplies which even the most simple community action requires and which these villages, being usually entirely subsistence, at present lack.

The second stage in the institutionalisation of Humanism tackled a different problem, that of ensuring that the modern urban economy benefited citizens rather than foreigners. In April 1967 the President admitted that at that stage Zambia had not yet answered certain vital economic questions, including who should own the means of producing wealth and how that wealth should be distributed.[82] But the following year he tackled one dimension of this issue: the role of foreign firms. He criticised them for 'gross under-capitalisation', 'excessive local borrowing', price rings and profiteering, huge remissions of funds overseas, a refusal to move away from southern African sources of supply, 'outdated management philosophies' and a reluctance to Zambianise.[83] His economic reforms, started in April 1968 and largely completed in November 1970, went a long way to remedying this situation. Their aim was 'to place the effective control and manipulation of the economy in truly Zambian hands and institutions'.[84] State participation in business was at the same time a means of arresting exploitation in society and of promoting the egalitarianism which was an essential element of Humanism by 'taking measures which strengthen and help the poor and weak'.[85]

It is this latter theme, the curbing of domestic exploitation, which has been the essence of the third stage in institutionalising Humanism. Most of the practical measures to carry through this stage only began to take shape at the end of 1970. They go some way towards answering the question which the President originally raised in 1967 as to who should own the means of producing wealth and how that wealth should be distributed. They therefore entail a fundamental re-ordering of class relations between Zambians themselves.

The President's argument is clear: there is a basic opposition between Humanism and capitalism as value systems.[86] Humanism,

82. Kaunda, *Humanism in Zambia, op. cit.*, p. 12.
83. Kaunda, *Zambia: towards Economic Independence, op. cit.*, pp. i–iii and 34.
84. President's address to Parliament, *Daily Parl. Deb.*, No. 25a, 8 January 1971, col. 13.
85. *Ibid.*, col. 11.
86. See Kaunda, *Humanism in Zambia, op. cit.*, pp. 3, 5, 6, 14; *Towards*

in line with 'the best tribal society', values all men just because they are human beings, whereas capitalism measures the worth of men by their economic position and power. Humanism believes in moral motivations—the power of conscience to summon people to self-discipline, self-sacrifice, and national service—whereas capitalism, with its 'price-tag phenomenon', undermines these motivations and replaces them with monetary incentives. Humanism stresses the values of mutual aid and communal effort, whereas capitalism stresses individualism and competition. Humanism believes in economic equality and social harmony, whereas capitalism institutionalises inequality and class conflict. Humanism therefore rejects capitalism: as an economic system because of the exploitation it involves, as a social system because of the class conflict it embodies, and as a political system because it provides the basis for a multi-party system. This rejection implies measures against foreign capital—measures that are relatively easy to take, since they do not excite domestic political opposition. But Humanism's rejection of capitalism also implies measures against domestic capitalists. Though the President made this clear in principle as early as April 1968, over two years elapsed before he began to reveal the practical measures which he contemplated to prevent 'the exploitation of man by man in whatever field'.

In November 1970 the President announced that the measures to be taken against capitalists include the development of a powerful State sector which will take over any Zambian firm which grows beyond a certain size; price control and enforcement of minimum wages to prevent profiteering and sweated labour; and a very steep income tax system and high indirect taxes on luxuries in order to curb the standard of living of the rich.[87] The government's wages policy has in fact encouraged faster salary rises at the lower than at the higher levels,[88] and the wealthy were 'soaked' by the budgets of both 1970 and 1971.[89] A change in worker–management relations is also contemplated: in 1971 legislation was passed to set up in most firms works councils which will have some power to approve certain decisions of management affecting employees.[90] Private

*Complete Independence, op. cit.,* p. 62; *Zambia: towards Economic Independence, op. cit.,* pp. 6 and 8; and *Take up the Challenge, op. cit.,* p. 35.

87. Kaunda, *Take up the Challenge, op. cit.,* pp. 41 and 42.
88. Mwanza, *Towards Income Policy in Zambia, op. cit.*
89. See ZIS press release No. 28/70, 30 January 1970, and *Daily Parl. Deb.,* No. 25i, 29 January 1971, cols 519 ff.
90. For the evolution of Dr Kaunda's ideas on this subject, see Kaunda, *Towards Complete Independence, op. cit.,* p. 50; his address to the second National Convention held at Kitwe, ZIS background paper No. 91/69, 12

ownership of land, which is another pillar of a capitalist system, is also to be modified, and the emergence of a class of landless peasants prevented. The unutilised land of absentee expatriate owners is being compulsorily acquired by the State; since late 1969 some half a million acres have been taken in this way. All land held under freehold tenure ($2\frac{1}{2}$ per cent of the total) is to be converted into leasehold, with the period of lease fixed at 100 years. Large-scale Zambian commercial farmers are not to be encouraged by the State, and a maximum size to any private land-holding is eventually to be introduced.[91] As for the 94 per cent of the country's land occupied under customary law, the party must ensure 'that those who are in a position to raise funds more easily do not acquire more and more land through the right of usage over a period of years to the exclusion of the rest of society'.[92]

Yet another measure contemplated by the President to limit the permeation of capitalist values through society is a code of leadership. This is a code of behaviour to be adhered to not only by UNIP leaders at all levels but also by senior civil servants, employees of parastatal bodies, and army and police officers. It was first outlined in very general terms in August 1969,[93] and in more concrete form in November 1970. Its provisions forbid any of those affected to receive more than one salary, to rent his own house while living in a government house, to hold directorships in private companies or even to own shares or conduct any private business venture.[94] A committee of eight Cabinet Ministers under Vice-president Chona was set up to work out the details of implementing the code. Before this committee had completed its work, the One-party Participatory Democracy Commission was asked to take it over. The government did not, however, immediately accept the commission's proposals for a severe and wide-ranging code of leadership when the proposals were made public in November 1972.

Another important step to curb the new middle class and protect the ordinary people was the abolition from 1 January 1971 of the remaining fee-paying schools and fee-paying sections of hospitals. This measure merely took further the already very extensive social

December 1969; his address to the Mufulira seminar, *Zambia Mail*, 21 March 1970; and Kaunda, *Take up the Challenge, op. cit.*, pp. 40 ff and 67 ff; and the Industrial Relations Act, No. 36 of 1971.

91. Kaunda, *Towards Complete Independence, op. cit.*, p. 40; *Take up the Challenge, op. cit.*, pp. 47–53; and ZIS background paper No. 12/69, 13 December 1969.

92. Kaunda, *Take up the Challenge, op. cit.*, p. 47.

93. Kaunda, *Towards Complete Independence, op. cit.*, pp. 62 and 63.

94. Kaunda, *Take up the Challenge, op. cit.*, p. 52.

welfare measures to protect and uplift the poor.[95] But it was a significant step in the implementation of Humanism not only because it meant that everybody could benefit from free State services[96] but also because it abolished the colonial practice whereby the State provided superior facilities to a tiny minority of civil servants at subsidised or no cost and to others who could afford to pay fees.

A number of points need to be made about this third stage in the institutionalisation of Humanism. Several measures have not yet been implemented, and await the further crystallisation of the ideas underlying them. No Zambian-owned company, with the exception of Mwaiseni Stores in 1968, has been nationalised. Price control is still not effective, and social security legislation in the field of minimum wages, contributions to the National Provident Fund and workmen's compensation payments are not fully enforced. Legislation on workers' participation was introduced only in late 1971, and remained unpromulgated a year later. A maximum size of private land-holding has not yet been fixed. And the code of leadership, which is likely to excite the most antagonism among the new middle class, has still to be worked out in detail. Indeed, President Kaunda came out with yet another set of proposals for the code of leadership in December 1972 and suggested a five-year moratorium on enforcement.[97]

Several of the measures which are intended to curb exploitation—such as the encouragement of Zambian companies rather than individual entrepreneurs and the widening of their opportunities by awarding them government contracts—seem likely to strengthen rather than weaken Zambian capitalists. So too does the new State-controlled Development Bank of Zambia, which is due to start assisting the Zambian private sector in 1973. Indeed, Humanism remains fundamentally ambivalent in its attitude to the private sector. Repeatedly, the President has stated, 'I do not want to create capitalism here'; but in the same breath he has gone on to say, 'I want Zambian businesses to expand and prosper,' for 'we have acknowledged . . . the importance of private capital's participation' and 'to a humanist there is nothing wrong in owning some property'.[98] The cause of this ambivalence stems from the

95. *Ibid.*, pp. 36 ff.
96. President's address to Parliament, *Daily Parl. Deb.*, No. 25a, 8 January 1971, col. 12.
97. *Zambia Daily Mail*, 4 December 1972.
98. See Kaunda, *Zambia: towards Economic Independence, op. cit.*, *passim*; ZIS background paper No. 91/69, 12 December 1969; and *Daily Parl. Deb.*, No. 25a, 8 January 1971, col. 17.

constraints imposed by the evolution of Humanism in a basically capitalist and colonialist economy.

Humanism is not so much the description of society as it is now, but a description of a society we are striving to achieve. For this reason we must be pragmatic and eclectic . . . We find that the entrepreneur can, in certain sectors of the economy, be of great benefit to Zambia now. If we insist on controlling everything through the state, we shall restrain our development. We do not have the administrative skills in sufficient quantity to be able to develop and control everything centrally.[99]

This ambivalence remains a basic question mark at the centre of Humanism. Its resolution will determine whether in fact the country is changing 'from a capitalist system to a socialist one', as the President claimed in 1967,[100] or whether the government restricts itself to creating a Welfare State with a large public sector in the midst of a basically private enterprise economy. Zambia will remain in the latter condition if the President is not successful in carrying through the measures he has announced. This will mean that class differences will become sharper, the rate of economic growth will continue to be erratic, and materialism will remain the dominant ethic.

For his own part, President Kaunda does seem determined to carry through the changes he regards as inherent in Humanism. But he has moved carefully, seeking to prepare people for impending changes. Take the example of land-holding. As early as April 1968 he said that government would 'not spend public money to create a few agricultural capitalists'; in August 1969 he went further, and hinted that 'thought must be given to what is a desirable maximum size of land which an individual may own', and repeated this warning more forcefully in November 1970.[101] Only in December 1972 did he spell out in detail his view of the country's future land tenure system. Even then, legislative action was not immediately taken. Or take the important example of Zambian private enterprise. In announcing the first economic reforms in April 1968 he warned Zambian entrepreneurs not to abuse the protection they were being given by exploiting employees or consumers: 'I do not want them to get rich at the expense of the nation.'[102] In August 1969 he devoted an important part of the speech in which he

99. Kaunda, *Towards Complete Independence, op. cit.*, p. 60.
100. Kaunda, *Humanism in Zambia, op. cit.*, p. 16.
101. Kaunda, *Zambia: towards Economic Independence, op. cit.*, p. 16; *Towards Complete Independence, op. cit.*, p. 40; and *Take up the Challenge, op. cit.*, p. 53.
102. Kaunda, *Zambia: towards Economic Independence, op. cit.*, p. 32.

launched the Matero economic reforms to the future of the Zambian private entrepreneur and to the question 'How can we control this group while at the same time allowing them the freedom to exercise their initiative?'[103] His answer at that time was confined to imposing limits on their earnings by taxation. It was only in November 1970 that he proposed a more comprehensive set of control measures.

President Kaunda is acutely aware of the magnitude of the task of institutionalising Humanism: 'We are engaged on a course of fundamental reconstruction of what institutions the people took over from the colonial rulers.' This involves 'a complete change of every citizen's attitude of mind', and requires 'a programme of persistent and constructive action'.[104] The President believes firmly that Humanism can be implemented, and is determined to succeed. As he stated in November 1970 when introducing the third stage, 'once you start on a revolutionary path, you have no alternative. Indeed, we seek no alternative. If you try to use any other method than the revolutionary path, you are bound to lose control of the ship and it will sink.'[105]

What, then, are the prospects for the successful carrying through of these radical steps? The obstacles are enormous. The basic problem is that, whereas the measures to implement Humanism by uplifting the rural areas and curbing foreign firms were popular among all classes of the Zambian population, the third-stage measures must antagonise the new local middle class. If fully implemented, they will cut the present high levels of consumption of members of that class; prevent many of them from entering the profitable realms of private capital accumulation; reduce their power even over their own businesses to the advantage of their employees; and eventually eliminate them once their firms reach a certain size. They no longer enjoy superior and segregated social services at the expense of the State. And their present penchant for buying up farms along the line of rail is threatened. Humanism clearly damages the interests of this new middle class.

President Kaunda is conscious of the threat which this class therefore poses to Humanism. There are, he has said, 'those who still seek to re-establish a capitalist order to the detriment of the people'.[106] They are to be condemned, and prevented from making Zambia 'a nation of workers on the one hand and capitalist masters

103. Kaunda, *Towards Complete Independence, op. cit.*, pp. 58 ff.
104. Kaunda, *Take up the Challenge, op. cit.*, pp. 8, 5 and 39.
105. *Ibid.*, p. 6.
106. *Ibid.*, p. 36.

on the other'.[107] Somewhat unrealistically, he has claimed that as
a result of the economic reforms which made government itself the
chief employer of labour, there is already 'a clear identity of
interest between workers and Government'. And he has pointed out
to employers in the private sector that the opportunities for co-
operation with their work force are more numerous than the
occasions for conflict.[108]

Nevertheless, classes obviously do exist in Zambia, both objectively
and as subjectively conscious groups. The new middle class which
has grown up since independence is largely the product of the
Africanisation of the civil service. Its numbers and power were
significantly swelled by the economic reforms. The latter benefited
particularly those few educated Zambian civil servants who switched
to lucrative posts in the expanding parastatal sector and those
emerging Zambian businessmen who were shielded by the State
from foreign competition. In little more than a year after the April
1968 reforms some 300 of the 850 foreign-owned shops changed
hands, while Zambianisation in the transport, contractor and certain
other fields reached 83 per cent.[109] It is a reflection of the basic
contradiction in Humanism's attitude to private enterprise that the
second phase in implementing the philosophy boosted the very class
which is increasingly hostile to further implementation. Another
irony is that the President was well aware of the problem which
was being created. As he himself said in August 1969 when extending wider protection to Zambian businessmen, the danger in introducing an element of free capitalism was that in a few years' time
it might be so entrenched that it would be impossible to eradicate.
Or, worse still, he said, we might 'find that we have become tainted
and have lost the desire to eradicate it'.[110]

As early as 1971 this prediction was being fulfilled. There was
mounting evidence of discontent among members of the middle
class. They did not like the abolition of fee-paying hospital and
school facilities in January. Several MPs opposed the increase in
vehicle licences in the 1971 budget. The Zambia Traders' Association repeatedly refused to accept the fact of a dominant public
sector and has demanded that the Industrial Development Corporation should divest itself of its rural retail outlets and hand them
over to private traders.[111] Many civil servants are hostile to the

107. Kaunda, *Towards Complete Independence*, *op. cit.*, pp. 42 and 44.
108. *Ibid.*, pp. 45–6.
109. *Ibid.*, pp. 9 and 11.
110. *Ibid.*, p. 60.
111. *Times of Zambia*, 26 March 1969, and 11 November 1969; *Zambia Mail*, 18 May 1970.

ruling party, and some of them have for years flouted the (humanist) ruling that a person cannot occupy government accommodation while renting out his own house at great profit.[112] As for the proposed code of leadership, even certain Cabinet Ministers have privately asserted that, if it is not dropped, it will merely be flouted. The problem of institutionalising Humanism is compounded by the fact that its values run counter to the dominant values in Zambian society. Among all classes materialism is more firmly entrenched than ever before as the supreme ethic. It is reflected in the conspicuous consumption and rise of corruption among certain administrative and political leaders, as well as in the general concern with promotion and pressure for wage increases—themselves the product of expectations created by the rapid growth of employment, upward occupational mobility, and rise in wages since 1964. 'Capitalism,' wrote President Kaunda, 'has been entrenched in this country whether you look at it from an economic, sociological, cultural, or indeed, political angle.'[113] And the State takeovers of private firms have not altered this situation, for shareholding in a company, on whatever scale, 'does not automatically constitute nor confer real or effective control'.[114] Indeed, the award of management contracts to the previous private owners has meant a continuity of personnel and policy at every, except the topmost, level of these companies, and has therefore ensured the continued predominance of a private enterprise ethic in the parastatal sector. Even the rural areas have not remained unaffected. The Land Commission reported in 1967 that traditional tenure was being undermined in certain areas: 'Land has been commercialised ... Under these conditions transfers *inter vivos* become common, sales of land emerge, and transmission of land rights on death is of regular occurrence.'[115]

The basic task still facing President Kaunda is therefore how far the values of Humanism can be instilled in what is still a predominantly private enterprise economy but with growing Zambian participation at the capital-owning and managerial levels. This task has been made even more difficult by the very nature of the historical process by which radicalism has been introduced into Zambia. While the widespread industrial unrest in 1966 may have been a

112. The ruling was first made in 1967 and has been repeated several times. See Cabinet Office circular No. 52 of 1967, 4 May 1967, and No. 67 of 1970, 30 November 1970.

113. Kaunda, *Humanism in Zambia, op. cit.*, p. 16.

114. President Kaunda's address to the National Assembly, *Daily Parl. Deb.*, No. 25a, 8 January 1971, col. 12.

115. *Report of the Land Commission* (Lusaka, August 1967), p. 40.

factor spurring the President to introduce Humanism, he cannot be said to have been acting under overwhelming mass pressure. On the contrary, nationalisation, the reform of worker–management relations and so on are not issues about which the ordinary people have felt strongly. This is indicated by the silence of the trade union movement on these issues until they were raised by the President. The fact that Dr Kaunda has acted largely on his own initiative makes the process of radicalisation peculiarly vulnerable to reversal.[116]

Nor has the President any powerful agency which he can use to educate the people to an enthusiastic support for his reforms or to coerce the middle class into at least a reluctant acquiescence. UNIP, we have seen, is not such an agency. Its top leaders are middle class in style of life: they draw high salaries, and many are now land-owners and entrepreneurs. Lower-level activists welcome the reforms, but neither understand the practical implications of the philosophy of Humanism[117] nor have the necessary skills to educate the people. The civil service is not a suitable agency, either. It is, in fact, itself the main base of the new middle class, and Zambia is *par excellence* a case of René Dumont's 'bureaucratic bourgeoisie'.[118] The special unit to further Humanism, the Ministry of National Guidance, has been staffed with only a handful of civil servants since its inception in early 1969 and has not had any perceptible impact. The army, too, cannot be expected to be a faithful executor of humanist values. Its officers have been trained almost entirely in the West and live a comfortable middle class existence. Unlike the civil service, the army has not been made subject to effective political control and may react violently to the civilian authorities if Humanism should seek to refashion it in a way unacceptable to its officer corps.

Another obstacle to the institutionalisation of Humanism is the growing indiscipline which has permeated society since independence. The economy has suffered from strikes, organised and wildcat, and from absenteeism, sleeping on duty, and other manifestations of labour indiscipline.[119] Unrest and disruption within the

116. This susceptibility to reversal of radical policies initiated by the chief executive in advance of popular pressure has been shown frequently in Africa, for example in post-Nkrumah Ghana.

117. President Kaunda, ZIS background paper No. 91/69, 12 December 1969.

118. Dumont, *False Start in Africa*, *op. cit.*, chapter 6.

119. *Livingstone Labour Conference—a Survey of Industrial Relations in Zambia* (Lusaka, 1967), p. v and *passim*.

trade union movement are also increasing.[120] Indiscipline in social
life is reflected in the rise in drunkenness: whereas 6,068 cases of
being drunk and incapable were reported in 1964, 14,968 were reported in 1970.[121] There has also been serious indiscipline, as we
have seen, in the ruling party and the civil service, with the middle
class especially showing no predisposition to accept the belt-tightening which both Humanism and economic growth demand. There is
clearly a general conflict in Zambia between the desire for increased
material standards of living and the widespread rejection of the
discipline which alone can make higher standards attainable.[122]
    Unfortunately, it is not likely that indiscipline will be greatly
reduced in the near future. Its causes are deep-seated and difficult
to remove. The origins lie in the independence struggle itself. If the
top nationalist leaders often found it difficult to control their colleagues, they found it even more difficult to control the field-level
activists of the party, in particular during UNIP's Cha Cha Cha
campaign in 1961 and over the issue of refraining from the use of
violence.[123] Moreover, the essence of the freedom struggle was
teaching people to reject colonial authority as legitimate. The
reversal in the distribution of power between Europeans and
Africans in 1962–64 reinforced this rejection. Hitherto Europeans
had monopolised authority roles in the public and private sectors
and in the political system. In 1962 they lost political power while
retaining their economic and administrative roles. It was now
possible for their African employees and subordinates to by-pass
the normal hierarchy and appeal to UNIP, whose leaders now controlled the government, for protection against disciplinary action.[124]
European employers and supervisors were additionally reluctant to
enforce discipline because few of them were Zambian citizens;
they were particularly vulnerable (even to the extent of deportation)
if racial discrimination was alleged against them.[125] Thus the new

120. The 1971 May Day rallies were an almost complete flop. Most
workers stayed away and dissident trade union leaders claimed that this
reflected worker dissatisfaction. *Zambia Daily Mail*, 3 May 1971.
    121. *Zambia Police Annual Reports for 1964 and 1969* (Lusaka, 1965 and
1971), appendix c.
    122. President Kaunda, at the second National Convention, ZIS back-
ground paper No. 91/69, 12 December 1969.
    123. Mulford, *Zambia: the Politics of Independence, op. cit.,* chapters iv
and v.
    124. Turner report, *op. cit.,* p. 15; and President Kaunda's speech at the
second Kitwe National Convention, ZIS background paper No. 91/69, 12
December 1969.
    125. President Kaunda, speaking at the first (1967) Kitwe National Con-

constitutional and political structure after 1962 not only ended whites' political power but undermined their authority in other roles as well. Nor were the new Zambian supervisors able to enforce discipline. They also had to contend with UNIP interference.[126] A further difficulty was the acute shortage of skilled and semi-skilled manpower. Incompetent people were rapidly promoted, and there was a great reluctance to lose men through dismissals or resignations. To sum up, 'the colonial system of labour discipline has broken down and nothing yet has developed to take its place'.[127]

In the face of these difficulties, how much further can President Kaunda take the institutionalisation of Humanism? His strategy so far has been to rely on exhortation. He tried to persuade the middle class to go along with his reforms in November 1970 by a mixture of moral appeal and rational argument: on the one hand, he stressed the evils of exploitation and, on the other, he pointed to 'the inevitable uprising by the exploited'.[128] Yet he himself has admitted that repeated calls for more discipline and productivity have evoked little positive response: 'we have developed the same type of resistance to them as insects develop to a much-used insecticide'.[129] One Minister of State frankly admitted that the President's words had fallen on deaf ears, and that 'we have taken them as a joke of the day'.[130]

We are forced to the conclusion that Humanism cannot be taken much further unless the level of coercion is increased. Humanism involves a revolution in the values of Zambian society and, therefore, a frontal attack on the interests of the middle class. Since the second world war, however, this class has been a determined defender of its position throughout most of the Third World, and there is no reason to think that it will react differently in Zambia. Until recently one would have said that it was difficult to see President Kaunda resorting to coercion. His style of government has rarely been coercive: its watchwords have been 'cajole' and 'compromise', not 'compel'; 'exhort' and not 'exact'. His speeches have been filled with 'I expect' and 'we must'.[131] Coercion also runs counter

vention, *National Convention on the Four-year Development Plan, op. cit.,* p. 12.

126. *Ibid.,* and statement by the General Secretary to the Mineworkers' Union of Zambia, Mr E. Thawe, *Times of Zambia,* 31 March 1971.

127. Turner report, *op. cit.,* p. 15.

128. Kaunda, *Take up the Challenge, op. cit.,* p. 45.

129. ZIS background paper No. 91/69, 12 December 1969.

130. Mr Ali Simbule, *Daily Parl. Deb.,* No. 25f, 26 January 1971, col. 318.

131. See, for example, his first announcement of the code of leadership. Kaunda, *Towards Complete Independence, op. cit.,* p. 62.

to Humanism as a philosophy. Humanism's high valuation of man leads to a belief in the efficacy of education, persuasion, and moral appeals to the better side of his nature. This is still Kaunda's theoretical position, and it is epitomised in such statements as: it is 'unthinkable for a humanist party to use strong-arm tactics to defeat its opponents',[132] and 'to a large extent the new system of industrial relations will put the onus on the workers to discipline themselves'.[133] However, the harsh treatment meted out to the UPP in 1971–72 indicates that the President is not averse to using coercion when he believes that circumstances warrant it. And he has gone back on his earlier pronouncements that the one-party State will rest only on a broad basis of voluntary acceptance, as expressed through the ballot box. These, certainly, are deviations from the path which Humanism prescribes. But they do not at all mean that Kaunda has abandoned this particular path for another. That he is still deeply committed to humanist values is reflected in his insistence that the one-party State must be democratic and in his rejection of the governmental regimentation which socialism in the Soviet Union involves.[134] Moreover, he does not have the agencies at his command which are competent or willing to coerce the rest of society. In these circumstances it may not prove possible to take much further the institutionalisation of humanist values.

## Conclusion

The prospect in Zambia is of growing instability. This arises from the widening gap between load and capacity. The process of tension management via radicalisation has now become an added source of tension, as it adversely affects the local middle class. And the absence of effective control over the army is a further matter for concern. Zambia is still in the initial stage of emerging from her colonial past. Only the first steps have so far been taken in diversifying and restructuring the economy, re-ordering social relations between classes and colour groups, and establishing autochthonous political and governmental institutions.

These institutions and the issues they are set up to resolve will necessarily be affected by the legal establishment of a one-party State. A central issue in any one-party system is, of course, that of political competition, which in turn affects the pace and pattern of economic and social change. The Zambian government has

132. Kaunda, *Ten Thoughts on Humanism, op. cit.*, p. 6.
133. ZIS background paper No. 91/69, 12 December 1969.
134. Kaunda, *Take up the Challenge, op. cit.*, p. 50.

given some indication of how candidates will be chosen in a general election. Following a primary election by the regional conference of the party in each local area, the central committee will choose between one and four of those nominated in each constituency. But it is still not certain how the central committee will exercise this discretion. We cannot, therefore, be categorical in answering certain key questions. How much competition will be judged legitimate in Zambia? Where, and within what limits, will competition be encouraged? How far will it be real or nominal? We have seen that when, in 1967, UNIP allowed the democratic election of central committee members, the result was an alarming increase in the sectional alignments of the politicians. Competition may therefore have to be reduced if intense factionalism is to be contained, and the result may be a one-party State which is less democratic than the President intends. This in turn may slow down the emergence of younger, more radical leaders who can replace their older and often more conservative colleagues. If this happens, the prospects for radical solutions to the country's problems recede even further.

Moreover, there is another potential obstacle to radical change. As Zambia continues to think out answers to the key economic, social and political problems of the 1970s, she will have to do so in increasingly difficult circumstances. But these do not only include the internal sources of instability and conservatism, analysed above. They also include external forces of reaction and subversion. Most of Zambia's main trading partners are capitalist States which do not even have social democrat or labour governments. They do not like socialist radicalism and are on occasion prepared to take a variety of measures against it.[135] Nearer home, Zambia also faces the crucial choice as to the pattern of her long-term relations with the white minority-ruled States to the south; and the growing aggressiveness of those States demands an urgent answer. Zambia can opt either to continue her existing policy of economic disengagement and political confrontation or pursue a policy of closer integration and friendly collaboration. If she chooses to follow the latter course, her options in other fields where choices must be made will be seriously limited: it is no accident that all the African States with which South Africa has already established friendly relations are conservative and authoritarian, favour private enterprise, and reject non-alignment as a viable foreign policy.

As Zambia enters a period characterised by increasing dissension as to the basic values which ought to underlie her way of life, her

135. R. J. Barnet, *Intervention and Revolution: the United States in the Third World* (New York, 1968).

decision as to her relations with the republic of South Africa will influence which values become dominant. This, in turn, will affect the kinds of institution that are created and will shape the answers given by government to the tough economic choices it faces. Should it move more towards a socialist mode of production, or relapse into its previous and very great dependence on private enterprise? As capital and foreign exchange become increasingly scarce, in which sectors should the main thrust of government-sponsored economic growth be concentrated? How much coercion is necessary and acceptable? On the initiative of the President, fairly radical answers have been given to these questions over the last six years. Yet the country has not been able to break decisively with its past in terms of either values or structures. Many African States have experienced an immediate, post-independence phase of radicalisation, only to revert under the pressure of Western-oriented military elites and local middle classes to more conservative economic and political patterns closer to their colonial heritage. The 1970s may well see Zambia, under the combined force of her middle class, both ex-patriate and local, and of the republic of South Africa, falling back along the same road. It would, in our view, be a tragic retrogression. Humanist values, which are beginning to be institutionalised, would be undermined by the resurgence of a harsher and more materialist ethic, and the liberation struggle in the subcontinent would suffer a grave setback. However, such a phase would be only temporary. In this, the most urbanised of sub-Saharan African States, the abandonment of humanist programmes would hasten the emergence of class conflict. It would herald a more bitter era in the country's history but one which, by its opposition of interests and values, would eventually embody once again the seeds of radical change.

# Bibliography[1]

## 1. *Manuscript sources*

### (a) *African National Congress, Lusaka*

'Address by the National President of Congress at the sixteenth annual conference, November 1965' (mimeo.).
'ANC approved constitution' (1968).
ANC files: applications for ANC candidature in the 1968 general elections.
ANC referendum leaflet, 17 April 1969.
ANC (Zambia) manifesto (n.d.).
Minutes of the post-election conference, 4 January 1969.

### (b) *Cabinet Office*

'Report of the committee appointed to review the emoluments and conditions of service of statutory boards and corporations and State-owned enterprises' (Lusaka: Cabinet Office, March 1970, mimeo.).

### (c) *Commonwealth Secretariat, London*

Commonwealth Prime Ministers' meeting: Rhodesia communique (September 1966, mimeo.).

### (d) *Government archives, Lusaka*

Annual reports on African affairs:

Balovale District, 1956, Sec./Nat. 66E.
Barotse Province, 1961, Sec./Nat. 66A.
Choma District, 1958, Sec./Nat. 66F.
Fort Jameson District, 1960, Sec./Nat. 66C.
Kalabo District, 1961, Sec./Nat. 66C.
Katete District, 1960, Sec./Nat. 66C.

1. Limited to documents cited in the text.

Mankoya District, 1961, Sec./Nat. 66A.
Mazabuka District, 1956, Sec./Nat. 66F.
Namwala District, 1957, Sec./Nat. 66F.
Serenje District, 1957, Sec./Nat. 66D.

## (e) *Establishment Division, Lusaka*

'Review of establishments and personnel work' (Lusaka: 1967, mimeo.).
Abridged staff list, December 1967 (Lusaka: 1968, mimeo.).
Administrative list, July 1968 (Lusaka: 1968, mimeo.).

## (f) *High Court, Lusaka*

'Judgement of the High Court in the matter of ten consolidated election petitions on diverse days in April, May and June 1969' (mimeo.).

## (g) *Ministry of Local Government and Housing*

Kabwe Rural Council: estimates file no. 102/49 (Offices of the Rural Council, Kabwe).
'Local government policy elections', Ministry of Local Government and Housing, file No. LGH 5010, part V.
'Local government elections policy', *ibid.*, vol. III.

## (h) *Office of National Development and Planning, Lusaka*

'Manpower: progress report and statistics, 1967' (Lusaka: Office of National Development and Planning, n.d., mimeo.).

## (i) *Offices of provincial Cabinet Ministers*

Minutes of the extraordinary meeting of the North-western Province Development Committee, 14 February 1969 (Solwezi).
Minutes of the fifth meeting of the Provincial Development Committee, Southern Province, 28 June 1966; Dev. 2/6, vol. I (Livingstone).
'Northern development plan: provincial progress report', 18 October 1967, Northern Province: Provincial Development Committee minutes, ADM 5/1/1 (Kasama).

## (j) *Registrar of Trade Unions*

'Report of the Registrar of Trade Unions for the year ended 31st December 1964' (Lusaka: n.d., mimeo.).

## (k) *United National Independence Party*

'A promise fulfilled' (Lusaka: UNIP Election Strategy Committee, 1968.).
Address by President Kaunda to the UNIP national council, 21 March 1969 (Lusaka, mimeo.).

'Choma District Governor's report to UNIP national council' (19 March 1969, mimeo.).

Constitution of the United National Independence Party, Zambia, adopted on 15 August 1967, and standing orders (Lusaka: n.d., mimeo.).

*Ibid.*, adopted on 9 May 1971 (Lusaka: n.d., mimeo.).

'General elections victory hand book for party workers' (Lusaka: UNIP Election Strategy Committee, Freedom House, 1968).

'General financial report to the Mulungushi conference of 15 August 1967' (Lusaka: mimeo., n.d.).

'Luapula Province: political report on the implementation of Humanism in Zambia', presented by M. Ngalande to the UNIP national council, November 1968 (mimeo.).

'Lundazi regional report to the UNIP national council' (March 1969, mimeo.).

'Mulungushi conference, 1967—proceedings of the annual general conference of UNIP, held 14 to 20 August 1967' (mimeo., n.d.).

'Report of the auditors upon the [UNIP] Accounts for the year ended 31 December 1969' (mimeo.).

'Road to Humanism in the Southern Province', report to UNIP national council, 5 November 1968 (mimeo.).

'The voice of UNIP' (Lusaka), May 1965.

'United National Independence Party: hand book for financial organisation' (Lusaka, December 1966).

UNIP national council minutes, 21–3 March 1969 (mimeo.).

— April 1969 (mimeo.).

'Western Province report to the national council of UNIP, 9–11 November 1968' (mimeo.).

'When UNIP becomes government' (Lusaka: n.d., mimeo.).


(l) *United Party*

'The Mirror' (Lusaka), March 1968, vol. 1, No. 1.
— May 1968, vol. 1, No. 3.


(m) *United Progressive Party*

Constitution of the United Progressive Party (mimeo., 1971).


(n) *Zambia Information Services*

'Report of body of public persons appointed to examine and report on the elections of the United National Independence Party offices, held at Mulungushi on 19th August 1967' (Lusaka: Zambia Information Services, 24 August 1967, mimeo.).

'Report on further investigation into police security arrangements consequent upon the discovery of voting papers from the United National

Independence Party Mulungushi elections in the neighbourhood of Broken Hill police station' (Lusaka: Zambia Information Services, 29 August 1967, mimeo.).


2. *Printed primary sources*

(a) *Northern Rhodesia/Zambia government publications (by the Government Printer, Lusaka, subject to the exceptions and additions shown. Entries are listed by year, and alphabetically within each year)*

*Annual report of the Department of Agriculture*, 1936.
*Report of the Commission appointed to inquire into the circumstances leading up to and surrounding the recent deaths and injuries caused by firearms in the Gwembe District and matters relating thereto*, 1958.
*Report of an inquiry into all the circumstances which gave rise to the making of the safeguard of elections and public safety regulations*, 1959.
*Report of the Commission of Inquiry into disturbances in certain African schools*, 1960.
*An account of the disturbances in Northern Rhodesia, July to October 1961*, 1961.
*Civil service staff list*, September 1962.
*Report of the Commission appointed to enquire into the mining industry in Northern Rhodesia* (Morrison report), 1962.
*Northern Rhodesia Gazette*, December 1963.
*Report of the Delimitation Commission*, 1963.
*Annual estimates of revenue and expenditure*, 1963–73.
Cabinet Office circulars, 1964–70 (Lusaka: Cabinet Office, some mimeo.).
*Government directory*, 1964–72 (Lusaka: Cabinet Office, normally issued twice a year).
*Government Gazette*, 1964–72.
Police annual reports, 1964–71.
*Establishment registers*, 1965–69 (Lusaka: Establishment Division).
*Annual report of the Provincial and District government, 1965*, 1966.
— *1966*, 1966.
*Economic report, 1966*, 1966.
*First National Development Plan, 1966–70*, July 1966.
*General orders*, 1966 edn.
*Manpower report: a report and statistical handbook on manpower, education, training and Zambianisation, 1965–66*, 1966.
*Public Service Commission report for 1965*, 1966.
*Report of the Commission of Enquiry into the mining industry, 1966* (Brown report), 1966.
*Humanism in Zambia and a guide to its implementation* (Lusaka: Zambia Information Services, n.d. [1967]).
*Livingstone Labour Conference—a survey of industrial relations in Zambia*, 1967.

*National convention on the four-year development plan, Kitwe, 11–13 January 1967*, 1967.

*Office of National Development and Planning: first National Development Plan, 1966–70. Progress report: 1 July 1966 to 1 March 1967* (n.d.).

*Report of the Land Commission* (Lusaka: Commissioner of Lands, August 1967).

*Report of the Tribunal on Detainees, 1967.*

*Candidates' guide* (Lusaka: Parliamentary Elections Office, 1968).

*Economic report, 1967* (1968).

*Establishment circulars, 1968* (Lusaka: Establishment Division, some mimeo.).

Parliamentary Elections Office 101/5/48/S, 2 October 1968 (Lusaka: Parliamentary Elections Office, 1968).

*Public Service Commission report for 1967* (1968).

*Report of the Electoral Commission (Delimitation of Constituency Boundaries)* (1968).

*The Friso report on rural agricultural credit in Zambia* (October 1968).

*Zambia: a picture progress report on the first four years of Zambian independence, 1964–68* (Lusaka: Cabinet Office, 1968).

*Zambia's plan at work, 1966–70* (Lusaka: Office of National Development and Planning, 1968).

*Budget address by the Vice-president, his honour S. M. Kapwepwe, M.P.* (1969).

*Economic report, 1968* (1969).

*Education in transition—report of the administrative working party appointed to examine certain aspects of the teaching service* (Lusaka: Ministry of Education, 1969).

Fifth summit conference of east and central African States, *Manifesto on southern Africa* (1969). [The Lusaka manifesto.]

*H.E. the President's address to Parliament on the opening of the first session of the second National Assembly, 22 January 1969* (1969).

International Labour Office, *Report to the government of Zambia on incomes, wages and prices in Zambia: policy and machinery* (the Turner Report) (1969).

*Monthly Digest of Statistics, 1969–72* (Lusaka: Central Statistical Office).

*Report of the Commission of Inquiry into the affairs of the Lusaka city council, November 1968* (1969).

*Statistical yearbook, 1968* (Lusaka: Central Statistical Office, 1969).

*The progress of Zambianisation in the mining industry: December 1968* (1969).

*Zambian manpower* (Lusaka: Development Division, Office of the Vice-president, 1969).

*Budget address by the Minister of Development and Finance, the Hon. E. H. K. Mudenda, M.P.* (1970).

*Census of population and housing, 1969—first report* (1970).

*Zambia: six years after* (Lusaka: Zambia Information Services, 1970).

*Dear Mr Vorster . . . Details of exchanges between President Kaunda of Zambia and Prime Minister Vorster of South Africa* (1971).

Government paper No. 1 of 1971: *Report of the Commission appointed to review the salaries, salary structure and conditions of service of the Zambia public service (including the Zambia police) and the defence force* (1971).

*Report of the Commission of Enquiry into the allegations made by Mr Justin Chimba and Mr John Chisata* (the Doyle report) (1971).

*Second National Development Plan: January 1972–December 1976* (Lusaka: Ministry of Development Planning and National Guidance,, December 1971).

*Village productivity and ward development committees: a pocket manual* (1971).

*Department of Labour: annual report for 1971* (1972).

*Report of the national Commission on the establishment of a one-party participatory democracy in Zambia* (1972).

— *Summary of recommendations accepted by government* (Government paper No. 1 of 1972) (1972).

(b) *Nothern Rhodesia/Zambia: parastatal sector*

*Foreign Affairs Bulletin, Tanzania*, vol. II, No. 1 (Dar es Salaam, January 1966).

(c) *Tanzania government publications*

*Rhodesia Railways reports and accounts*, 30 June 1965.
*Prospects for Zambia's mining industry* (Lusaka: Mindeco, 1970).

3. *Printed secondary sources*

Angi, C., and Coombe, T., 'Primary school leavers and youth programmes in Zambia', in *Education in Eastern Africa* (Nairobi, 1970), vol. 1, No. 2.

Anglin, D. G., 'Confrontation in southern Africa: Zambia and Portugal', *International Journal*, vol. xxv, No. 3 (summer 1970).

— 'Zambia and the recognition of Biafra', *African Review*, vol. 1, No. 2 (September 1971).

Apter, D. E., *The politics of modernization* (Chicago: University of Chicago Press, 1965).

— (ed.), *Ideology and discontent* (New York: Free Press, 1964).

Austin, D. G., *Politics in Ghana, 1946–60* (London: Oxford University Press, 1964).

— *Britain and South Africa* (London: Oxford University Press, 1966).

Baldwin, R. E., *Economic development and export growth: a study of Northern Rhodesia, 1920–60* (Berkeley and Los Angeles: University of California Press, 1966).

Bancroft, J. A., *Mining in Northern Rhodesia* (London: British South Africa Company, 1961).

Barber, W. J., *The economy of British central Africa: a case study of economic development in a dualistic society* (Stanford: Stanford University Press, 1961).
— 'Federation and the distribution of economic benefits', in Leys, C., and Pratt, C. (eds), *A new deal in central Africa* (London: Heinemann, 1960).
Barnes, J. A., *Politics in a changing society: a political history of the Fort Jameson Ngoni* (Manchester: Manchester University Press, second edition, 1967).
Barnet, R. J., *Intervention and revolution: the United States in the Third World* (New York: World Publishing Company, 1968).
Bates, R. H., *Unions, parties, and political development—a study of mineworkers in Zambia* (New Haven: Yale University Press, 1971).
— 'Input structures, output functions and systems capacity: a study of the Mineworkers' Union of Zambia', *Journal of Politics*, vol. 32 (November 1970).
Berg, E. J., and Butler, J., 'Trade unions', in Coleman, J. S., and Rosberg, C. G. (eds), *Political parties and national integration in tropical Africa* (Berkeley and Los Angeles: University of California Press, 1964).
Bienen, H., *Tanzania: party transformation and economic development* (Princeton: Princeton University Press, 1967).
Bostock, M., and Harvey, C. (eds), *Economic independence and Zambian copper: a case study of foreign investment* (New York: Praeger, 1972).
Bowman, L. W., 'Rhodesia since UDI', *Africa Report*, vol. 12, No. 2 (February 1967).
Brass, P. R., 'Political participation, institutionalisation and stability in India', *Government and Opposition*, vol. 4, No. 1 (1969).
Brelsford, W. V., *The tribes of Zambia* (Lusaka: Government Printer, second edition, n.d.).
Brown, R., 'Zambia and Rhodesia: a study in contrast', *Current History*, vol. 48 (April 1965).
Brzezinski, Z. K., *The Soviet bloc, unity and conflict* (revised and enlarged, London: Cambridge University Press, 1967).
Caplan, G. L., 'Barotseland: the secessionist challenge to Zambia', *Journal of Modern African Studies*, vol. 6, No. 3 (October 1968).
— *The elites of Barotseland, 1878–1969: a political history of Zambia's Western Province* (Berkeley and Los Angeles: University of California Press, 1970).
Cartwright, J., 'Shifting forces in Sierra Leone', *Africa Report*, vol. 13, No. 9 (December 1968).
Chisiza, D. K., 'Africa—what lies ahead?', quoted in Dumont, R., *False start in Africa* (New York: Praeger, 1966; London: Sphere Books, 1968).
Clegg, E., *Race and politics: partnership in the Federation of Rhodesia and Nyasaland* (London: Oxford University Press, 1960).
Coleman, J. S., and Rosberg, C. G. (eds), *Political parties and national integration in tropical Africa* (Berkeley and Los Angeles: University of California Press, 1964).

Colson, E., and Gluckman, M. (eds), *Seven tribes of British central Africa* (Manchester: Manchester University Press, 1951).

Davidson, J. W., *The Northern Rhodesian Legislative Council* (London: Faber & Faber, 1948).

Davies, D. H. (ed.), *Zambia in maps* (London: University of London Press, 1971).

Decke, B., 'What is tribalism?', *Africa and the world* (September 1970).

Dotson, F. and L. O., *The Indian minority of Zambia, Rhodesia and Malawi* (New Haven: Yale University Press, 1968).

Dresang, D. L., 'The civil service in Zambia' (forthcoming).

Dumont, R., *False start in Africa* (New York: Praeger, 1966; London: Sphere Books, 1968).

Eckstein, H., and Apter, D. E. (eds) *Comparative politics: a reader* (New York: Free Press, 1963).

Elliott, C., *et al.*, *Some determinants of agricultural labour productivity in Zambia* (University of Zambia/University of Nottingham Agricultural Labour Productivity Study, mimeo., November 1970).

— (ed.), *Constraints on the economic development of Zambia* (Nairobi: Oxford University Press, 1971).

— 'The Zambian economy' (Lusaka, 1968, mimeo.).

Epstein, A. L., *Politics in an urban African community* (Manchester: Manchester University Press, 1958).

Faber, M. L. O., and Potter, J. G., *Towards economic independence: papers on the nationalisation of the copper industry in Zambia* (London: Cambridge University Press, 1972).

Fagan, B. M. (ed.), *A short history of Zambia from the earliest times until A.D. 1900* (Nairobi: Oxford University Press, 1966).

Fernandez, J. W., 'The Lumpa uprising: why?', *Africa Report*, vol. 9, No. 10 (November 1964).

Festinger, L., *A theory of cognitive dissonance* (London: Tavistock Publications, 1957).

Fortman, B. de G. (ed.), *After Mulungushi: the economics of Zambian Humanism* (Nairobi: East African Publishing House, 1969).

Fourie, D., *War potentials of the African States south of the Sahara* (Johannesburg: South African Institute of International Affairs, 1968).

Franck, T. M., *Race and nationalism: the struggle for power in Rhodesia–Nyasaland* (London: Allen & Unwin, 1960).

Fry, J., review article on the Turner report, *Eastern Africa Economic Review* (December 1970).

Gann, L. H., *The birth of a plural society: the development of Northern Rhodesia under the British South Africa Company, 1894–1914* (Manchester: Manchester University Press, 1958).

— *A history of Northern Rhodesia: early days to 1953* (London: Chatto & Windus, 1964).

Geertz, C., 'Ideology as a cultural system', in Apter, D. E. (ed.), *Ideology and discontent* (New York: Free Press, 1964).

Gertzel, C., *The politics of Independent Kenya* (London: Heinemann, 1970).

— 'The provincial administration in Kenya', *Journal of Commonwealth Political Studies*, vol. IV, No. 3 (November 1966).

Gluckman, M., 'The Lozi of Barotseland in north-western Rhodesia' in Colson, E., and Gluckman, M. (eds)., *Seven tribes of British central Africa* (Manchester: Manchester University Press, 1951).

— 'Anthropological problems arising out of the African industrial revolution', in A. W. Southall (ed.), *Social change in modern Africa* (London: Oxford University Press, 1961).

Goodman, S. H., 'Investment policy in Zambia', in Fortman, B. de G. (ed.), *After Mulungushi: the economics of Zambian Humanism* (Nairobi: East African Publishing House, 1969).

Gray, R., *The two nations: aspects of the development of race relations in the Rhodesias and Nyasaland* (London: Oxford University Press, 1960).

Greenfield, C. C., 'Manpower planning in Zambia', *Journal of Administration Overseas*, vol. VII, No. 4 (October 1968).

Gupta, A., 'The Zambian National Assembly: study of an African legislature', *Parliamentary Affairs*, vol. XIX, No. 1 (winter 1965–66).

Haefele, E. T., and Steinberg, E. B., *Government controls on transport: an African case* (Washington, D.C.: Brooking's Institution, 1965).

Hailey, W. M., *An African survey* (London: Oxford University Press, 1957).

Hall, R., *Zambia* (London: Pall Mall Press, 1965).

— *The high price of principles: Kaunda and the white south* (London: Hodder & Stoughton, 1969).

— 'Zambia and Rhodesia: links and fetters', *Africa Report*, vol. II, No. 1 (January 1966).

Harvey, C. R. M., 'The fiscal system', in Elliott, C. (ed.), *Constraints on the economic development of Zambia* (Nairobi: Oxford University Press, 1971).

Hazlewood, A., and Henderson, P. D., *Nyasaland: the economics of federation* (Oxford: Blackwell, 1960).

Hellen, J. A., *Rural economic development in Zambia, 1890–1964* (Munich: Weltforum-Verlag, 1968).

Herskovitz, M., *The human factor in changing Africa* (New York: Knopf, 1962).

Hodgkin, T., *African political parties* (Harmondsworth: Penguin, 1961).

Huntington, S. P., 'Political development and political decay', *World Politics*, vol. XVII, No. 3 (1965).

Johns, S. W., 'Parastatal bodies in Zambia: a survey' (forthcoming).

Jolly, R., 'The skilled manpower constraint', in Elliott, C. (ed.), *Constraints on the economic development of Zambia* (Nairobi: Oxford University Press, 1971).

— 'The Seers report in retrospect', *African Social Research*, No. 11 (June 1971).

— 'How successful was the first National Development Plan?', in 'Six years after', supplement to the *Zambia Mail*, November 1969.

Jorre, J. de St, 'Zambia's economy: progress and perils', *Africa Report*, vol. 12, No. 9 (December 1967).

Kasfir, N., 'The decline of cultural sub-nationalism in Uganda', in Olorunsola, V. A. (ed.), *The politics of cultural sub-nationalism in Africa* (New York: Doubleday–Anchor, 1972).

Kaunda, K. D., *Zambia shall be free: an autobiography* (London: Heinemann, 1962).

— *A humanist in Africa: letters to Colin Morris from Kenneth Kaunda, President of Zambia* (London: Longmans, 1966).

— *Zambia: independence and beyond. The speeches of Kenneth Kaunda*, ed. Legum, C. (London: Nelson, 1966).

-- *Installation address by the Chancellor*, University of Zambia inauguration ceremony, July 1966 (Lusaka, n.d.).

— *Zambia's guidelines for the next decade* (Lusaka: Government Printer, 1968).

— *Economic revolution in Zambia* (Lusaka: Government Printer, 1968).

— *Towards economic independence* (Lusaka: Government Printer, 1968).

— *Towards complete independence* (Lusaka: Government Printer, 1969).

— *I wish to inform the nation* (Lusaka: Government Printer, 1969).

— *Take up the challenge* (Lusaka: Government Printer, 1970).

— *Ten thoughts on Humanism* (Kitwe: Veritas Corporation, 1970).

— *Address to Parliament on the opening of the third session of the second National Assembly, 8 January 1971* (Lusaka: Government Printer, 1971).

— *A path for the future*, 8 May 1971.

Kay, G., *A social geography of Zambia: a survey of population patterns in a developing country* (London: University of London Press, 1967).

Keatley, P., *The politics of partnership: the Federation of Rhodesia and Nyasaland* (Harmondsworth: Penguin, 1963).

Kelman, H. C., 'Patterns of personal involvement in the national system—a social psychological analysis of political legitimacy', in Rosenau, J. N. (ed.), *International politics and foreign policy* (New York: Free Press, 1969).

Kilson, M., *Political change in a west African State* (Cambridge, Mass.: Harvard University Press, 1966).

Kirkman, W., *Unscrambling an empire—a critique of British colonial policy, 1956–66* (London: Chatto & Windus, 1966).

Koff, D., 'Notes on the Kenya general election, 1966—the contradiction of opposition', *East Africa Journal*, vol. III, No. 5 (August 1966).

Kuper, L., and Smith, M. G. (eds), *Pluralism in Africa* (Berkeley and Los Angeles: University of California Press, 1969).

Langworthy, H. W., *Zambia before 1890: aspects of pre-colonial history* (London: Longman, 1972).

Legum, C. (ed.), *Zambia: independence and beyond. The speeches of Kenneth Kaunda* (London: Nelson, 1966). (See also Kaunda, K. D.)

— and Drysdale, J. (eds), *Africa contemporary record: annual survey and documents, 1968–69* (London: Africa Research, 1969).

Lewis, W. A., *Politics in west Africa* (London: Allen & Unwin, 1965).

Leys, C., and Pratt, C. (eds), *A new deal in central Africa* (London: Heinemann, 1960).

Lipset, S. M., *Political man* (New York: Doubleday–Anchor, 1963).

Long, N., *Social change and the individual: a study of the social and religious responses to innovation in a Zambian rural community* (Manchester: Manchester University Press, 1968).

Luckham, R., 'A comparative typology of civil–military relations', *Government and Opposition*, vol. 6, No. 1 (winter 1971).

Mackinson, I., 'The National Institute of Public Administration', *Service*, (December 1967).

Martin, A., *Minding their own business: Zambia's struggle against Western control* (London: Hutchinson, 1972).

Mason, P., *Year of decision: Rhodesia and Nyasaland in 1960* (London: Oxford University Press, 1960).

Mazrui, A. A., 'Pluralism and national integration', in Kuper, L., and Smith, M. G., *Pluralism in Africa* (Berkeley and Los Angeles: University of California Press, 1969).

Meebelo, H., *Reaction to colonialism: a prelude to the politics of independence in northern Zambia, 1893–1939* (Manchester: Manchester University Press, 1971).

Miller, N. N., 'The rural African party: political participation in Tanzania', *American Political Science Review*, vol. 64, No. 2 (1970).

Miracle, M. P., 'Plateau Tonga entrepreneurs in historical inter-regional trade', *Rhodes-Livingstone Journal*, No. 26 (December 1959).

Mitchell, J. E., 'Electricity supply in Zambia'—an address (mimeo., 1967).

Mlenga, K. G. (ed.), *Who's who in Zambia, 1967–68* (Lusaka: Zambia Publishing Co., n.d. [1968]).

Molteno, R. V., *The Zambian community and its government* (Lusaka: Neczam, 1974).

— 'Our university and our community', *Jewel of Africa*, vol. 2, Nos 3 and 4 (1970).

— *Africa and South Africa—the implications of South Africa's 'outward-looking' policy* (London: Africa Bureau, 1971).

— 'South Africa's forward policy in Africa', *Round Table*, No. 243 (July 1971).

— 'Zambia and the one-party State', *East Africa Journal*, vol. 9, No. 2 (February 1972).

— 'National security and institutional stability' (forthcoming).

Morgenthau, R. S., *Political parties in French-speaking west Africa* (Oxford: Clarendon Press, 1964).

Morris-Jones, W. H., 'Dominance and dissent: their inter-relations in the Indian party system', *Government and Opposition*, vol. 1, No. 4 (July–September 1966).

Mtshali, B. V., 'South Africa and Zambia's 1968 election', *Kroniek van Afrika*, No. 2 (1970).

— 'Zambia's foreign policy', *Current History*, vol. 58, No. 343 (March 1970).

Mulford, D. C., *The Northern Rhodesian general election, 1962* (Nairobi: Oxford University Press, 1964).
— *Zambia: the politics of independence, 1957–64* (London: Oxford University Press, 1967).
— 'Northern Rhodesia—some observations on the 1964 elections', *Africa Report*, vol. 9, No. 2 (February 1964).
Mwanakatwe, J. M., *The growth of education in Zambia since independence* (Lusaka: Oxford University Press, 1968).
Nkwabilo, K. H., 'Remarks on manpower and Zambianisation' (Lusaka: University of Zambia, mimeo., 26 June 1969).
Olorunsola, V. A. (ed.), *The politics of cultural sub-nationalism in Africa* (New York: Doubleday–Anchor, 1972).
Omer-Cooper, J. D., *The Zulu aftermath* (London: Longman, 1966).
Ostrander, F. T., 'Zambia in the aftermath of Rhodesian UDI. Logistical and economic problems', *African Forum*, vol. 2, No. 3 (winter 1967).
Oyediran, O., 'The role of ethnicity and partisanship in the politics of Nigerian students', *ODU—University of Ife Journal of African Studies*, vol. 4, No. 2 (January 1968).
Palmer, N. D., *The Indian political system* (London: Allen & Unwin, 1961).
Palombara, J. La (ed.), *Bureaucracy and political development* (Princeton: Princeton University Press, 1963).
Panter Brick, S. K., 'The right of self-determination: its application to Nigeria', *International Affairs*, vol. 44, No. 2 (1968).
Pratt, R. C., 'The administration of economic planning in a newly independent State: the Tanzanian experience, 1963–66', *Journal of Commonwealth Political Studies*, vol. v, No. 1 (March 1967). (See also Leys, C.)
Ranger, T. O. (ed.), *Aspects of central African history* (London: Heinemann, 1968).
Rasmussen, T., 'Political competition and one-party dominance in Zambia', *Journal of Modern African Studies*, vol. 7, No. 3 (October 1969).
Roberts, A. D., 'The nineteenth century in Zambia' and 'The political history of twentieth century Zambia', in Ranger, T. O. (ed.), *Aspects of central African history* (London: Heinemann, 1968).
— 'White judges under attack', *Round Table*, No. 236 (October 1969).
— 'The Lumpa Church of Alice Lenshina', in Rotberg, R. I., and Mazrui, A. A. (eds), *Protest and power in black Africa* (New York: Oxford University Press, 1970).
Rosenau, J. N. (ed.), *International politics and foreign policy* (New York: Free Press, 1969).
Rotberg, R. I., 'The Lenshina movement of Northern Rhodesia', *Rhodes-Livingstone Journal*, vol. xxix (1963).
— *The rise of nationalism in central Africa: the making of Malawi and Zambia, 1873–1964* (Cambridge, Mass.: Harvard University Press, 1965).
— 'Tribalism and politics in Zambia', *Africa Report*, vol. 12, No. 9 (December 1967).

— and Mazrui, A. A. (eds), *Protest and power in black Africa* (New York: Oxford University Press, 1970).

Rothchild, D., 'Rural–urban inequities and resource allocation in Zambia', *Journal of Commonwealth Political Studies*, vol. x, No. 3 (1972).

Scarritt, J. R., 'Adoption of political styles by African politicians in the Rhodesias', *Midwest Journal of Political Science*, vol. x, No. 1 (February 1966).

— 'The Zambian election—triumph or tragedy?', *Africa Today*, vol. 16, No. 1 (February–March 1969).

Schurman, F., *Ideology and organisation in communist China* (Berkeley and Los Angeles: University of California Press, 1966).

Scott, I., and Molteno, R. V., 'The Zambian general elections', *Africa Report*, vol. 14, No. 1 (January 1969).

Shils, E., 'The concept and function of ideology', a reprint from vol. 7 of *International Encyclopedia of the Social Sciences* (New York: Macmillan and Free Press, 1968).

Shonfield, A., *Modern capitalism: the changing balance of public and private power* (London: Oxford University Press, 1965).

Sklar, R. L., 'Political science and national integration—a radical approach', *Journal of Modern African Studies*, vol. 5, No. 1 (1967).

— 'Zambia's response to UDI', *Mawazo* vol. 1, No. 3 (June 1968).

— 'On returning to the road of legality in Rhodesia', *Pan-African Journal*, vol. 1, No. 4 (autumn 1968).

Soremekun, F., 'The challenge of nation-building: neo-humanism and politics in Zambia, 1967–69', *Genève-Afrique*, vol. ix, No. 1 (1970).

Southall, A. W. (ed.), *Social change in modern Africa* (London: Oxford University Press, 1961).

Sutcliffe, R. B., 'Crisis on the Copperbelt', *The World Today*, vol. 22, No. 12 (December 1966).

— 'Zambia and the strains of UDI', *The World Today*, vol. 23, No. 12 (December 1967).

— *Sanctions against Rhodesia* (London: Africa Bureau, 1966).

Thomas, P. A., 'Zambian economic reforms', *Canadian Journal of African Studies*, vol. 2, No. 1 (spring 1968).

The London *Times* news team, *The black man in search of power* (London: Nelson, 1968).

Tordoff, W., *Government and politics in Tanzania* (Nairobi: East African Publishing House, 1967).

— 'Provincial and District government in Zambia', *Journal of Administration Overseas*, vol. viii, Nos 3 and 4 (July and October 1968).

— 'Provincial and local government in Zambia', *Journal of Administration Overseas*, vol. ix, No. 1 (January 1970).

— 'Political crisis in Zambia', *Africa Quarterly*, vol. x, No. 3 (October–December 1970).

Vansina, J., *The kingdoms of the Savanna* (Madison: University of Wisconsin Press, 1966).

Wallerstein, I., *Africa: the politics of independence* (New York: Random House, 1961).

— 'Ethnicity and national integration in west Africa', in Eckstein, H., and Apter, D. E. (eds), *Comparative politics* (New York: Free Press, 1963).

Weiss, H. F., *Political protest in the Congo* (Princeton: Princeton University Press, 1967).

Williams, S., *Central Africa: the economics of inequality* (London: Fabian Commonwealth Bureau, 1960).

Wills, A. J., *An introduction to the history of central Africa* (London: Oxford University Press, 1964).

Worsley, P., *The Third World* (London: Weidenfeld & Nicolson, 1964).

Young, C., *Politics in the Congo* (Princeton: Princeton University Press, 1965).

Young, R., and Fosbrooke, H. A., *Smoke in the hills: political tension in the Morogoro district of Tanganyika* (Evanston: Northwestern University Press, 1960).

Young, R. A., 'The 1968 general elections', in Davies, D. H. (ed.), *Zambia in maps* (London: University of London Press, 1971).

Zacklin, R., 'Challenge of Rhodesia', *International Conciliation* No. 575 (November 1969).

Zolberg, A. R., *Creating political order: the party States of west Africa* (Chicago: Rand McNally, 1966).

— 'The structure of political conflict in the new States of tropical Africa', *American Political Science Review*, vol. LXII, No. 1 (March 1968).

Zulu, J. B., *Zambian Humanism* (Lusaka: Neczam, 1970).

## 4. *Miscellaneous*

### (a) *Anonymous publications*

*About Zambia*, No. 6: *History* (Lusaka: Zambia Information Services, n.d.). [Author: Parsons, Q. N.]

*Copperbelt of Zambia mining industry year book, 1968* (Kitwe: Copper Industry Service Bureau, n.d.).

### (b) *Conference papers*

Hesse, C., 'Some political aspects of development planning and implementation in Zambia, with particular reference to the Eastern and Luapula Provinces', paper presented to the University of East Africa Social Science Conference, Dar es Salaam, January 1968.

Mwanza, J. M., 'Towards income policy in Zambia', paper presented to the University of East Africa Social Science Conference, Nairobi, December 1969.

Subramaniam, V., 'The social background of Zambia's higher civil servants and undergraduates', paper presented to the University of East Africa Social Science Conference, Nairobi, December 1969.

(c) *Election manifestoes*

Mitchley, H. R. E., election manifesto, 1968.
Musole, J. W., election manifesto, 1968.

(d) *Legislation*

Cap. 45 of *The laws of Zambia* (1965 edition).
Constitution of Zambia: appendix 3 to *The Laws* (1965 edition).

(e) *Newspapers, research bulletins and press releases*

East and Central Africa:

> *Central African Examiner*, 1962 (Salisbury).
> *East African Standard*, 1967 (Nairobi).

South Africa:

> *Southern Africa News Week*, 1968.
> *Sunday Times*, 1971 (Johannesburg).

United Kingdom:

> *Africa Digest*, 1967–69 (London).
> *Africa Research Bulletin*, Political, Social and Cultural series, and Economic, Financial and Technical series, 1964–72 (Exeter).
> *The Economist*, 1967 (London).
> *Financial Times*, 1965–69 (London).
> *The Guardian*, 1969–71 (London).
> *The Observer*, 1969 (London).
> *The Times*, 1966–69 (London).

United States:

> *New York Times*, 1965 (New York).
> — (international edition) 1966 (New York).

Zambia:

> *Business and Economy*, 1967 (Ndola).
> *Political Orbit*, June 1969 (mimeo.).
> *Sunday Times of Zambia*, 1971 (Ndola).
> *The Mirror*, March–May 1968 (Lusaka).
> *The Voice of UNIP*, 1965 (Lusaka).
> *Times of Zambia*, 1965–72 (Ndola).
> *Zambia Mail*, 1965–70 (Lusaka).
> *Zambia Daily Mail*, 1970–72 (Lusaka).
> Zambia Information Services (Lusaka):
>
>> Background papers, 1964–72.
>> Press releases, 1964–72.
>> Zambia District News, 1967–68.
>> Zambia News, 1966–70.

(f) *Parliamentary records*

Northern Rhodesia/Zambia:
Biographical and other records: Speaker's Office, National Assembly (Lusaka).
*Daily parliamentary debates*, 1971–72 (Lusaka).
*Legislative Council debates*, 1964 (Lusaka).
*National Assembly debates*, Hansard Nos 1–28, 1964–71 (Lusaka).
*National Assembly standing orders, 1967* (Lusaka).
*Reports of the Public Accounts Committee*, Hansard Nos 7–16, 1966–1968 (Lusaka).

United Kingdom:
*Parliamentary Debates*, House of Commons official report, Hansard: vols 718–22, November–December 1965 (London).

(g) *Theses*

Bates, R. H., 'Unions, parties, and development: a study of government policy toward the mineworkers of Zambia' (Massachusetts Institute of Technology: Ph.D., 1969). Subsequently published: see above.
Bull, M. M., 'A history of the Lozi people to 1900' (University of London: Ph.D., 1968).
Dresang, D. L., 'The Zambia civil service: a study in development administration' (University of California, Los Angeles: Ph.D., 1971).
Helgerson, J., 'The Northern Rhodesian Council, 1959–63' (Duke University: M.A., 1968).
Langworthy, H. W., 'A history of Undi's kingdom to 1890' (Boston University: Ph.D., 1969).
Meebelo, H., 'African reaction to European rule in the Northern Province of Northern Rhodesia, 1895–1939' (University of London: Ph.D., 1969). Subsequently published: see above.
Mubako, S. V. S., 'The presidential system in the Zambian constitution' (University of London: M.Phil., 1970).
Roberts, A., 'A political history of the Bemba, north-eastern Zambia, to 1900' (University of Wisconsin: Ph.D., 1966).

(h) *United Nations*

*Economic survey mission on the economic development of Zambia: report of the UN/ECA/FAO mission* (Ndola: Falcon Press, 1964).
United Nations Security Council, official records: S/PV. 1331, 8 December 1966; S/PV. 1332, 9 December 1966; S/PV. 1336, 13 December 1966.
United Nations resolution S/RES/253 of 29 May 1968, under chapter VII of the United Nations' charter.
'Report by the Secretary General in pursuance of resolution 235 (1968)', UN doc. S/8786/ Add. 2, 10 October 1968.
*United Nations Monthly Chronicle*, vol. VI, No. 7 (July 1969) and vol. VII, No. 4 (April 1970). United Nations resolution condemning the proclamation of republican status in Rhodesia, S/RES/277 of 18 March 1970.

# Index